*Also by* **Ashgate**

**JOHN HARLEY**
Orlando Gibbons and the Gibbons Family of Musicians

**DAVID WYN JONES**
Music in Eighteenth-Century Britain

**HERMINE WEIGEL WILLIAMS**
Francesco Bartolomeo Conti: His Life and Music

**MICHAEL I. WILSON**
Nicholas Lanier: Master of the King's Musick

**DAVID LASOCKI and ROGER PRIOR**
The Bassanos: Venetian Musicians and Instrument Makers
in England, 1531–1665

*and in the Collected Studies Series*

**MICHAEL TALBOT**
Venetian Music in the Age of Vivaldi

**RICHARD SHERR**
Music and Musicians in Renaissance Rome and Other Courts

**CHRISTOPHER PAGE**
Music and Instruments of the Middle Ages: Studies on Texts and Performance

**ERNEST H. SANDERS**
French and English Polyphony of the 13th and 14th Centuries:
Style and Notation

**ROGER BOWERS**
English Church Polyphony: Singers and Sources from the 14th to
the 17th Century

**RUTH STEINER**
Studies in Gregorian Chant

**DAVID FALLOWS**
Songs and Musicians in the Fifteenth Century

**RICHARD L. CROCKER**
Studies in Medieval Music Theory and the Early Sequence

VARIORUM COLLECTED STUDIES SERIES

# Monteverdi and
# his Contemporaries

Tim Carter

---

# Monteverdi and
# his Contemporaries

---

## Ashgate
### VARIORUM

Aldershot · Burlington USA · Singapore · Sydney

**Published in the Variorum Collected Studies Series by**

Ashgate Publishing Limited
Gower House, Croft Road,
Aldershot, Hampshire GU11 3HR
Great Britain

Ashgate Publishing Company
131 Main Street,
Burlington, Vermont 05401–5600
USA

Ashgate website: http://www.ashgate.com

ISBN 0–86078–823–7

**British Library Cataloguing-in-Publication Data**
Carter, Tim
    Monteverdi and his Contemporaries. – (Variorum Collected Studies Series: CS690)
    1. Monteverdi, Claudio, 1567–1643 – Criiticism and Interpretation. 2. Song – Italy –
    History – 17th Century. 3. Song – Italy – History and Criticism. 4. Music – Italy –
    17th Century – History and Criticism.
    I. Title.
    782'.00945'09032

**US Library of Congress Cataloging-in-Publication Data**
Carter, Tim
    Monteverdi and his Contemporaries / Tim Carter.
        p.    cm – (Variorum Collected Studies Series: CS690)
    Includes bibliographical references and index.
    1. Music – Italy – 16th Century – History and Criticism. 2. Music – Italy –
    17th Century – History and Criticism. 3. Monteverdi, Claudio, 1567–1643 –
    Criticism and Interpretation. I. Title. II. Collected Studies; CS690.
    ML290.2.C22   2000
    780'.945.09032–dc21                                                        00–061798

The paper used in this publication meets the minimum requirements of the
    American National Standard for Information Sciences – Permanence of
    Paper for Printed Library Materials, ANSI Z39.48–1984.        ∞  ™

Printed by St Edmundsbury Press, Bury St Edmunds, Suffolk

VARIORUM COLLECTED STUDIES SERIES C690

# CONTENTS

This volume contains xii + 256 pages

# INTRODUCTION

Taking a retrospective view of one's publications suggests in several senses a journey both through the material that has nurtured and focussed a scholarly career and also in matters autobiographical. The two become inextricably intertwined – for all that autobiography will scarcely interest the general reader – and thus each help explain the other: perhaps, then, I can be forgiven for placing these essays in various contexts that have determined their nature in revealing and (it now appears to me) striking ways.

The contents of this collection – and of a first on *Music, Patronage and Printing in Late Renaissance Florence* published in this same series – span some twenty years of publishing in a wide range of periodicals and books; they range from my days as a doctoral student under Nigel Fortune at the University of Birmingham (1975–79) through my employment at the Universities of Leicester (1978–79) and Lancaster (1980–87) – with leave to take up fellowships at the Harvard Center for Italian Renaissance Studies, Villa I Tatti, Florence (1984–85) and at the Newberry Library, Chicago (1986) – and at Royal Holloway, University of London (1987– ). They were all influenced to varying degrees by my teachers, colleagues, students and friends, and also by trends in the discipline which I would not claim to have shaped but to which I have certainly responded. My selection for these two volumes is not all-inclusive – it omits three book-chapters,[1] an essay on Mozart (my other field of research),[2] innumerable dictionary articles, material more 'popular' in focus, and a large number of reviews – although it forms something of an *opera omnia* of articles and essays that have appeared up to and including 1998. It also presents a body of material that might, I hope, add up to more than the sum of its parts.

*Monteverdi and his Contemporaries* might best be seen as subdivided into two sections, 'Issues in Early Seventeenth-Century Solo Song' (I–IV) and 'Monteverdi Studies' (VI–XII); my essay on concepts of 'aria' in the late sixteenth and early seventeenth centuries (V) provides the link between the two. The volume marks something of new direction in my work from the late 1980s, in contrast to the strongly archival basis of much of my doctoral and post-doctoral research (as seen in *Music, Patronage and Print-*

*ing in Late Renaissance Florence*), although the seeds were sown earlier. I was no longer in a position to spend long stretches of time in the archives, and if truth be told, I was becoming somewhat disenchanted by the way in which contemporary documents often seem to distance us from, rather than bring us closer to, the music. I had also been commissioned to write something of a textbook on the period which by its nature needed to be predominantly musical rather than source-based.[3] It was almost inevitable that I would have to start looking at music in a different light, for all the continuities of interests from my previous work.

One such continuity is the issue of music printing and publishing: a broader statistical treatment of the output of Italian music printers in this period had already raised intriguing questions about the relationship between supposedly 'old' and 'new' styles and repertories (I), and I have since become interested in the way in which a 'print culture' might be seen as having influenced the course of contemporary theoretical debate (VI) and musical practice.[4] Another continuity is my work on the so-called 'new music' for solo voice and basso continuo which had already figured in my doctoral dissertation,[5] a repertory rich in interpretative problems ranging from performance (II) to analysis and criticism (IV). It was also becoming clear that generic and other labels attached to this music by modern scholars do not always square easily either with contemporary perceptions or with other evidence; this can be illustrated by close attention to the surviving sources – as, for example, in the case of Caccini's famous song 'Amarilli, mia bella' (III) – or by a careful analysis of a number of quite distinct pieces in different styles that in fact share closely related musical structures (V).

Around the time of writing these particular essays, I was also involved in two large-scale Monteverdi projects, revising Denis Arnold's 'Master Musicians' study of the composer and translating Paolo Fabbri's monograph on him.[6] This was a good moment for Monteverdi scholars, given the conferences and performances in 1993 celebrating the 350th anniversary of his death. Anyone working on music in late Renaissance and early Baroque Italy must inevitably come to terms with the greatest composer of the period, and I have chosen to do so in two ways: first, by looking at issues of musical poetics and aesthetics (in particular, the question of signification; VII–IX); and second, by submitting each of his dramatic works to close analysis in new historical and critical contexts (X–XII), an ongoing project that seems set to produce a book.[7] Here my earlier interest in aria in terms of style, structure and genre took on a new focus in the context of changing notions of resemblance and representation that, like many of the 'new' musicologists (not least, Gary Tomlinson), I construe in somewhat (too?) trendy Foucauldian terms (VIII), and also, more recently, in the light of developments in gender studies (XI).[9] But my readings also have an empirical basis both within the music – for all the controversy caused by the application of neo-Schenkerian techniques to this repertory – and within its poetry. My attention to verse–music relationships in Monteverdi's theatrical works – such that one can discuss music with some confidence even if only a text survives (X) – stems most obviously from my work on Mozart's operas, although it also harks back to more primitive efforts in this area in dealing with Peri's *Euridice* in my dissertation. I also find myself returning to and re-reading archival and other documents in intriguing ways to put these rich works in environments that still remain to be fully understood (XII).[10] Thus it seems likely that my future work will seek to reintegrate and synthesize the separate strands in my work seen in these two collections of essays.

As with the previous volume, in preparing and ordering these essays for reprinting, I have not undertaken a serious process of correction and revision – nor have I paid attention to places where material is (occasionally) repeated from one essay to another – and the wise reader will examine the footnotes of later essays to discover the more recent work of scholars in the light of which my earlier work will need to be reconsidered. They are presented roughly in chronological order of writing (and hence not entirely in order of publication), although I have altered the sequence for the sake of thematic groupings (XI was written between VI and VII, and I have reversed I and II, and VIII and IX).

In terms of recording my debts of gratitude, the first footnotes of each of these essays bear witness to the institutions, libraries, colleagues and friends who have supported my work in innumerable ways. Many of these essays were tried out as papers presented before the Biennial Conference on Baroque Music (UK) and the annual meetings of the Society for Seventeenth-Century Music (USA), while my students at Royal Holloway have often acted as unwitting guinea-pigs in lectures and seminars; the feedback accruing thereby may not always have made its presence felt, but it was appreciated nonetheless. Wendy Heller and I seem to take great delight in pipping each other to various posts, and likewise Massimo Ossi; our emulation, competition and homage is, for me, of the best scholarly kind. One name appears in all of these essays after 1995, my beloved wife Annegret Fauser, to whom I dedicate this collection.

TIM CARTER

*Royal Holloway, University of London,*
*March 2000*

# Endnotes

[1] 'The North Italian Courts', in C. Price (ed.), *Man & Music: The Early Baroque Era; from the Late 16th Century to the 1660s* (London, Macmillan, 1993), 23–48; '[Opera in] The Seventeenth Century', in R. Parker (ed.), *The Oxford Illustrated History of Opera* (Oxford & New York, Oxford University Press, 1994), 1–46; 'Secular Vocal Music', in R. Bray (ed.), *The Blackwell History of Music in Britain*, ii: *The Sixteenth Century* (Oxford, Blackwell, 1995), 147–209

[2] 'Mozart, da Ponte and the Ensemble: Methods in Progress?', in S. Sadie (ed.), *Wolfgang Amadè Mozart: Essays on his Life and his Music* (Oxford, Clarendon Press, 1996), 241–9.

[3] *Music in Late Renaissance & Early Baroque Italy* (London, Batsford [Portland, Oregon, Amadeus Press], 1992).

[4] For the latter, see my 'Printing the "New Music"', in K. van Orden (ed.), *Music and the Cultures of Print* (New York & London, Garland, 2000), 3–37.

[5] *Jacopo Peri (1561–1633): His Life and Works* (PhD dissertation, University of Birmingham, 1980; repr. New York & London, Garland Publications, 1989).

[6] D. Arnold, *Monteverdi*, rev. T. Carter, 'The Master Musicians' (3rd edn., London, Dent, 1990); P. Fabbri, *Monteverdi*, trans. T. Carter (Cambridge, Cambridge University Press, 1994).

[7] The saga continues in 'Lamenting Ariadne?', *Early Music*, 27 (1999), 395–405; 'New Light on Monteverdi's *Ballo delle ingrate* (Mantua, 1608)', *Il saggiatore musicale* (forthcoming [2000]); 'Singing *Orfeo*: On the Performers of Monteverdi's First Opera', *Recercare* (forthcoming [2000]).

[8] See also, most recently, my 'Finding a Voice: Vittoria Archilei and the Florentine "New Music"', in L. Hutson (ed.), *Feminism and Renaissance Studies*, 'Oxford Readings in Feminism' (Oxford, Clarendon Press, 1999), 450–67.

[9] W. A. Mozart: 'Le nozze di Figaro', 'Cambridge Opera Handbooks' (Cambridge, Cambridge University Press, 1987).

[10] See also my *Polemics on the 'Musica moderna': Agostino Agazzari, 'La musica ecclesiastica'; Marco Scacchi, 'Breve discorso sopra la musica moderna'*, ed. Z. Szweykowski & T. Carter, trans. T. Carter, 'Practica musica', 1 (Kraków, Musica Iagellonica, 1993); *Composing Opera: From 'Dafne' to 'Ulisse errante'*, ed. Z. Szweykowski & T. Carter, trans. T. Carter, 'Practica musica', 2 (Kraków, Musica Iagellonica, 1994).

# ACKNOWLEDGEMENTS

Grateful acknowledgement is made to the following for their kind permission to reproduce the essays included in this volume: the Royal Musical Association, London (I); Oxford University Press (II, III, VIII, IX, XII); Libreria Musicale Italiana, Lucca (IV); Basil Blackwell Ltd., Oxford (V); Pendragon Press, Stuyvesant, NY (VI); Leo S. Olschki, Florence (VII); Accademia Nazionale Virgiliana di Scienze, Lettere e Arti, Mantua (VII); University of Chicago Press (X); Cambridge University Press (XI).

# PUBLISHER'S NOTE

The articles in this volume, as in all others in the Collected Studies Series, have not been given a new, continuous pagination. In order to avoid confusion, and to facilitate their use where these same studies have been referred to elsewhere, the original pagination has been maintained wherever possible.

Each article has been given a Roman numeral in order of appearance, as listed in the Contents. This number is repeated on each page and quoted in the index entries.

# I

# MUSIC PUBLISHING IN ITALY, c.1580–c.1625:
# SOME PRELIMINARY OBSERVATIONS

Many scholars have attempted to come to terms with the stylistic diversification and experimentation that characterises Italian sacred and secular music at the turn of the sixteenth century. Changes in aesthetic attitudes and musical styles are both seen as typical of the transition from the Renaissance to the Baroque periods. However, an important source for documenting this transition–the activities of the major music publishing houses in Italy centred largely in Venice, Rome, Milan and Naples–has been unduly neglected. To what extent did these activities reflect, or even influence, the course of musical development during this period, and how can an account of them aid the scholar in solving the complex historical problems of this transitional age?

The splendid bibliographical researches of Emil Vogel, Claudio Sartori, Howard Mayer Brown and, of course, the compilers of the *Répertoire international des sources musicales* have resulted in listings of the sacred, secular and instrumental publications that survive from the sixteenth and seventeenth centuries.[1] Their catalogues are variously organized either by composer or chronologically. The composer-listings of the New Vogel and RISM Series A/I are clearly useful to scholars seeking information on individual musicians. However, they reflect a composer-orientated view of music history that can be limiting. For scholars seeking to come to terms with compositional trends, chronological listings are much more relevant. My aim, therefore, is to demonstrate the potential of reorganizing the New Vogel and RISM Series A/I into chronological order, thereby providing, in conjunction with other catalogues, a year-by-year survey of music publishing in Italy over the 1600s. This study, which concentrates on the publishing of secular vocal music, represents the first fruits of a long-term research project. Thus my remarks are best regarded as preliminary and somewhat tentative. Nor am I the first to embark on this path. Anne-Marie Bautier-Regnier has studied the output of Italian music publishers from 1501 to 1563, and, more recently, Angelo Pompilio has presented statistics covering this output from 1550 to 1650.[2] I am indebted to their work. However, I hope that the presentation and analysis of the more detailed statistics given here will raise further questions and offer possible solutions.[3]

It is worth discussing general trends in Italian music publishing of the period 1550–1640 to provide a broad context in which to place my more detailed comments on the publishing of secular vocal music over the 1600s. Most accounts of music publishing in Italy at the end of the sixteenth century paint a picture of an industry in decline. According to Donald Krummel, Venetian music publishing reached its heyday in the decades leading up to 1580, whereupon there began a period of slow decline that can be linked to economic recession in the republic as it moved into the new century. Furthermore, as Venetian music publishing ebbed, Roman publishers came into the ascendant.[4] Iain Fenlon describes the 1590s as 'a period in which Italian publishing has already begun to experience the difficulties that would seriously besiege it in the first years of the seventeenth century. . . . It is more or less certain that towards the end of the [sixteenth] century the great Venetian printers became noticeably less adventurous in their repertoire'.[5]

Table 1 gives details of music publications for every fifth year from 1550 to 1640.[6] In the light of the above remarks, it might be seen as containing some surprising figures. Column 1 gives the total

Table 1: Total number of music publications issued by Italian publishers, 1550–1640 (every fifth year)

| Year | 1<br>Total | 2<br>Re-editions | 3<br>Gardano/Scotto/<br>Amadino/Vincenti |
|---|---|---|---|
| 1550 | 18 | 8  [44.4%] | 16  [88.9%] |
| 1555 | 30 | 7  [23.3%] | 22  [73.3%] |
| 1560 | 36 | 17  [47.2%] | 33  [91.7%] |
| 1565 | 37 | 20  [54.1%] | 33  [89.2%] |
| 1570 | 56 | 15  [26.8%] | 48  [85.7%] |
| 1575 | 40 | 7  [17.5%] | 32  [80%] |
| 1580 | 56 | 14  [25%) ] | 42  [75%] |
| 1585 | 99 | 23  [23.2%] | 77  [77.8%] |
| 1590 | 81 | 25  [30.9%] | 61  [75.3%] |
| 1595 | 67 | 16  [23.9%] | 52  [77.6%] |
| 1600 | 92 | 28  [30.4%] | 72  [78.3%] |
| 1605 | 78 | 21  [26.9%] | 60  [76.9%] |
| 1610 | 83 | 24  [28.9%] | 59  [71.1%] |
| 1615 | 90 | 23  [25.6%] | 68  [75.6%] |
| 1620 | 97 | 23  [23.7%] | 63  [64.9%] |
| 1625 | 56 | 12  [21.4%] | 41  [73.2%] |
| 1630 | 42 | 4  [ 9.5%] | 24  [57.1%] |
| 1635 | 35 | 6  [17.1%] | 22  [62.9%] |
| 1640 | 58 | 7  [12.1%] | 39  [67.2%] |

number of sacred, secular and instrumental publications for the year, column 2 the number of re-editions, and column 3 the number of volumes issued by the four major Venetian houses of Gardano, Scotto and (after 1583) Amadino and Vincenti. The figures in columns 2 and 3 are also expressed as percentages of the total in column 1. Column 1 presents Italian music publishing as being in a fairly healthy state for the bulk of the period under discussion. There appears to be an increase in activity until the mid-1580s. Thereafter the number of publications seems to remain at a high level until the mid-1620s, with a decline in the 1630s and a slight increase in activity in 1640. The total annual number of publications was in the 90s in 1585, 1600, 1615 and 1620.

From column 3, it does appear that the percentage share of the Italian market held by the four major Venetian publishing houses did indeed decline slightly from the late 1570s. Therefore, Krummel's and Fenlon's observations may to some extent be justified. Moreover, such figures are no indication of the quality of the prints they represent: whether this declines in terms of content or presentation is another matter. However, although it is clear that the Venetian houses were facing increased competition over the 1600s, their actual output does not seem to have decreased significantly until the economic slump of the early 1620s. Certainly, there is little evidence to suggest a serious decline in their activities until this time: on the contrary, 1585–1620 appears to be the peak period of Venetian music publishing.[7] There is no doubt that these Venetian publishers were facing economic difficulties in the early seventeenth century, and, for example, it may have been these difficulties which led Amadino to cease publishing music more or less completely in 1617. However, in 1620, the Gardano firm (now headed by Bartolomeo Magni) issued at least 30 volumes compared with 19 in 1615, and the Vincenti 33 compared with 31.

I

Although the general level of activity of Italian publishing houses may have remained reasonably stable from the mid-1580s until the 1620s, it is clear that the nature of these activities changed considerably. Fig.1 compares the number of sacred and secular publications for each year given in Table 1 (instrumental publications have been omitted).[8] A remarkable picture emerges. In the sample years from 1550 to 1575, secular publications clearly outweigh sacred ones, and the latter remain at a fairly low level. This confirms the trend noted by Lewis Lockwood as beginning in the late 1530s, when the printing of sacred music went into decline and that of secular music rapidly increased.[9] The publication of sacred music in the sample years between 1580 and 1600 is healthier, although secular publications still predominate (and particularly in 1585). However, in the first decades of the seventeenth century the situation changes considerably. The publication of sacred music increases still further, and in the sample years after 1610 it decisively outweighs that of secular music.[10] It would appear that from the 1580s to the early 1620s, a number of publishers fundamentally reorientated their activities from secular music towards sacred music. The point is emphasised by comparing the output of particular publishing houses for three of the 'peak' years seen in Table 1, 1585, 1600 and 1620 (see Table 2).[11]

Table 2: Music publications issued by Italian publishers in 1585, 1600 and 1620

|  |  | 1585 | | | 1600 | | | 1620 | | |
| --- | --- | --- | --- | --- | --- | --- | --- | --- | --- | --- |
|  |  | sacred | secular | instrumental | sacred | secular | instrumental | sacred | secular | instrumental |
| Venice | Gardano | 8 | 17 | 1 | 6 | 20 | 0 | 22 | 7 | 1 |
|  | Scotto | 4 | 19 | 0 | 5 | 2 | 0 | — | — | — |
|  | Amadino | 8 | 18 | 2 | 8 | 13 | 1 | — | — | — |
|  | Vincenti | see Amadino* | | | 5 | 11 | 1 | 21 | 10 | 2 |
| Other |  | 9 | 12 | 1 | 11 | 8 | 1 | 19 | 13 | 2 |
| | Total | 29 | 66 | 4 | 35 | 54 | 3 | 62 | 30 | 5 |

*In 1585, Amadino and Vincenti held a joint company in partnership.

It is not clear to what extent this reorientation was caused simply by a decline of market interest, and therefore publishing activity, in secular music. For example, some of the new secular styles for solo voice(s) and basso continuo may have been seen as too difficult for the average amateur musician, and therefore as less saleable. On the other hand, a number of other factors may also come into account. Only a few can be broached here. The relative paucity of sacred publications until the 1570s is rather surprising, given the known level of musical activity in at least the major ecclesiastical institutions in Italy in the first two-thirds of the sixteenth century. However, it is possible that many *cappelle* relied largely on manuscript sources for their performing material: witness the rich manuscript collections of sacred music stemming from Bologna, Casale Monferrato, Ferrara, Mantua, Modena, Trent and the Vatican. Quite apart from the matter of cost, manuscript choirbooks may have been easier to use and more reliable than prints. Indeed, there is evidence to suggest that even in the early seventeenth century, some institutions were buying single copies of sacred prints and having them transcribed into manuscript.[12] Furthermore, manuscripts allowed individual *maestri di cappella* to compose, select and order musical items as befitted the particular liturgical needs of their institutions. The lack of such flexibility must have counted against prints, which could only contain the most basic and widespread liturgical repertoires.

In this light, it may be significant that the upturn in the publishing of sacred music appears to occur shortly after the Conciliar reformers had settled their opinions on the role of music within the liturgy, and, perhaps more importantly, on a standard liturgy to be practised throughout the Catholic

I

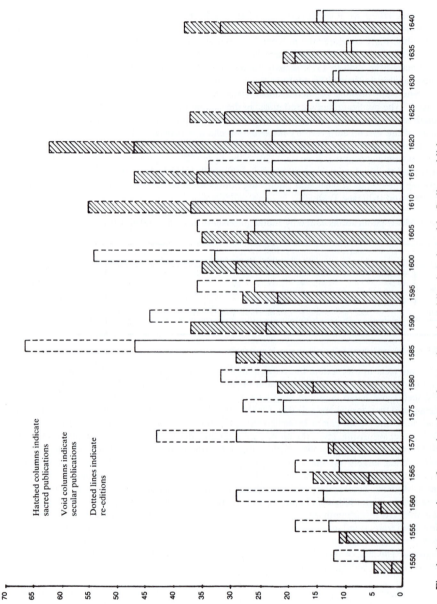

Fig. 1: A comparison of sacred and secular vocal music publications issued by Italian publishers, 1550–1640 (every fifth year)

Church. The standardisation of the liturgy was no doubt useful to Italian music publishers, offering them a more predictable and stable market for their wares. The nature of sacred publications after Trent suggests that publishers were quick to turn this to their advantage. Moreover, in mid-century, publishers may have been reluctant to commit themselves financially to issuing sacred music while the status of music within the Church was so uncertain. Thus they were no doubt encouraged by the decisions of the Councils in the mid-1560s. Furthermore, the increasingly splendid activities of the Church in Counter-Reformation Italy as ecclesiastical institutions entered a new period of stability must have indicated to music publishers that expanding their activities in the field of sacred music could produce favourable financial results.

However, this may not entirely explain the marked increase in the publishing of sacred music in the early seventeenth century. Here the advent of the new styles for small vocal forces and basso continuo must surely be taken in account.[13] The apparently rapid adoption of these styles may have been due to economic no less than purely musical pressures, for there is some evidence to suggest that at least some ecclesiastical institutions were reducing their commitment to music over the 1600s owing to their being in financial and other difficulties.[14] Whatever the case, one can suggest that the new styles, although appealing in themselves, were also intended to sustain, if not encourage, the performance of multi-part sacred music within or outside the Church. Lodovico Grossi da Viadana referred to this in the preface to his *Cento concerti ecclesiastici* of 1602, and the *Cento concerti* received at least seven editions before 1612 and was emulated by numerous other publications. Much archival work remains to be done before we may postulate any change in the level and nature of musical activity resulting from (or leading to) the gradual replacing of the polyphonic idiom of the *stile antico* with the perhaps more accessible and more popular *stile moderno* in sacred music over the 1600s. However, the activities of Italian music publishers suggest that some changes did occur.

There are obvious dangers in drawing firm conclusions from the data thus far presented. The sample years chosen here may or may not be typical, and indeed the publishing of sacred music appears to have increased in the 1590s more than Fig.1 would suggest. (In 1599, for example, sacred publications outnumbered secular publications by 41 to 28.) 1607 marked a further peak in secular publications (60 secular publications compared with 48 sacred). However, the broad picture presented here is confirmed by the statistics presented by Pompilio.[15] It must also be remembered that these figures refer only to what has survived as ascertainable from recent bibliographical catalogues, and thus may not give an accurate indication of the real output of Italian publishing houses. However, publishers' catalogues from the period by and large support the above remarks. For example, the Gardano and Vincenti catalogues of 1591 each list publications of sacred and secular music roughly in the proportion 1:2.[16] Similarly, the catalogue issued by the heirs of the Florentine printer and bookseller Filippo Giunta in 1604/5 contains sacred and secular music in the proportion 7:11.[17] In contrast, the Vincenti catalogue of 1621, which lists well over three times as many items as that of 1591, contains sacred and secular music in the proportion 11:7.[18] The situation is similar in the Vincenti catalogue of 1649.[19]

Figs.2(a) and 2(b) provide a more detailed year-by-year analysis of the output of secular publications.[20] The three superimposed graphs indicate the number of re-editions, new editions and the total output for each year. They flesh out the picture presented in Fig.1, although it must be remembered that the decline in secular publications apparent in Fig.2(b) should be taken in the context of the reorientation of publishing activities discussed above. There is a steady build up in activity until the late 1560s, both in terms of increased output and of the issuing of new music (the change in proportion of re-editions and new editions is remarkable). In the 1570s, however, music

I

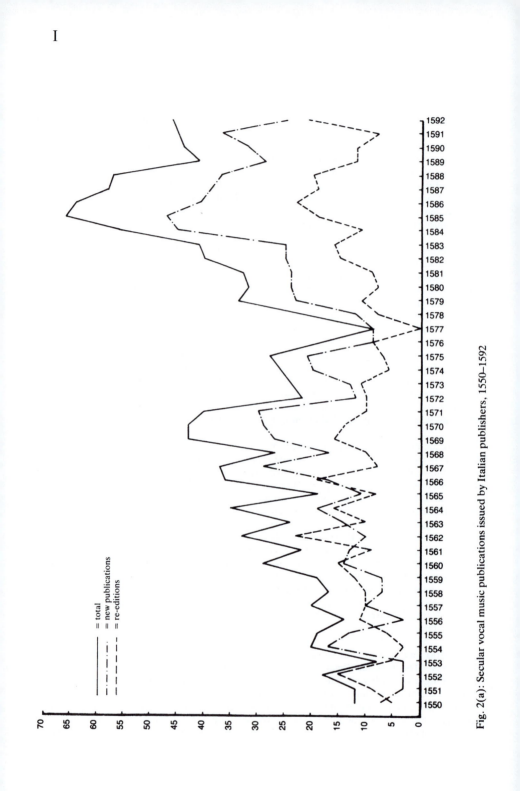

Fig. 2(a): Secular vocal music publications issued by Italian publishers, 1550–1592

I

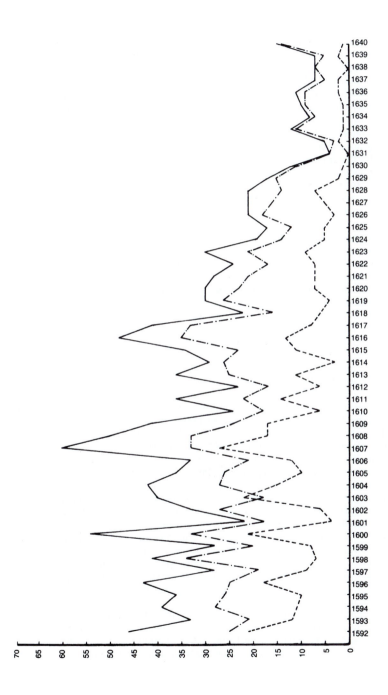

Fig. 2(b): Secular vocal music publications issued by Italian publishers, 1592–1640

publishers (and particularly the Venetian houses) appear to have been affected firstly by the war against the Turks from 1570 to 1573, and then by the outbreak of plague in 1575, 1576 and 1577. It may also be significant that during the plague years, the publishing of lighter genres (three- and four-part villanellas, etc.) declined quite markedly, and more so than that of the five- and six-part madrigal. From the trough in 1577, we see a dramatic increase up to the mid-1580s, which was no doubt encouraged in its later stages by the appearance in 1583 of the publishing company run jointly by Ricciardo Amadino and Giacomo Vincenti (who formed separate companies in 1586). After the peak of 1585-8, the graphs level out, with smaller peaks in 1600 (perhaps caused by a large-scale reprinting programme apparently initiated by the Gardano and Vincenti houses), 1607 (aided by the brief life of Alessandro Raverii's publishing house from 1600 to 1609) and 1616 (also a peak year in the issuing of sacred publications). Secular output decreases from 1618 or 1619, and this decline continues through the 1620s, a period of economic depression in northern Italy. Output reaches a very low ebb in the first years of the 1630s, when plague was again besetting the peninsula, and only gradually recovers during the rest of the decade, although it never again reaches its former heights.

It is comparatively easy to detect general trends in Fig.2 and to identify the immediate effects of major crises such as war or plague, or the healthier periods when existing publishing houses boosted their output and new ones came into existence. However, there are great dangers in attempting to account for the more localised variations between individual years or groups of years without greater knowledge of the economics and practice of music publishing in this period. It is very tempting to relate the annual variations in output to the general economic conditions prevailing in a given year, and indeed in the case of Venice there does seem to be a correlation between the activities of the major publishing houses and fluctuations in the Venetian economy.[21] However, some caution is necessary in accepting any direct relationship: first, because economic statistics are not yet available in the depth of detail necessary for such an exercise; and second, because the methods of financing music publishing in the republic are by no means clear. For example, Richard Tilden Rapp has convincingly demonstrated that the so-called economic decline of Venice in the early seventeenth century is something of a myth, and that instead there was a reorientation of the Venetian economy away from international trade and manufacturing towards services and 'luxury' goods.[22] Thus the extent to which music publishing may have suffered from this reorientation, if it suffered at all, is unclear. One conclusion that can be firmly drawn, however, is that the major changes in secular styles which music historians deem to be so important over the 1600s took place against a backdrop of stasis, if not gradual decline, in secular music publishing, and indeed, as we have seen, in the face of a reorientation of the activities of a number of publishing houses towards sacred music.

One advantage of a chronological listing of publications is that it allows us to examine firstly the relative distribution of particular types of publications (and therefore particular musical genres) in any given year, and secondly, the durability or otherwise of individual genres, forms and styles. Table 3 gives a breakdown of secular publications without an obligatory basso continuo (whether in whole or in part) from 1580 to 1625 according to the number of voices in each publication.[23] Thus we can see the frequency of three-, four-, five- and six-part publications for each year during this period. In performing this breakdown, a certain degree of flexibility has been necessary. For example, a print of five-part madrigals will often contain one or more six- or eight-part pieces at the end, and these pieces may or may not be advertised on the title-page. For the present purpose, such a print counts as a five-part publication. However, a publication specifically titled, for example, *Il primo libro de madrigali a cinque et a sei voci* has not been included in either column 3 or column 4. Nevertheless, such 'mixed' volumes, and also spiritual madrigals, two-part collections, volumes such as madrigal comedies and the like, and, after 1600, volumes with an obligatory basso continuo, have been

Table 3: Secular vocal music publications issued by Italian publishers, 1580–1624, classified according to scoring

| Year | 1<br>a3 | 2<br>a4 | 3<br>a5 | 4<br>a6 | 5<br>Sub-total<br>(1+2+3+4) | 6<br>Total |
|---|---|---|---|---|---|---|
| 1580 | 3 (3) | 6 (5) | 15 (9) | 3 (3) | | 32 (24) |
| 1581 | 1 (1) | 5 (2) | 17 (14) | 7 (5) | | 33 (24) |
| 1582 | 8 (5) | 7 (3) | 17 (12) | 7 (4) | | 40 (25) |
| 1583 | 1 (1) | 7 (3) | 23 (14) | 7 (4) | | 41 (25) |
| 1584 | 6 (6) | 11 (7) | 22 (19) | 11 (9) | | 56 (45) |
| | 19 [9.4%] | 36 [17.8%] | 94 [46.5%] | 35 [17.3%] | 184 [91.1%] | 202 |
| 1585 | 4 (3) | 14 (7) | 35 (28) | 6 (3) | | 66 (47) |
| 1586 | 7 (2) | 13 (7) | 29 (21) | 7 (5) | | 64 (41) |
| 1587 | 12 (8) | 11 (6) | 23 (18) | 7 (3) | | 58 (39) |
| 1588 | 11 (9) | 10 (6) | 23 (16) | 2 (0) | | 57 (37) |
| 1589 | 8 (6) | 5 (3) | 19 (13) | 5 (4) | | 41 (29) |
| | 42 [14.7%] | 53 [18.5%] | 129 [45.1%] | 27 [9.4%] | 251 [87.8%] | 286 |
| 1590 | 9 (6) | 7 (3) | 15 (11) | 5 (5) | | 44 (32) |
| 1591 | 9 (6) | 6 (5) | 17 (14) | 8 (7) | | 45 (37) |
| 1592 | 10 (7) | 8 (2) | 15 (9) | 8 (4) | | 46 (25) |
| 1593 | 5 (4) | 7 (6) | 13 (7) | 4 (1) | | 33 (21) |
| 1594 | 11 (7) | 4 (3) | 17 (12) | 5 (4) | | 39 (28) |
| | 44 [21.3%] | 32 [15.5%] | 77 [37.2%] | 30 [14.5%] | 183 [88.4%] | 207 |
| 1595 | 5 (3) | 6 (3) | 17 (15) | 5 (3) | | 36 (26) |
| 1596 | 7 (3) | 7 (3) | 20 (14) | 4 (2) | | 43 (25) |
| 1597 | 6 (3) | 4 (2) | 12 (9) | 0 (0) | | 28 (19) |
| 1598 | 4 (1) | 4 (2) | 24 (22) | 1 (1) | | 41 (34) |
| 1599 | 5 (3) | 2 (1) | 11 (9) | 2 (1) | | 28 (20) |
| | 27 [15.3%] | 23 [13.1%] | 84 [47.7%] | 12 [6.8%] | 146 [83%] | 176 |
| 1600 | 15 (8) | 6 (5) | 22 (12) | 3 (1) | | 54 (33) |
| 1601 | 5 (4) | 3 (2) | 5 (4) | 4 (4) | | 22 (18) |
| 1602 | 5 (3) | 2 (0) | 18 (16) | 1 (1) | | 33 (27) |
| 1603 | 7 (3) | 6 (1) | 18 (11) | 4 (1) | | 40 (18) |
| 1604 | 8 (3) | 4 (3) | 20 (14) | 3 (3) | | 42 (27) |
| | 40 [20.9%] | 21 [11%] | 83 [43.5%] | 15 [7.9%] | 159 [83.2%] | 191 |
| 1605 | 7 (6) | 1 (0) | 15 (10) | 3 (2) | | 36 (26) |
| 1606 | 4 (3) | 2 (1) | 17 (10) | 0 (0) | | 33 (21) |
| 1607 | 7 (3) | 6 (5) | 25 (9) | 2 (1) | | 60 (33) |
| 1608 | 6 (5) | 6 (2) | 20 (12) | 0 (0) | | 50 (33) |
| 1609 | 1 (1) | 1 (1) | 24 (13) | 1 (0) | | 41 (24) |
| | 25 [11.4%] | 16 [7.3%] | 101 [45.9%] | 6 [2.7%] | 148 [67.3%] | 220 |
| 1610 | 3 (2) | 1 (1) | 3 (2) | 1 (0) | | 24 (18) |
| 1611 | 5 (4) | 2 (1) | 17 (10) | 0 (0) | | 36 (22) |
| 1612 | 3 (3) | 1 (0) | 12 (9) | 0 (0) | | 23 (17) |
| 1613 | 3 (3) | 5 (2) | 10 (5) | 0 (0) | | 36 (25) |
| 1614 | 4 (4) | 0 (0) | 7 (4) | 0 (0) | | 29 (26) |
| | 18 [12.2%] | 9 [6.1%] | 49 [33.1%] | 1 [0.7%] | 77 [52%] | 148 |
| 1615 | 7 (4) | 1 (0) | 10 (9) | 0 (0) | | 34 (23) |
| 1616 | 4 (4) | 2 (1) | 14 (8) | 0 (0) | | 48 (35) |
| 1617 | 2 (2) | 2 (0) | 12 (7) | 1 (1) | | 41 (33) |
| 1618 | 2 (1) | 0 (0) | 5 (3) | 0 (0) | | 22 (16) |
| 1619 | 2 (2) | 1 (1) | 7 (5) | 0 (0) | | 30 (26) |
| | 17 [9.7%] | 6 [3.4%] | 48 [27.4%] | 1 [0.6%] | 72 [41.1%] | 175 |
| 1620 | 1 (0) | 1 (0) | 4 (3) | 0 (0) | | 30 (23) |
| 1621 | 1 (1) | 1 (0) | 5 (2) | 1 (1) | | 28 (21) |
| 1622 | 0 (0) | 1 (1) | 4 (2) | 0 (0) | | 24 (17) |
| 1623 | 0 (0) | 1 (1) | 2 (2) | 0 (0) | | 30 (21) |
| 1624 | 2 (1) | 0 (0) | 2 (1) | 0 (0) | | 19 (14) |
| | 4 [3.1%] | 4 [3.1%] | 17 [13%] | 1 [0.8%] | 26 [19.8%] | 131 |

included in the figure in column 6, which therefore gives the total output for the year (compare with Fig.2). Two further points should be made. First, I have focussed on the total number of publications in a particular scoring in any particular year, including re-editions. This has some implications which will be discussed below, but for present purposes it does seem that re-editions should not be excluded from any attempt to discover fluctuating patterns in the activity of secular music publishing or, for that matter, changing tastes in the market for which publishers were catering. Nevertheless, to provide complete information, I have given the number of new editions in each category in parentheses. Thus the difference between this number in parentheses and the figure preceding it indicates the number of re-editions in the category in the year. Second, although this breakdown is according to the number of voices required by any given publication, it is also a reasonably reliable indicator of the attention devoted to particular genres. Thus the great majority of three-part publications contain lighter genres such as the villanella or canzonetta, with, at least in this period, three-part madrigals being in a very definite minority. Similarly, the five- and six-part publications by and large consist of madrigals. The situation is less clear in the case of four-part publications, which can contain either madrigals or villanellas, canzonettas and related genres, though madrigals tend to predominate.

As one might expect, in the last quarter of the sixteenth century five-part publications (and therefore five-part madrigals) consistently form a major part of the output of each year, followed by three- and four-part prints and then six-part ones. This situation lasts well into the 1600s. However, in the case of three- and four-part publications, the latter appear to decline as the period progresses, while the former overtake them for a time and appear to last longer. The six-part publication has a rather uneven existence, disappearing almost completely after 1605. It is possible that in the first two decades of the new century, three- and five-part scorings became the staple format for those composers preferring not to adopt the new secular styles with basso continuo. However, perhaps the most remarkable feature of Table 3 is the relative stability of five-part publications that continues well into the second decade of the seventeenth century. There are peaks in the output of five-part pieces in the mid-1580s, late 1590s and 1607. (In the case of 1607, the peak is caused in part by the large number of re-editions issued primarily by Alessandro Raverii.) In the early 1590s, five-part publications lost some ground to three-part ones (and indeed, the period 1587 to 1594 appears to represent a flourishing of the three-part genres, and in particular the canzonetta). However, five-part publications regain their position between 1595 and 1600 (at the expense of three-part ones), and, with the exception of 1601, 1610 and 1614, they remain in a reasonably high profile until 1618. To be sure, 1585-86 represents the real high point for five-part prints. Nevertheless, it seems clear that the five-part madrigal held its own against the inroads of the newer styles for much longer than one might expect.

This is clearly cause for comment. There is no doubt that the first decade of the seventeenth century saw a number of major stylistic changes come to fruition, as can be seen in the publication of new genres with basso continuo (for example, the solo song, duet and continuo madrigal) from 1602 onwards. However, in the context of the overall secular output of this decade, such changes only gradually make themselves apparent. Indeed, comparing the figures for 1600–1609 with each preceding decade, there are few marked differences, and in the case of five-part publications (and therefore the five-part madrigal) there is even a notable recovery, if not increase, when compared with the output of the 1590s. The five-part madrigal does not appear to have suffered significantly from the competition of the newer genres with basso continuo at least until the second decade of the century. Rather, on the basis of these figures one could argue that the newer styles gained ground

I

more at the expense of lighter genres such as the canzonetta than of the serious five-part madrigal. In other words, the solo song and duet may initially have been seen as lighter genres themselves and not as serious competitors with the polyphonic idiom. This is borne out by the contents of a number of publications of the first decade of the century containing monodies and duets, for example by Domenico Maria Melli, Domenico Brunetti, Lodovico Bellanda, Francesco Lambardi, Giovanni Ghizzolo and Enrico Radesca da Foggia. The survival of the five-part madrigal and the possible equating of the solo song and duet with lighter genres are ironic, to say the least, given the high-minded ideals of many of the first protagonists of the new styles of the early Baroque period. However, one should not press the point too strongly.

This evidence for the stability of the five-part madrigal presents a picture that is a little at odds with that offered by most music histories of the period. However, on reflection it should not be too surprising. The five-part madrigal without basso continuo is unlikely to have been abandoned overnight, even if one might reasonably expect the process to have taken less than fifteen years. One must first question the speed with which publishers responded to changes in musical supply and demand. It is not clear to what extent they kept abreast of compositional developments and audience tastes in this period, even if they would have been foolish to ignore them completely. Indeed, it is possible that publishers rather artificially preserved the traditional genres in the face of market forces whether for economic or other reasons or out of a rather cautious business sense. Thus some may have been reluctant to issue volumes in newer styles until they could be sure of the outcome of what might have been seen as a conflict between the *stile antico* and the *stile moderno*. Furthermore, there is no doubt that the five-part madrigal retained a prestige afforded it by tradition. Thus it may have remained common for a composer to issue at least one set of old-style polyphonic madrigals in his career (and in particular at its outset) in order to prove to the world his musical skills and seriousness of purpose. Finally, it is clear that the preservation of the five-part madrigal was due in no little part to the appearance of re-editions, and if one does not take these into account a decline in five-part publications is perhaps apparent earlier in the seventeenth century (see the figures in parentheses in Table 3, column 3). Nevertheless, the point remains that a market for five-part madrigals appears to have existed well into the second decade of the new century.

Although Table 3 is concerned primarily with secular publications without continuo, it does give some indication of the effect of the newer styles on the more established genres. The difference between the figures in column 5 (the sub-total) and column 6 (the total output) indicates the number of publications which do not fit into the classifications in columns 1–4. From 1580 to 1604, this difference is slight, albeit gradually increasing. However, the difference becomes greater from the middle of the first decade of the seventeenth century, largely because of the appearance of publications with basso continuo. Thus in 1600–1604, publications devoted each mainly to three-, four-, five- and six-part pieces without basso continuo take up 83.2% of the total output for that period, in 1605–1609, 67.3%, 1610–14, 52%, 1615–19, 41.1%, and 1620–24, 19.8%. It is clear that the newer styles were gradually taking over. Nevertheless, in 1610–14, publications in the standard scorings without basso continuo still outnumbered those with basso continuo, and the figures for such publications without basso continuo remain reasonable healthy until about 1617 and 1618.

This can be seen more clearly in Fig.3, which superimposes two graphs indicating the number of secular publications with and without basso continuo.[24] Thus these graphs also give a rough indication of the relative weight of 'old'- and 'new'-style publications in the period. Caution is necessary here, for there are obvious dangers in categorising publications with basso continuo as 'modern' and those without as 'conservative'. When the basso continuo is used as a simple *basso seguente*, it has little

I

Fig. 3: The appearance of a basso continuo in secular vocal music publications issued by Italian publishers, 1600–1635

- - - - - = publications without basso continuo

———— = publications with basso continuo

stylistic relevance. Furthermore, there is more to the *stile moderno* than simply the use of a basso continuo, and, conversely, some publications (for example, of five-part madrigals) without basso continuo might still exhibit, if not inaugurate, many features of the new styles. Nevertheless, the results seen in Fig.3 are significant. Obviously there is no doubt that publications without basso continuo gradually decline in the first three decades of the seventeenth century, and that those with basso continuo increase. However, it does seem that the adoption of the basso continuo (and therefore on the whole the adoption of the new styles) in secular publications was a slow process. After a 'false start' in the early 1600s there is a gradual rise to 1608, but only from 1613 onwards do publications with basso continuo regularly equal or outnumber those without, and indeed not until 1617 or 1618 do publications with basso continuo dominate to any great extent. The attention devoted by historians of secular music in the early 1600s to the rise of the newer solo song, duet and continuo madrigal may be warranted in terms of the music itself, but it is perhaps disproportionate when viewed in the context of the activities of music publishers during this period.

From Fig.3, it appears that the basso continuo did not become standard in secular publications until after 1617, even if it had been asserting itself in the early 1610s. It does seem that the situation in sacred music was slightly different. Table 4 gives details of sacred and secular publications with and without basso continuo for each of the sample years between 1610 and 1635 included in Table 1 and Fig.1.[25] The slow appearance of the basso continuo in secular music discussed above is clearly apparent. However, in 1605 well over half of sacred publications contained a part for basso continuo (compared with one-seventh of secular publications), and differences between sacred and secular publications are similarly marked in 1610 and 1615. It seems that a basso continuo part was provided more frequently in sacred publications than in secular ones, at least until the end of the second decade of the century. This is confirmed by the contemporary publishers' catalogues mentioned above. Of course, this is no proof that the *stile moderno* made itself felt more quickly in sacred music than in secular music, although I shall be offering further evidence below to suggest that this was indeed the case. As I have said, the presence or absence of a basso continuo part does not necessarily provide a reliable indication of the modernity or otherwise of the music in a given publication. This is especially the case in sacred publications, where the use of the basso continuo as a *basso seguente* was more prevalent, given that church musicians necessarily had an instrument to hand, and indeed where such a basso continuo part was often an optional aid to, rather than an essential ingredient of, the performance. On the other hand, in secular circles music for voice(s) and basso continuo may have been regarded as 'difficult' (or unsociable?), amateurs may have preferred the old ways, and an

Table 4:  Sacred and secular vocal music publications with and without a basso continuo part issued by Italian publishers, 1600–1635 (every fifth year)

| Year | Sacred | | Secular | |
|------|--------|----------------------|-------|----------------------|
|      | Total  | With basso continuo  | Total | With basso continuo  |
| 1600 | 35 | 5  [14.3%] | 54 | 4  [7.4%]  |
| 1605 | 35 | 21  [60%]  | 36 | 5  [13.9%] |
| 1610 | 55 | 47  [85.5%] | 24 | 12  [50%] |
| 1615 | 47 | 43  [91.5%] | 34 | 17  [50%] |
| 1620 | 62 | 62  [100%]  | 30 | 25  [83.3%] |
| 1625 | 37 | 35  [94.6%] | 17 | 14  [82.4%] |
| 1630 | 27 | 24  [88.9%] | 12 | 11  [91.7%] |
| 1635 | 21 | 21  [100%]  | 10 | 10  [100%] |

instrument may not always have been available. Thus the adoption of the basso continuo in sacred and secular music was probably made at different times and according to different needs.

As we have seen, Table 3 gives details of secular prints without basso continuo classified according to the scorings adopted in individual publications. It is difficult to provide a similar table for secular prints with basso continuo, partly because of the greater stylistic and generic diversification apparent in secular publications in the early 1600s. Thus in 1580–85, 91.1% of secular publications were clearly divided into three-, four-, five- and six-part prints. In the 1600s, however, it is noticeable that the format of secular publications becomes much less standardised and composers appear to have exercised a greater freedom of choice in their publications, not only in the decision of whether or not to use a basso continuo (and therefore, on the whole, whether or not to write in the *stile moderno*), but also in the question of the nature and number of scorings to be adopted in an individual publication. Furthermore, *stile moderno* publications exclusively devoted to a single scoring (for example, solo songs, duets) are not common. This diversification, which is indeed a marked feature of secular music publishing in the first decades of the seventeenth century, is not surprising in a period of stylistic change, but it does make it difficult to discern clear and consistent trends.

Nevertheless, some features can be noted. Fig.4 compares the output of publications containing five-part pieces without basso continuo (whether or not in volumes devoted exclusively to that scoring) with that of those containing solo songs and duets.[26] Publications of spiritual madrigals, madrigal comedies and operas have been excluded. These graphs reinforce the point made in connection with Table 3, that the five-part madrigal continued to flourish well into the seventeenth century. Again, one is impressed by the durability of the older genre and by the slowness with which the solo song and duet gained a foothold in secular music, and indeed the solo song and duet only established themselves in the second decade of the century. 1610 was not a good year for the five-part madrigal, but it recovered, and only from 1618 did the new genres inexorably take over from the older one. Moreover, it is worth noting that even in the last years of the second decade of the century, publications including solo songs and duets barely took up 50% of the total secular output of each year. Again this offers a corrective to the traditional focus of most historians of this period. However, 1618 appears to have been a crucial year for the transition between old and new styles in Italian secular music of the early seventeenth century. As well as signalling the final demise of the five-part madrigal without basso continuo, it also saw the appearance of two publications which perhaps confirmed the new trend in secular music publishing, the first of a series of volumes of canzonettas for solo voice and continuo edited by Giovanni Stefani (*Affetti amorosi*, Venice, 1618; RISM 1618[15]), and the first volume of Remigio Romano's series *Raccolta di bellissime canzonette musicali* (Vicenza, 1618; RISM 1618[17]) containing texts and guitar letters. Furthermore, it is precisely from 1618 that Nigel Fortune traces the decline of the solo madrigal in contemporary songbooks.[27] Some scholars, myself included, have suggested that the solo madrigal might best be viewed as an extension of, rather than a substitute for, the polyphonic madrigal.[28] If so, it declined with its polyphonic counterpart.

Once again, differences between sacred and secular music publications are apparent. Table 5 gives details of sacred and secular prints containing music for one or two voices and basso continuo (excluding operas and spiritual madrigals) for each of the sample years between 1600 and 1635 listed in Table 1 and Fig.1.[29] In 1610, eighteen sacred prints contained pieces for one or two voices and basso continuo, compared with eight secular prints, although the percentage share of the respective total

I

= total (see Fig. 2(b))

= publications containing five-part
pieces without continuo

= publications containing solo songs
and duets with continuo

Fig. 4: A comparison of secular vocal music publications containing five-part pieces without basso
continuo and those containing solo songs and duets with basso continuo issued by Italian
publishers, 1600–1625

Table 5: Sacred and secular vocal music publications containing pieces for one or two voices and basso continuo issued by Italian publishers, 1600–1635 (every fifth year)

| Year | Sacred | | Secular | |
|---|---|---|---|---|
| | Total | 1,2vv., bc | Total | 1,2vv., bc |
| 1600 | 35 | 1 [2.9%] | 54 | 54 [0%] |
| 1605 | 35 | 4 [11.4%] | 36 | 2 [5.6%] |
| 1610 | 55 | 18 [32.7%] | 24 | 8 [33.3%] |
| 1615 | 47 | 19 [40.4%] | 34 | 5 [14.7%] |
| 1620 | 62 | 33 [53.2%] | 30 | 15 [50%] |
| 1625 | 37 | 20 [54.1%] | 17 | 11 [64.7%] |
| 1630 | 27 | 12 [44.4%] | 12 | 10 [83.3%] |
| 1635 | 21 | 12 [57.1%] | 10 | 9 [90%] |

outputs is similar. In 1615, such pieces are present in at least 40.4% of sacred prints, compared with 14.7% of secular ones. Perhaps 1615 is an unrepresentative year as regards the publishing of secular solo songs and duets (see Fig.4). Thus in 1616, volumes containing solo songs and duets took up 35.4% of the total secular output, although this remains lower than the equivalent figure for sacred prints (45.1%). A balance is perhaps reached by 1620, although the difference in number of prints in the sacred and secular outputs (33 compared with fifteen) is significant. However, after the mid-1620s, the proportion of secular prints containing solo songs and duets appears to have increased as compared with sacred publications. One conclusion that may be drawn from these figures (and which is confirmed by other years) is that pieces for one or two voices with basso continuo were initially more readily accepted in sacred rather than secular prints. However, solo songs or duets did not come to dominate sacred publications to the same extent as they did secular ones from the mid-1620s onwards, for obvious reasons: there was still a significant place for larger-scale works in sacred music of the second quarter of the seventeenth century. There is another intriguing possibility that arises from these figures, and one which I believe can be supported by examining the careers of a significant number of early monodists: when it came to fostering and disseminating a general awareness of the new styles for solo voice(s) and basso continuo (whether in the minds of composers, publishers or the buyers of printed music) in the first two decades of the seventeenth century, sacred music was more influential than secular.

The obvious dangers of statistics of this kind require that any assessment of their significance should be undertaken with great caution. I have already discussed the difficulties of determining the real, as opposed to the surviving, output of Italian publishing houses, although the fact that these findings can be confirmed by a careful analysis of contemporary publishers' catalogues offers some encouragement. However, there are other problems. To take such an overview of music publishing in Italy is to obscure regional trends in favour of a geographical area the unity of which is a tenuous, albeit tenable, concept. There is no doubt that the consideration of place as well as year of publication is likely to reveal the existence of certain regional differences in the publishing of both sacred and secular music, differences that this preliminary report has not been able to specify. For example, there are grounds for suggesting that the Venetian houses lessened their interest in new publications of five-part madrigals without basso continuo quite early on in the century, and that the continued appearance of such publications was due at least in part to publishers more on the periphery of Italian music publishing in Rome and particularly Naples. Similarly, the different policies and relative fortunes of individual houses (or of composers associated with these houses) no doubt affected the constitution of the total output of secular music publications in this period. Angelo Pompilio has begun to confront these questions.[30] In time, it may be more useful to present statistical analyses based on an itemisation of the pieces in individual publications (with additional allowance for variations in scoring, etc., that might have been permissible in terms of contemporary performance practice), although this appears an impossibly arduous task. Dates of publication are scarcely reliable indicators of dates of composition, and thus they can only be used to detect trends in the dissemination, rather than the first appearance, of particular genres and styles. Again, to take an example only from the field of secular music, it is likely that Caccini was writing some of his solo songs at least seventeen years before the appearance of *Le nuove musiche* in 1602. Similarly, not everything that was composed appeared in print, and so publishing statistics ignore both music that remained in manuscript for reasons of choice or necessity (its quality, limited geographical relevance, or other factors that made printed publication inappropriate), and music that was improvised. Finally, we need to know much more about the economics and general practices of music publishing in Italy during this period. Can publications be distinguished according to who provided the financial support for their appearance (the composer, patron, publisher or some other)? What was the print run of an individual edition? What was the cost of a printed volume, and how did it compare with, say, a manuscript copy? For whom were publishers producing their editions? These are only some of the questions that need to be answered before any figures relating to publishers' output can be given an adequate interpretation.

The approach adopted here raises many controversial issues to do with matters of methodology as much as of interpretation. Such quantitative methods assume a direct link between the producers and users of printed music and move all too readily from the global to the particular. They also ignore more qualitative judgements on the nature and agents of change in musical style. Nevertheless, it does seem that the data presented here suggest some revision of the usual historical interpretations of this period. Most historians seeking to document the stylistic changes occuring over the 1600s tend to focus on the appearance of new genres and styles, and in particular those involving the solo song and duet with basso continuo, in secular music of the period. In so doing, they present an incomplete, if not inaccurate, picture. Fundamental questions have yet to be asked. Perhaps our search for answers will initiate renewed attempts to come to terms with the complex problems of music in late sixteenth- and early seventeenth-century Italy.

## NOTES

[1]  The following catalogues have been used in preparing this study: Claudio Sartori, *Bibliografia della musica strumentale italiana stampata in Italia fino al 1700* (Florence, 1952; supplement: 1968); RISM B/I/1: *Recueils imprimés, XVIᵉ-XVIIᵉ siècles*, ed. François Lesure (Munich, 1960); Nigel Fortune, 'A Handlist of Printed Italian Secular Monody Books, 1602–1635, *Royal Musical Association Research Chronicle*, 3 (1963), 27–50 (Supplement: 4 (1964), 98) (henceforth '*Handlist*'); Howard Mayer Brown, *Instrumental Music Printed Before 1600: a Bibliography* (Cambridge, Mass., 1965) (henceforth 'Brown 1965'); Emil Vogel, Alfred Einstein, François Lesure and Claudio Sartori, *Bibliografia della musica italiana vocale profana pubblicata dal 1500 al 1700* (Pomezia, 1977) (henceforth 'New Vogel'); RISM Series A/I: *Einzeldrucke vor 1800*, ed. Karlheinz Schlager et al. (Kassel, 1971–81); John Whenham, *Duet and Dialogue in the Age of Monteverdi* (Ann Arbor, 1982), vol.2, 25–164 ('An Analytical Catalogue of Italian Secular Duets and Dialogues c.1600 to c.1643') (henceforth '*Catalogue*'). I am most grateful to Dr Nigel Fortune, Dr Jerome Roche, Elizabeth Roche and Dr Graham Dixon for their helpful comments and suggestions. This study has also benefitted from the responses of participants at the Durham (U.K.) Conference on Baroque Music, 13–16 July 1984, at which a first version was presented.
[2]  Anne-Marie Bautier-Regnier, 'L'édition musicale italienne et les musiciens d'outremonts au XVIᵉ siècle (1501–1563)', *Entretiens d'Arras, 17–20 juin 1954: La renaissance dans les provinces du nord*, ed. François Lesure (Paris, 1956), 27–49; Angelo Pompilio, 'Editoria musicale a Napoli e in Italia nel cinque–seicento', *Musica e cultura a Napoli dal XV al XIX secolo*, ed. Lorenzo Bianconi and Renato Bossa (Florence, 1983), 79–102.

[3] Some general points on the statistics presented here should be made:
(i) I have relied only on publications which have survived either in whole or in part, or whose existence can otherwise be confirmed by recent catalogues. Publications mentioned only in late sixteenth- or early seventeenth-century catalogues have not been included. When a publication spans two years, the later year has been counted as the year of publication. I have not attempted to modify old-style dates, with the exception of Jacopo Peri, *Le musiche sopra L'Euridice* (Florence, 1600), which has been included under 1601. Giulio Caccini, *Le nuove musiche* (Florence, 1601), has been included under 1602 due to the delay in its appearance.
(ii) The classification into sacred and secular categories has been done largely according to text (Latin and Italian/French respectively) rather than function. Publications of *madrigali spirituali* are classified as 'secular'; publications of *laudi* are classified as 'sacred'. Mixed volumes (for example, of motets and madrigals, madrigals and instrumental music, etc.) have been classified according to the majority of their contents.
(iii) Publications containing text and guitar letters only (e.g. RISM 1618[17]) have not been included in these statistics.
(iv) I use the term 're-edition' to indicate reprints, second and subsequent editions (whether from the same or a different publisher) and compilations where a significant corpus of the volume is taken from one or two previously published sources. Anthologies, however, are not counted as re-editions except where they are themselves reprints.
(v) Classification according to genre, scoring and the presence or absence of a basso continuo part is sometimes difficult, and in a small number of cases I have had to make some rather arbitrary decisions. For this and other reasons, my figures cannot be guaranteed to be wholly accurate. However, the margin of likely error is not such that it would fundamentally alter the picture presented here.

[4] Donald W. Krummel, 'Printing and Publishing of Music: II', *The New Grove Dictionary of Music and Musicians*, ed. Stanley Sadie (London, 1980), vol. 15, 265: 'In summary, the history of music publishing before 1700 is one of early brilliance and extended decline. The peak was reached before 1580, in Venice, Nuremberg, Paris and Antwerp. The decline was apparent by 1600 and is reflected in a diminished output, in printing that is less spacious, less craftsmanlike and less original...'.

[5] Iain Fenlon, 'Il foglio volante editoriale dei Tini, circa il 1596', *Rivista italiana di musicologia*, 12 (1977), 238.

[6] Table I is compiled from RISM A/I and RISM B/I/1 (cross-checked with Brown 1965, New Vogel).

[7] See also the graph in Pompilio, op.cit., 96.

[8] Fig.1 is compiled from RISM A/I and RISM B/I/1 (cross-checked with New Vogel).

[9] Lewis Lockwood, *The Counter-Reformation and the Masses of Vincenzo Ruffo* (Florence, 1970), 145–6; see also Bautier-Regnier, op.cit..

[10] See also Pompilio, op.cit., 98.

[11] Table 2 is compiled from RISM A/I and RISM B/I/1 (cross-checked with Brown 1965, New Vogel).

[12] James H. Moore, *Vespers at St Mark's: Music of Alessandro Grandi, Giovanni Rovetta and Francesco Cavalli* (Ann Arbor, 1981), vol.1, 86.

[13] See Jerome Roche, 'North Italian Liturgical Music in the Early 17th Century' (Ph.D. dissertation, University of Cambridge, 1968).

[14] Jerome Roche, 'Music at S. Maria Maggiore, Bergamo, 1614–1643', *Music & Letters*, 47 (1966), 296–312.

[15] Pompilio, op.cit., 84–5, 98.

[16] Oscar Mischiati, *Indici, cataloghi e avvisi degli editori e librai musicali italiani dal 1591 al 1798* (Florence, 1984), 83–98.

[17] Mischiati, op.cit., 110–34.

[18] Mischiati, op.cit., 135–53. There has been some confusion over the date of this catalogue (earlier sources have assumed 1619), but Mischiati's arguments (op.cit., 19–20) in favour of 1621 are convincing.

[19] Mischiati, op.cit., 163–86. An apparent exception to these relative weightings of sacred and secular publications is provided by the Tini catalogue of c.1596 (transcribed by Fenlon, op.cit.). Here sacred prints outnumber secular prints in the proportion roughly 2:1. This may be explained by the fact that the Tini firm was based in Milan, an important centre for the ecclesiastical reforms of the last quarter of the sixteenth century.

[20] Fig.2 is compiled from New Vogel (with additions from RISM A/I, Fortune, *Handlist*, supplement) and RISM B/I/1.

[21] Brian Pullan, *Rich and Poor in Renaissance Venice: the Social Institutions of a Catholic State, to 1620* (Oxford, 1971), 14–21.

[22] Richard Tilden Rapp, *Industry and Economic Decline in Seventeenth-Century Venice* (Cambridge, Mass., 1976).

[23] Table 3 is compiled from New Vogel (with additions from RISM A/I, Fortune, *Handlist*, supplement) and RISM B/I/1.

[24] Fig.3 is compiled from New Vogel (with additions from RISM A/I, Fortune, *Handlist*, supplement) and RISM B/I/1. Publications are classified according to the presence or absence of a basso continuo part, a written-out accompaniment for lute, chitarrone or keyboard, or the mention of a basso continuo on the title-page. Publications in which the basso continuo is described as being optional have been included in the 'with basso continuo' graph.

[25] Table 4 is compiled from RISM A/I, RISM B/I/1 and New Vogel. The classification is according to the principles adopted for Fig.3. The data for sacred publications is not always reliable. Therefore, here and in Table 5, the figures for sacred publications should be regarded as *minima*.

[26] Fig.4 is compiled from New Vogel (with additions from RISM A/I, Fortune *Handlist*, supplement), RISM B/I/1, Fortune, *Handlist* and Whenham, *Catalogue*. The graph of five-part publications without basso continuo includes those in which the basso continuo is described on the title-page as being optional, or where it is not necessary for all the pieces therein.

[27] Nigel Fortune, 'Madrigal: III', *The New Grove Dictionary of Music and Musicians*, ed. Stanley Sadie (London, 1980), vol.11, 477.

[28] Tim Carter, 'Jacopo Peri (1561–1633): Aspects of his Life and Works', *Proceedings of the Royal Musical Association*, 105 (1978–9), 58.
[29] Table 5 is compiled from RISM A/I, RISM B/I/1, New Vogel, Fortune, *Handlist* and Whenham, *Catalogue*. In the case of sacred publications, I have had to rely on the description of the contents on the title-page as transcribed in RISM.
[30] Pompilio, op.cit., 85–9, 99–102.

# II

# On the composition and performance of Caccini's *Le nuove musiche* (1602)

1 A dinner party: painting (Italy, c1620) by Gerard van Honthorst (1590–1656) (Florence, Galleria Uffizi; photo London, Mansell Collection)

In an article in this journal, Howard Mayer Brown firmly placed the songs for solo voice and continuo which Giulio Caccini published as *Le nuove musiche* (Florence, 1602) in a 16th-century perspective.[1] It is clear that the claims for originality and innovation made in Caccini's title-page and preface should be accepted only with reservation. Indeed, they should be read in the context both of his vanity and of his antagonism towards his Florentine colleagues. *Le nuove musiche* may not even have been the first printed book of monodies; that honour should perhaps go to Domenico Maria Melli's *Musiche* (Venice, 1602). Melli's volume probably preceded Caccini's by some three months because the appearance of *Le nuove musiche* was delayed by the death of Caccini's publisher,

Giorgio Marescotti.[2] Melli, a lawyer and amateur composer from Reggio Emilia, produced a rather routine collection of solo madrigals. Significantly, however (and unlike Caccini), he issued his volume with what appears to have been a minimum of fuss. Throughout the 16th century, and before, solo vocal performance to the lute or other accompanying instrument(s) was well known. It is documented by contemporary accounts and manuscripts and by a number of publications from 1509 onwards containing original songs and arrangements of polyphonic pieces scored for one voice and accompaniment in lute tablature.[3] The manuscripts and prints must represent the tip of the iceberg: no doubt the practice of solo singing was widespread. The monodies of Melli and Caccini, then, clearly belong to a long-standing tradition.

Vincenzo Giustiniani's manuscript treatise *Discorso sopra la musica* (*c*1628) presents an account of the changing styles of music in Italy from 1570 to the late 1620s. He says that the musicians of five cities in particular contributed to a new style of singing and of solo song that appeared from about 1575 onwards: Naples, Ferrara, Mantua, Rome and Florence.[4] Caccini had connections with all five. His teacher, Scipione del Palla, spent much of his career in Naples before returning to his native Tuscany to take up a post at the grand-ducal court in Florence.[5] Caccini visited Ferrara, home of the much famed *concerto delle donne*, at least three times, in 1583, 1592 and 1594.[6] Florence had close political and cultural ties with Mantua, and during the 1580s Caccini worked with Alessandro Striggio, the Mantuan nobleman and composer who spent much of his career in Florence.[7] Similarly, in the early 1590s Caccini went to Rome, the city of his childhood, perhaps to see his old patron Giovanni de' Bardi, and he performed his songs there to great applause.[8] Solo songs to the lute, however, were not new to Rome, even if, as Caccini remarked, his audience was now hearing independently composed pieces for the medium rather than arrangements. For example, in the last two decades of the century the city saw four volumes of three- and four-part canzonets issue from the presses of Simone Verovio in a format that allowed the possibility, among others, of performance by solo voice with lute or keyboard accompaniment.[9]

There is enough evidence to question the extent to which Caccini's style departs from established practice. He deserves credit for bringing a new sophistication to 16th-century solo song. There are close links, however, between his simpler monodies and the songs in, for example, the Bottegari Lutebook.[10] Even in the case of the more complex pieces, the differences are more apparent than real, for Caccini writes into his score details of interpretation previously left to the performer. This is made explicit in the title of his *Nuove musiche e nuova maniera di scriverle* (Florence, 1614): 'New compositions *and a new way of writing them out*'. For example, an important feature of *Le nuove musiche* of 1602 is that Caccini notates a significant amount of the ornamentation to be performed by the singer. Even though this ornamentation is related to some of the patterns presented in such treatises as Giovanni Battista Bovicelli's *Regole, passaggi di musica, madrigali et*

*motetti passeggiati* (Venice, 1594), Caccini takes unusual care over the quality and extent of such embellishments.[11] Similarly, the rhythmic and melodic subtlety apparent in the printed versions of his songs may well be the result of attempts to codify a manner of performance that was applied to the rather four-square writing of earlier solo songs. In common with a number of composers of the late 16th century, Caccini thus exhibits a tendency to insist upon his right to exercise greater control over the performance of his music than had previously been the case. What was once improvised is increasingly composed into the score. This gives an important insight into the emergence of the Baroque style from that of the Renaissance in both sacred and secular music.

In the preface to *Le nuove musiche*, Caccini explained that he had found it necessary to publish his songs because they were circulating in Italy 'tattered and torn' and because singers were destroying his music by adding inappropriate and excessive ornamentation.[12] Bartolomeo Barbarino gave the same reasons for issuing his *Il secondo libro de madrigali... da una voce sola* (Venice, 1607), adding, as Caccini perhaps implied, that his music was being plagiarized and his authorship ignored. In the case of *Le nuove musiche*, no fewer than 17 of the collection's 23 pieces survive in one or more manuscript copies. The main sources are two related manuscripts: Brussels, Bibliothèque du Conservatoire Royal de Musique, Codex 704, and Florence, Biblioteca Nazionale Centrale, Magl.XIX.66. The other manuscripts are in collections in Florence, Bologna, Modena, London and Tenbury (the last is now in the Bodleian Library, Oxford). A number of these manuscripts are probably contemporary with, if they do not predate, the publication of *Le nuove musiche*.

Caccini tells us that some of the songs published in *Le nuove musiche* (specifically, *Perfidissimo volto, Vedrò'l mio sol, vedrò prima ch'io muoia* and *Dovrò dunque morire*) were composed some 15 years earlier. This places them in the mid-1580s, when Giovanni de' Bardi's camerata was nearing the end of its activities in Florence.[13] The fact that another song, *Fere selvaggie*, survives incomplete in the Bottegari Lutebook, which contains material from the mid-1570s and 1580s, confirms that Caccini composed, and presumably re-composed, his songs over a number of years before bringing them into print.[14] Some of the manuscript versions of these songs can therefore be seen as illuminating Caccini's compositional process, and as such they have been discussed by Nancy Maze, William Porter and H. Wiley

Ex.1 Giulio Caccini, Perfidissimo volto: (a) **Brussels 704**, p.41; (b) Le nuove musiche (**1602**), **p.8**

Ex.2 **Caccini**, Ardi, cor mio: (a) **Brussels 704**, p.77; (b) Le nuove musiche, **p.28**

Hitchcock.[15] The fact that the Brussels manuscript has now been issued in facsimile means that significant alternative versions of Caccini's songs are now readily available to performers and scholars.[16] It is worth reviewing the lessons to be learnt from it.

Brussels 704 contains 140 pieces from the late 16th (and perhaps early 17th) century. It is of Florentine provenance and shares a scribe and numerous songs with the now incomplete Florence XIX.66. Measuring 27 by 21 cm, Brussels 704 appears to consist of three fascicles, and one can detect at least three hands distributed through the manuscript. There are 12 staves per page, and on all but a few pages every third staff consists of six lines for lute tablature. The manuscript mostly contains chamber monodies, though there is one dialogue, and one duet (Jacopo Peri's *Intenerite voi, lacrime mie* for two tenor voices and continuo). There are also a number of theatre pieces from Florentine court entertainments dating from at least 1579 onwards. As Porter has shown, these include extracts from Jacopo Corsi and Jacopo Peri's *Dafne* of 1598.[17] All but the duet are notated for solo voice and unfigured bass, and 46 also have the bass realized in lute tablature. In the other songs the tablature staves have been left blank. Most of the songs are anonymous, though there are attributions to Corsi, Peri and Alessandro Striggio. Other composers can be deduced from concordances, notably Caccini, Francesco Rasi and Piero Strozzi. In the case of Caccini, the manuscript contains 15 of the songs included in *Le nuove musiche* and 11 of those in the 1614 *Nuove musiche*.[18]

Of the 15 songs from *Le nuove musiche* in Brussels 704, nine use the same clef combinations as the print, three (*Movetevi à pietà del mio tormento, Fortunato augellino* and *Occh'immortali*) have the vocal line in the tenor clef instead of Caccini's soprano clef, one (*Perfidissimo volto*) has soprano clef for tenor clef, one (*Ardi, cor mio*) has soprano and bass clefs for treble and baritone clefs, and one (*Sfogava con le stelle*) has the unusual combination of treble and bass clefs for the more standard treble and baritone clefs of the print. There is no apparent reason for these differences in clef. But they may not be significant: for example, Bartolomeo Barbarino, in the preface to his *Il secondo libro de madrigali*, stated that the vocal line of a song in the soprano clef could be sung an octave lower by a tenor voice (and presumably vice versa). Nine of the songs are in the same 'key' as the versions in *Le nuove musiche*, five (*Vedrò'l mio sol, vedrò prima ch'io muoia, Fere selvaggie, Fillide mia, se di beltà sei vaga, Udite, udite,*

*amanti* and *Occh'immortali*) are a tone lower ('F major' for 'G major') and one (*Perfidissimo volto*) is a tone higher ('A minor' for 'G minor'). As with the clefs, these differences may be somewhat arbitrary. Indeed, it seems that the actual 'key' of a song was of little importance to Caccini; according to his preface, the one to choose was that which best suited the chest voice of the performer.

One of the *Le nuove musiche* songs in Brussels 704, *Perfidissimo volto*, appears to confirm Caccini's complaint that singers were ruining his songs primarily by adding excessive ornamentation. In several places, elaborate figuration is replaced in the print by more restrained ornamental patterns. These patterns are each of a type that occurs frequently in Caccini's volume (ex. 1).[19] Similarly, the final cadence of *Dovrò dunque morire* is more ornamented in Brussels 704 than in the print. In the manuscript as a whole, however, such ornamentation is generally reserved for the theatre pieces. In fact, the Brussels 704 versions of Caccini's songs are usually much simpler than those published (ex. 2). Caccini's claim to have improved upon earlier ornamentation practices (in his preface he complains of 'the multitude of *passaggi* on both short and long syllables and in every sort of piece')[20] must therefore be examined carefully. He may have paid attention to the ideals of Bardi's camerata, but he was first and foremost a singer, and apparently a singer who delighted in showing off his talents to an appreciative audience. Thus he seems to have sought a compromise between the camerata's asceticism and his own natural flamboyance. To be fair to Caccini, however, he employs ornamentation much more discriminately than may have been the norm, usually reserving it for appropriate (long) syllables and with due regard for the presentation of the text. His patterns of ornamentation are also more refined and subtle than those to be found in most earlier ornamentation treatises. Finally, it must be said that although most of the Brussels 704 songs are much simpler than their printed counterparts, this is no guarantee that they would have been so in performance, given a singer seeking to add improvised ornamentation whenever and wherever possible.

Many of the differences between the versions of a song in Brussels 704 and *Le nuove musiche* can be seen as examples of how Caccini might have tidied up his compositions for publication. In the print, the delivery of the text is tauter (through speeding up the short syllables and using dotted rhythms) and the rather four-square rhythmic patterns found in the manuscript

Ex.3 Caccini, Fortunato augellino: (a) **Brussels 704**, p.13; (b) Le nuove musiche, **p.14**

Ex.4 Caccini, Movetevi à pietà del mio tormento: (a) **Brussels 704**, p.55; (b) Le nuove musiche, **p.1**

cadences to emphasize their importance to the structure of the song (ex.3). In addition, in *Le nuove musiche* Caccini often writes out a repeat of the second section of a song, whereas in the manuscript the repeat is indicated only by a sign or is omitted. Sometimes, and to marvellous effect in *Amarilli mia bella*, he also adds an extended final cadence. There are some alternative readings in the verse, but no more than is common in several versions of individual solo songs. Indeed, Brussels 704 sometimes provides a better reading of the poem than the print.

Most of the songs common to the manuscript and the print bear a close resemblance, with the manuscript providing what can be seen as skeletal versions of Caccini's final product. This is especially the case with the arias, which are the simpler pieces in the volume and which are most closely linked to the 16th-century solo song tradition. In some of the madrigals, however, we find more extensive differences. For example, the opening of *Movetevi à pietà del mio tormento* in Brussels 704 diverges significantly from the version in *Le nuove musiche* (ex.4). In Brussels 704, the 'G minor' imperfect cadence in bars 3–4 is succeeded by a number of cadences on G throughout the song, creating a conflict with the main tonal centre, A. In *Le nuove musiche*, Caccini consistently and skilfully avoids these cadences, improving the song's tonal structure (ex.5). There are similar examples in both *Perfidissimo volto* and *Dolcissimo sospiro*.

are more elegantly shaped to give a subtler grace, or *sprezzatura* ('a certain noble negligence of song')[21] to the melody. Similarly, Caccini generally adds written embellishments and provides long notes for *esclamazioni* and other such vocal effects that he expected the singer to employ. The vocal line is often liberated from the bass, whereas the manuscript versions have both moving closely together (this tendency was perhaps inherited from earlier solo songs). The more obvious consecutives are also avoided. The bass lines themselves are more effective, particularly through the increased use of first-inversion chords. Caccini also makes a point of giving some interest to the bass at

Although Caccini attempted to notate as much as possible in the versions of his songs published in *Le nuove musiche*, his preface makes it clear that much was still left to the performer(s). The singer needs to add

2 An angel playing a lute: pen and ink drawing by Francesco Mazzuchelli (1571/3–1626) (Darmstadt, Hessisches Landesmuseum)

cadential *trilli* and *gruppi* and to employ such vocal devices as the *esclamazione*, the *crescere e scemare della voce* and perhaps other ornaments, according to advice given in the preface. Even more freedom is granted in the realization of the bass. Caccini adopted the relatively new system of figured bass, with the additional refinement of a notational device (also used by Peri and other monodists) to indicate when harmony notes are to be struck or re-struck over a held bass note. As in the case of a number of early printed monody books (for example, collections by Melli and Peri), Caccini took care to explain this system in his preface. Nevertheless, for all its remarks on the style of singing to be used in his songs, Caccini's preface is rather uninformative on the nature of the accompaniment. This is understandable, given that he clearly felt that the accompaniment had a secondary role to play as a discreet background and support to the voice. Caccini acknowledged the imprecision of figured bass in his

Ex.5 Caccini, Movetevi à pietà del mio tormento: (a) **Brussels 704, pp.55–6**; (b) Le nuove musiche, p.1

preface. Short of printing the accompaniment in tablature, however, this was the most efficient method, he said, of presenting his intentions. Improvising a chordal accompaniment above a bass line, whether figured or unfigured, was common enough in the late 16th century. Indeed, we have records of Caccini himself doing just this in the 1580s.[22] However, the modern performer of Caccini's songs is left with little guidance on matters of accompanimental style and technique.

An important feature of Brussels 704 is that it is one of a few manuscripts to contain solo song accompaniments in lute tablature. The general characteristics of these realizations have been summarized by John Walter Hill in this journal and need not be repeated here.[23] Seven of the songs common to the manuscript and *Le nuove musiche* have such accompaniments. For the most part they are chordal rather than contrapuntal, often excessively so, and the texture is generally somewhat thicker than is usual in earlier songs for solo voice and lute. The figured bass of the print suggests a more sophisticated harmonic vocabulary than that found in the tablature (for example, in its use of 6-3 chords and suspensions) and there are some differences in the placing of major and minor 3rds. As Hill remarks, there are many examples of irregularly treated suspensions and 7ths, and of parallel 5ths and octaves. Cadential suspensions indicated in the print are occasionally not present in the tablature, and other suspensions are generally avoided; 7–6 suspensions are sometimes replaced by 5–6 motions over a sustained bass. However, we do find a specific cadential pattern that Caccini was to adapt in his own figured bass (ex.6).

Even without the discrepancies between the tablature and Caccini's figured bass, the rather uncertain status of Brussels 704 would prompt some caution in claiming these accompaniments to be worthy of imitation. As we have seen, the somewhat four-square vocal writing in the manuscript may betray a rather primitive style of monody that has close links with 16th-century solo song forms. The same could be said of the accompaniments, with their chordal textures which often move in the rhythm of the voice.[24] Furthermore, the fact that in the print Caccini liberates the vocal line from the bass may mean that he intended his accompaniments to be slightly more flexible than the tablature of Brussels 704 suggests. However, in some of the songs in the manuscript one can detect the beginnings of a more sophisticated approach to realizing the bass. Here the support offered to the voice exhibits a greater

Ex.6 Caccini, Ardi, cor mio: (a) **Brussels 704, p.77**; (b) Le nuove musiche, **p.28**

subtlety in rhythm, harmony and texture. A good example is provided by the Brussels 704 reading of *Fillide mia, se di beltà sei vaga* (ex.7), here given in parallel with the version published in *Le nuove musiche* (transposed down a tone). The comparison illustrates the small but significant differences in the vocal and bass lines of the types discussed above. The tablature also offers solutions to certain problems of accidentals and figuring in the print and, in some cases, alternative readings. The several 6-3 chords that remain unfigured in *Le nuove musiche* are worthy of note, as is the 5–6 progression in bar 1. There is a tierce di picardie at the cadence in bar 11, while elsewhere 3rds are omitted (particularly at the cadences in bars 5, 14 and 19). Similar examples, whether in 'major' or 'minor' keys, are common throughout the manuscript. The texture of the accompaniment also deserves comment. In bars 2–3, 14–15 and 17–18, it thins out to two parts moving in 10ths, and in bars 7–8 the bass is left on its own. This allows the return to a fuller texture to reinforce the vocal line at cadences. It must be admitted that these contrasts are the exception rather than the rule in Brussels 704. However, in *Fillide mia* at least, we see a slightly more polished manner of accompanimental writing that may well mark a new trend in the performance of monody, a trend that was to take the solo song firmly away from its 16th-century forbears.

We cannot be certain that Caccini knew the readings of his songs contained in Brussels 704, or that he would

Ex.7 **Caccini**, Fillide mia, se di beltà sei vaga: **(a) Brussels 704**, p.67; (b) Le nuove musiche, **p.33 (transposed down a tone)**

(ex.7 continued)

‡ rhythm unclear to end in tablature

3 A concert: painting, ?Venetian school, 16th century (London, National Gallery)

have sanctioned the intabulated accompaniments therein. However, there is probably no single 'correct' version of a Caccini song. His scores should be seen as frozen improvisations which need interpretative flexibility, and above all *sprezzatura*, to bring them to life. *Le nuove musiche* may well provide a clearer view of Caccini's intentions than the various manuscript sources of his songs. Nevertheless, Brussels 704 offers an insight into Caccini's compositional process, possible solutions to some of the many performance problems associated with his music, and a glimpse of the stylistic ferment of the late 16th century.[25]

[1]H. M. Brown, 'The geography of Florentine monody: Caccini at home and abroad', *EM*, ix (April 1981), pp.147–68

[2]The dedication of *Le nuove musiche* is dated 1 February 1601 (n.s. 1602), but the imprimatur is dated 1 July 1602. The discrepancy is explained in a note by Giorgio Marescotti's son and successor to his publishing firm, Cristofano. Melli's dedication is dated 26 March 1602.

[3]See Brown, *Instrumental Music Printed before 1600* (Cambridge, Mass., 1965).

[4]Ed. and Eng. trans. C. MacClintock, Musicological Studies and Documents, ix (Rome, 1962), pp.69–71

[5]On Scipione del Palla, see Brown, 'The geography of Florentine monody', p.148.

[6]A. Newcomb, *The Madrigal at Ferrara, 1579–1597*, 2 vols. (Princeton, NJ, 1980), i, pp.199–203. The 1592 and 1594 visits (the latter with Jacopo Corsi and Ottavio Rinuccini to celebrate the wedding of Carlo Gesualdo) are also documented by letters in Florence, Archivio di Stato, Mediceo del Principato, 1689, ff.382, 415 and 1013. Alfonso II, Duke of Ferrara, made frequent attempts to have Caccini enter his employment.

[7]Newcomb, *op cit*, i, pp.55–6

[8]The visit to Rome is described in the preface to *Le nuove musiche*, ed. H. W. Hitchcock (Madison, Wisc., 1970), pp.45–6. It may have taken place in 1592 (see C. Casellato, 'Caccini', *Dizionario biografico degli italiani*, xvi (1973), pp.25–33). Caccini's career was affected by his patron Giovanni de' Bardi's move to Rome in 1592. He was dismissed from court service in July 1593, ostensibly on the grounds of a dispute with one Antonio Salviati, but according to the composer's own account his dismissal was due to the persecution of his rivals. He contemplated leaving Florence to live in Rome, Ferrara or Genoa, and visited these cities. However, he remained domiciled in Florence (see Newcomb, *op cit*, i, pp.202–3, and Brown, 'The geography of Florentine monody', p.158). He was reinstated into court service from 1 October 1600, perhaps as a result of his contribution to the festivities held that month to celebrate the marriage of Maria de' Medici and Henry IV of France.

[9]*Diletto spirituale* (1586), *Ghirlanda di fioretti musicali* (1589), *Canzonette a quattro voci* (1591) and *Lodi della musica* (1595) were issued in Rome by Verovio, whose important publications are discussed in G. L. Anderson, *The Canzonetta Publications of Simone Verovio, 1586–1595* (DMA diss., U. of Illinois, 1976).

[10]Modena, Biblioteca Estense, C311; ed. MacClintock, *The Bottegari Lutebook*, Wellesley Edition, viii (Wellesley, Mass., 1965). See also MacClintock, 'A Court Musician's Songbook: Modena MS C311', *JAMS*, ix (1956), pp.177–92.

[11]Hitchcock, 'Vocal Ornamentation in Caccini's *Nuove Musiche*', *MQ*, lvi (1970), pp.389–404

[12]Caccini, preface to *Le nuove musiche*, ed. Hitchcock, p.43

[13]Caccini, preface to *Le nuove musiche*, ed. Hitchcock, p.45; dedication to *L'Euridice* (Florence, 1600), given in A. Solerti, *Le origini*

*del melodramma* (Turin, 1903/R1969), pp.50–52, and translated in O. Strunk, *Source Readings in Music History* (New York, 1950), pp.370–72. See also C. V. Palisca, 'The "Camerata Fiorentina": a Reappraisal', *Studi musicali*, i (1972), pp.203–36.

[14]The second stanza of *Fere selvaggie, Fillide mia*, is no.35 in *The Bottegari Lutebook*, ed. MacClintock.

[15]N. C. Maze, *The Printed and Manuscript Sources of the Solo Songs of Giulio Caccini* (PhD diss., U. of Illinois, 1956); W. V. Porter, *The Origins of the Baroque Solo Song: a Study of Italian Manuscripts and Prints from 1590–1610* (PhD diss., Yale U., 1962), pp.82–95; Hitchcock, 'Vocal Ornamentation', *passim*

[16]*Musiche de vari autori, XVIIe siècle*, Thesaurus musicus, new series, A/3 (Brussels, 1979). The manuscript is described and catalogued in Porter, *op cit*, pp.67–70 and 259–70. Porter has done valuable work on this manuscript and his dissertation is an important study, to which I am indebted.

[17]Porter, 'Peri and Corsi's *Dafne*: some New Discoveries and Observations', *JAMS*, xviii (1965), pp.170–96

[18]The songs from *Le nuove musiche* in Brussels 704 are listed below in the order in which they appear in the print. Those marked with an asterix are provided with an accompaniment in tablature. For convenience, I have adopted the numberings and spellings of *capoversi* given in *Le nuove musiche*, ed. Hitchcock.

1 *Movetevi à pietà del mio tormento*, pp.55–6
3 *Dolcissimo sospiro*, pp.7–8
6 *Perfidissimo volto*, pp.41–2
7 *Vedrò'l mio sol, vedrò prima ch'io muoia*, p.29*
8 *Amarilli mia bella*, p.46*
9 *Sfogava con le stelle*, pp.159–60
10 *Fortunato augellino*, pp.13–14
11 *Dovrò dunque morire*, p.45*
15 *Ardi, cor mio*, pp.77–8*
16 *Ard'il mio petto misero*, pp.195, 197 and 199
17 *Fere selvaggie*, pp.113–16*
18 *Fillide mia, se di beltà sei vaga*, pp.67–8*
19 *Udite, udite, amanti*, pp.81–2*
20 *Occh'immortali*, pp.69–70
22 *Belle rose porporine*, pp.227 and 231–2

All but nos. 9, 16 and 22 are in the hand of the first scribe of the manuscript.

[19]In the music examples, I have retained the original note-values. The texts follow the original orthography, though I have modified the punctuation and capitalization to clarify the verse. All examples from *Le nuove musiche* have been transcribed from the facsimile of the print (Rome, 1934), and thus differ in some details from *Le nuove musiche*, ed. Hitchcock.

[20]Caccini, preface to *Le nuove musiche*, ed. Hitchcock, p.44

[21]*Ibid*, pp.44–5

[22]Newcomb, *op cit*, i, pp.55–6

[23]J. W. Hill, 'Realized continuo accompaniments from Florence c1600', *EM*, xi (April 1983), pp.194–208

[24]See the example in Hill, *op cit*, p.198.

[25]Two further studies relevant to Caccini and Brussels 704 appeared after this article was in proof: S. Willier, 'Rhythmic Variants in Early Manuscript Versions of Caccini's Monodies', *JAMS*, xxxvi (1983), pp.481–97; W. V. Porter, 'A Central Source of Early Monody: Brussels, Conservatory 704 (I)', *Studi musicali*, xii (1983), pp.239–79.

# III

# Caccini's *Amarilli, mia bella*: Some Questions (and a Few Answers)

*AMARILLI, mia bella* is the best known of the solo madrigals that Giulio Caccini included in his *Le nuove musiche* of 1602.[1] The text was by Alessandro Guarini, who no doubt saw in his poem the *brevità, acutezza, leggiadria, nobiltà* and *dolcezza* that he claimed were most characteristic of modern madrigal verse.[2] Similarly, the *leggiadria* and *dolcezza* of

I am grateful to the staff of the libraries mentioned in this study for their generous assistance, and particularly the Bibliothèque du Conservatoire royal de musique, Brussels, the Biblioteca universitaria, Bologna, the British Library, London, and the Bodleian Library, Oxford, for permission to reproduce the photographs herein. Preliminary research for this study was undertaken during my fellowship at the Newberry Library, Chicago, and it has also benefited greatly from the ideas and guidance of Nigel Fortune, to whom it in part belongs. Personal thanks are also due to Jane A. Bernstein, Lucy Carolan, Frank Dobbins, Iain Fenlon, John Milsom and Christopher Wilson for their help with particular points of information. Libraries are cited by the following sigla: B-Bc, Brussels, Conservatoire royal de musique; B-Gu, Ghent, Rijksuniversiteit, Centrale bibliotheek; D-Bds, Berlin (East), Deutsche Staatsbibliothek, Musikabteilung; GB-Cfm, Cambridge, Fitzwilliam Museum; GB-Ckc, Cambridge, Rowe Music Library, King's College; GB-Lbl, London, British Library; GB-Ob, Oxford, Bodleian Library; GB-Och, Oxford, Christ Church; I-Bu, Bologna, Biblioteca universitaria; I-Fn, Florence, Biblioteca nazionale centrale; I-MOe, Modena, Biblioteca estense; NL-DHgm, The Hague, Gemeentemuseum; US-NYp, New York, Public Library at Lincoln Center, Library and Museum of the Performing Arts. Printed anthologies cited by date and superscript number (e.g. 1601[5]) follow the listing in *Recueils imprimés XVIᵉ-XVIIᵉ siècles*, I: *Liste chronologique*, ed. François Lesure, *Répertoire international des sources musicales*, BI/1 (Munich, 1960).

[1] *Le nuove musiche* was printed by the Marescotti press in Florence. The dedication is dated 1 February 1601 (*stile fiorentino*, i.e. 1602), but the licence to print is dated 1 July 1602. The delay in appearance, due to the death of the head of the press, Giorgio Marescotti, is explained in a note by his son, Cristofano. The volume was also printed in Venice in 1607 (by Alessandro Raverii) and in 1615 (by Giacomo Vincenti). For a modern edition, see *Giulio Caccini: Le nuove musiche*, ed. H. Wiley Hitchcock, Recent Researches in the Music of the Baroque Era, 9 (Madison, 1970); *Amarilli, mia bella* is given on pp. 85–8.

[2] The text has occasionally been ascribed to Giovanni Battista Guarini, but the attribution to Alessandro (Giovanni Battista's son) is clear in I-Fn Magl. VII.359, f. 92, and Alessandro declares his authorship of the poem in an (undated) letter to the Marchese of Carrara included in his *Delle lettere del Sig. Alessandro Guarini*, p. 125, in *Prose del Signor Alessandro Guarini* (Ferrara, 1611). In this letter, Alessandro includes a *risposta* to the poem, 'Alessi, se novella / fiamma credo in quel core, ab ben oblio'. Alessandro Guarini's biography is unclear – see Luigi Napoleone Cittadella, *I Guarini, famiglia nobile Ferrarese oriunda di Verona: Memorie* (Bologna, 1870); 'Guarini, Alessandro', in *Dizionario enciclopedico della letteratura italiana* (Bari, 1967), ii, 211. He was born in Ferrara in *c*.1565; by 1584 he was a student at the University in Perugia; and later Duke Alfonso II d'Este appointed him an ambassador to Florence (therefore before 1597). Caccini would have had plenty of opportunity to meet him, whether in Florence or in Ferrara (which the singer visited on several occasions). Later, Alessandro Guarini was in service in Mantua and Venice, and he also made trips to Flanders, Austria and Bavaria. He died on 13 August 1636. In this light, it seems unlikely that the text of *Amarilli, mia bella* was written much before the late 1580s or early 1590s, which would perhaps place Caccini's song among the later of his pieces included in *Le nuove musiche*. For Alessandro Guarini's comments on modern poetry, see his preface for Luzzasco Luzzaschi's *Il sesto libro de madrigali a cinque voci* (Ferrara, 1596), most accessible in Anthony Newcomb, *The Madrigal at Ferrara, 1579–1597* (Princeton, 1979), i, 118.

Caccini's setting have marked it out for prominence: *Amarilli, mia bella* was one of the first of his songs to be disseminated widely through Italy and Europe, and its distinction is reflected in its frequent appearance (often in less than satisfactory editions) in vocal antholo- gies up to the present day. But the song is far from being a straightforward example of Caccini's style. Indeed, a study of its sources in contemporary manuscripts and prints raises intriguing questions about the supposed innovations of Caccini's music and about the ways in which Florentine monody became known both south and north of the Alps.[3]

Despite the claims on the title-page and in the dedication and preface of *Le nuove musiche*, recent scholars have instead tended to play down Caccini's purported originality, placing his music firmly in the broader context of the solo songs and solo singing that were popular throughout the Renaissance, and also in the specific context of the new styles of singing that Vincenzo Giustiniani (in his *Discorso sopra la musica* of *c*.1628) claimed had developed in northern Italy in the mid-1570s.[4] Caccini's volume was not even the first book of solo songs to be published: the dedication of Domenico Maria Melli's *Musiche . . . per cantare nel chittarone, clavicembalo, & altri instrumenti* (Venice, 1602) is dated 26 March 1602, that is, some three months before Caccini's volume finally appeared. Moreover, the absence of any self- aggrandizing fanfares in Melli's rather routine collection suggests that, Caccini's wishful thinking apart, there was nothing particularly striking about a volume of songs for solo voice and instrumental

---

[3] The following sources of *Amarilli, mia bella* were used for this study. Prints: *Ghirlanda di madrigali a sei voci* (Antwerp, Pierre Phalèse, 1601[5]), f. 4 in all partbooks, for six voices (C1, C2, C3, C4, F4 clefs; the *quinto* partbook is now lost), unattributed; Giulio Caccini, *Le nuove musiche* (Florence, Giorgio Marescotti, 1601 [*recte* 1602]; repr. Venice, Alessandro Raverii, 1607; Giacomo Vincenti, 1615), pp. 12–13, for solo voice (G2 clef) and figured bass; Robert Dowland, *A Musicall Banquet* (London, Thomas Adams, 1610), no. 19, for solo voice (G2 clef) and unfigured bass (the bass is also realized in (English) lute tablature), attributed to 'Giulio Caccini detto Romano'; Johann Nauwach, *Libro primo di arie passeggiate a una voce* (Dresden, [n.p.], 1623), for solo voice (C1 clef) and figured bass, unattributed; Jacob van Eyck, *Der fluyten lust-hof*, i (Amsterdam, Paulus Matthysz, 1646), two versions for solo recorder (in D minor with two doubles; in G minor with three doubles) and one for two (in D minor), unattributed. Manuscripts (in alphabetical order by library sigla): B-Bc MS 704, p. 46, for solo voice (G2 clef) and unfigured bass (the bass is also realized in (Italian) lute tablature), unattributed; GB-Cfm 32.g.29 (the Fitzwilliam Virginal Book), p. 155, arrangement for keyboard (dated 1603) by Peter Philips (also in D-Bds Lynar Al, p. 318), attributed to 'Julio Romano'; GB-Lbl Add. MS 15117, f. 6, for solo voice (C1 clef, with text as 'Miserere my.maker') and accompaniment in (English) lute tablature, unattributed; GB-Lbl Egerton 2971, ff. 28ᵛ–29, embellished for solo voice (C1 clef) and accompaniment in tablature for lyra viol, unattributed; GB-Lbl Egerton 3665 (the 'Tregian' manuscript), pp. 22–3 (no. 106), for three voices (C1, C2, F4 clefs), attributed to 'Julio Romano'; GB-Lbl Royal Appendix 55, ff. 10ᵛ–11, for solo voice (C4 clef) and unfigured bass, unattributed; GB-Ob Tenbury MS 1018, f. 39, for solo voice (C1 clef) and unfigured bass, unattributed; I-Bu MS 177/IV, f. 49, one voice part (C1 clef) of three or four, unattributed; I-Fn Magl. XIX.66, f. 18, for solo voice (G2 clef) and unfigured bass, unattributed. I have been unable to see the keyboard arrangement in the collection (1625) by Vincentius de la Faille; see below, n. 26.

[4] For Giustiniani, see *Ercole Bottrigari: Il desiderio; Vincenzo Giustiniani: Discorso sopra la musica*, trans. Carol MacClintock, Musicological Studies and Documents, 9 (Rome, 1962), 69–71. This is discussed further in Tim Carter, 'On the Composition and Performance of Caccini's *Le nuove musiche* (1602)', *Early Music*, 12 (1984), 208–17.

accompaniment. Frottolas had appeared in print in formats allowing this manner of performance, likewise the madrigals of Verdelot, and so too Roman and north-Italian canzonettas and lighter madrigals of the 1580s and early 1590s.[5] These and other repertories were also frequently performed in this way, even if they are preserved in standard partbooks.

Caccini himself placed some of the songs in *Le nuove musiche* in the mid-1580s, linking them specifically to the activities of the Camerata sponsored in Florence by Giovanni de' Bardi.[6] As is well known, the Camerata promoted a classicizing movement that sought to produce a kind of music more faithful to the text than contemporary polyphony. Caccini, whether jumping on a bandwagon or not, felt that his songs did just this: he had learnt more from the Camerata, he said, than from 30 years of counterpoint. He reports that his songs were received with acclaim in Florence, and that they spread quickly across Italy to the extent that it was now necessary for him to reassert his claims to his music through the medium of print.

> If I have not heretofore published the musical studies I made after the noble manner of singing learned from my famous master Scipione del Palla, nor other compositions of divers madrigals and airs made by me at various times, it is because I esteemed them but little. It seemed to me that these pieces of mine had been honoured enough – indeed, much more than they merited – by being constantly performed by the most famous singers of Italy, male and female, and by other noble persons who are lovers of the profession. But now I see many of them circulating tattered and torn; moreover I see ill-used those single and double roulades – rather, those redoubled and intertwined with each other – developed by me to avoid that old style of *passaggi* formerly in common use (one more suited to wind and stringed instruments than to the voice); and I see vocal crescendos-and-decrescendos, *esclamazioni*, tremolos and trills, and other such embellishments of good singing style used indiscriminately. Thus I have been forced (and also urged by friends) to have these pieces of mine published, and in this first publication to explain to my readers by means of the present discourse the reasons that led me to such a type of song for solo voice.[7]

Thus *Le nuove musiche* was designed to 'set the record straight' in terms of Caccini's originality in inventing a 'new' music, in terms of the readings of songs that had become 'tattered and torn', and in terms of

---

[5] Prints of polyphonic music arranged for solo voice(s) (in mensural notation) and lute (in tablature) are listed in Howard Mayer Brown, *Instrumental Music Printed before 1600: A Bibliography* (Cambridge, Mass., 1965).

[6] As examples of his earliest compositions, Caccini mentions specifically *Perfidissimo volto, Vedrò'l mio sol, vedrò prima ch'io muoia, Dovrò dunque morire* and the now-lost *Itene à l'ombra de gli ameni faggi* (from an eclogue by Sannazaro) both in the dedication of his *L'Euridice composta in musica in stile rappresentativo* (Florence, 1600) and in the preface to *Le nuove musiche*; see *Giulio Caccini: Le nuove musiche*, ed. Hitchcock, 45. Parts of another song in *Le nuove musiche*, *Fere selvaggie*, survive in I-MOe MS Mus. C.311 (f. 14ᵛ), a manuscript which bears the date 1575; see *The Bottegari Lutebook*, ed. Carol MacClintock, The Wellesley Edition, 8 (Wellesley, 1965).

[7] Translated in *Giulio Caccini: Le nuove musiche*, ed. Hitchcock, 43.

the new styles of vocal performance developed by the Florentine singer.

The survival of a number of songs from *Le nuove musiche* in contemporary manuscripts supports Caccini's claims about the circulation of his music. These manuscript sources also reveal how Caccini may have 'tidied up' his songs for publication.[8] In the case of *Amarilli, mia bella*, the song survives scored for solo voice and unfigured bass in two closely related manuscripts, I-Fn Magl. XIX.66 and B-Bc MS 704 (see Figure 1; here the bass is also realized in lute tablature).[9] The differences between these manuscript versions and the one printed in 1602 are not as striking as in the case of some of the other songs by Caccini surviving in similar circumstances, perhaps because *Amarilli, mia bella* is so tautly conceived (and easily remembered?). The printed version adds some melodic and rhythmic refinements, and the implied harmonic progressions are somewhat more elegantly handled. Most striking, however, is the addition of a brief coda at the end of the song, which appears in only one of the other sources of *Amarilli, mia bella* surveyed in this study, the version printed in Robert Dowland's *A Musicall Banquet* of 1610. This coda makes a fine conclusion to the setting.

More interesting from the point of view of the early sources of *Amarilli, mia bella*, however, is the survival of two apparently contemporary multi-part versions of the song. The anthology *Ghirlanda di madrigali a sei voci, di diversi eccellentissimi autori de nostri tempi, raccolta di giardini di fiori odoriferi musicali*, issued in 1601 by the Antwerp printer Pierre Phalèse the younger (RISM 1601[5]),[10] contains a straightforward version for six voices: this is in fact the first printed source of Caccini's piece (see Example 1).[11] Here the setting is fairly homophonic, occasionally enlivened by a few contrapuntal entries. In contrast, I-Bu MS 177/IV contains a much freer adaptation (a parody?) that

---

[8] Comparisons between manuscript and printed versions of Caccini's songs have been made in Nancy C. Maze, 'The Printed and Manuscript Sources of the Solo Songs of Giulio Caccini' (Ph.D. dissertation, University of Illinois, 1956); William V. Porter, 'The Origins of the Baroque Solo Song: A Study of Italian Manuscripts and Prints from 1590–1610' (Ph.D. dissertation, Yale University, 1962); H. Wiley Hitchcock, 'Vocal Ornamentation in Caccini's *Nuove musiche*', *The Musical Quarterly*, 56 (1970), 389–404; Stephen Willier, 'Rhythmic Variants in Early Manuscript Versions of Caccini's Monodies', *Journal of the American Musicological Society*, 36 (1983), 481–97; Carter, 'On the Composition and Performance of Caccini's *Le nuove musiche*'.

[9] B-Bc MS 704 has been reproduced in facsimile (*Musiche de vari autori, XVII* siècle, Thesaurus musicus, new series, A/3 (Brussels, 1979)), and has been discussed in William V. Porter, 'A Central Source of Early Monody: Brussels, Conservatory 704', *Studi musicali*, 12 (1983), 239–79; 13 (1984), 139–67.

[10] The rather fanciful title is typical of Phalèse anthologies. Its apparent reference to the *Fiori del giardino di diversi eccellentissimi autori à quattro, cinque, sei, sette, otto, & novi voci* (Nuremberg, 1597[13]) is not matched by any shared madrigals (except for Marenzio's *Lucida perla, a cui fu conca il cielo*). Of 1601[5], GB-Lbl holds copies of the *canto, alto, tenore* and *basso* partbooks, B-Gu has the *alto, basso* and *sesto* partbooks, and NL-DHgm has the *canto* (incomplete), *tenore, basso* and *sesto* partbooks. The *quinto* partbook is now lost.

[11] In the examples presented here, I have 'silently' corrected obvious errors, standardized accidentals, and added punctuation, etc. to the texts. Dotted bar-lines are editorial, as are accidentals and other matter in square brackets.

254

Figure 1.    B-Bc MS 704, p. 46.

would appear to be for three or four voices (see Figure 2).[12] In both of these sources, the song is presented in the form ‖:A:‖:B:‖ (in 1601[5] the repeats are written out and slightly altered) rather than the A‖:B:‖ of the Florence and Brussels manuscripts and written out in the 1602 print.

[12] I-Bu MS 177/IV is a single *canto* (so styled) partbook, for the most part of villanella/canzonetta-type strophic pieces (with the first strophe laid under the music and subsequent

Example 1.   *Amarilli, mia bella*, from *Ghirlanda di madrigali a sei voci* (Antwerp, 1601[5]), beginning (*quinto* partbook lost; all parts have text).

The dating of these multi-part settings is by no means clear. I-Bu MS 177/IV appears largely to contain canzonettas from the 1580s and 1590s. Some of the pieces also have letter tablature for a guitar accompaniment, which would suggest a date of at least the second decade of the seventeenth century (although it is not clear exactly when the tablature was added). As for the six-part version, 1601 is clearly a *terminus ad quem* (Phalèse's dedication of the anthology to Giovanni Le Blon is dated 27 January), but the print has a number of curious features that make it difficult to trace Phalèse's source(s) for its music. There are 33 madrigals by 25 named composers: the only unattributed setting is, curiously enough, *Amarilli, mia bella*. A good number of these composers (Baccusi, Bati, Bertani, Carletti, Cavaccio, Coma, Croce, Eremita, A. Ferrabosco, Gastoldi, Guami, Malvezzi, Marenzio, del Mel, de Monte, Pallavicino, Philips, Sabino, Sweelinck, Tigrini, Vecoli, Verdonck, Vinci, Virchi, Zanotti) featured regularly in Italian and northern madrigal anthologies of the late 1580s and 1590s:

strophes on the facing page). It contains 40 pieces, including Luca Marenzio's *Dicemi la mia stella* (f. 10, first printed in his *Il primo libro delle villanelle . . . a tre voci* (Venice, 1584)), an adaptation of Paolo Quagliati's *La prima volta ch'io* (f. 36ᵛ, first printed in his *Canzzonette . . . a tre voci . . . libro secondo* (Rome, 1588)), and Orazio Vecchi's *Mentre io campai contento* (f. 51, first printed in his *Canzonette . . . libro primo a quattro voci* (Venice, 1580)). There are enough indications in the manuscript to suggest that it is likely to have been one of a set of partbooks rather than a self-contained volume of melodies compiled as an *aide-mémoire*, although it remains unclear how many partbooks are missing from the set, or how many voices were used in the version of *Amarilli, mia bella*.

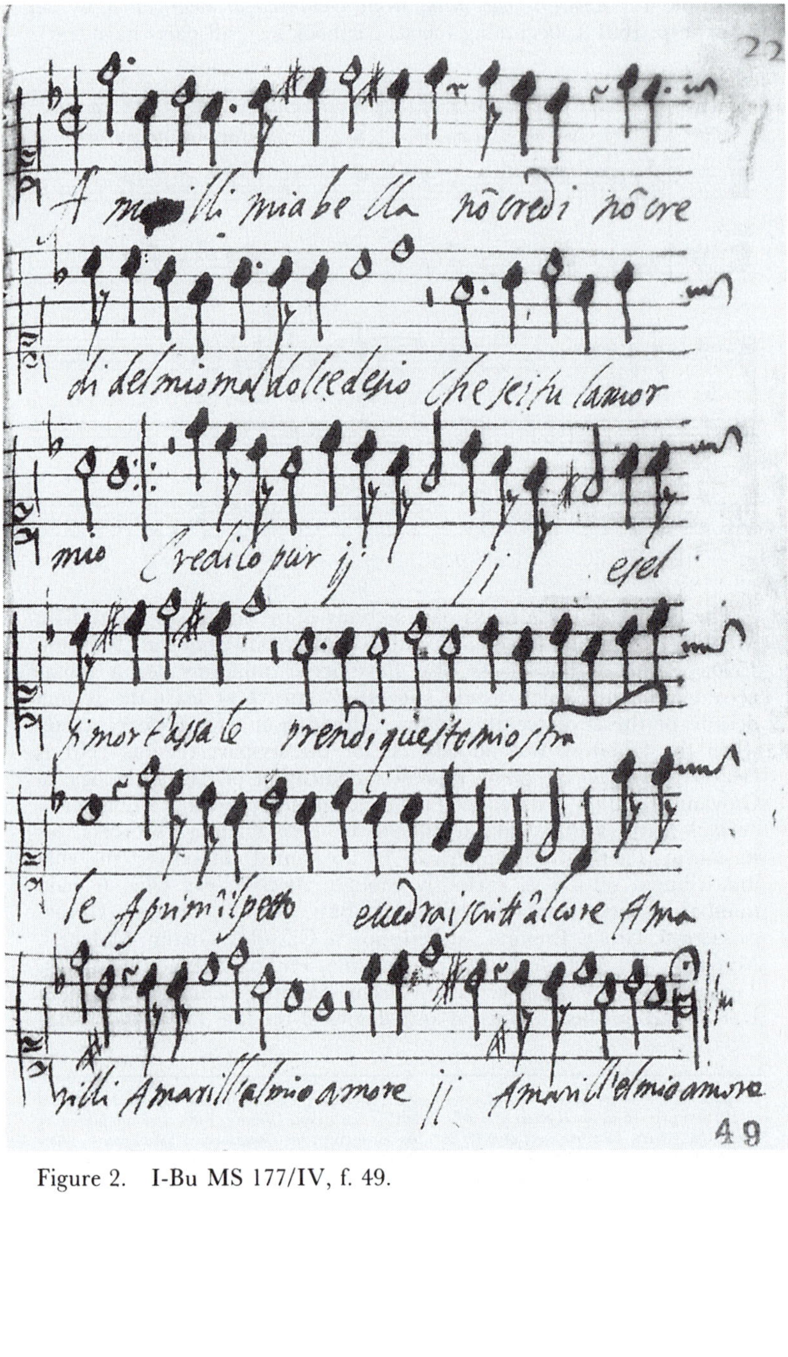

Figure 2. I-Bu MS 177/IV, f. 49.

III

indeed 18 of these 25 had already appeared in one or more Phalèse prints. But of the 33 madrigals in the anthology, only 16 are known from earlier Italian printed sources. This is unusual for Phalèse. His normal practice was to pirate Italian publications (whether by individual composers or anthologies) for his own collections: thus his anthologies (unlike Italian anthologies) contain predominantly music already in print. Typical examples are his *Paradiso musicale di madrigali et canzoni a cinque voci* (1596[10]) and *Il vago alboreto di madrigali et canzoni a quattro voci* (1597[15]). Of the 41 madrigals in 1596[10], only four are not known from Italian prints (and of these four, two are by composers closely associated with Phalèse, Peter Philips and Cornelis Verdonck). The 37 other madrigals were all first printed in Italy between 1574 and 1592. Similarly, in 1597[15] there are 43 madrigals, of which only three (including one by Verdonck) were new to the press, with a repertory spreading from 1580 to 1595. Moreover, 1597[15] contains six madrigals from Ricciardo Amadino's anthology *Novelli ardori: Primo libro de madrigali a quatro voci, di diversi eccell. auttori* (Venice, 1588[18]) and 16 from Amadino's *Di XII. autori vaghi e dilettevoli madrigali a quatro voci* (Venice, 1595[5]). Thus Phalèse generally takes his repertory from Italian prints that had appeared anything from two (more usually, four or five) to 30 years before. 1601[5] appears to be the exception, unless there were one or more Italian six-part prints (perhaps just one anthology) which Phalèse pirated and which are now lost. Such a hypothesis explains the apparent anomaly of 1601[5]. It also suggests that the six-part version of *Amarilli, mia bella* could have first appeared in an Italian (probably Venetian) print in the 1580s or 1590s, unless, that is, Phalèse received the piece through private hands.

The six-part *Amarilli, mia bella* seems to be less a madrigal than a canzone, a rather old-fashioned genre by 1601, and, as was common in this repertory, it might itself be an adaptation of a three-part model. (The existence of a three-part *Amarilli, mia bella* would perhaps account for the parody-like nature of the version in I-Bu MS 177/IV as well as Francis Tregian's curious three-voice transcription discussed below.)[13] Nor is it clear whether this six-part version can be associated directly with Caccini. The inclusion in 1601[5] of madrigals by Luca Bati and Cristofano Malvezzi gives the volume a slender Florentine link (and Bati rarely figures in Italian or northern anthologies), although this is no guarantee that Caccini himself wrote or sanctioned the six-part *Amarilli, mia bella*. But these problems apart, the survival of an ostensibly archetypal solo song in one version apparently for three or four voices and another for six clearly raises important questions

---

[13] The six-part *Amarilli, mia bella* fits closely the definition of a canzone given in Ruth I. DeFord, 'Musical Relationships between the Italian Madrigal and Light Genres in the Sixteenth Century', *Musica disciplina*, 39 (1985), 107–68 (see pp. 115–16), and DeFord notes that Phalèse tended not to distinguish canzoni from madrigals in his anthologies. She also discusses various multiple versions of popular settings in the late sixteenth century, suggesting a common practice that clearly relates to the situation with *Amarilli, mia bella* discussed here.

about the nature of the Florentine 'new music'. Caccini himself claimed that one of the innovatory features of his style was precisely the fact that his songs were conceived from the start for a solo singer. In his preface to *Le nuove musiche*, he recounts that after his success in Florence he went to Rome (in the early 1590s, it seems) to try out his pieces there:

> The aforesaid madrigals and the air were performed in Signor Nero Neri's house for many gentlemen assembled there (and notably Signor Lione Strozzi), and everyone can testify how I was urged to continue as I had begun, and was told that never before had anyone heard music for a solo voice, to a simple stringed instrument, with such power to move the affect of the soul as these madrigals. (This was both because of their new style and because, accustomed then to hearing as solos madrigals published [originally] for multiple voices, they did not think a soprano part sung by itself alone could have any affect whatsoever, without the artful interrela-tionships of [all] the parts.)[14]

But even if Caccini wished to emphasize the novelty of moving 'the affect of the soul' through solo song 'without the artful interrelation-ships of [all] the parts', at least some of his contemporaries could easily assimilate his music into conventional genres, namely the three- or four-part villanella/canzonetta and the six-part canzone/madrigal.

Of course, multiple versions of particular pieces are by no means uncommon in Renaissance sources, and they were also a characteris-tic feature of Renaissance performing practice. They seem to have been particularly prevalent in the villanella/canzonetta/canzone repertory, where the same setting can appear reworked in three-, four-, five- and even six-part scorings as well as perhaps deriving from a solo-voice prototype.[15] Other details also place Caccini's 'new' music firmly in the context of these 'light' sixteenth-century genres. It seems that the 'noble manner of singing' developed by Caccini's teacher, Scipione delle Palle, emerged in the context of the Neapoli-tan villanella repertory.[16] The ‖:A:‖:B:‖ structure of *Amarilli, mia bella* as presented in I-Bu MS 177/IV and in 1601[5] is typical of the villanella/canzonetta/canzone, as is its clear melodic and harmonic structure (which is also reminiscent of the stock formulas of the sixteenth century, particularly the romanesca). Moreover in I-Bu MS 177/IV *Amarilli, mia bella* is grouped with Roman- and north-Italian-style

---

[14] Translated in *Giulio Caccini: Le nuove musiche*, ed. Hitchcock, 45–6.

[15] For example, see *Giovanni Ferretti: Il secondo libro delle canzoni a sei voci (1575)*, ed. Ruth I. DeFord, Recent Researches in the Music of the Renaissance, 57–8 (Madison, 1983). 'Arrange-ments' in the villanella tradition are also discussed in Donna G. Cardamone, *The Canzone villanesca alla napolitana and Related Forms, 1537–1570* (Ann Arbor, 1981), i, 179–208.

[16] Howard Mayer Brown, 'The Geography of Florentine Monody: Caccini at Home and Abroad', *Early Music*, 9 (1981), 147–68. Giustiniani, in his *Discorso sopra la musica*, also emphasizes the importance of the villanella for the new styles of singing in the 1570s. Further links with the Neapolitan style, and also details of Caccini's arrival in Florence, are discussed in Tim Carter, 'Giulio Caccini (1551–1618): New Facts, New Music', *Studi musicali*, 16 (1987), 13–31.

canzonettas. There is also other evidence to suggest that the new solo song was initially perceived by music printers and their public as lying close to such 'light' genres.[17] Certainly, to the compilers of I-Bu MS 177/IV and 1601[5], Caccini's song was easily seen to fit fair and square into tradition.

The connections between seemingly 'old' and seemingly 'new' secular genres over the 1600s suggested by these multi-part versions of *Amarilli, mia bella* have tended to be ignored by modern historians, who, for example, often regard the polyphonic madrigal and the solo song as representing diametrically opposed stylistic and aesthetic poles. However, Act 2 of Monteverdi's *Orfeo* (1607) contains music that is first presented as a solo-voice recitative and is then re-arranged in a five-part context. Similarly, on 24 August 1609, Monteverdi wrote in response to a request from the Mantuan court secretary and librettist of *Orfeo*, Alessandro Striggio:

> I received a letter from Your Lordship together with certain words to be set to music, as a commission from His Highness, and they arrived yesterday . . . . I shall start to work on them as soon as possible, and when they are all done I shall inform Your Lordship or bring them myself to Mantua, because I want to be back in service shortly. I thought first of setting these words for a solo voice, but if later on His Highness orders me to re-arrange the air for five voices, this I shall do.[18]

Indeed, we have at least one concrete example of Monteverdi 'setting . . . words for a solo voice' and then deciding to 're-arrange the air for five voices'. His *Lamento d'Arianna*, the solo-voice lament that was the climax of his opera *Arianna* of 1608, reappears in a five-part version in Monteverdi's *Il sesto libro de madrigali a cinque voci* of 1614.[19] Similarly, solo songs by Caccini and his contemporaries are presented as four-part madrigals in a curious collection issued by the Sicilian Pietro Maria Marsolo in 1614,[20] and there are also examples in the works of Sigismondo d'India of pieces that started life for solo voice and basso continuo and later appeared as five-part madrigals.[21] The process also seems to have worked the other way, whether as a formal part of the compositional process or as an informal aspect of contem-

---

[17] See Tim Carter, 'Music Publishing in Italy, *c*.1580–*c*.1625: Some Preliminary Observations', *RMA Research Chronicle*, 20 (1986–7), 19–37, esp. pp. 28–9.

[18] For the original, see *Claudio Monteverdi: Lettere, dediche e prefazioni*, ed. Domenico de' Paoli (Rome, 1973), 40–2. My translation differs slightly from *The Letters of Claudio Monteverdi*, trans. Denis Stevens (London, 1980), 64.

[19] In 1608, Arianna's lament was 'accompagnato da viole et violini'; see the comments in Gary Tomlinson, *Monteverdi and the End of the Renaissance* (Oxford, 1987), 138. The nature of this accompaniment is unclear, although it seems unlikely to have extended to the polyphonic elaboration of the 1614 arrangement.

[20] *Pietro Maria Marsolo: Secondo libro de' madrigali a quattro voci*, ed. Lorenzo Bianconi, Musiche rinascimentali siciliane, 4 (Rome, 1973).

[21] I-MOe F1530, f. 6, gives the *alto* part of a five-part arrangement of the solo-voice lament *Infelice Didone*, published by Sigismondo d'India in his *Le musiche . . . libro quinto* (Venice, 1623). For another example of music presented in a solo-voice and multi-part format, see Paolo Quagliati's *Il primo libro de' madrigali a quattro voci* (Venice, 1608).

III

porary performing practice. Thus Sigismondo d'India's *Le musiche . . . da cantar solo* of 1609 contains two monodies that appear to be reworkings of settings first published in his *Il primo libro de madrigali a 5 voci* of 1606.[22]

Interrelationships between the solo song and the polyphonic madrigal are also apparent in pieces that are not direct or indirect translations from one medium to the other. Although the Florentine solo song may have been promulgated initially by singers rather than composers, a number of monodists did in fact bring to the 'new' music various structural and expressive devices initially developed within the polyphonic madrigal. Significantly, these composers – including Sigismondo d'India and Marco da Gagliano – were equally at home in polyphonic and solo-voice writing.[23] Similarly, the polyphonic madrigal of the late 1590s and early 1600s became increasingly influenced by the solo song in terms of declamatory freedom and heightened expressiveness: this, of course, is one key to Monteverdi's *seconda prattica*. Such interactions offer important lessons for historians seeking to come to terms with secular music in late sixteenth- and early seventeenth-century Italy.

*Amarilli, mia bella* seems to have achieved some fame in at least parts of northern Italy. Not only does it survive in manuscript sources there, as we have seen, but its opening was also imitated in settings of texts that themselves appear to echo Alessandro Guarini's poem. For example, both I-Fn Magl. XIX.66 (f. 16) and B-Bc MS 704 (p. 97) contain a solo-voice setting of Ottavio Rinuccini's 'Amarillide mia, dirò mio sole' which begins in a manner strikingly reminiscent of *Amarilli, mia bella* (see Example 2). A very similar opening also appears in five-part settings of 'Amarillide mia, dirò mio sole' by two Sienese composers, in Tommaso Pecci's *Madrigali a cinque voci* (Venice, 1602) and in Agostino Agazzari's *Il secondo libro de madrigali a cinque voci* (Venice, 1606). However, Caccini himself may have tired of such obvious associations: his setting of 'Amarill'io mi parto' (in Girolamo Montesardo's *L'allegre notti di Fiorenza* (Venice, 1608)) almost self-consciously avoids any direct allusion to the song.[24]

[22] *Intenerite voi, lagrime mie* and *Cruda Amarilli, che col nome ancora*. For the 1606 volume, see *Sigismondo d'India: Il primo libro de madrigali a cinque voci*, ed. Federico Mompellio, I classici musicali italiani, 10 (Milan, 1942); for the 1609 volume, see *Sigismondo d'India: Il primo libro di musiche da cantar solo*, ed. Federico Mompellio, Instituta et monumenta, I/4 (Cremona, 1970).

[23] This point is explored further in Tim Carter, 'Jacopo Peri (1561–1633): Aspects of his Life and Works', *Proceedings of the Royal Musical Association*, 105 (1978–9), 50–62 (see pp. 54–5).

[24] The Montesardo volume is discussed in Tim Carter, 'Serate musicali in Early Seventeenth-Century Florence: Girolamo Montesardo's *L'allegre notti di Fiorenza* (1608)', *Renaissance Studies in Honor of Craig Hugh Smyth*, ed. Andrew Morrogh et al. (Florence, 1985), i, 555–68; and *Amarill'io mi parto* is transcribed in Carter, 'Giulio Caccini (1551–1618): New Facts, New Music', 29–31. I am grateful to Nigel Fortune for informing me that the song is also included (anonymously) in *Il maggio fiorito: Arie, sonetti, e madrigali, à 1.2.3. de diuersi autori, posta in luce da Gio. Battista Rocchigiani* (Orvieto, 1623[8]). Three other settings of 'Amarilli, mia bella' were published in the first decade of the seventeenth century: Giuseppe Palazotto in Antonio Il Verso, *L'ottavo libro de madrigali a cinque voci* (Venice, 1603); Francesco Genvino in *Libro secondo di madrigali a cinque voci* (Naples, 1605); Giovanni Vincenzo Macedonio di Mutio in *Il secondo libro de madrigali a cinque voci* (Naples,

Example 2.   *Amarillide mia, dirò mio sole*, from B-Bc MS 704, p. 97.

But *Amarilli, mia bella* seems to have become even more established north of the Alps. As we have seen, the first printed source of the song (in six parts) appeared in Antwerp in 1601. In 1623, Johann Nauwach included a much ornamented version of *Amarilli, mia bella* as the last piece in his *Libro primo di arie passeggiate a una voce* printed in Dresden (see Example 3).[25] It is unlikely that Nauwach's source for the song was the 1602 print: there is no coda, and various other features of the second half of the song are closer to manuscript readings of *Amarilli, mia bella* than to the print (compare Example 3 with B-Bc MS 704 in Figure 1). The song also became well known in the Low Countries, as spiritual *contrafacta* and other arrangements in Dutch and Flemish sources reveal.[26] What is not clear, however, is exactly how it was transmitted across the Alps. The dissemination of *Amarilli, mia bella* does not appear to have been due to Caccini himself: he made only one trip outside Italy, to Paris from September 1604 to May 1605 (there were also plans to extend his tour to England, but they were dropped).[27] Nor does the 1602 print appear to have had a significant part to play in the process (with the exception of Robert Dowland's edition discussed below): it is likely that the edition that appeared from the Marescotti press was limited in size and did not achieve an

---

1606). I have been able to see only Palazotto's setting, which bears no relation to Caccini's, although it is curious in the light of the Neapolitan connections mentioned above that 'Amarilli, mia bella' should have been popular with this group of composers working in Naples.

[25] Nauwach's version is compared with Caccini's in Alfred Einstein, 'Ein unbekannter Druck aus der Frühzeit der deutschen Monodie', *Sammelbände der Internationalen Musik-Gesellschaft*, 13 (1911–12), 286–96 (see pp. 294–5).

[26] Some of these *contrafacta* are discussed in Florimond van Duyse, *Het oude Nederlandsche lied: Wereldlijke en geestelijke liederen uit vroegeren tijd teksten en melodieen* (Antwerp, 1903), pp. xxxiv–xxxv, 2568–70. A similar fate seems to have befallen Gioseppino (?Cenci)'s *Fuggi, fuggi da questo cielo*, which was taken up with some enthusiasm in Dutch *contrafacta*. Further evidence of the circulation of *Amarilli, mia bella* in the Low Countries is offered by the variations on it by Jacob van Eyck (see notes 3, 30), and also by the arrangement in the keyboard manuscript, dated 1625, by the Flemish Vincentius de la Faille, discussed in Charles van den Borren, 'Le Livre de clavier de Vincentius de la Faille (1625)', *Mélanges de musicologie offerts à M. Lionel de la Laurencie*, Publications de la Société française de musicologie, 2nd series, 3–4 (Paris, 1933), 85–96. This manuscript, formerly in the Écorcheville collection, can no longer be traced. According to van den Borren, this arrangement is very different from Philips's in the Fitzwilliam Virginal Book.

[27] Angelo Solerti, 'Un viaggio in Francia di Giulio Caccini', *Rivista musicale italiana*, 10 (1903), 707–11; Ferdinand Boyer, 'Giulio Caccini à la cour d'Henri IV (1604–1605) d'après des lettres inédites', *La Revue musicale* (1926), 241–50. Caccini's plan to spend a month in England is mentioned in his letter from Paris to Belisario Vinta, 19 February 1605, in Solerti, 'Un viaggio in Francia', 710–11.

262

Example 3. *Amarilli, mia bella*, from Johann Nauwach, *Libro primo di arie passeggiate* (Dresden, 1623), beginning of the second half.

extensive circulation. (The 1607 and 1615 editions from Venice may have gained wider currency.)[28] An intriguing candidate for transmitting the song is the author of the text, Alessandro Guarini, who spent some time in Flanders (possibly between 1607 and 1615).[29] But it seems most likely that the song's dissemination was achieved largely by way of manuscripts passing through the hands of Italian musicians and/or music-lovers travelling to the north, or northern musicians and/or music-lovers visiting Italy. Indeed, some of the curious corruptions in both text and music that appear in the course of the song's dissemination suggest some manner of aural rather than textual transmission.

However, it is clear that the medium of print was important for the transmission of *Amarilli, mia bella* in at least some of its sources. For example, Jacob van Eyck's three versions for recorder(s) are closely related (with only minor rhythmic changes) to the six-part version

---

[28] See my comments in Tim Carter, 'Music-Printing in Late Sixteenth- and Early Seventeenth-Century Florence: Giorgio Marescotti, Cristofano Marescotti, Zanobi Pignoni', *Early Music History* (forthcoming).

[29] According to the entry in the *Dizionario enciclopedico della letteratura italiana* (see above, n. 2), Alessandro Guarini 'militò nelle guerre di Fiandra sotto i Bentivogli'. The most likely candidate from the Ferrarese Bentivoglio family is Guido Bentivoglio, who was papal nuncio to the Spanish Netherlands from August 1607 until 1615. The wars in the Low Countries formally ceased with the Twelve-Year Truce of 1609.

printed in Antwerp by Phalèse in 1601.[30] Similarly, at least two
English sources of the song are related to the Phalèse print. Antwerp
was an important staging post for the transmission of music from Italy
to England, not just because of its geographical proximity but also
because the city, and indeed the Spanish Netherlands as a whole, was
host to a large English community, including Catholics who, whether
out of choice or necessity, had left Protestant England. Phalèse prints
were certainly available in England (indeed, perhaps more so than
prints emanating from the Italian presses): in mid-1599, William
Cavendish, Earl of Devonshire, spent 18*s* 18*d* in London 'for singing
books', including two Phalèse anthologies first printed in 1583, *Musica
divina* and *Harmonia celeste*, and music by Philips (also printed by
Phalèse) and Orazio Vecchi.[31] Similarly, Joseph Kerman has noted
the extent to which Phalèse anthologies appear to have influenced the
content and presentation of Nicholas Yonge's *Musica transalpina* of
1588.[32] It is clear, too, that Phalèse prints were important sources for
Francis Tregian's anthologies of contemporary secular, sacred and
instrumental music (GB-Lbl Egerton 3665, the 'Tregian' manuscript,
continued in US-NYp Drexel 4302, the 'Sambrooke' manuscript).

The two versions of the song in English sources that appear directly
related to the six-part version printed by Phalèse are the keyboard
arrangement by Peter Philips in the Fitzwilliam Virginal Book (the
arrangement is dated 1603 and also survives in another source, D-Bds
Lynar A1), and the three-part version included in GB-Lbl Egerton
3665.[33] Philips, who had lived in Antwerp between 1590 and 1597, was
closely associated with Pierre Phalèse: all his major music prints were
issued by him. He also seems to have acted for a time as something of
a general music editor for the press: he compiled at least one Phalèse
anthology, the *Melodia olympica* of 1591, and he may have had a hand in
others. Philips was indeed an ideal editor. Apart from his obvious
musical skills, he had also spent at least three years at the English
College in Rome between 1582 and 1585, and it is possible that
Philips was the source of at least some of the Italian music that
Phalèse included in his later anthologies. Philips's keyboard arrangement of *Amarilli, mia bella* is clearly an intabulation of the six-part
version, taken either from the Phalèse print (although Philips adds the

[30] For the three versions of *Amarilli, mia bella*, see *Jacob van Eyck: Der fluyten lust-hof*, ed. Gerritt
Vellekoop (Amsterdam, 1957–8), i, 41–2, 71–3; ii, 90–1. The first has some variants in the first
half. These variation sets are discussed briefly in Thurston Dart, 'Four Dutch Recorder Books',
*The Galpin Society Journal*, 5 (1952), 57–60.

[31] See the accounts transcribed in Walter L. Woodfill, *Musicians in English Society from Elizabeth I
to Charles I* (Princeton, 1953; repr. New York, 1969), 253–4.

[32] Joseph Kerman, *The Elizabethan Madrigal: A Comparative Study* (New York, 1962), 48–50.

[33] Philips's arrangement of *Amarilli, mia bella* is in *The Fitzwilliam Virginal Book*, ed. J. A. Fuller
Maitland and William Barclay Squire (Leipzig, 1899; repr. New York, 1963), i, 329–31. GB-Lbl
Egerton 3665 is discussed in Bertram Schofield and Thurston Dart, 'Tregian's Anthology', *Music
and Letters*, 32 (1951), 205–16; Elizabeth Cole, 'L'Anthologie de madrigaux et de musique
instrumentale pour ensembles de Francis Tregian', *La Musique instrumentale de la renaissance*, ed.
Jean Jacquot (Paris, 1955), 115–26.

correct attribution to 'Julio Romano') or from a common source (see Example 4). (There is little to support the tempting suggestion that it was Philips who provided, or perhaps even arranged, the six-part version for Phalèse.)[34] Philips adds embellishments and makes a few minor changes, but he follows the six-part version closely, even down to the altered repeats of each half of the song.[35] The discovery of a six-part version of *Amarilli, mia bella* as the source for Philips's arrangement removes any need to explain the apparent anomaly of a keyboard composer transcribing and elaborating a solo song rather than, as was more usually the case, a polyphonic madrigal.

Example 4(a).   *Amarilli, mia bella*, from *Ghirlanda di madrigali a sei voci*, beginning of the second half (first time).

The Fitzwilliam Virginal Book was copied by Francis Tregian apparently after his conviction of recusancy in 1609 and subsequent imprisonment in the Fleet until his death in 1619. His other big collection (now split between GB-Lbl Egerton 3665 and US-NYp Drexel 4302) seems to have been compiled in similar circumstances.

[34] Philips did adapt two three-part canzonettas by Ruggiero Giovanelli in his *Madrigali a otto voci* (Antwerp, 1598); see DeFord, 'Musical Relationships', 144. But whether he did the same for *Amarilli, mia bella* can only remain speculation.

[35] The B♭ chord in bar 5 of Example 4(b), and also the curious B♮ in the bass of bar 12 of the Fuller Maitland edition, may be misreadings by Tregian. I am grateful to Lucy Carolan for informing me that the other source for Philips's arrangement, D-Bds Lynar A1, p. 318, has respectively a G minor chord and a B♭ in these two places, making the Lynar version a more exact transcription of the six-part madrigal in 1601⁵.

Example 4(b). *Amarilli, mia bella*, arranged by Philips, from the Fitzwilliam Virginal Book (after Fuller Maitland), beginning of the second half (first time).

Tregian could have collected at least some of the music for his anthologies while he was living on the continent. (He was in Rome in the early 1590s and lived in Brussels from at least 1603 until 1606 or 1607.)[36] Philips may also have been an important source for Tregian's manuscripts, whether when they were both in Brussels or by sending him music after his return to London: Henry Peacham remarked in 1622 that Philips regularly sent music from the continent to England.[37] Certainly the connections between Philips and Tregian are well documented – Tregian's manuscripts contain a good deal of his keyboard, consort and vocal music – and of course they were both Catholics. The three-part version of *Amarilli, mia bella* in Egerton 3665, attributed to 'Julio Romano', comes at the end of a series of three-part canzonettas by Roman and north-Italian composers of the 1580s and 1590s.[38] However, this version is almost certainly a reduction of the six-part version printed by Phalèse in 1601 and arranged by Philips in 1603. Tregian knew Phalèse's 1601 anthology: he scored eight six-part madrigals (but not, significantly, *Amarilli, mia bella*) from it later in his

---

[36] Pearl A. Boyan and George R. Lamb, *Francis Tregian, Cornish Recusant* (London, 1955), 103–5.

[37] In *The Compleat Gentleman* (1622), given in Oliver Strunk, *Source Readings in Music History* (London, 1952), 336.

[38] On these canzonettas and their one-time attribution to Caccini, see Carter, 'Giulio Caccini: New Facts, New Music', 26–7.

266

collection (US-NYp Drexel 4302, pp. 502–18 (nos. 105–15)). For his version of *Amarilli, mia bella*, Tregian (or his source) scores the parts given in Phalèse's *canto, sesto* and *basso* partbooks to create a three-part piece. This produces some curious gaps that suggest that Tregian (or his source) was not copying a version intended for just three voices (see Example 5, and compare Example 4(a)). Tregian (or his source) also ignores the written-out (and slightly altered) repeats of each half in 1601[5], replacing them with a repeat sign. However, in the process of making this adaptation to the six-part version, Tregian (or his source) appears to have confused the first and second endings of the second half, producing an ending in his copy that is unworkable (see Example 6). It is significant that this three-part setting of *Amarilli, mia bella* should share contextual (but not musical) similarities with the version in I-Bu MS 177/IV: in both cases the settings are grouped with late sixteenth-century canzonettas, and both are presented in the ‖:*A*‖:*B*:‖ format. However, it is not clear why Tregian (or his source) should have reduced a six-part madrigal to three voices, unless he knew of, or suspected, the existence of a three-voice model on which the six-voice version was based.

*Amarilli, mia bella* first appeared in print in England in Robert Dowland's *A Musicall Banquet* of 1610, scored for solo voice and (unfigured) bass plus an accompaniment intabulated for lute.[39] Here, too, the source seems clear: Robert Dowland based his version of the

Example 5. *Amarilli, mia bella*, from GB-Lbl Egerton 3665, pp. 22–3, beginning of the second half (text laid under the bass part only).

---

[39] A facsimile edition is edited by Diana Poulton (Menston, 1973); for a modern edition, see *Robert Dowland: A Musicall Banquet (1610)*, ed. Peter Stroud, The English Lute-Songs, second series, 20 (London, 1968). *A Musicall Banquet* also includes Caccini's *Dovrò dunque morire* (from *Le nuove musiche*, also in GB-Ob Tenbury MS 1018), Domenico Maria Melli's *Se di farmi morire* (from Melli's *Le seconde musiche . . . à una & due voci* (Venice, 1602)), and the anonymous *O bella più che le stelle Diana* (also in GB-Lbl Egerton 2971).

Example 6(a). *Amarilli, mia bella,* from *Ghirlanda di madrigali a sei voci,* ending of the second half (first time, continuation of Example 4(a)).

Example 6(b). *Amarilli, mia bella,* from *Ghirlanda di madrigali a sei voci,* ending of the second half (second time).

Example 6(c). *Amarilli, mia bella,* from GB-Lbl Egerton 3665, pp. 22–3, ending of the second half (continuation of Example 5).

song on the 1602 print (not, it seems from the underlay and other typographical details, the edition printed by Alessandro Raverii in Venice in 1607), with the exception that the bass part is given in the F4 clef rather than Caccini's F3. Dowland follows the 1602 print's placing of bar-lines, even though this causes some irregularities because of differences in the line-breaks; the variant readings can be explained by unclear passages in the original (he corrects some and confuses others); the realization of the bass for lute follows Caccini's figuring in the 1602 print exactly; and the song has its 1602 coda.

Clearly Caccini's print had reached England (or at least Robert Dowland) by 1610, and Dowland's edition no doubt indicates the popularity of Caccini's music there in the first decades of the seventeenth century. Testimony of this popularity is also offered by English manuscript sources of his songs, and particularly *Amarilli, mia bella*, some if not all of which arguably come from the second decade of the century. It is striking, however, that as with the continental sources of *Amarilli, mia bella*, these manuscripts present a 'family' of readings of the song existing quite independently of the 1602 print and Dowland's 1610 edition. There are at least four English manuscripts containing *Amarilli, mia bella* as a solo song: GB-Lbl Add. MS 15117 (for soprano voice and lute tablature, with the English text 'Miserere my maker'), GB-Lbl Egerton 2971 (a heavily embellished version for soprano voice and lyra viol tablature), GB-Lbl Royal Appendix 55 (see Figure 3; for tenor voice and unfigured bass), and GB-Ob Tenbury MS 1018 (see Figure 4; for soprano voice and unfigured bass).[40] The readings in Egerton 2971, Royal Appendix 55 and Tenbury MS 1018 have slight differences but are closely related (witness the added chromaticism at the end), while Add. MS 15117, although with more variants, is at least partly linked to them.

The dating of the versions of *Amarilli, mia bella* in these manuscripts remains unclear. The *contrafactum* in Add. MS 15117 and the embellished setting in Egerton 2971 seem likely to be later readings than the straightforward versions of the song in Royal Appendix 55 and Tenbury MS 1018.[41] In the case of Tenbury MS 1018, the music by Alfonso Ferrabosco II for two masques by Ben Jonson from 1611 in the same layer of the manuscript as *Amarilli, mia bella* suggests that it was

[40] For GB-Lbl Royal Appendix 55, see Charles W. Warren, 'The Music of Derick Gerarde' (Ph.D. dissertation, Ohio State University, 1966), i, 49, 204; Iain Fenlon and John Milsom, '"Ruled Paper Imprinted": Music Paper and Patents in Sixteenth-Century England', *Journal of the American Musicological Society*, 37 (1984), 139–63, esp. p. 160. For GB-Ob Tenbury MS 1018 (which contains 13 songs by Caccini, nine of which are attributed), see Nancy C. Maze, 'Tenbury MS 1018: A Key to Caccini's Art of Embellishment', *Journal of the American Musicological Society*, 9 (1956), 61–3. For GB-Lbl Egerton 2971, see Mary Cyr, 'A Seventeenth-Century Source of Ornamentation for Voice and Viol: British Museum MS Egerton 2971', *RMA Research Chronicle*, 9 (1971), 53–72 (a transcription of *Amarilli, mia bella* is given on pp. 70–1). For GB-Lbl Add. MS 15117, see Mary Joiner, '"Amarilli, mia bella": Its Influence on "Miserere my maker"', *The Lute Society Journal*, 10 (1968), 6–14, and 'British Museum MS Add. 15117: A Commentary, Index and Bibliography', *RMA Research Chronicle*, 7 (1969), 51–109. 'Miserere my maker', a text evoking Psalm 51, is also set for solo voice and lute in GB-Ckc Rowe MS 2, ff. 12ᵛ–13 (see Joiner, 'British Museum MS Add. 15117', pp. 90–1), and for six voices in GB-Och MSS 56–60, no. 31. The setting in Rowe MS 2 is arguably related to GB-Lbl Add. MS 15117, but the one in GB-Och (attributed to Thomas Foorde) is very different. GB-Lbl Egerton 2971 and GB-Ob Tenbury MS 1018 share another Caccini song, *Dolcissimo sospiro* (also printed in *Le nuove musiche*), and the anonymous *Crud'Amarilli* (2p, 'Ma grideran per me le piaggi e monti').

[41] Joiner, 'British Museum MS Add. 15117', 51–3, and Mary Chan (i.e. Joiner), *Music in the Theatre of Ben Jonson* (Oxford, 1980), 16, 97, 105, place the manuscript in or shortly after 1616, although it clearly contains much earlier pieces. However, it may be later still. Cyr, 'A Seventeenth-Century Source of Ornamentation', 54–5, places Egerton 2971 in the second decade of the seventeenth century.

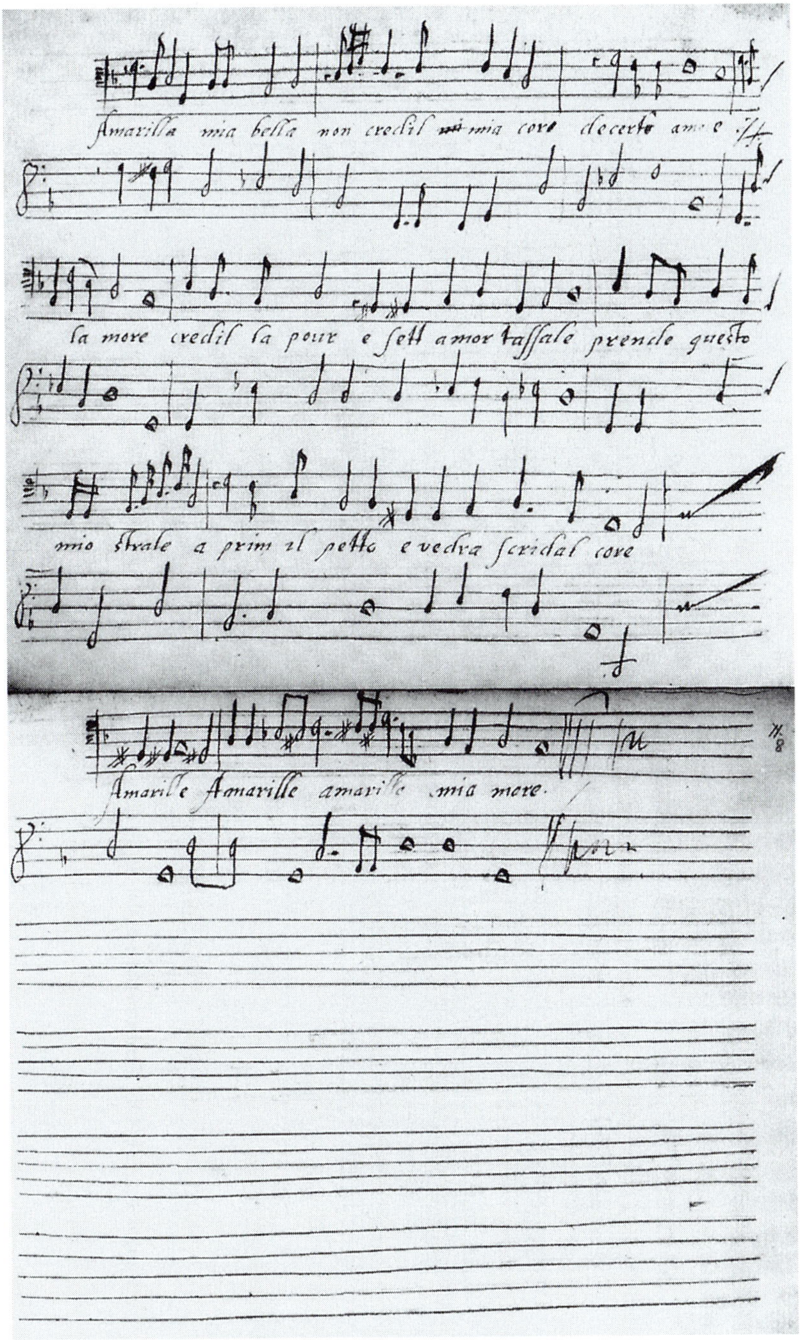


Figure 3. GB-Lbl Royal Appendix 55, ff. 10ᵛ–11.

III

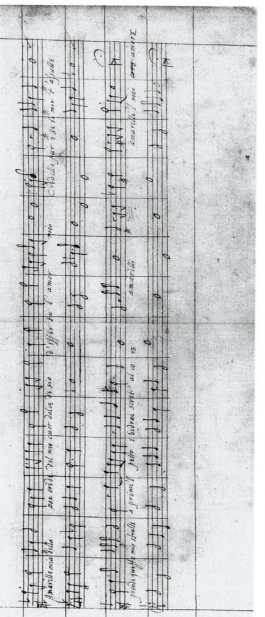

Figure 4.   GB-Ob Tenbury MS 1018, f. 39 (bottom half).

copied a short time after the Dowland edition of 1610 appeared.[42] Royal Appendix 55 has been assigned a somewhat earlier date, but this remains open to question, even if the manuscript could still perhaps be the first source for Caccini's song in England. It is generally assumed to be one of a number copied by the Flemish Derick Gerarde and held in the library of John, Lord Lumley (d. 1609), son-in-law of the noted music collector Henry Fitzalan, Earl of Arundel (d. 1580). Thus the manuscript, a rather rough-and-ready collection of French *airs* (mostly just the soprano line and text), has been associated with the lively musical activity in the Arundel/ Lumley home at Nonsuch Palace.[43] However, the Lumley provenance is not entirely proven, and the evidence for some or all of the manuscript being in Gerarde's hand (which, admittedly, fluctuated quite markedly) is equivocal. Paper-type and other evidence led Iain Fenlon and John Milsom to place the manuscript in 'the 1590s or slightly later'.[44] This would make it a very late Gerarde compilation: he seems to have been most active in the third quarter of the sixteenth century, although his biography remains hazy. The repertory also argues for a late dating: 11 of the chansons have concordances in prints that appeared between 1609 and 1611, including Gabriel Bataille's second and third books of *Airs de différents autheurs, mis en tablature de luth* (Paris, 1609[13], 1611[10]) and Pierre Ballard's *Second livre d'airs à quatre de différents auteurs* (Paris, 1610[13]).[45] Moreover, *Amarilli, mia bella* itself appears to be a later addition to the manuscript, and in a hand that bears even less similarity to Gerarde's. The text of the song is corrupted in a manner suggesting reproduction from memory by someone more used to French than to Italian. ('Amarilli' is given as 'Amarille', and the second half of the song begins 'Credil la pour e sett amor tassale'; the texts in Egerton 2971 and Tenbury MS 1018 are less obviously corrupt.) This is perhaps evidence for some manner of north-European transmission.[46] As for the date (and still assuming a Lumley provenance), it is possible that the song was copied into the manuscript even after the death of Lord Lumley in 1609, when his library passed over to Henry, Prince of Wales, and thence to the Royal

---

[42] Chan, *Music in the Theatre of Ben Jonson*, 42, 234–40, 267.

[43] For Fitzalan, see Kerman, *The Elizabethan Madrigal*, 45, and Charles W. Warren, 'Music at Nonesuch', *The Musical Quarterly*, 54 (1968), 47–57.

[44] Fenlon and Milsom, '"Ruled Paper Imprinted"', 160. George F. Warner and Julius P. Gilson, *Catalogue of Western Manuscripts in the Old Royal and King's Collections* (London, 1921), ii, 393–4, dates Royal Appendix 55's Nicolas le Blé paper as 1560–90.

[45] I am grateful to Jane Bernstein and Frank Dobbins for this information. Of the chansons in the manuscript (following the numbering in Augustus Hughes-Hughes, *Catalogue of Manuscript Music in the British Museum* (London, 1906–9), ii, 466), nos. 2 (by Antoine Boësset), 13–15 and 16 (by Pierre Guédron) are in 1609[13]; nos. 1–3, 5, 9 and 14–15 are in 1610[13]; and nos. 6 (by Guédron) and 7 are in 1611[10].

[46] It is perhaps worth noting that Gerarde seems to have been reasonably fluent in Italian: see his madrigals in GB-Lbl Royal Appendix 23–5 (no. 37), and Royal Appendix 26–30 (nos. 1–3 and 9).

Library.[47] Thus the version of *Amarilli, mia bella* here may be at least contemporaneous with the Dowland 1610 print and the copying of the song into Tenbury MS 1018, if not later still.

This brief survey of the sources of *Amarilli, mia bella* has left a number of questions unanswered – in particular, much more work needs to be done on the dating and interrelationships of the manuscripts discussed here – but it has also raised a number of important questions about the origins of the 'new' style of Florentine solo song, about the networks of transmission that spread across Europe and enabled one Italian song to become well known in Italy, Germany, the Netherlands and England, and about the role of manuscripts in what is generally taken as the age of printing. The picture presented here is a complex one that opens up several avenues for further enquiry. But there is perhaps another, more fundamental, issue at stake. Caccini's song survives in several versions for solo voice, in at least one three-voice version, in another version apparently for three or four voices, and in a version for six voices, not to mention numerous *contrafacta* and instrumental arrangements. Where or what is the 'authentic' *Amarilli, mia bella*?

The question may seem curious. The 'authentic' *Amarilli, mia bella* is obviously that which has the authority of the composer, that is, the song as published in *Le nuove musiche* of 1602. Caccini was indeed anxious to assert this authority, although it is striking that the 1602 print seems to have been markedly ineffective in 'fixing' his music. Any editor will no doubt rightly give priority to *Le nuove musiche* as the primary source for the song, regarding the other versions of it variously as 'secondary' or 'corrupt', or as 'arrangements'. But modern techniques of categorizing sources, although obviously important, may well miss a point. *Amarilli, mia bella* could exist equally well in several different guises. Moreover, the common factor between these guises is less the song as Caccini wished to have it notated than its 'aria', taking the term in its broadest sense.[48] Good 'aria' was an aesthetic quality much sought by those composers of the sixteenth century who set themselves apart from the polyphonic tradition; it also transcends distinctions of genre or performing medium and need scarcely be affected by them. Finally, it is a quality independent of a given piece's manifestations in notated scores. *Amarilli, mia bella*, with its taut construction and easily remembered line, fills the bill well, however it might be presented for performance. Thus the different

[47] On the fate of the Lumley collection, see Warren, 'The Music of Derick Gerarde', i, 46. Prince Henry had some interest in Italian music, and he employed Angelo Notari in 1610 or 1611. However, the copy of *Amarilli, mia bella* in Royal Appendix 55 is clearly not in Notari's hand (compare GB-Lbl Add. MS 31440, a manuscript copied by Notari).

[48] See the discussion of the term 'aria' in Nino Pirrotta, 'Early Opera and Aria', *Music and Theatre from Poliziano to Monteverdi*, trans. Karen Eales (Cambridge, 1982), 237–80, esp. pp. 247–8; and Franklin B. Zimmermann, 'Air: A Catchword for New Concepts in Seventeenth-Century English Music Theory', *Studies in Musicology in Honor of Otto E. Albrecht*, ed. John W. Hill (Kassel, 1980), 142–57.

versions of the song discussed in this study reveal more than just the flexibility of contemporary attitudes towards musical works. They also emphasize the point that if there was an important stylistic shift in music of the late Renaissance and early Baroque periods, it was less one of changing genres and performing media than a reorientation of the musical qualities deemed to be essential for effective and affective composition.

# IV

## NEW SONGS FOR OLD?
## GUARINI AND THE MONODY

The influence of Battista Guarini on the late Cinquecento madrigal has long been acknowledged. Indeed, the connections were noted at the time: when (in 1596) Alessandro Guarini spoke of the new styles of modern madrigal verse – its *brevità, acutezza, leggiadria, nobiltà* and *dolcezza* – that had brought in their train new styles of music,[1] he was surely referring to the poetry of his father as set by composers in the Ferrarese and Mantuan circles with which both father and son were closely associated. Gary Tomlinson, too, has made considerable claims for the influence of Guarini upon the developing madrigal style of Claudio Monteverdi.[2] Guarini's epigrammatic madrigals, he argues, had a decisive influence on the affective and stylistic gains in Monteverdi's *Il quarto libro de madrigali a cinque voci* (Venezia, Amadino, 1603). And texts drawn from *Il pastor fido* – already well known to have caused significant changes of direction in the work of Luca Marenzio, Giaches de Wert and Benedetto Pallavicino – allowed Monteverdi to formulate a new «musical speech» in his *Il quinto libro de madrigali a cinque voci* (Venezia, Amadino, 1605). Both aspects of Guarini's art – the epigrammatic and the dramatic – are thus brought into the ambit of the text-oriented *seconda pratica* that Monteverdi claimed distinguished his style and that of his more enlightened contemporaries from the more purely musical concerns of the *prima pratica*.

Monteverdi's formulation of the *seconda pratica* stood contemporary with an even more radical rethinking of musical style and aesthetics in Florence, the birth of the so-called 'new music'. It is well known, of course, that the 'new music' was scarcely new. Less certain are the connections between this 'new music' and the *seconda pratica*, even though Monteverdi cites some of his Florentine colleagues in his defence of his new style.[3] Nevertheless, both movements appear to share common aims (whether or

---

[1] In the dedication to L. LUZZASCHI, *Sesto libro de' madrigali a cinque voci*, Ferrara, Baldini, 1596, given in A. NEWCOMB, *The Madrigal at Ferrara, 1579-1597*, Princeton, Princeton University Press, 1980, I, p. 118.

[2] G. TOMLINSON, *Monteverdi and the End of the Renaissance*, Oxford, Clarendon Press, 1987, pp. 73-147.

[3] Jacopo Peri and Giulio Caccini are included among composers who have followed Cipriano de Rore in developing the style of the *seconda pratica*, see Giulio Cesare Monteverdi's *Dichiaratione di una lettera, che si*

not through similar means), enlisting the support of late Renaissance Humanism so as to create new directions in musical style and aesthetics. Accordingly, one would expect the verse of Guarini to have had no less an input into the changes created by the solo song (monody) than was evidently the case in the polyphonic madrigal. However, this was not to be. Solo-song composers never became enthusiastic over Guarini in the same way as contemporary madrigalists, and for reasons that lay at least partly in the content and structure of his verse. Conversely, when they did set Guarini, his verse exposed the inherent weaknesses of early seventeenth-century monody, forcing composers to confront precisely the tensions between old and new that arguably lie at the heart of the 'new music'.

Monodists certainly set Guarini, and with some regularity: the 100 or so music-prints containing solo songs published between 1602 and 1620 contain well over 100 Guarini settings for solo voice and basso continuo (in fact, the figure is probably significantly higher).[4] It is clear that for monodists, Guarini and Marino remained the two most popular poets for their music: settings of their poetry far and away outnumber those of, say, Rinuccini or Chiabrera, while Tasso comes well towards the bottom of any list. But this output of Guarini settings, however significant in numerical terms, gives an impression of diffuseness that contrasts with the more focussed approach to Guarini in many polyphonic madrigal prints. As one might expect, Guarini settings tend to be concentrated in collections by monodists with clear 'literary' tendencies, and/or who have practical experience of the polyphonic madrigal as well as the solo song, and/or who associated their music with specific academies or salons. An obvious example is Lodovico Bellanda's *Musiche* published in Venice in 1607: the volume – with nine Guarini settings – is dedicated to a member of the Accademia Filarmonica of Verona, Alberto Fabriani. But Guarini never dominates a single monody book in the same way as in madrigal books by, say, Marenzio, Wert, Pallavicino, Salomone Rossi or Monteverdi, and with only a few exceptions, Guarini sequences or cycles (again, not uncommon in madrigal books) rarely appear in the output of monodists. Nor do traditions become established (again, as in madrigal books) of emulatory settings of particular texts.

One can suggest a number of possible reasons for the apparent reluctance of monodists to confront Guarini. For example, the solo song may not have been (or may

---

*ritrova stampata nel Quinto libro de suoi madrigali* (in C. MONTEVERDI, *Scherzi musicali a tre voci*, Venezia, Amadino, 1607) given in C. MONTEVERDI, *Lettere, dediche e prefazioni*, ed. D. De' Paoli, Roma, De Santis, 1973, pp. 393-407. The connections between Monteverdi's *Orfeo* (1607) and Peri's *Euridice* (1600) are obvious enough. For Monteverdi and Caccini, see I. HORSLEY, *Monteverdi's Use of Borrowed Material in «Sfogava con le stelle»*, «Music & Letters», LIX, 1978, pp. 316-328.

[4] The best accounts of the repertory are N. FORTUNE, *Italian Secular Monody from 1600 to 1635: An Introductory Survey*, «The Musical Quarterly», XXXIX, 1953, pp. 171-195; ID. *Italian Secular Song from 1600 to 1635: The Origins and Development of Accompanied Monody*, Ph.D. diss., University of Cambridge, 1954; W. V. PORTER, *The Origins of the Baroque Solo Song: A Study of Italian Manuscripts and Prints from 1590-1610*, Ph.D. diss., Yale University, 1962. My survey is largely restricted to printed sources, most of which are inventoried in E. VOGEL - A. EINSTEIN - F. LESURE - C. SARTORI, *Bibliografia della musica italiana vocale profana pubblicata dal 1500 al 1700*, [Pomezia-Genève], Staderini-Minkoff, 1977 (henceforth NV), but the text attributions are notoriously inaccurate. Facsimiles of a number of these prints can be found in the seven volumes of *Italian Secular Song, 1606-1636*, ed. G. Tomlinson, New York & London, Garland, 1986.

not have been seen to be) a genre appropriate for high-flown literary texts that had already become well established in the province of the polyphonic madrigal (and certainly some of the more overtly 'popular' monodists were not of a kind to bother with such texts anyway). Moreover, the flowering of monody publications (from 1609 onwards) comes some time after the Guarini 'craze', which was arguably most intense between the mid 1590s and mid 1600s (prompted in part by the long-awaited performances of *Il pastor fido* in Mantua in 1598 and the publication of the *Rime* in Venice in the same year).[5] Similarly, the main centres for early monody – Florence, the Papal States, the Veneto, Milan – remain geographically and politically distinct from the cities that took the lead (at least after the secession of Ferrara in 1598) in Guarini settings, Mantua and (to a somewhat lesser extent) Naples.

Florence is an intriguing case, however, for Guarini was certainly in some manner of contact with Florentine circles: *Il pastor fido* was reviewed by Lionardo Salviati and mooted for performance at the wedding of Grand Duke Ferdinando de' Medici and Christine of Lorraine in 1589;[6] as a secretary, Guarini received a salary of 20 *scudi* per month from the Medici court from April 1599 until 1601;[7] he was involved in the festivities for the wedding of Maria de' Medici and Henry IV of France in October 1600;[8] and he was a member of the Accademia della Crusca. Accordingly, Giulio Caccini includes four Guarini settings in his *Le nuove musiche* (Firenze, Marescotti, 1602),[9] *Amor io parto, Non più*

---

[5] For the performances and critical fortunes of *Il pastor fido*, the basic text remains V. ROSSI, *Battista Guarini ed «Il pastor fido». Studio biografico-critico con documenti inediti*, Torino, Loescher, 1886. The Mantua productions are discussed in I. FENLON, *Music and Patronage in Sixteenth-Century Mantua*, I, Cambridge, Cambridge University Press, 1980, pp. 146-157 (tr. it. *Musicisti e mecenati a Mantova nel '500*, Bologna, Il Mulino, 1992). For the performance before Margherita of Austria, see also *A Briefe Discourse of the Voyage and Entrance of the Queene of Spaine into Italy* [translated from the French and Dutch by «H. W.»], London, n.d., p. 10: «The morrow after being Sunday, the 22. of Nouember [1598] there was done nothing except at night: about 5. of the clocke there was vpon a great round Theater (wherein euery one might stand) played an excellent Comedy, which dured from the said fiue of the clocke vntill 3. houres after midnight, without any one beeing wearied with seeing or hearing, for the great singularities of inexplicable artificies which were shewed in the same: which vnto all seemed so admirable, so rare and so excellent, that in the iudgements of them all, it should seeme impossible, (as long as the world shal stand) to represent a Comedy more excellent and pleasant, where (ouer and aboue the said artificies and admirable rarieties,) there was betweene euery enterlude, heard most rare musicke of many partes, with diuers instruments, accompanied with angelical & delicate voyces, insomuch that it seemed rather a diuine, the[n] humane thing, or at least wise, that the voices of heauen had intermixed themselues with the entire perfection of that of men, and the spirits of this age. Being in fine a thing so rare, that it is impossible to set the same in writing, except the author therof, or the inuentor of the artificies should doe it himselfe: The said comedy, besides the castle of artificial fireworkes, and besides the triumphall arkes which were in good number excellent well made, and ouer and aboue the present of the litter, did cost aboue 25000. crownes of gold [...]».

[6] For the proposed Florentine performance, see V. ROSSI, *op. cit.*, pp. 93-94; S. J. LEDBETTER, *Luca Marenzio: New Biographical Findings*, Ph.D. diss., New York University, 1971, p. 201. Documents concerning the obtaining of a Florentine privilege for the print of *Il pastor fido* – Guarini sought and gained exemption from the usual payment for such a privilege – are in Florence, Archivio di Stato, «Auditore delle Riformagioni», 17, no. 132 (22 January 1589/90); «Mediceo del Principato», 1689, fol. 7r.

[7] His appointment on 1 April 1599 is noted in Florence, Archivio di Stato, «Depositeria Generale», 389 («Ruolo della Casa del Ser.mo Ferdinando Medicj Cardinale Gra. Duca di Toscana»), appendix, no. 375.

[8] Guarini provided the text of Emilio de' Cavalieri's *Giunone e Minerva* performed at the wedding banquet on 5 October.

[9] The volume is edited in G. CACCINI, *Le nuove musiche (1602)*, ed. H. W. Hitchcock, Madison, A-R Editions, 1970 («Recent Researches in the Music of the Baroque Era», IX).

*guerra, pietate* and *Perfidissimo volto* in the main body of the print, and *Cor mio, deh non languire* in the preface as an illustration of his ideal performance style. Girolamo Montesardo also includes two solo-voice Guarini settings in his collection glorifying the delights of Florence, *L'allegre notti di Fiorenza ... Musiche a una, due, tre, quattro e cinque voci* (1608).[10] But the two other Florentine monodists publishing in the first decade of the seventeenth century, Severo Bonini and Jacopo Peri (a 'literary' composer if ever there was one), remain reluctant to confront Guarini, while Francesco Rasi's *Madrigali di diversi autori*, printed in Florence in 1610, avoids the poet altogether.

Caccini's selection of Guarini texts is revealing. He opts almost entirely for his longer discursive poems rather than the epigrammatic ones that Tomlinson notes were so influential for the madrigals of Monteverdi's *Quarto libro*. The one Guarini text shared between Caccini's *Le nuove musiche* and Monteverdi's *Quarto libro*, *Non più guerra, pietate*, is, as Tomlinson points out, typical of Guarini's old-fashioned «rhetorically heightened discursive style».[11] And although Caccini's choice of the long version of *Perfidissimo volto* rather than the shorter, more epigrammatic reworking published in the 1598 *Rime* may be due to other reasons – Caccini places the song among the earliest of his works from the mid 1580s[12] – it is somehow emblematic: the version of *Perfidissimo volto* sanctioned by Guarini in 1598 had to wait until 1611 for a solo-voice setting, and a feeble one at that, by Pietro Benedetti.[13] Indeed, monodists as a whole seem to have been reluctant to broach Guarini's epigrams.

One can see why. *Cor mio, deh non languire*, set by Caccini in 1602, is the longest of the 'family' of *Cor mio* poems in Guarini's output. One of the shortest is *Cor mio, mentre i' vi miro*. This text, and the variant *Donna, mentre i' vi miro*, received some eighteen settings between 1586 and 1619, but only two for solo voice and continuo, by Francesco Rasi (*Vaghezze di musica per una voce sola*, Venezia, Gardano, 1608) and Sigismondo D'India (*Le musiche ... da cantar solo*, Milano, Tini e Lomazzo, 1609).[14] The poem is typical of the Guarini epigram – eight predominantly short verses divided into two sections (*expositio* and *acumen*) with a witty 'point' at the end:[15]

> Cor mio, mentre i' vi miro,
> visibilmente i' mi trasformo in voi;
> e trasformato poi
> in un solo sospir l'anima spiro.

---

[10] See T. CARTER, «*Serate musicali*» *in Early Seventeenth-Century Florence: Girolamo Montesardo's «L'allegre notti di Fiorenza» (1608)*, in *Renaissance Studies in Honor of Craig Hugh Smyth*, ed. A. Morrogh *et al.*, Firenze, Giunti Barbera, 1985, I, pp. 555-568.

[11] G. TOMLINSON, *op. cit.*, p. 87.

[12] See G. CACCINI, *Le nuove musiche (1602)* cit., p. 45.

[13] P. BENEDETTI, *Musiche*, Firenze, Marescotti, 1611. The two versions of the poem are discussed in G. TOMLINSON, *op. cit.*, p. 87.

[14] D'India's volume is edited in S. D'INDIA, *Il primo libro di musiche da cantar solo*, ed. F. Mompellio, Cremona, Fondazione Claudio Monteverdi, 1970 («Instituta et monumenta», 1/4), and ID., *Le musiche a una e a due voci. Libri I, II, III, IV e V (1609-1623)*, ed. J. Joyce, Firenze, Olschki, 1989 («Musiche rinascimentali siciliane», IX).

[15] B. GUARINI, *Opere*, ed. M. Guglielminetti, 2nd ed., Torino, UTET, 1971, p. 267 f., gives the version in Guarini's *Rime* (Venezia, Ciotti, 1598), *Donna, mentre i' vi miro* (and lines 5 and 6 are reversed).

Ex. 1 – FRANCESCO RASI, *Cor mio, mentre i' vi miro*, in *Vaghezze di musica per una voce sola*, Venezia, Gardano, 1608, fol. [2v]-3r.

O bellezza mortale,
o bellezza vitale,
poi che sì tosto un core
per te rinasce, e per te nato more.

It is hard not to recall Monteverdi's splendid setting in his *Quarto libro*, a setting that seems to mark the peak of Monteverdi's epigrammatic style.[16] Rasi's efforts (Ex. 1) evoke Monteverdi's, particularly at the exclamation in line 5 (but his text reads «O fierezza mortale», destroying the anaphora). Yet he palls in comparison: in particular the feeble repetitions at the end – however necessary to give the setting a viable length – make nonsense of Guarini's delightful paradox.

Of course, Rasi had concerns other than the stylish and rhetorically effective presentation of a text: his *Vaghezze di musica* is primarily a 'singer's' collection, with the main aim seemingly to display (as far as contemporary notation would allow) the tenor's virtuoso technique. But other more 'composerly' monodists seem to have had no

---

[16] See the discussion in G. TOMLINSON, *op. cit.*, pp. 89-91.

Ex. 2 – GIOVANNI GHIZZOLO, *Oimè, se tanto amate*, in *Madrigali et arie ... a una et due voci*, Venezia, Raverii, 1609, p. 10.

less difficulty with the Guarini epigram. *Ohimè, se tanto amate*, another poem celebrated in Monteverdi's *Quarto libro*, receives only two solo-voice settings (compared with fifteen for more than one voice), by Giovanni Ghizzolo (*Madrigali et arie ... a una et due voci*, Venezia, Raverii, 1609) and Giulio Romano (*Fuggilotio musicale ... a una et due voci*, Venezia, Vincenti, 1613).[17] Ghizzolo is braver than most other monodists in confronting Guarini throughout his three books of *Musiche*: indeed, the *Giuoco della cieca* from *Il pastor fido* also receives a fully-fledged setting in the 1609 volume. This particular book is associated specifically with the «ridotto musicale» hosted by the dedicatee, Michelangelo Marchesi, Archdeacon and Canon of the Cathedral of Novara, and the emphasis on Guarini makes it somewhat untypical for its time. Moreover, Ghizzolo clearly knows Monteverdi's madrigals, whether through the original prints or through the spiritual *contrafacta* published by Aquilino Coppini in nearby Milan in 1607-9. Thus Ghizzolo's *Oimè, se tanto amate* contains numerous echoes of Monteverdi's setting, not least in the ending (Ex. 2). But despite Ghizzolo's efforts to

---

[17] For Giulio Romano, see H. W. HITCHCOCK, *Depriving Caccini of a Musical Pastime*, «Journal of the American Musicological Society», XXV, 1972, pp. 58-78.

extend the final cadence, again the result is too laboured to come off successfully. It seems clear that often the epigrammatic madrigal simply did not offer enough scope – or for that matter, enough words (see Rasi's repetitions) – for the reduced scale of a solo song: while Monteverdi was able to turn concise texts to his (polyphonic) advantage, monodists were left with no room for play. Moreover, Tomlinson notes that for a successful musical setting, the epigram required «a precise control of musical continuity (and discontinuity)», and the ability «to respond to poetic articulations of different weights with an array of musical analogues».[18] Such control and analogues were simply not available to the monodist.[19]

The difficulties facing monodists in setting Guarini's epigrammatic verse are easily explained by the affective and structural constraints of such verse for solo-voice setting: they tended to prefer more discursive and more immediately emotional texts that allowed them to exploit free declamation in the framework of the *stile rappresentativo*. Two obvious, and fairly popular, examples by Guarini are *Occhi, un tempo mia vita* – with solo-voice settings by Bartolomeo Barbarino (*Madrigali ... Per cantare ... da una voce sola*, Venezia, Amadino, 1606), Antonio Cifra (*Li diversi scherzi ... a una, a due et tre voci. Libro secondo*, Roma, Robletti, 1613), «Gioseppino» (Cenci?; in Pietro Maria Marsolo's *Li madrigali a quattro voci opera decima*, Venezia, Vincenti, 1614),[20] and Vincenzo Calestani (*Madrigali et arie ... a una e due voci*, Venezia, Vincenti, 1617) – and *Voi pur da me partite, anima mia*, set by Francesco Rasi (*Vaghezze di musica* cit., 1608), Pietro Benedetti (*Musiche*, Firenze, Marescotti, 1611), and Domenico Belli (*Il primo libro dell'arie a una e a due voci*, Venezia, Amadino, 1616). Of course, it is precisely these latter qualities that were inherent in Guarini's *Il pastor fido* and which allowed Monteverdi to develop his new «musical speech». But despite the fact that *Il pastor fido* texts were seemingly much better suited to solo-voice setting than the Guarinian epigram, monodists again remained reluctant to confront the play.

The vogue for *Il pastor fido* is well documented in contemporary madrigal books: indeed, a good number proclaim their allegiance to the play on their title-page.[21] In

---

[18] G. TOMLINSON, *op. cit.*, p. 82.

[19] The case of another *Cor mio* poem even shorter than *Cor mio, mentre i' vi miro, Cor mio, deh non piagnete* (B. GUARINI, *Opere* cit., p. 286 f.) is no less revealing, if for different reasons:

Cor mio, deh non piagnete,
ch'altro mal io non provo, altro martire,
che 'l veder voi del mio languir languire.
Dunque non vi dolete,
se sanar mi volete;
che quell'affetto, che pietà chiamate,
s'è dispietato a voi, non è pietate.

This offers even less scope for settings of an appropriate length. But significantly, its rhetoric is more straightforward, with an uncomplicated progression towards the final line. Monodists must have felt happier with the clarity of the argument: the poem was set as a solo song by Domenico Maria Melli (*Musiche*, Venezia, Vincenti, 1602), Pietro Benedetti (*Musiche ... Libro secondo*, Venezia, Amadino, 1613) and Claudio Saracini (*Le seconde musiche*, Venezia, Vincenti, 1620).

[20] See P. M. MARSOLO, *Secondo libro de' madrigali a quattro voci*, ed. L. Bianconi, Roma, De Santis, 1973 («Musiche rinascimentali siciliane», IV).

[21] For example, prints by Gabriele Fattorini (*La cieca. Il primo libro de madrigali a cinque voci*, Venezia, Amadino, 1598), Philippe de Monte (*Musica sopra Il pastor fido*, Venezia, Gardano, 1600), Giovanni Piccioni

comparison, the output of solo songs setting texts from *Il pastor fido* appears thin. Mirtillo's lament *Udite, lagrimosi spirti d'Averno* (III, 6) achieved some popularity, with published settings by Domenico Brunetti (*L'Euterpe ... a una, due, tre et quattro voci,* Venezia, Amadino, 1606), Lucia Quinciani (in Marc'Antonio Negri's *Affetti amorosi ... libro secondo,* Venezia, Amadino, 1611), and Bartolomeo Barbarino (among the solo songs in his *Madrigali a tre voci,* Venezia, Amadino, 1617), plus a fine version dedicated to Monteverdi by Claudio Saracini (*Le seconde musiche,* Venezia, Vincenti, 1620): its thirteen lines have all the characteristics of the discursive madrigal. But in the case of *O Mirtillo, Mirtillo anima mia* (III, 4) – the *Pastor fido* cycle that stands near the head of Monteverdi's *Quinto libro* – of the twenty or so settings published between 1595 and 1626, only two are by monodists, in Giovanni Ghizzolo's *Il terzo libro delli madrigali, scherzi et arie. A una et due voci* (Milano, Lomazzo, 1613) and Giovanni Boschetto Boschetti's *Strali d'Amore ... Con alcuni madrigali, dialoghi e villanelle a una, due et tre voci* (Venezia, Vincenti, 1618). Moreover, Ghizzolo's setting of Amarilli's poignant speech owes little to the spirit, or even the practice, of the play: it is a setting for bass (!) voice with florid passages (ranging from $B'$ to $e'$) as sung by the Milanese virtuoso Ottavio Valera.[22] It is even more striking that the extract from the play that seems almost emblematic of a '*Pastor fido*' composer, *Ah dolente partita* (III, 3), is broached only once by a monodist, in a setting attributed to Caccini in a late (1610s) English manuscript.[23] The evident reluctance to set *Ah dolente partita* may be due to the fact that in both structure and content it is very close to a Guarini epigram. Nevertheless, the paradox remains that if *Il pastor fido* enabled composers to create a new «musica rappresentativa», to quote Monteverdi's contemporaries,[24] or a new «musical speech», to quote Tomlinson, these issues were explored only in a style and genre seemingly inimical to representing «musical speech», the polyphonic madrigal, and not in the one style and genre precisely where representing «musical speech» was claimed to lay at the heart of the matter, the solo song.[25]

---

(*Il pastor fido musicale ... Il sesto libro di madrigali a cinque voci,* Venezia, Vincenti, 1602), Marsilio Casentini (*La cieca. Madrigali a cinque voci ... libro quarto,* Venezia, Vincenti, 1609), Claudio Pari (*Il pastor fido. Secondo libro de' madrigali a cinque voci,* Palermo, Maringo, 1611), Biagio Tomasi (*Corisca ... Il secondo libro de madrigali a cinque et a sei voci,* Venezia, Magni, 1613) and his colleague Giovanni Nicolò Mezzogorri (*Il pastor fido armonico ... Secondo libro de madrigali a cinque voci,* Venezia, Magni, 1617), Scipione Cerreto (*L'Amarillide a tre voci,* Napoli, Vitale, 1621), and Tarquinio Merula (*Satiro e Corisca, dialogo musicale a due voci,* Venezia, Vincenti, 1626). For a general discussion, see A. HARTMANN jr, *Battista Guarini and «Il pastor fido»,* «The Musical Quarterly», XXXIX, 1953, pp. 415-425.

[22] For Ottavio Valera, see also F. ROGNONI TAEGGIO, *Selva de varii passaggi parte seconda,* Milano, F. Lomazzo, 1620, pp. 72-75, which gives two settings (*Sfogava con le stelle, Tempesta di dolcezza*) each headed «Musica del Molto Illustre Signor Ottauio Valera, & da lui Cantata, con gli istessi Passaggi».

[23] Oxford, Bodleian Library, Tenbury MS 1018. The manuscript is inventoried in W. V. PORTER, *op. cit.,* and the Caccini songs have most recently been discussed in S. WILLIER, *Rhythmic Variants in Early Manuscript Versions of Caccini's Monodies,* «Journal of the American Musicological Society», XXXVI, 1983, pp. 481-497. On the dating, however, see T. CARTER, *Caccini's «Amarilli, mia bella»: Some Questions (and a Few Answers),* «Journal of the Royal Musical Association», CXIII, 1988, pp. 250-273: 268, note 41. Firenze, Biblioteca Nazionale Centrale, Magl. XIX. 66, also originally contained a setting of *Ah dolente partita* (perhaps the same one) according to its contemporary index.

[24] See the preface of *Il secondo libro della musica di Claudio Monteverde e d'altri autori a cinque voci fatta spirituale da Aquilino Coppini,* Milano, Tradate, 1608, given in NV 1946.

[25] Compare the remarks on Monteverdi's *Quinto libro* in A. EINSTEIN, *The Italian Madrigal,* Princeton, Princeton University Press, 1949, II, p. 853: «Is it not strange that Monteverdi uses the old a cappella style

Ex. 3 – GIOVANNI FRANCESCO CAPELLO, *M'è più dolce il penar per Amarilli,* in *Madrigali et arie a voce sola,* Venezia, Vincenti, 1617, p. 1 f.

The reluctance of monodists to come to terms with *Il pastor fido* may again be due to a number of reasons: the problematic reception of a play always prone to academic and religious controversy; the expectations of the genre; fast-changing preferences in poetic styles; and the inability or reluctance on the part of solo-song composers to broach the high ground already occupied by more serious and better established musical forms. But again, too, the problem may lie in the verse itself. If Guarinian epigrams were too short for solo-song composers, some of the speeches from *Il pastor fido* may have been too long for a genre that had neither the desire nor the ability to work on a large scale: it is significant that the setting of Mirtillo's speech *Ch'io t'ami, e t'ami più della mia vita* (III, 3) included in Raffaello Rontani's *Le varie musiche ... a una due e tre voci ... libro primo* (Firenze, Pignoni, 1614), and whether by accident or design, turns the single speech into a two-section dialogue for tenor and soprano voices respectively. Moreover, as well as the question of length, there is also the issue of the intensity required to depict Guarini's emotional verse. Cultivating such intensity had become a hallmark of the modern madrigal, but composers of solo songs were hard-pressed to match the varied expressive vocabulary of polyphony, whether because of their sometimes limited competence or because of the restricted possibilities of one voice and continuo. Monodists confronting Guarini had to work hard to give their settings full effect, and often they outstretched both themselves and their medium. Giovanni Francesco Capello's setting of *M'è più dolce il penar per Amarilli* in his *Madri-*

---

precisely for the 'dramatic' texts, the monologues and dialogues from the *Pastor fido.* [...] One might sup-pose that he would have used the *stile nuovo* and the basso continuo to make his music more 'dramatic' and naturalistic than ever. But here just the opposite is the case».

*gali et arie a voce sola* (Venezia, Vincenti, 1617) is a case in point (Ex. 3): despite the dissonances, the angular vocal lines and the chromaticism, the setting simply lacks the affective range that one might expect to find in even the most average multi-voice setting.

The recognition that the most powerful emotional moments required music for more than just one voice may seem strange – it also gives the lie to the wishful thinking of many early monodists – but it is perhaps not surprising in the context of traditions developed through some fifty years of madrigal writing. In his own limited way, Giovanni Ghizzolo makes precisely this point in the curious *Mentre la notte al suo bel manto il lembo* in his *Madrigali et arie* of 1609.[26] The poem combines narration and direct speech in a manner similar to Ottavio Rinuccini's well known *Sfogava con le stelle* (which Ghizzolo also sets here). The opening is treated as conventional recitative for soprano and continuo. But at the shift to direct speech (a shepherd's invocation to the stars) a bass voice enters (doubled by the continuo) to produce a soprano-bass duet. This unexpected shift to a duet texture has some significance within the structure of the book as a whole: the setting divides off the opening solo songs from the two- and three-part pieces. The effect is also reminiscent of Monteverdi's setting of *Sfogava con le stelle* in his *Quarto libro*, where psalmodic 'recitative' for the opening narration leads to rich counterpoint for the lover's exclamation («O immagini belle»). But Ghizzolo completely reverses the expectations of the genre: precisely where one would expect solo song to come into its own – at a powerful personal invocation – the composer turns his back on the medium. Significantly, too, the very next piece in the book is a duet (soprano and bass) setting of Mirtillo's intense speech *Or consolato io moro* (*Il pastor fido*, V, 3). In the case of *Mentre la notte al suo bel manto il lembo*, Ghizzolo's tactics may well be the result simply of an attempt to distinguish the two parts of the poem through textural distinctions well established within the madrigalian tradition. But perhaps the monody is *too* personal for character-based statements within lyric and/or pastoral genres. And perhaps the free and flexible structures of the solo madrigal were felt to lack the formal underpinning increasingly thought necessary for the fullest affective expression.

Of course, Guarini still had something to offer monodists. Indeed, those of his madrigals that make specific reference to singing had some popularity. *Deh com'in van chiedete* (a *risposta* to Rinuccini's *A me, che tanto v'amo*) is set by Giulio Caccini – in Marsolo's *Li madrigali a quattro voci* (cit. 1614; this volume also contains Caccini's setting of the *proposta*) – and by Camillo Orlandi (*Arie, a tre, due et voce sola*, Venezia, Vincenti, 1616) and Raffaello Rontani (*Le varie musiche ... a una et due voci ... Libro terzo*, Roma, Soldi, 1619): Orlandi's setting is typical, with its roulades at «d'udir, bella Sirena, il canto mio» and «al suon de' vostri accenti». Other examples include *O come sei gentile*, set by Caccini (again in Marsolo's *Li madrigali a quattro voci*), Bartolomeo Barbarino (*Madrigali* cit., 1606), Vincenzo Calestani (*Madrigali et arie* cit., 1617) and Raf-

---

[26] The text is attributed to Guarini in NV 1193, but it is by Orsina Cavaletta, see the *Rime di diversi celebri poeti dell'età nostra*, Bergamo, Ventura, 1587, p. 213. I am indeed grateful to Antonio Vassalli for this information.

faello Rontani (*Le varie musiche a una a due e tre voci ... Libro secondo*, Roma, Roblet-ti, 1618);[27] and *Al partir del mio sole*, set by Lodovico Bellanda (*Musiche* cit., 1607) and Claudio Saracini (*Le terze musiche*, Venezia, Vincenti, 1620).[28] Moreover, serious monodists (or those with pretensions to seriousness) were still expected to set Guarini – Giulio Caccini and Domenico Maria Melli made the point with their Guarini settings in the first published songbooks issued in 1602 – and those particularly who had some experience of handling polyphonic textures did not necessarily set Guarini badly. Sigismondo D'India is a good example. His *Le musiche* of 1609 includes a fine setting of that other archetypal *Pastor fido* madrigal, *Crud'Amarilli, che col nome ancora* (I, 2). Significantly, the song makes clear reference to D'India's own five-part setting includ-ed in his *Il primo libro de madrigali a cinque voci* (Milano, Tradate, 1606),[29] and gains much of its expressive intensity from techniques – careful harmonic planning (also emphasised by sequential repetition), well gauged contrasts of pace, and intense disso-nance and chromaticism – that had been forged within the *seconda pratica* madrigal. A similar sense of D'India's compositional craft is apparent in his *O primavera, gioventù de l'anno* also in the 1609 volume: here the whole of Mirtillo's speech from the opening of Act III of *Il pastor fido* is set in a long cycle, where the careful harmonic planning and rhythmic pacing extends over five *partes* in a manner that merits close analysis.

Raffaello Rontani's setting (*Le varie musiche ... libro primo* cit., 1614) of *O primav-era, gioventù de l'anno* (also in five *partes*, with each *pars* further subdivided) is much less impressive: the composer rushes through the text for 96 bars of the most banal kind of Florentine recitative (D'India's setting, significantly, lasts 175 bars). But Ron-tani appears to have prompted some rival Florentine settings of greater interest: Domenico Visconti included a setting of the first fourteen lines of *O primavera* in his *Il primo libro de arie a una e due voci* (Venezia, Amadino, 1616), and Giovanni Bettini a setting of the same text (set in so similar a way to Visconti as to suggest direct modelling) in Calestani's *Madrigali et arie* (1617). Visconti begins in a conventional madrigal style, but at «tu torni ben, ma teco / non tornano i sereni / e fortunati dì de le mie gioie», he introduces a more structured *arioso* constructed over a 'walking bass' (Ex. 4). The whole setting lasts 48 bars, the same space filled by two *partes* – 22 lines of verse – of Rontani's setting. The appearance of the 'walking bass' may be prompted by word-painting («tu torni ...»), and later contrasts between walking-bass sections and more flexible 'recitative' seem to set off the invocation of spring from the state of the lover. But as a result, Mirtil-lo's speech is also given a much more formal, much less spontaneous guise.

One might well decry Visconti's *O primavera, gioventù de l'anno* as yet one more example of the way in which early seventeenth-century composers lost sight of poetry as poetry – in favour of a more neutral *poesia per musica* – at the waning of the 'golden age' of the madrigal. But although Visconti's setting certainly appears affectively more

[27] There is a further solo-voice setting in Bologna, Civico Museo Bibliografico Musicale, MS Q140, fols. 10r-11r.

[28] Curiously, however, *Mentre vaga Angioletta* receives only one monodic setting, in J. H. KAPSBERGER's *Libro primo di arie passeggiate a una voce*, Roma, n.p., 1612.

[29] The volume is edited in S. D'INDIA, *Il primo libro de madrigali a cinque voci*, ed. F. Mompellio, Milano, Fondazione E. Bravi, 1942 («I classici musicali italiani», X).

Ex. 4 – DOMENICO VISCONTI, *O primavera, gioventù de l'anno,* in *Il primo libro de arie a una e due voci,* Venezia, Amadino, 1616, p. 4 f.

neutral than a solo-voice recitative, it might instead be interpreted as an attempt to offer to monody precisely the formal quality long available to polyphony but not yet so to the solo madrigal. Furthermore, Visconti offers this quality not by appropriating polyphonic techniques – which was D'India's inherently old-fashioned solution – but by adopting a structural guise that was both inherent and unique to monody, that of the aria. Visconti's *O primavera* is not an aria in the (early seventeenth-century) technical sense of the term: the text is, and is set as, a madrigal. But the stylistic devices adopted by Visconti here are precisely those which had been developed within the strophic settings designated as arias in the period: the setting is certainly aria-like, as indeed Visconti suggests by his title-page. Moreover, the formal quality of aria-writing is scarcely as emotionally neutral as might be believed. Monteverdi was only one of many composers to realise the fact that the most intense emotional expression was best achieved through musical techniques that aimed less for an immediate but all too deluding naturalism than for an aesthetic distancing that, paradoxically, allows a far more powerful identification with the emotions at hand. He made the point in *Sfogava con le stelle* by contrasting 'naturalistic' declamation, on the one hand, with intensely emotional counterpoint on the other. He did so, too (and to choose only the most obvious example), in the *Lamento della ninfa* (in his *Madrigali guerrieri et amorosi ... Libro ottavo,* Venezia, Vincenti, 1638) by contrasting the 'naturalistic' recitative-madrigal of the shepherds (*Non avea Febo ancora*) with the intensely emotional triple-time ground-bass aria of the nymph. The lesson is the same, even if the means through which it is applied are different. And it is arguably this new use of aria styles that marks the emotional and musical maturity of the monody as a genre in its own right.

Triple time writing was the most obvious musical gesture associated with aria in the early seventeenth century, and it is not surprising that triple time sections start appearing with some frequency in solo madrigals (including Guarini settings) from the second decade of the century. Short passages of triple time were of course not unusual in earlier polyphonic and solo madrigals, whether to provide figurative word-painting or to match some metric shift in the verse (or both): for monody, Bellanda provides some useful (and quite extended) examples in his 1607 *Musiche*.[30] But by the 1610s, a number of polyphonic and monodic settings start to focus on longer triple-time sections designed to emphasise the musical (and also textual) 'point' of the setting. Filippo Vitali's setting for two sopranos and continuo of *T'amo mia vita, la mia cara vita* in his *Musiche ... a due tre e sei voci libro primo* (Firenze, Pignoni, 1617), for example, is symptomatic of the change. It is a fine setting: again, two voices are better than one. More to the present point, there are also ten bars of triple-time writing at «Prendila tosto Amore, / stampala nel mio petto» which although perhaps prompted by the accentuation of the text also give some urgency to the lover's request, focussing our attention in ways distinct from the prevailing 'recitative'. The trend becomes even more apparent by the 1630s. Giovanni Felice Sances's dialogue setting of *Tirsi morir volea* (*Cantade ... a doi voci ... Libro secondo. Parte seconda*, Venezia, Magni, 1633) is a splendid example.[31] This text, another Guarini 'classic', had largely been ignored by monodists (the exception is Giacomo Fornaci's flaccid setting in his *Amorosi respiri musicali ... A una, due e tre voci*, Venezia, Vincenti, 1617). But Sances rehabilitates the poem with a vengeance to produce a stylish miniature operatic *scena*. The narrative portions of the text are assigned to a third character, Festauro, a virtuoso bass; Filli's two speeches are set in duple-time arioso; and Tirsi's one speech «Et io, mia vita, moro» is then combined with Filli's last words «Mori, cor mio, ch'io moro» for a brief duple-time duet (the phrases are interchanged between the two voices). The last three lines of the madrigal «Così moriro i fortunati amanti» – its 'point' – are then set for all three voices as a glorious trio in the most up-to-date Venetian triple-time. It is a long section – 53 bars – which Sances also directs should be repeated, providing a fine climax to the setting.

But Sances's successful treatment of Guarini is perhaps more the exception than the rule for the 1630s. In the same year as Sances's *Cantade ... a doi voci*, Benedetto Ferrari also included two Guarini settings in his *Musiche varie a voce sola* (Venezia, Magni, 1633).[32] This is a surprisingly 'literary' collection (there are also four Marino settings), which perhaps reflects the courtly links with Alfonso III, Duke of Modena, proclaimed in Ferrari's dedication. Again one notes the association of high-flying literary texts with specific cultured circles: significantly, Ferrari's *Musiche varie a voce sola ...*

---

[30] For example, *Questa invitta guerriera*, with triple time at the mention of singing in the text, and *Baciai, ma che mi valse*, at «dolcissimi i baci».

[31] Edited in J. WHENHAM, *Duet and Dialogue in the Age of Monteverdi*, Ann Arbor, UMI Research Press, 1982, II, pp. 438-447.

[32] Ferrari's three books of *Musiche* are discussed in A. MAGINI, *Le monodie di Benedetto Ferrari e «L'incoronazione di Poppea»: un rilevamento stilistico comparativo*, «Rivista Italiana di Musicologia», XXI, 1986, pp. 266-299.

IV

Ex. 5 – BENEDETTO FERRARI, *Cor mio, tu ti nascondi*, in *Musiche varie a voce sola*, Venezia, Magni, 1633, pp. 8-11.

*Libro secondo* (Venezia, Magni, 1637), dedicated to the English ambassador to Venice, Basil Feilding, inhabits a palpably different (and much more modern) poetic world. The setting of Guarini's *Mentre v'adoro e voi m'avete a schivo* is an *ottava rima* treated to a fairly feeble set of strophic variations for bass voice and continuo. The second song sets another of Guarini's *Cor mio* poems written in typically discursive vein:[33]

---

[33] B. GUARINI, *Opere* cit., p. 269.

IV

Cor mio, tu ti nascondi
a l'apparir del nostro amato sole?
E inanzi a sì bel foco
mi lasci freddo e fioco?
Quando a formar parole,
per domandar mercede,
l'anima tormentata ardir ti chiede,
che paventi codardo?
Fuggi tu forse il folgorar del guardo,
per fuggir il tuo fato?
Non sai morir beato.

But if the choice of text appears conservative, the music is emphatically not so. Ferrari attempts to turn his setting into a recitative-aria combination, shifting to a triple-time aria (lasting 69 bars) for the last four lines (Ex. 5). However, there is no real excuse in either the content or the presentation of the text for the change, and the words have to be extensively repeated: the result is a very curious, dislocated setting where the discomfort caused by the verse becomes palpable in the music. One might also detect the same problems in Sances's *Tirsi morir volea*, for all its wit and charm. Here, too, one feels a clash betweeen the demands of the text and Sances's ambitions for the music: the direct speeches are not long enough to produce a truly dramatic *scena* (again reflecting the problems of the epigrammatic style for monodists), and the final three lines are not strong enough to support such an extensive 'aria'. The new musical styles of the 1630s required very different kinds of texts in terms of both content and structure.

The resulting tensions between text and music, and between old and new, give these late Guarini settings a curious ambivalence. But ambivalence is typical of all attempts by monodists to come to terms with the phenomenon of Guarini. Moreover, such ambivalence in turn reflects the fundamental stylistic and aesthetic paradoxes that lay at the heart of the 'new' (or is it the 'old'?) music. In the first decades of the seventeenth century, neither the affective nor the structural qualities of Guarini's verse seem always to have been suitable for monody. But by the time monody had reached a maturity granting it the potential for dealing with Guarini, the needs of composers had changed: the poet was now too old fashioned to meet the requirements of a new generation. This seems too negative a conclusion to reach at the end of a paper, or indeed a conference, devoted to «Guarini e la musica». At the same time, however, it is precisely through the issue of «Guarini e la musica» that we can start to come to terms with the complex stylistic issues underpinning music in late Renaissance and early Baroque Italy.

# V

## 'AN AIR NEW AND GRATEFUL TO THE EAR': THE CONCEPT OF *ARIA* IN LATE RENAISSANCE AND EARLY BAROQUE ITALY

Most accounts of music in early seventeenth-century Italy conventionally begin with opera and the so-called 'new music' in Florence. But opera and solo song formed only a minor part of the gamut of music-making in a period when secular music as a whole was coming under pressure from the ideological and pragmatic demands of the Counter-Reformation. And even within secular music, writing for solo voice and continuo was but one of a surprising variety of techniques occupying the attention of composers whose wide-ranging activities often demonstrate a healthy lack of concern over generic and stylistic propriety, or over any apparent anachronism resulting from the mixture of seemingly old and seemingly new compositional techniques.

This rich and complex tapestry gives the lie to the neat categorizations and clear focuses promoted by modern historians. Giulio Caccini's solo song 'Amarilli, mia bella', a quintessential example of the 'new music', in fact survives in a variety of formats for a range of performing media, including a six-part setting published one year before the 'authorized' version for solo voice and basso continuo in *Le nuove musiche* (Florence: Heirs of Giorgio Marescotti, 1602).[1] In turn, two five-part madrigals published in Claudio Monteverdi's *Il quinto libro de madrigali a cinque voci* (Venice: Ricciardo Amadino, 1605), 'Ecco, Silvio, colei che in odio hai tanto' and 'Ch'io t'ami e t'ami più de la mia vita', sit quite happily as duets for two sopranos and continuo in a manuscript copied by Angelo Notari (London, British Library, Add. MS 31440, ff. 53v-62v), while Act II of Monteverdi's *Orfeo* (1607) contains music that is first presented as a solo-voice recitative and is then re-arranged in a five-part context ('Ahi, caso acerbo'). In 1608, Paolo Quagliati published a collection of four-part madrigals which can also be performed as solo songs,[2] and solo songs by Caccini and his contemporaries are presented as four-part madrigals in *Il secondo libro de madrigali a quattro voci* (Venice: Giacomo Vincenti, 1614) by the Sicilian Pietro Maria Marsolo.[3] And in broader terms, there are clear examples of cross-fertilization between polyphonic madrigals, duets

V

and solo songs as regards declamatory, expressive and structural techniques.[4] All this suggests a community of musical discourse in early seventeenth-century secular music that belies the attempts of modern historians to classify and divide the repertory according to potentially anachronistic stylistic, generic and medium-related criteria.

The point is clear in a well-known letter from Monteverdi to Alessandro Striggio dated 24 August 1609:

> I received a letter from Your Lordship together with certain words to be set to music, as a commission from His Highness, and they arrived yesterday.... I shall start to work on them as soon as possible, and when they are all done I shall inform Your Lordship or bring them myself to Mantua, because I want to be back in service shortly. I thought first of setting these words for a solo voice, but if later on His Highness orders me to re-arrange the air [*aria*] for five voices, this I shall do.[5]

Indeed, we have at least one concrete example of Monteverdi setting words for a solo voice and then re-arranging the 'air' for five voices: his *Lamento d'Arianna*, the solo-voice lament that marked the climax of his opera *Arianna* of 1608, appears in a five-part version in the composer's *Il sesto libro de madrigali a cinque voci* of 1614.[6]

Monteverdi's term *aria* invokes a complex web of interlocking meanings that cannot always be untangled.[7] It can indicate a genre (as in *aria per cantar ottave* or the strophic arias in early seventeenth-century songbooks); it can be used simply to mean 'melody'; and it can (as in English) have the more general sense of demeanour, manner or character. But problems of definition notwithstanding, *aria* seems to have become something of a catchword in contemporary musical discussion. For example, the protagonists in the Artusi–Monteverdi controversy each agreed – to different effect – that Monteverdi's music displayed 'a new *aria*, a new appeal to the ear struck by fast and slow movement, and now roughly and now sweetly according to the *aria*'.[8] This notion of new kinds of *aria* is also taken up by Vincenzo Giustiniani in his *Discorso sopra la musica* (*c.*1628). The significance of Giustiniani's treatise has been downplayed by recent historians, largely, one suspects, because it fails to accord with traditional perceptions of style-change in music over the 1600s. Ironically, however, it is precisely Giustiniani's challenge to these traditional perceptions that makes him so intriguing.[9]

Vincenzo Giustiniani (1564-1637) was a nobleman, dilettante and amateur musician living in Rome, and his discourse was intended to provide an account of music in his lifetime presumably for the benefit of gentlemen seeking guidance in civilized conversation. This account is obviously biased in favour of Rome, of Giustiniani's patrons (notably Cardinal Montalto and the Barberini family)[10] and doubtless of his favourite musicians. Nevertheless, his perceptions of contemporary music, however inexpert and prejudiced, are not without interest. Giustiniani certainly senses significant changes in musical style during the period he is covering, but inevitably this is seen less as a transition from one period of music history to another than as simply a matter of fashion 'just as in the manner of dress, which continually adopts new styles as they are introduced in the courts of princes, as, for example, [the spread] through Europe of dress according to the manner of France or of Spain'. More to the point, Giustiniani perceives as many continuities as discontinuities over the 1600s, and he attaches little weight to issues that figure prominently in modern accounts of the period, notably the shift towards music for solo voice and basso continuo at the expense of equal-voice polyphony.

What changes do occur are articulated in very different terms. Giustiniani says that as a child he went to music school and noted that the compositions most in favour were by Arcadelt, Lassus, Alessandro Striggio, Cipriano de Rore and Philippe de Monte. But:

> In a short space of time, musical taste changed, and there appeared the compositions of Luca Marenzio and Ruggiero Giovanelli, with newly delightful invention as much in music to be sung by several voices as in [music] for solo voice to some instrument. Their excellence lay in an air new and grateful to the ear [*una nuova aria et grata all'orecchie*], with some simple fugues and without extraordinary artifice. And at the same time, Palestrina, Soriano and Giovanni Maria Nanino composed things to sing in church with a facility in good, sound counterpoint, with a good air and with a fitting decorum [*con buon'aria e con decoro condecente*], in sign of which even today one places their compositions before those of other moderns, who all learnt from them and who have sought to vary [their style] more with delightful ornaments than with fundamental and substantial artifice.

Giustiniani makes several important points here: first, the music of Marenzio and Giovanelli is characterized by a 'new and grateful' air,[11] and that of Palestrina, Soriano and Nanino, by a 'good' air; second, Marenzio and Giovanelli's new air existed in music both for several voices and for solo voice and instrumental accompaniment; third, modern composers have varied older styles only in matters of ornament and not in substance.

Later in the *Discorso*, Giustiniani associates *aria* with an equally resonant and no less difficult term, 'grace' (*grazia*). Three things are necessary to produce praiseworthy compositions: first, good, rich counterpoint; second, an avoidance of overtly learned or pedantic devices; and third, 'they should be full of air [*ariose*] and with singular grace'. Compositions that exhibit the first two qualities will still fail if they lack the third, 'and this is also necessary in other compositions which are called arias to be sung by one or a few more voices to instruments'. He continues:

V

From what I have already said, perhaps there arises in you a desire and curiosity to understand what is 'aria' and 'grace' in music and in compositions, which act in such a way that they delight and please those who hear them when they are sung and played. Anticipating the request you make of me, and given the desire I have to satisfy you, I will say, that a precise reply is very difficult, even for persons more expert than me.

Giustiniani is forced to fudge the issue – he senses a new or good *aria* in a piece of music, but cannot explain it – and is sidetracked into a discussion of divine providence (which grants grace) and good singing. Ultimately, it is hard to pin down why a given piece of music or a given performance has good *aria* or grace, just as, Giustiniani says, it is impossible to explain why those who frequent bordellos in Spain and Africa sometimes prefer women who appear ugly to an Italian. *Aria* and grace are not necessarily to do with superficial beauty: they are less tangible qualities that underpin, even belie, surface appearances.

Giustiniani's use of visual analogies in his attempt to grasp the notion of *aria* may owe something to Petrarch's well-known discussion of imitation in his letter to Boccaccio in the *Familiares* (23.19):

> A proper imitator should take care that what he writes resemble the original without reproducing it. The resemblance should not be that of a portrait to the sitter – in that case the closer the likeness is the better – but it should be the resemblance of a son to his father. Therein is often a great divergence in particular features, but there is a certain suggestion, what our painters call an 'air' [*aer*], most noticeable in the face and eyes, which makes the resemblance.... Thus we writers must look to it that with a basis of similarity there should be many dissimilarities. And the similarity should be planted so deep that it can only be extricated by quiet meditation. The quality is to be felt rather than defined. Thus we may use another man's conceptions and the colour of his style, but not his words. In the first case, the resemblance is hidden deep; in the second it is glaring. The first procedure makes poets, the second makes apes.[12]

But Giustiniani falters when it comes to translating this visual image into aural terms. Nor is he alone: precisely the same dilemma of defining *aria* in musical terms was faced by much more expert musicians than he (from Nicola Vicentino to Roger North). The issue exposes a crucial *lacuna* in contemporary theory, the need for a thorough account of the art and craft of modern musical expression, a true poetics of music.[13]

However, various passages devoted, however hazily, to the notion of *aria* in contemporary treatises suggest lines of inquiry that might focus the 'quiet meditation' needed to determine precisely what Giustiniani found 'new and grateful' in the music of Marenzio and his contemporaries. For example, in his *L'antica musica ridotta alla moderna prattica* (Rome: Antonio Barré, 1555) Nicola Vicentino noted that three things were necessary to compose: first, a knowledge of melodic writing; second, a knowledge of consonances and dissonances; and third,

> Then one will give the appropriate movement [*moto*] to that [musical] subject which is suitable to the words, or to other thoughts. And this movement is commonly called 'aria': whence if some [setting of] words, or some composition without words, has its appropriate movement, then some say that this composition has a beautiful aria, but it is an improper use [of the term]. And one can use this aria or movement in many ways, as will be understood from the chapter on movement . . .[14]

By *moto*, Vicentino is referring to rhythm and pacing (the 'chapter on movement' – Book II, Chapter 31 – deals with the selection and combination of note-values), which are to be matched appropriately to the affective content of the text being set: this is improperly called *aria*. Again, Vicentino does not enlighten us on what is a proper use of the term. But in Book IV of his treatise – significantly, precisely the one that deals with issues of musical poetics – Vicentino introduces the notion of the *procedere* ('the manner of proceeding') of a given piece. It seems likely that this is what he has in mind for *aria*, broadening the focus of *moto* to embrace melodic profile and harmonic and tonal structure. Vicentino is clear on the role of the bass in defining the *procedere*,[15] but he also allocates a significant role to the soprano. So, too, does Zarlino, in his *Le istitutioni harmoniche* (Venice: 1558):

> the soprano – being the highest of the parts – is most penetrating to the ear and is heard above all the others. As fire nourishes and is the cause of all natural things produced for the ornamentation and conservation of the world, the composer strives to have his upper voice be decorative, beautiful, and elegant, so that it will nourish and satisfy the souls of listeners. As the earth is the foundation of the other elements, the bass has the function of sustaining and stabilizing, fortifying and giving growth to the other parts. It is the foundation of the harmony and for this reason is called bass, as if to say the base and sustenance of the other parts. If we could imagine the element of earth to be lacking, what ruin and waste would result in universal and human harmony! Similarly a composition without a bass would be full of confusion and dissonance and would fall into ruin.
>
> Therefore, when a composer composes the bass of his music, he proceeds with rather slow, somewhat leaping movements, rather wider than in the other parts. This permits the middle voices to progress with

elegant and conjunct movements, most of all the soprano, for this is its nature.[16]

In both cases, it is hard to ignore what seems to be a significant anticipation of the soprano-bass polarity that was to become a characteristic feature of music in the last quarter of the century. And both Zarlino and Vicentino allocate specific functions – and specific types of motion – to the soprano and bass parts which may well indicate where we, in turn, should look for airs 'new and grateful to the ear'.

At first sight, Giustiniani's emphasis on Marenzio and Giovanelli as protagonists of a new style appears somewhat curious: it might be dismissed simply as a result of his pro-Roman prejudices. When Monteverdi searched for the founder of the new style that he called the *seconda prattica*, he went back to an earlier madrigalist, Cipriano de Rore; and modern historians would tend to look for 'new and grateful' airs in the 'new music' of Giulio Caccini and his Florentine colleagues. But it is indeed possible that Marenzio and his contemporaries focused the development of new compositional models that were changed only in matters of ornament, not substance, in the early seventeenth century. Such models may be most readily apparent in Marenzio's three-part villanellas (he published five oft-reprinted books in his lifetime): 'Se il dolce sguardo del divin tuo volto' (Ex. 1) from his *Il primo libro delle villanelle a tre voci* (Venice: Giacomo Vincenti and Ricciardo Amadino, 1584) is a useful example. The analysis in Ex. 3a [see p.137] maps the piece in terms of a background descent through a fifth, from $d^2$ to $g^1$ through $b\flat^1$: this *diapente* descent contributes (with the cleffing, final and signature) to defining a specific tonal type that in turn represents the so-called transposed Dorian mode (on G).[17] The descent is preceded effectively by a prolongation of the primary note, $d^2$, first by a middleground descent to $b\flat^1$ and then (in bs 6-11) by a registral transfer to the lower octave. Each note of the soprano (with only one or two minor exceptions) receives consonant support, but structurally significant notes on the middleground and background are further emphasized by cadential and other articulations: the consecutive fifths characteristic (indeed, indicative) of the genre are present in the middleground but not (in fact, somewhat unusually) in the foreground or background.

Of course, we cannot know whether the clearly articulated descents, the directed tonal motion and the consonant support in this villanella are what Giustiniani would have identified with his 'new and grateful' air. However, it may be significant that another theorist, the Florentine Vincenzo Galilei, focuses on precisely these issues (if not, inevitably, in precisely this way) in his own account of the 'new air' required of music to avoid the manifest defects of contemporary polyphony. Galilei is well known as a member of the so-called Florentine Camerata and the author of the *Dialogo della musica antica, et della moderna* (Florence: Giorgio Marescotti, 1581), a

V

Ex. 1   Luca Marenzio, 'Se il dolce sguardo del divin tuo volto' (*Il primo libro delle villanelle a tre voci* (1584), no. 19; all parts have text)

treatise that, among other things, presents a violent polemic against Renaissance compositional styles and theoretical traditions. He also continued to explore these issues in a more measured manner in his late manuscript treatises.[18]

The defects of modern music were obvious enough:

> Today the singing in harmony of many voices is considered the summit of perfection; among the ancients solo singing had this reputation. And if the singing of many together was also esteemed, it was the singing of one air and not of so many. Today the quantity of consonances is greatly prized, and unisons are undervalued, while then the latter were prized and the former deprecated. Today, touching many and diverse notes is in esteem; then, few and the same notes, and they did not use more notes in singing than in speaking, except enough to distinguish the two. Today many varied time-values are used, both slow and fast. Then there were used only the long and the short as is customary naturally in speaking, although I believe that instruments when played alone used more. Today runs of *gorgia* and many other artifices are prized which the ancients, the better composers especially, preferring simplicity, deplored as lascivious and effeminate. Today by imitation of the words is understood not the

133

V

complete thought and the meaning of the words and of the whole text, but the significance of the sound of one only.... The end of music today is nothing but the delight and pleasure of the senses. Among the ancients it was to move and dispose the soul to virtue.[19]

This preference for the 'singing of one air' over the 'many' airs of contemporary polyphony left open the question of whether the only solution was monophony pure and simple, or whether there was still room for harmony. Logic dictated the former, but Galilei, practising musician that he was, was unable to take the crucial step, for, he said, 'is not depriving music of [consonances] ... the same as depriving painting of colours?'[20]

He sought a compromise, invoking Plato's recommendation in the *Laws* that students of the lyre should be taught to accompany a singer only in the *proschorda* manner, and not *synphonon*, i.e. in unison and not in consonance. Galilei's strategy was to focus on this distinction between *proschorda* and *synphonon* in an argument which, though scarcely sound in terms of scholarly rigour, provided a neat solution to his problem:

Plato principally condemned many singing together in consonance with a diversity of airs as is customary today, first because the diversity of those airs heard at the same time mix up their proper and particular nature one and the other, and thus each of those airs cannot pursue its end; moreover, given that the words are not understood by the listeners, therefore they cannot produce any affect in them. The same Plato condemned one voice singing to the instrument in consonance, and he praised singing to it in unison, the true import of which ruling I interpret in this way. One can sing in unison to the instrument in two ways. The first and simplest is that the instrument makes only one sound and touches one string, which is in unison with the voice of him who sings to the instrument, and this is the manner which I believe was used when music began, to wind and string instruments, and before men knew how to sing without them and came to understand the consonances and the way of making use of them. The second manner of singing in unison was introduced in my view after the use of consonances, and this is when one sings solo to the instrument, of which many strings are struck among which is the part of him who sings at the same time, arranged so that between them they produce diverse consonances. This can equally be done in two ways, one, which is first and true, results every time that the air of him who sings to the instrument is in a manner uniform with the consonances of the instrument that it seems a single body, and one same sound.... The other manner results whenever that body of diverse consonances produced by the instrument is not perfectly proportioned and united to the aria of the singer ... and this is the manner condemned by

Plato, and the first is the one praised [by him] as none other than
singing in unison albeit with the use of consonances, but in a manner
so uniform among themselves that to the ear they present, in a manner
of speaking, one single sound.[21]

Plato's distinction between singing *proschorda* and singing *synphonon* is
recast as a distinction between different kinds of harmonic support and
tonal projection: the ideal is for the harmony to support and reinforce the
air so perfectly that one hears, as it were, only one sound. Galilei gives two
brief examples to illustrate the point (Ex. 2). In the first (*proschorda*), the
melody is supported by primary triads in root position and with a clear
harmonic motion. In the second (*synphonon*), secondary triads are
introduced, some in inversion, and the harmonic motion is less clear.
Moreover, a background descent is much more clearly articulated in the
first example than in the second (the treatment of the implied $\hat{2}$ at the end
is particularly interesting). We have here, in effect, examples of 'good' and
'bad' air.

Ex. 2 Vincenzo Galilei, *Dubbi intorno a quanto io ho detto dell'uso
dell'enharmonio, con la solutione di essi,* Florence, Biblioteca
Nazionale, MS Ant. di Galileo 3, f. 66r

a) 'Unison' (*Proschorda*)

b) 'Consonance' (*Synphonon*)

It is no surprise to observe similarities between Galilei's brief example
and the kinds of strategies discerned in Marenzio's 'Se il dolce sguardo':
Galilei himself firmly advocated 'popular' genres such as the villanella –
indeed specific such pieces – as models for his proposed musical reform.
Moreover, the lesson was not lost on the composer most influenced by
Galilei, Giulio Caccini: Caccini claimed (in the preface to *Le nuove
musiche*) to have learnt more from the Camerata than from thirty years of

counterpoint, and his solo songs included in *Le nuove musiche* are the main musical product of the Camerata's speculations. Thus Caccini's songs reveal (especially in the pared-down versions often surviving in manuscript sources) close relationships with the villanella tradition.[22] Moreover, at least one near-contemporary theorist, the Florentine Giovanni Battista Doni, made a further connection between the new music and earlier (Roman) repertories: 'Luca Marenzio, Giulio Romano [Caccini] and the like began to have the parts sung with beautiful grace and to make the words better understood than previously'.[23]

Linking Caccini with Marenzio does not seem unreasonable in the light of Ex. 3, a comparison of Marenzio's 'Se il dolce sguardo' and Caccini's quintessential 'Amarilli, mia bella'.[24] The comparison reveals striking similarities in terms both of the background structure and of middleground features: for example, note the prolongations of $\hat{5}$ through a registral transfer and cadence on the dominant ('Se il dolce sguardo', b.11; 'Amarilli, mia bella', b.20). Certainly Caccini's song involves more elaborate projections of the simple structures and techniques seen in Marenzio's villanella: particularly striking is the more extended exploration, on various levels, of the 'authentic' division of the $d^2$-$d^1$ octave ($d^2$-$a^1$-$d^1$) as an alternative to the 'plagal' ($d^2$-$g^1$-$d^1$) division appropriate to the mode of the piece. Moreover, Caccini adopts the rather looser approach to harmonic support typical of the monodic-recitative style. But the two works are of a piece. They are also projections of two closely related airs.

The *diapente* descents elaborated in Marenzio's villanella and Caccini's song derive from still more basic models drawn from improvisatory traditions (which variously influenced both the villanella and the Florentine new music): for example, the standard bass patterns for improvisatory recitation in the sixteenth century (the basis for *arie per cantar ottave* and the like) – the *Romanesca*, *Passo e mezzo* and, later, the *Ruggiero* and *folia* – all support melodic lines that are straightforward elaborations of a *diapente* descent. But even if the strategies discerned in Marenzio's 'Se il dolce sguardo' are not new to the villanella repertory, the fact that they start to encroach upon more 'serious' genres is clearly cause for comment, both from Giustiniani and from modern scholars. For example, in the 1580s the structural procedures of the villanella and canzonetta are clearly adopted within the middleground strategies and background structures (not to mention foreground features) of the so-called canzonetta- or hybrid-madrigal characteristic of the Roman and, to a lesser extent, Ferrarese schools: here Marenzio (followed by Giovanelli and Vecchi) seems to have taken an important lead in cross-breeding 'popular' and 'serious' genres.[25] It is also clear that such *diapente*-structures and their newly elaborate prolongations had a profound effect on the *seconda prattica* madrigals of Monteverdi and his contemporaries.[26]

The evident parallels between Monteverdi's 'Anima mia, perdona' (in

Ex. 3   a) Marenzio, 'Se il dolce sguardo'; b) Giulio Caccini, 'Amarilli, mia bella' (*Le nuove musiche* (1602), no. [8])

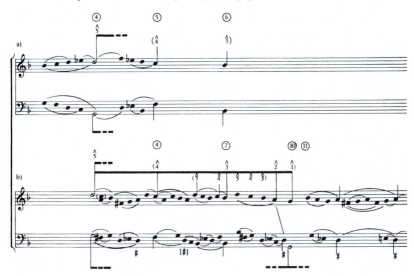

his *Il quarto libro de madrigali a cinque voci*, Venice: Ricciardo Amadino, 1603) and 'Amarilli, mia bella' (and thus, one step removed, Marenzio's 'Se il dolce sguardo') make the point clear (Ex. 4).[27] These parallels extend far beyond the presence of the same background descent from $d^2$ to $g^1$ (through $bb^1$), which simply reflects two settings in similar tonal types.[28] Both pieces have a clearly articulated middleground *diapente* descent leading to a cadence on G that marks the end of the first poetic and musical paragraph. The second section is structured as a dominant prolongation supporting an implied $\hat{5}$ (with registral transfer) but focusing on an inner-voice $a^1$ (exploiting the alternative authentic division of the $d^2$-$d^1$ octave, the possibility of which is established in both cases in the opening phrase). This in turn leads to a return to the primary note of the Fundamental Line ($d^2$), then a transfer of this $d^2$ to the lower octave, then a final restoration of the $d^2$ for the last (background) descent through the *diapente* to $g^1$. There are also some intriguing similarities closer to the foreground. For example, in the initial middleground descent, note the replications of the descent from the initial $\hat{5}$ once the descent itself has begun – this is especially striking in the Monteverdi. However, in the case of the shift to the lower octave $d^1$ (emphasized by a clear cadence) in the second halves of both settings, Monteverdi's strategy is significantly closer to Marenzio's 'Se il dolce sguardo' than to the Caccini. In part, this reflects the fact that both Monteverdi and Marenzio are writing for more than one voice. Caccini arrives at his low $d^1$ through the arpeggiation of a single line ($d^2$-$a^1$-$f^1$-$d^1$; the $g^1$ is noticeably absent). But both Marenzio and Monteverdi prepare their lower $d^1$ by a subsidiary *diapente* descent from $a^1$ to $d^1$, with the $a^1$ coming from a second voice. Above this $a^1$-$d^1$ descent, and quite separate from it, both settings have a $d^2$-$c^2$ neighbour-note pattern, with the $c^2$ left hanging: it resolves only by implication at the cadence on the low $d^1$ (there is an implied chromatic ascent of $c^2$-$c\sharp^2$-$d^2$). In all three cases, the motivation for this shift to a lower register seems to be both musical (it is a convenient way of extending the structure) and textual: the shift reflects a particular crux in the verse (Marenzio, 'non porge a le mie pene alcuna aita', 'does not offer any help to my pain'; Caccini, 'aprimi il petto, e vedrai scritto al core', 'open my breast, and you will see written on my heart'; Monteverdi, 'Deh, qual vendetta aver puoi tu maggiore / del tuo proprio dolore?', 'Ah, what greater revenge can you have than your own grief?').

Of course, there are also differences in 'Anima mia, perdona' that reflect issues of genre, of the expressive demands of the text, and, for that matter, of Monteverdi's compositional skill. The initial prolongation of $\hat{5}$ is more artfully worked out, in part because of the greater textural possibilities permitted by five voices; the initial middleground descent to $bb^1$ is less strongly articulated, maintaining the flow to the end of the section; this opening section also reveals a number of intriguing motivic relationships at foreground and middleground level; and the prolongation of the middle-

Ex. 4 Claudio Monteverdi, 'Anima mia, perdona' (*Il quarto libro de madrigali a cinque voci* (1603), no. 6a)

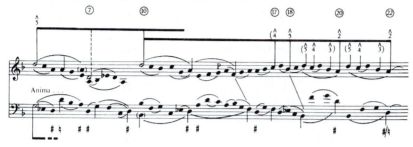

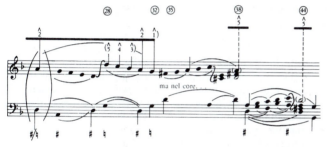

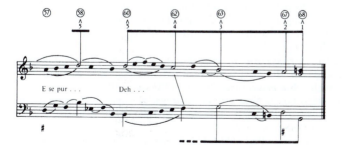

V

ground $\hat{2}$ in bs 22-31 involves a splendid, if entirely characteristic, example of a descent that 'breaks back' on itself through registral transfer before resolving to $\hat{1}$ (typically, precisely the same process is exploited on a larger scale in bs 49-58).[29] Such examples could be multiplied throughout the piece.

Nevertheless, Monteverdi's 'Anima mia, perdona', Caccini's 'Amarilli, mia bella' and Marenzio's 'Se il dolce sguardo', despite the evident differences of style, genre, scoring and technique, clearly belong to the same family (of course, just one of several possible families in late Renaissance and early Baroque music). Moreover, it seems reasonable to assume that this relationship would have been perceived by the likes of Nicola Vicentino as a matter of their *procedere* – that is, in terms of their strikingly similar *arie* – or, in modern parlance, of their use of common foreground, middleground and background strategies associated with a specific tonal type. Finally, it is but a short step to argue that the processes elaborated here, with their clear and precise articulation of *diapente* descents, would have been associated by Giustiniani with the 'air new and grateful to the ear' that he perceived in music of the 1580s, and which was neither fundamentally nor substantially altered by modern musicians during his lifetime. This new *aria*, in turn, was indeed essentially independent of the distinctive styles, genres and performing media that are used to map out traditional accounts of this music in history textbooks. It is precisely here that we can identify some of the core procedures that generated a community of musical discourse in late sixteenth- and early seventeenth-century Italy. And it is precisely thanks to a rather obscure Roman critic of the 1620s that we can find new ways of coming to terms with the complex issues affecting secular music in the late Renaissance and early Baroque periods.[30]

NOTES

1. See Tim Carter, 'Giulio Caccini's *Amarilli, mia bella*: Some Questions (and a Few Answers)', *Journal of the Royal Musical Association*, Vol. 113 (1988), pp.250-73. The song is in Giulio Caccini, *Le nuove musiche*, ed. H. Wiley Hitchcock, 'Recent Researches in the Music of the Baroque Era', Vol. 9 (Madison: A-R Editions, 1970), pp.85-8.

2. Paolo Quagliati, *Il primo libro de' madrigali a quattro voci* (Venice: Giacomo Vincenti, 1608). See the discussion in Alfred Einstein, 'Das Madrigal zum Doppelgebrauch', *Acta musicologica*, Vol. 6 (1934), pp.110-16.

3. Pietro Maria Marsolo, *Secondo libro de' madrigali a quattro voci, opera decima (1614)*, ed. Lorenzo Bianconi, 'Musiche rinascimentali siciliane', Vol. 4 (Rome: Edizioni De Santis, 1973).

4. See Tim Carter, 'Jacopo Peri (1561-1633): Aspects of His Life and Works',

*Proceedings of the Royal Musical Association*, Vol. 105 (1978-9), pp.50-62, for further discussion of these issues.

5. For the original, see *Claudio Monteverdi: Lettere, dediche e prefazioni*, ed. Domenico de' Paoli (Rome: Edizioni De Santis, 1973), pp.40-2. My translation largely follows *The Letters of Claudio Monteverdi*, trans. Denis Stevens (London: Faber, 1980), p.64.

6. The original lament was written for Arianna accompanied by a consort of viols – see Gary Tomlinson, *Monteverdi and the End of the Renaissance* (Oxford: Clarendon Press, 1987), pp.138-9 – but survives only in versions for solo voice and basso continuo. For the music, see *Claudio Monteverdi: Tutte le opere*, ed. Gian Francesco Malipiero *et al.* (2nd edn, Vienna: Universal, 1954-68), Vol. 6, pp.1-21; Vol. 11, pp.161-7.

7. An important preliminary discussion of the term is in Nino Pirrotta, 'Early Opera and Aria', in *New Looks at Italian Opera: Essays in Honor of Donald J. Grout*, ed. William W. Austin (Ithaca: Cornell University Press, 1968), pp.39-107; this also appears, with some changes, in Pirrotta, *Music and Theatre from Poliziano to Monteverdi* (Cambridge: CUP, 1981), pp.237-80. See also Franklin B. Zimmermann, 'Air: A Catchword for New Concepts in Seventeenth-Century English Music Theory', in *Studies in Musicology in Honor of Otto E. Albrecht*, ed. John Walter Hill (Kassel: Bärenreiter, 1980), pp.142-57. This is not the place for a full account of the term *aria* and its relatives in contemporary texts: such an account forms part of a longer-term research project.

8. The remark is made in a letter from Giovanni Maria Artusi to L'Ottuso, the unknown academic who defended Monteverdi, and is repeated in the reply from L'Ottuso to Artusi, both quoted in Artusi's *Seconda parte dell'Artusi overo Delle imperfettioni della moderna musica* (Venice: Giacomo Vincenti, 1603), pp.9, 14: 'noua aria, noua sollecitudine dell'udito, percossa dalla prestezza, et tardanza del moto, hor aspramente, & hor soauemente secondo l'aria ... '.

9. The treatise is edited in Angelo Solerti, *Le origini del melodramma: testimonianze dei contemporanei* (Turin, 1903, repr. Hildesheim: Olms, 1969), pp.98-128, and translated in Carol MacClintock, *Hercole Bottrigari, 'Il Desiderio ... '; Vincenzo Giustiniani, 'Discorso sopra la musica'*, 'Musicological Studies and Documents', Vol. 9 (American Institute of Musicology: 1962), pp.63-80. My translations sometimes differ.

10. See James Chater, 'Musical Patronage in Rome at the Turn of the Seventeenth Century: The Case of Cardinal Montalto', *Studi musicali*, Vol. 16 (1987), pp.179-227.

11. MacClintock translates *aria* as 'melody'. This is not an isolated view of Marenzio. Thomas Morley, for example, similarly praises his madrigals 'for good air and fine invention': see his *A Plain & Easy Introduction to Practical Music* [1597], ed. R. Alec Harman (London: Dent, 1952), p.294. Morley also mentions Giovanelli (and Orazio Vecchi, Stefano Venturi and Giovanni Croce) as worthy of imitation in the field of the madrigal, and Marenzio and Giovanni Ferretti in that of the canzonet. Similarly, Henry Peacham, in *The*

*Compleat Gentleman* (1622), praised Marenzio 'for delicious air and sweet invention' and Vecchi for 'goodnesse of air': see Oliver Strunk, *Source Readings in Music History: From Classical Antiquity to the Romantic Era* (London: Faber, 1952), pp.335, 336. And in his *Trattato della musica scenica* (*c.*1633-5), Giovanni Battista Doni says that 'Luca Marenzio . . . è stato il primo nello stile madrigalesco a fare camminare le parti con bell'aria; poichè avanti a lui, purchè il concento fosse sonoro e soave, di poco altro si curavano' ('Luca Marenzio . . . was the first in the madrigal style to make the parts move with beautiful air; for before him, provided that the concent was sonorous and sweet, they paid attention to little else'), see Doni, *De' trattati di musica . . . tomo secondo*, ed. Anton Francesco Gori (Florence: Stamperia Imperiale, 1763), p.24 (this extract is also given in Solerti, *Le origini del melodramma*, p.212).

12. Translated in Thomas M. Green, 'Petrarch and the Humanist Hermeneutic', in *Italian Literature: Roots and Branches; Essays in Honor of Thomas Goddard Bergin*, ed. Giose Rimanelli and Kenneth J. Atchity (New Haven: Yale University Press, 1976), pp.211-12.

13. I have raised some of the issues in 'Artusi, Monteverdi and the Poetics of Modern Music', in *Studies in the Legacy of Musical Humanism: Essays in Honor of Claude Palisca*, ed. Nancy Kovaleff Baker and Barbara Russano Hanning (Stuyvesant: Pendragon, 1992), pp.171-94.

14. *L'antica musica ridotta alla moderna prattica*, f. 27r: 'allhora si darà il moto conveniente sopra à quel suggietto, che sia in proposito delle parole, overo sopra altri pensieri; & questo moto appresso il vulgo è detto aria, onde s'alcune parole, overo compositioni senza parole, hanno il suo moto conveniente, allhora alcuni dicono questa compositione ha una bell'aria, & è parlar improprio: questo aria, overo moto, si può usare in molti modi, come nel Cap[itolo] del moto s'intenderà . . . '

15. *Ibid.*, f. 55v: 'Il Lettore dè avvertire che il Basso, è quello che regge, & dà la gratia del bel procedere & a varietà dell'Armonia à tutte le parti, si al procedere per andare alle cadentie come anchora per andare ad altri passaggi' ('The reader should note that the bass is that [part] which rules and gives the grace of good *procedere* as regards the variety of the harmony to all the parts, as much in the *procedere* for leading to the cadences as in leading to other passages').

16. Gioseffo Zarlino, *The Art of Counterpoint: Part Three of 'Le istitutioni harmoniche', 1558*, trans. Guy A. Marco and Claude V. Palisca (New Haven: Yale University Press, 1968), p.179.

17. For the concept of tonal type, see Harold S. Powers, 'Tonal Types and Modal Categories in Renaissance Polyphony', *Journal of the American Musicological Society*, Vol. 34 (1981), pp.428-70. My methods here owe an obvious debt to Felix Salzer, 'Heinrich Schenker and Historical Research: Monteverdi's Madrigal *Oimè, se tanto amate*', in *Aspects of Schenkerian Theory*, ed. David Beach (New Haven: Yale University Press, 1983), pp.135-52. I have also benefited from Susan K. McClary, 'The Transition from Modal to Tonal

Organization in the Works of Monteverdi' (Diss., Harvard University, 1976), for all its lack of methodological underpinning in ways that the present essay attempts to correct. Another useful example is Saul Novack, 'Tonality and the Style of Palestrina', in *Music and Civilization: Essays in Honor of Paul H. Lang*, ed. Edmond Strainchamps and Maria Rika Maniates (New York: Norton, 1984), pp.428-43. Novack's analysis of the first Kyrie from Palestrina's *Missa brevis*, with its clear middle- and background descents, would seem to confirm Vincenzo Giustiniani's comment on Palestrina given above (p. 129). But too few modern scholars (and for that matter, teachers of harmony and counterpoint) have noticed that at least in terms of the treatment of opening points of imitation (sequence of voices, entry pitches, etc.), the *Missa brevis* is entirely untypical of Palestrina's four-part output.

18. Transcribed and discussed in Claude V. Palisca, 'The Beginnings of Baroque Music: Its Roots in Sixteenth Century Theory and Polemics' (Diss., Harvard University, 1953); Frieder Rempp, *Die Kontrapunkttraktate Vincenzo Galileis*, 'Veröffentlichungen des Staatlichen Instituts für Musikforschung, Preussischer Kulturbesitz', Vol. 9 (Cologne: Volk, 1980). See also Palisca, 'Vincenzo Galilei's Counterpoint Treatise: A Code for the *Seconda Pratica*', *Journal of the American Musicological Society*, Vol. 9 (1956), pp.81-96.

19. Galilei, *Il primo libro della prattica del contrapunto intorno all'uso delle consonanze*, trans. in Palisca, 'The Beginnings of Baroque Music', pp.217-19.

20. Vincenzo Galilei, *Dubbi intorno a quanto io ho detto dell'uso dell'enharmonio, con la solutione di essi*, Florence, Biblioteca Nazionale, MS Ant. di Galileo 3, f. 65r: 'Oltre che il privare la musica dell'uso loro non è egli . . . l'istesso che privare la pittura della vaghezza de colori?'

21. *Ibid.*:

Dannava principalmente Platone il cantare in consonanza molti insieme con diversità d'arie come si costuma hoggi; prima perche la diversita di esse arie udite nel medesimo tempo, si corrompono la natura propria et particulare loro l'un all'altra, et cosi alcuna di loro [f. 65v] non puo conseguire il suo fine; oltre che le parole non sendo ben intese dagl'uditori non possano conseguente-mente operare in essi alcuno affetto. Dannava il medesimo Platone il cantar un solo allo strumento in consonanza, et lodava il cantare ad esso all'unisono; il sentimento vero della qual legge, interpreto io di questa maniera. Puossi al strumento cantare all'unisono in due modi, il primo et il piu semplice e che lo strumento non faccia piu d'un solo suono col tocchare una sola corda la quale sia unisone con la voce; di quello che ad esso strumento canta; et questo si fatto modo crederò io che fusse usato in quelli primi principii sopra gli strumenti di fiato et di corde, ma avanti pero che gl'huomini sapessero senza esso cantare et che si venissero in cognitione delle consonanze et del modo di servirsi dell'uso di loro. Il secondo modo di cantare all'unisono s'introdusse per mio avviso dopo l'uso delle consonanze; et questo è quando un solo canti allo strumento, del quale siano percosse molte corde tra le quali sia ancora la parte di quello che canta nel tempo medesimo, sposte si che faccino tra di loro diverse consonanze; et ciò parimente si puo fare in due maniere una che è la principale et la vera, segue tutta volta che l'aria di quello che canta allo strumento sia di maniera uniforme alle consonanze di quello che paia tutto un corpo, et un is-[f. 66r] tesso suono; ... segue l'altra maniera tutte volte che quel tal corpo di consonanze diverse che cagiona lo strumento, non sia con l'aria di cantate perfetamente proportionato et unito; ... che quella è dannata da Platone, et approvata la prima non altramente che all'unisono cantante seben con l'uso delle consonanze; ma di maniera tra di loro uniformi che all'udir rappresentano per modo di favellare un solo suono.

See also the discussion of this passage (and the examples given here in Ex. 2) in Claude V. Palisca, 'Vincenzo Galilei and Some Links Between "Pseudo-Monody" and Monody', *The Musical Quarterly*, Vol. 46 (1960), pp.344-60.

22. See Howard Mayer Brown, 'The Geography of Florentine Monody: Caccini at Home and Abroad', *Early Music*, Vol. 9 (1981), pp.147-68. The sources are discussed in William V. Porter, 'The Origins of the Baroque Solo Song: A Study of Italian Manuscripts and Prints from 1590-1610' (Diss., Yale University, 1962); H. Wiley Hitchcock, 'Vocal Ornamentation in Caccini's *Nuove musiche*', *The Musical Quarterly*, Vol. 56 (1970), pp.389-404; Stephen Willier, 'Rhythmic Variants in Early Manuscript Versions of Caccini's Monodies', *Journal of the American Musicological Society*, Vol. 36 (1983), pp.481-97.

23. Doni, *Trattato della musica scenica* (c.1633-5), in *De' trattati di musica . . . tomo secondo*, p.17: 'Luca Marenzio, Giulio Romano, e simili, hanno cominciato a far cantare con bella grazia le parti, e fare intendere alquanto meglio le parole, che non si faceva prima . . . '.

24. My reading draws on the analysis in McClary, 'The Transition from Modal to Tonal Organization in the Works of Monteverdi', pp.42-6, 74-6, although it seeks a somewhat clearer focus. I have graphed Caccini's song to the end of the second section; there follows a repeat of this section (bs 28-44=11-27) and a 'coda' (bs 44-50) consisting of a straightforward descent from $d^2$ (with a neighbour note $e^2$) to $g^1$ (but through $b\natural^1$).

25. For the hybrid-madrigal, see Ruth I. DeFord, 'The Evolution of Rhythmic Style in Italian Secular Music of the Late Sixteenth Century', *Studi musicali*, Vol. 10 (1981), pp.43-74; 'Musical Relationships between the Italian Madrigal and Light Genres in the Sixteenth Century', *Musica disciplina*, Vol. 39 (1985), pp.107-68.

26. See McClary, The Transition from Modal to Tonal Organization in the Works of Monteverdi', *passim*; Geoffrey Chew, 'The Perfections of Modern Music: Consecutive Fifths and Tonal Coherence in Monteverdi', *Music Analysis*, Vol. 8, No. 3 (October 1989), pp.247-73.

27. Monteverdi, *Tutte le opere*, Vol. 4, pp.26-30. The piece is also analysed – to somewhat different effect – in McClary, 'The Transition from Modal to Tonal Organization in the Works of Monteverdi', pp.136-59. For present purposes I treat this madrigal, the first of a two-part setting, as a structurally discrete entity. Note that I do not intend to argue that these pieces are directly

modelled one on another, although the kinds of issues discussed here are certainly open to questions of imitation and emulation (see Howard Mayer Brown, 'Emulation, Competition, and Homage: Imitation and Theories of Imitation in the Renaissance', *Journal of the American Musicological Society*, Vol. 35 (1982)) or, for that matter, of intertextuality (see Kevin Korsyn, 'Towards a New Poetics of Musical Influence', *Music Analysis*, Vol. 10, Nos 1-2 (March-July 1991)). Moreover, one scholar, at least, has detected clear cases of competition between Monteverdi and Caccini; see Imogene Horsley, 'Monteverdi's Use of Borrowed Material in "Sfogava con le stelle"', *Music and Letters*, Vol. 59 (1978), pp.316-28.

28. 'Amarilli, mia bella' is in fact in a high-clef tonal type (g2-$\flat$-G) – in contrast to 'Anima mia, perdona' and 'Se il dolce sguardo' (c1-$\flat$-G) – although for no apparent reason. The soprano parts of the three pieces occupy similar ranges.

29. Cf. Chew, 'The Perfections of Modern Music', p.259.

30. Early versions of this paper were presented at the University of Reading (1989), '*Analisi e fortuna del madrigale polifonico': Convegno di studi* (Como, 1991) and the Fourth Music Analysis Conference (City University, London, 1991). I am particularly grateful to Geoffrey Chew for his advice at various stages of the proceedings, and to the members of the study group on sixteenth- and early seventeenth-century Italian music at Royal Holloway and Bedford New College for the discussions that gave some focus to these ideas.

# VI

# ARTUSI, MONTEVERDI, AND THE POETICS OF
# MODERN MUSIC

My essay is intended as little more than a footnote, or a series of
footnotes, to Claude Palisca's exemplary account of the Artusi-Monteverdi controversy first published in 1968.[1] But it also marks the first,

---

[1]Revised in Claude V. Palisca, "The Artusi-Monteverdi Controversy," *The New Mon-
teverdi Companion*, eds. Denis Arnold and Nigel Fortune (London: Faber and Faber,
1985) 127–58. See also Robert Mario Isgro, "The First and Second Practices of
Monteverdi: Their Relation to Contemporary Theory" (D.M.A. diss., University of
Southern California, 1968); Anthony Newcomb, "Alfonso Fontanelli and the Ancestry
of the *Seconda pratica* Madrigal," in *Studies in Renaissance and Baroque Music in
Honor of Arthur Mendel*, ed. Robert L. Marshall (Kassel: Barenreiter, 1974) 47–68;
Paolo Fabbri, *Monteverdi* (Turin: EDT/Musica, 1986) 48–65; and Gary Tomlinson,
*Monteverdi and the End of the Renaissance* (Oxford: Clarendon Press, 1987) 21–28.
The broader material in Claude V. Palisca, "The Beginnings of Baroque Music: Its
Roots in Sixteenth-Century Theory and Polemics" (Ph.D. diss., Harvard University,
1953) and *idem*, Humanism in Italian Renaissance Musical Thought (New Haven and
London: Yale University Press, 1985) is also crucial. Monteverdi's letter to his "Studiosi
lettori" appended to *Il quinto libro de madrigali a cinque voci* (Venice: Ricciardo
Amadino, 1605) and Giulio Cesare Monteverdi's *Dichiaratione* appended to the *Scherzi
musicali a tre voci* (Venice: Ricciardo Amadino, 1607) are transcribed in Domenico de'
Paoli, *Claudio Monteverdi: lettere, dediche e prefazioni* (Rome: Edizioni De Santis,

tentative steps towards a broader study of the complex theoretical and critical issues facing composers and their audiences in late-Renaissance and early-Baroque Italy.

## CHRONOLOGY

In 1590 or 1591, Monteverdi moved to Mantua to join the musicians of the court of Duke Vincenzo Gonzaga; he dedicated *Il terzo libro de madrigali a cinque voci* (Venice: Ricciardo Amadino) to the duke in 1592. The Third Book brought to an end a remarkably prolific series of publications marking Monteverdi's studies with Marc'Antonio Ingegneri and his first maturity as a composer. There followed eleven-years' silence, at least in terms of publishing: *Il quarto libro de madrigali a cinque voci* (Venice: Ricciardo Amadino) appeared only in 1603, and *Il quinto libro* (Venice: Ricciardo Amadino) in 1605. This silence may have been at least partly due to the pressure of Monteverdi's duties in Mantua. He was closely involved in the day-to-day musical life of the court and also accompanied Duke Vincenzo on at least two trips to foreign parts: a military campaign in Hungary in 1595, and a health cure to Spa in Flanders in 1599. Monteverdi also had no need to think about publishing given that he had already achieved one of its aims, the securing of a post in a prestigious musical center.

But there may be other reasons for the composer's "silence." This seems to have been a time when Monteverdi explored and assimilated new idioms; Marenzio and Luzzaschi had similar breaks in their publishing careers. The mid-1590s saw the appearance of Giaches de Wert's pioneering *L'undecimo libro de madrigali a cinque voci* (Venice: Angelo Gardano, 1595), and also an important series of madrigal prints emerging from Ferrarese circles, by Alfonso Fontanelli, Carlo Gesualdo, and Luzzasco Luzzaschi (from 1594 to 1596). All these developments must have had considerable impact on Monteverdi. Indeed, he was in direct contact with Ferrara, and some of his new madrigals were performed at the house of Antonio Goretti there on, it seems, 16 November 1598.[2]

---

1973) 390–407; translations of the *Dichiaratione* and other relevant documents are in Oliver Strunk, ed., *Source Readings in Music History: From Classical Antiquity to the Romantic Era* (London: Faber and Faber, 1952).

[2] The occasion is described (and dated) in Giovanni Maria Artusi, *L'Artusi, overo Delle imperfettioni della moderna musica* (Venice: Giacomo Vincenti, 1600) fol. 39r. Artusi's dialogue is "set" in the period of the festivities in Ferrara (and before Pope Clement VIII) for the wedding of Margherita of Austria and Philip III of Spain (12–18 November), which explains the presence of the Austrian, Luca. According to Artusi, Luzzaschi and Ippolito Fiorino were present at the performance on 16 November, but given that this gathering (if it actually happened) was less than a week before a large-scale staging

His music thus came to the attention of Giovanni Maria Artusi, a Bolognese theorist and pupil of Zarlino. In late 1600, Artusi published a treatise, *L'Artusi, overo Delle imperfettioni della moderna musica* (Venice: Giacomo Vincenti; the dedication is dated 20 November); the dialogue between "Vario" ("a gentleman from Arezzo" as spokesman for Artusi) and "Luca" is divided into two *ragionamenti* exploring the evident "imperfections" of modern music. The first discusses the combination of instruments in *concerti* and systems of tuning and temperament; here Artusi covers ground similar to (and sometimes at odds with) Ercole Bottrigari's *Il Desiderio, overo De' concerti di varii strumenti musicali* (Venice: Ricciardo Amadino, 1594). In the second *ragionamento*, Artusi deplores the irregular melodic, harmonic, and modal practices of some modern composers who thereby satisfy neither sense nor reason; in particular, he examines passages from anonymous madrigals later published by Monteverdi. It is not clear why Artusi picks on the young composer, although compared with, say, Fontanelli, Gesualdo, Luzzaschi, and Wert, he may have been perceived as a relatively easy target. Bottrigari was reportedly quick to produce a counter-treatise, *L'ante Artusi*.[3] However, Monteverdi decided (if, that is, he had a choice) to keep silent; perhaps he was anxious not to affect his standing in Mantua. But the composer was already being defended by the unknown "L'Ottuso Accademico" in an exchange of letters with Artusi begun, the latter said, in 1599.

In summer 1602, Artusi wrote a critique of Bottrigari's *Il Patricio, overo De' tetracordi armonici* (Bologna: Vittorio Benacci, 1593), which

---

of Guarini's *Il pastor fido* (itself in honor of Margherita) in Mantua on 22 November, it seems unlikely that Monteverdi was present. For the Mantuan production, see Iain Fenlon, "Music and Spectacle at the Gonzaga Court, c.1580–1600," *Proceedings of the Royal Musical Association* CIII (1976–77) 90–105.

[3] Bottrigari had further grounds for grievance in Artusi's accusation of his having appropriated Annibale Melone's *Il Desiderio*; see the preface to Alemanno Benelli, *Il Desiderio*, ed. Giovanni Maria Artusi (Milan: Stampatori Archiepiscopali, 1601). *L'ante Artusi* is mentioned in the dedication of Artusi's *Seconda parte dell'Artusi overo Delle imperfettioni della moderna musica* (Venice: Giacomo Vincenti, 1603) fol. A2v. The dedication and preface to the *Seconda parte dell'Artusi* also refer to Artusi's planned edition of Zarlino's *De re musica* (also promised in Zarlino's own *Sopplimenti musicali* [Venice: Francesco de' Franceschi, 1588]), which seems never to have appeared.

had taken issue with Francesco Patrizi's interpretations of Aristoxenus.[4] This critique was then included in the *Seconda parte dell'Artusi overo Delle imperfettioni della moderna musica* (Venice: Giacomo Vincenti, 1603; the dedication is dated 25 March). The *Seconda parte dell'Artusi* is made up of two (separately paginated) elements that were almost certainly prepared at different times (and their conjunction leads to oddities of presentation in the print). First, there is the mischievous dedication (to Bottrigari) and preface (outlining Artusi's grievances against his dedicatee), plus the *Considerationi musicali*, focussed primarily on the opinions of the (anonymous) author of *Il Patricio* (although Monteverdi and the moderns again come in for criticism). Second, between the preface and the *Considerationi* we have *L'Artusi: Della imperfettione della moderna musica, parte seconda*. The inclusion of the latter may have been prompted by the appearance of Monteverdi's *Il quarto libro de madrigali a cinque voci* (the dedication is dated 1 March 1603), which includes one madrigal criticized by Artusi in 1600. Artusi now returns to the ground of the second *ragionamento* of his first treatise, reproducing part of his correspondence with L'Ottuso and further criticizing Monteverdi and the moderns.

Thus far, the main butt of Artusi's attack appears to be Ercole Bottrigari, and the latter further responded in 1604 with his *Aletelogia di Leonardo Gallucio ai benigni, e sinceri lettori, lettera apologetica D[el] M[olto] I[llustre] S[ignor] C[avaliere] H[ercole] B[ottrigari]* (Bologna, Civico Museo Bibliografico Musicale, MS B–43). But Monteverdi now entered the fray as well with a statement to his "Studious Readers" appended to *Il quinto libro de madrigali a cinque voci* of 1605 (the dedication is dated 30 July). This short letter mentions Artusi by name (something Artusi had not yet done for Monteverdi) and promises a full account of his new art in a treatise to be called *Seconda pratica, overo Perfettione della moderna musica*. That the letter is directed specifically at the *Seconda parte dell'Artusi* seems clear from Monteverdi's use of the singular "Perfettione" in his reworking of Artusi's title; similarly, Giulio Cesare Monteverdi later said that Monteverdi first contemplated taking up the pen in 1603. A (now lost) response to this statement was

[4] In Francesco Patrizi, *Della poetica: la deca istoriale* (Ferrara: Vittorio Baldini, 1586). Artusi had promised his critique in the preface to his edition of *Il Desiderio* (1601); its date can be deduced from the dedication of the *Seconda parte dell'Artusi* (1603).

then prepared by one Antonio Braccino da Todi, generally thought to be a pseudonym for Artusi. This "discorso" prompted a defense of Monteverdi by his brother, Giulio Cesare, included in Monteverdi's *Scherzi musicali a tre voci* (Venice: Ricciardo Amadino, 1607; the dedication is dated 21 July): a "Dichiaratione" of, or a virtual gloss on, Monteverdi's 1605 letter, which interleaves his brother's text with his own commentary. Close reading of the *Dichiaratione* suggests that it is intended at least partly as a point-by-point rebuttal of Braccino's *discorso*, but Giulio Cesare also broadens the debate, embracing issues and arguments going back to 1600. Significantly, too, the title of Monteverdi's planned treatise is now *Seconda pratica, overo Perfetioni della moderna musica*, shifting from "Perfettione" (after Artusi in 1603) to the plural "Perfetioni" (compare Artusi in 1600).

Braccino again responded with a *Discorso secondo musicale* (Venice: Giacomo Vincenti, 1608). This marks the end of the debate; Monteverdi was perhaps too embroiled in his work for Mantua, and also in various personal crises, to be able to offer a further response. But the affair still rankled if we are to believe the dedication of Monteverdi's *Sanctissimae Virgini missa . . . ac vespere* (Venice: Ricciardo Amadino, 1610), where the composer seeks to "silence those mouths that utter unjust clauses against Claudio" ("claudantur ora in Claudium loquentium iniqua"). Meanwhile, in 1609 Adriano Banchieri referred to the debate in his *Conclusioni nel suono dell'organo* (Bologna, Heirs of Giovanni Rossi), and further echoes of the controversy appear in various writings of the 1610s and beyond. Even in the 1630s and up until his death, Monteverdi was still planning to write his treatise on the *seconda pratica*. But the composer claimed that Artusi eventually reconciled himself to the modernist stance,[5] and the storm seems to have passed with little or no damage to Monteverdi's reputation and career, at least to judge by his appointment as *maestro di cappella* of St. Mark's, Venice, in 1613.

The evident intensity of the Artusi-Monteverdi controversy is striking. Even though it sits squarely within frames of reference established by the polemics between Nicola Vicentino and Vicente Lusitano in the 1550s, and Vincenzo Galilei and Gioseffo Zarlino in the 1580s,

---

[5]In his letter to Giovanni Battista Doni, Venice, 22 October 1633, in de' Paoli, *Claudio Monteverdi: lettere, dediche e prefazioni*, 319–24; see 321.

no prior theoretical dispute had kept the presses so busy, with at least six printed statements appearing in the space of only eight years. The heat of battle becomes even clearer if one takes into account the amount of Monteverdi's music printed in the first decade of the century: his chief printer, Ricciardo Amadino, alone brought out no less than fourteen editions, reprinting the Third Book of Madrigals (1600, 1604, 1607), printing and reprinting the Fourth (1603, 1605, 1607) and Fifth Books (1605, 1606, 1608, 1610) and the *Scherzi musicali* (1607, 1609), and issuing *Orfeo* (1609) and the *Sanctissimae Virgini missa . . . ac vespere* (1610). Certainly Artusi was litigious by nature; he had already tackled the Florentine theorist Vincenzo Galilei in (now lost) treatises, and his various campaigns against Ercole Bottrigari ranged widely through the media and the law courts. But one also wonders whether the intensity of the debate itself reflects a new perception of the power of the press; even though the musical materials of the Artusi-Monteverdi controversy initially circulated in manuscript, the emerging "print culture" for music in the sixteenth and early seventeenth centuries both encouraged and facilitated the subjection of individual composers to close scrutiny in the public eye.[6]

Indeed, it seems possible that the controversy was fuelled precisely by the presses themselves as a way of drawing attention to, and therefore enhancing the market for, their wares. Artusi is consistently published by the Venetian printer Giacomo Vincenti, and Monteverdi (like, for that matter, a good number of his *seconda pratica* colleagues) is closely allied with Vincenti's erstwhile partner and now rival, Ricciardo Amadino. Amadino also published the treatise by Ercole Bottrigari viewed with such distaste by Artusi, *Il Desiderio* (1594). Artusi's 1600 treatise bears all the signs of a private publication: it is a high-quality edition with, on the title page, a special block presenting the arms of Artusi's dedicatee, Cardinal Pompeo Arrigoni. The title page also proclaims the author's identity, plus his origins, rank and position. But

---

[6]We are only beginning to come to terms with notions of a "print culture" for music in sixteenth- and early seventeenth-century Italy; see the discussion in Mary S. Lewis, *Antonio Gardano, Venetian Music Printer, 1538–1569: A Descriptive Bibliography and Historical Study*, in progress (New York and London: Garland, 1988– ) I: 3–16.

in the 1603 treatise, the author is barely mentioned on the title page,[7] and the main decoration is Vincenti's own device. By the third (now lost) and fourth treatises, Artusi has withdrawn even further, disappearing behind the pseudonym Antonio Braccino da Todi. Monteverdi, in turn, is slow to enter the argument, and his defense is largely undertaken by two other figures: L'Ottuso and his brother. The reticence of the chief duellists, and the use of (real or imaginary) seconds, gives a curious impression of shadow-boxing; the only names that constantly recur are those of the printers emblazoned on the title pages of these various treatises and music prints. Was Vincenti actively encouraging a polemic the thrust of which was designed to favor the "middle-of-the-road" path also characteristic of his output as a whole over the more "avant-garde" works published by his rival? Did Amadino in turn respond by printing and re-printing Monteverdi's music and by encouraging statements such as the 1605 letter and the 1607 *Dichiaratione*? Certainly, Amadino must also have had a hand in obtaining for the 1607 *Scherzi musicali* something which appears in a Monteverdi print for the very first time, a privilege to protect against infringements of copyright.[8] All this is circumstantial, to say the least. But even if Vincenti and Amadino were not actively involved in the controversy, there is no reason why they should have discouraged it. The result was obviously good for business.

## A FLORENTINE CONNECTION?

Standing even further in the wings of this shadow-play are a number of other figures, some named, others not. One is Francesco Patrizi, who is

---

[7] The point was noted by the censor, who seems to have requested a number of changes to the volume; see Palisca, "The Artusi-Monteverdi Controversy," 136, n. 16. I have not yet been able to collate the surviving copies of the *Seconda parte dell'Artusi* to distinguish (if possible) its various states, but as a whole the print seems to merit close bibliographical scrutiny. For example, the title page has "Nuouamente Ristampata," with (at least in the copy in London, British Library, Hirsch I.36) the "Ri-" then blanked out.

[8] Obtaining a privilege was a relatively simple matter after legislative changes in 1603; see Richard J. Agee, "The Venetian Privilege and Music-Printing in the Sixteenth Century," *Early Music History* III (1983) 1–42. But of the seven first editions of secular music issued by Ricciardo Amadino in 1607 (Emil Vogel *et al.*, *Bibliografia della musica italiana vocale profana pubblicata dal 1500 al 1700* ("Il nuovo Vogel"), 3 vols. [Pomezia: Staderini, 1977] nos. 9, 11, 242, 624, 1013, 1348, 1950), only two claim privileges on their title pages: Monteverdi's *Scherzi musicali*, and Bartolomeo Barbarino's *Il secondo libro de madrigali . . . da una voce sola.* Both are folio volumes (the others are part-books), and curiously, both have dedications dated 21 July.

defended by Artusi and whose vast *Della poetica* of the late 1580s (part printed and part in manuscript) may offer significant insights into a wide range of issues, some debated by Artusi and Monteverdi, and others later to concern the composer in his search for "the natural path to imitation."[9] Another figure, and perhaps significantly a friend of Patrizi, is Giovanni de' Bardi, head of the so-called Florentine Camerata. Bardi and his protégé, Vincenzo Galilei, both supported by their "mentor," the noted philologist Girolamo Mei, had prompted extensive discussions on the defects of contemporary polyphony.[10] Moreover, Vincenzo Galilei's late treatises on counterpoint and dissonance treatment presented ground rules for good practice in the modern style that, had they been better known, could indeed have provided a "code" for the *seconda pratica*.[11] The Florentines offer a well-defined set of humanist ideas on music against which the Artusi-Monteverdi controversy can be measured. And even if their solutions to the evident imperfections of modern music—solo song was one answer—were never wholeheartedly adopted by Monteverdi, their shared aesthetic stances, and their profound admiration for the madrigals of Cipriano de Rore, are similar enough to prompt a search for at least some connection.[12] But the timing

[9]In his letter to Doni of 22 October 1633, Monteverdi describes his difficult search for "la via naturale alla immitatione." The issue is explored in Gary Tomlinson, "Madrigal, Monody, and Monteverdi's *via naturale alla immitatione," Journal of the American Musicological Society* XXXIV (1981) 60–108.

[10]See Claude V. Palisca, "The 'Camerata Fiorentina': a Reappraisal," *Studi musicali* I (1972) 203–36; *idem*, "Girolamo Mei: Mentor to the Florentine Camerata," *The Musical Quarterly* XL (1954) 1–20; *idem, The Florentine Camerata: Documentary Studies and Translations* (New Haven and London: Yale University Press, 1989). Ironically, Artusi cited Girolamo Mei in his own defense in the *Seconda parte dell'Artusi* (1603) 31, 52.

[11]See Claude V. Palisca, "Vincenzo Galilei's Counterpoint Treatise: a Code for the *Seconda pratica," Journal of the American Musicological Society* IX (1956) 81–96; *idem*, "The Beginnings of Baroque Music," 204–358. Galilei's late treatises are transcribed in Freider Rempp, *Die Kontrapunkttraktate Vincenzo Galileis*, "Veröffentlichungen des Staatlichen Instituts für Musikforschung, Preussischer Kulturbesitz," IX (Cologne: Arno Volk, 1980).

[12]The citations of Rore by Giovanni de' Bardi and Giulio Cesare Monteverdi, and their seemingly different motivations—for clarity of text presentation and intensity of text expression respectively—are discussed in Jessie Ann Owens, "Mode in the Madrigals of Cipriano de Rore," in *Altro Polo: Essays on Italian Music in the Cinquecento*, ed. Richard Charteris (Sydney: Frederick May Foundation for Italian Studies, 1990) 1–15. For Vincenzo Galilei's comments on Rore, see Palisca, "The Beginnings of Baroque Music," 225–27. According to Bardi (who knew Rore personally) in his *Discorso mandato a Giulio Caccini detto romano sopra la musica antica, e 'l cantar bene* (?1578) (translated in Palisca, *The Florentine Camerata*, 114), "had he not been taken from us

of events does not seem in favor of any direct link—Bardi's Camerata was active chiefly in the 1570s and 1580s, Galilei died in 1591, and Bardi himself left Florence for Rome in 1592—and although Monteverdi saw a copy of the main treatise to emerge from the group, Galilei's *Dialogo della musica antica, et della moderna* (Florence: Giorgio Marescotti, 1581), he did so, it seems, only in the 1610s.[13]

There were close enough connections between Florence and Mantua as a result of Duke Vincenzo Gonzaga's marriage to Eleonora de' Medici in 1584, and indeed Giulio Cesare Monteverdi included two Florentine musicians in his list of composers who followed the *seconda pratica* "renewed in our notation" by Rore, Jacopo Peri and Giulio Caccini. Claudio Monteverdi may have come into direct contact with Peri and Caccini when visiting (if he did) Florence in 1600 as part of the retinue of Duke Vincenzo Gonzaga to participate in the festivities for the marriage of Maria de' Medici and Henri IV of France; certainly, he knew the opera premiered at these festivities, Peri's *Euridice*.[14] Thus Peri and Caccini could have been conduits for the earlier ideas of Bardi and Galilei.  But Bardi's departure for Rome did not put an end to

---

by death, he would have, in my opinion, brought this genre of music of several airs to such perfection that others would have been easily able to raise it to the true and perfect condition so much praised by the ancients." Luca similarly praises Rore in *L'Artusi, overo Delle imperfettioni della moderna musica* (1600) fols. 19v–20r: "È stato iudicioso compositore M. Cipriano, & ha dato gran lume à pratici; & se io dicessi, che fosse stato il primo, che hauesse incominciato ad accomodare bene le parole, & con bell'ordine, non direi bugia; essendo da suoi antecessori, & nel medesimo tempo, molto in vso il fare de' barbarismi."

[13]In his letter to Giovanni Battista Doni, Venice, 2 February 1634, Monteverdi says that he saw Galilei's treatise "anzi venti anni fa"; see de' Paoli, *Claudio Monteverdi: lettere, dediche e prefazioni*, 326.

[14]Alessandro Striggio, Mantuan court secretary and librettist of *Orfeo*, was certainly present in Florence in October 1600; his presence in the entourage of the Duke of Mantua is noted by the major-domo of the Medici court, Giovanni del Maestro (Florence, Archivio di Stato, Carte Strozziane, I, 27, fol. 38[bis]v). Del Maestro's list also includes unspecified servants; given that Monteverdi is known to have travelled with the duke, these may have included the composer. Peri's opera was published as *Le musiche sopra l'Euridice* (Florence: Giorgio Marescotti, 1600 [=1601]), and both text and music of Monteverdi's *Orfeo* owe a clear debt to it. For Monteverdi and Caccini, see Imogene Horsley, "Monteverdi's Use of Borrowed Material in 'Sfogava con le stelle', " *Music & Letters* LIX (1978) 316–28.

likely contact with Monteverdi.[15] His precise movements thereafter until his return to Florence in 1606 remain unclear, but as *maestro di camera* (and lieutenant-general of the pontifical guard) to Pope Clement VIII (Ippolito Aldobrandini), he could well have visited Ferrara after the secession of the city to the papacy in 1598. There is also one specific occasion when Bardi and Monteverdi seem to have been in the same place at the same time, on the battlefields of Hungary in 1595: Bardi was among the papal troops (under Gian Francesco Aldobrandini) joined by Duke Vincenzo Gonzaga and his retinue (including a small group of musicians headed by Monteverdi) at the siege of Viszgrad in late summer.

Vincenzo Gonzaga's campaign in Hungary was scarcely auspicious, but the trip allowed Monteverdi to see Venice and Vienna, both cities that played a significant part in his later career. At first sight, too, it would seem unlikely for a servant-musician to meet a lieutenant-general in the heat of battle. However, battle was far from many minds in the stand-off between the Christian forces and the Turks, and Vincenzo Gonzaga had no scruples over using the occasion to display his princely attributes:

> Here it is not seemly to ignore that in his pavilions, which were many and beautiful, the Lord Duke stood and had himself served in the grand manner, for as well as a standard guard of arquebusiers which he kept around his person, he also had with him a most numerous and complete household, and in particular a large group of titled knights and gentlemen, wherefore he continually and to his great splendor maintained a most abundant table. Moreover, His Highness often sumptuously banqueted many lords and barons of the army, who for the better part of the day would come to pass the time in a friendly manner with His Highness, on whose order not just on feast days but every day four or five masses were said in his quarters, and he lived in a catholic manner, but on the solemn [days] Vespers were sung with music by singers and organ which he had brought with him, to the infinite pleasure not, I say, of those who were serving His Highness, but of other catholics in the army, who gathered there, it also occurring

---

[15]For Bardi's career, see his entry in the *Dizionario biografico degli italiani*, in progress (Rome: Società Grafica Romana, 1960– ) VI: 300–303, and the summary in Palisca, *The Florentine Camerata*, 1–11.

many times that the Most Serene Archduke had music performed for
his entertainment by the same singers.[16]

It would be intriguing if Bardi and Monteverdi actually met and discussed the Camerata's reforms; it would also explain the echoes of
Florentine thought—half remembered, as it were—in later statements
on the *seconda pratica*. Perhaps it was Monteverdi's encounter with
Bardi in Hungary that further encouraged the composer to enter the
humanist paths that he explored in Mantua and Ferrara shortly after his
return from the field. Bardi, too, may have had some reaction to the
meeting: soon after his return to Rome, he sent to the Duke of Ferrara
a madrigal done "according to my usual method, keeping the line intact,
and with the expression of the words and the conceit."[17]

### THE 1607 *DICHIARATIONE*

It is surprising to find Giulio Cesare Monteverdi's *Dichiaratione della
lettera stampata nel quinto libro de' suoi madrigali* following the can-
zonetta-type pieces in Claudio Monteverdi's *Scherzi musicali a tre voci*;
they scarcely seem comfortable bedfellows. Giulio Cesare focusses on
the madrigal, not the canzonetta, and although he mentions the *scherzi*,
this is only in an aside offering further proof of his brother's originality
in matters musical (the point at issue is the term *seconda pratica*). Failing
a convincing demonstration of some connection between the aesthetic
premises of the *Dichiaratione* and the textual and musical content of the
*scherzi* themselves,[18] one can only assume that the link between the

---

[16]Fortunato Cardi, *Relatione del primo viaggio che il ser.mo sig. duca di Mantova fece
alla guerra d'Ongheria l'anno 1595* (Mantua, Archivio di Stato, Archivio Gonzaga, *busta*
388) fol. 11, transcribed in Fabbri, *Monteverdi*, 45. Vincenzo Gonzaga's campaigns in
Hungary are discussed in Vincenzo Errante, "Forse che sì, forse che no," *Archivio
storico lombardo* XLII (1915) 15–114.

[17]Bardi to the Duke of Ferrara, Rome, 3 October 1595, given in Angelo Solerti, *Gli
albori del melodramma*, 3 vols. (Milan: Fratelli Bocca, 1904; reprint Hildesheim: Georg
Olms, 1969) I: 47, note 4; translated in Palisca, "The 'Camerata Fiorentina', " 224.

[18]Massimo Ossi's as yet unpublished paper "*Un ordine novo, bello, et gustevole*: Formal
Synthesis in Claudio Monteverdi's First Volume of *Scherzi musicali*" attempts just such
a demonstration. Note also the broader discussion in Ossi, "Claudio Monteverdi's
Concertato Technique and its Role in the Development of his Musical Thought" (Ph.D.
diss., Harvard University, 1989). I am grateful to Professor Ossi for sharing some of his
ideas with me.

VI

182

*Scherzi musicali* and the *Dichiaratione* is less conceptual than pragmatic: Monteverdi needed to defend himself against Antonio Braccino da Todi's first *discorso*, and the *Scherzi musicali* was the first print to give him a chance to do so. The *Dichiaratione* could just as easily have been coupled with *Orfeo* had the opera been printed in the year of its first performance.

The faulty typesetting in the reference to the *Dichiaratione* on the title page of the *Scherzi musicali* might suggest a hasty, if not late, addition to the print. Collating the signatures and gathering structure of the first edition may offer further clues. But the presence of the *Dichiaratione* in each subsequent edition of the *Scherzi musicali* (Venice: Ricciardo Amadino, 1609, 1615; Bartolomeo Magni, 1628)— even though reprints often omit text material (dedications, prefaces, etc.) present in a first edition—suggests that the *Dichiaratione* certainly was eventually viewed, even if not first conceived, as an integral and important part of the volume. Clearly the Monteverdi brothers and their printers thought the *Dichiaratione* of enough value to merit devoting time, effort, and money to setting and re-setting four pages of close-knit text. Moreover, even if the *Dichiaratione* and the *scherzi* seem mismatched, other aspects of the print give a suitable impression of seriousness. The presence of a privilege—unprecedented for Monteverdi—has already been noted. It is also striking that Giulio Cesare Monteverdi and Ricciardo Amadino eschew the standard (and least costly) part-book format in favor of a single volume in folio with each piece presented on facing pages in "choir-book" layout. There are precedents for issuing canzonettas in this manner—for example, the engraved collections issued in Rome by Simone Verovio in the 1580s and 1590s[19]—but even so, the presentation seems more luxurious than warranted by the essentially light-hearted nature (if it is) of the musical contents.

For all its significance, the *Dichiaratione* itself is no model of logic, and the arguments are not always clear. Quite apart from Giulio Cesare Monteverdi's grasp of the issues, the reader is hampered by the presentation (interleaving passages from Claudio Monteverdi's 1605 letter

---

[19]*Diletto spirituale* (1586), *Ghirlanda di fioretti musicali* (1589), *Canzonette a quattro voci* (1591), *Lodi della musica* (1595); see Gary Lee Anderson, "The Canzonetta Publications of Simone Verovio, 1586-1595" (D.M.A. diss., University of Illinois, 1976).

with commentary), and even by the confusing references to "the opponent" (*l'oppositore,* who is sometimes, but by no means consistently, to be identified with Antonio Braccino da Todi) and "the adversary" (*l'aversario,* sometimes, but by no means consistently, Artusi).[20] This in turn may reflect the fact that although Artusi's two treatises of 1600 and 1603 were clearly in Giulio Cesare Monteverdi's sights, his primary aim was specifically to respond to Braccino's first *discorso.* Indeed, the contents, perhaps even the layout, of the *Dichiaratione* may owe more than hitherto suspected to Braccino's now lost text. Both L'Ottuso and Artusi had offered lessons in how to handle an epistolary polemic in the *Seconda parte dell'Artusi* of 1603; L'Ottuso's second letter is a point-by-point refutation of Artusi's letter to him, and Artusi similarly refutes L'Ottuso. In this *modus operandi,* the refutation tends to combine verbal nit-picking with discussion of specific theoretical and broader philosophical issues according to a (not always logical) agenda dictated by the document being refuted. It is often left to the reader to provide a synthesis of the ideas thus presented. Braccino likely adopted a similar format, quoting Monteverdi's 1605 statement and offering a gloss on each successive point. This in turn may have prompted Giulio Cesare Monteverdi to proceed as he did. We cannot know whether he also followed Braccino in interleaving lines from the original with passages of commentary (in 1603, Artusi had kept original and commentary separate), although it seems likely given that the technique appears rather old-fashioned, perhaps even scholastic. Whatever the case, Giulio Cesare's gloss on his brother's text seems intended first as a refutation of an earlier gloss on that text, and only second as a clarification of Monteverdi's 1605 letter and/or a new position-statement rebutting Artusi (not just Braccino) in the broader controversy. Indeed, the need to refute Braccino point-by-point (and by Braccino's own mode of argument), and also the tendency towards fragmentation in the mode of presentation, doubtless hindered Giulio Cesare from even attempting (if he were able) to present a rounded view of his brother's aesthetic stance.

---

[20] Giulio Cesare Monteverdi certainly knew that Antonio Braccino was a false name ("finto," he says), and he may have guessed that Braccino and Artusi were one and the same, but there is some attempt in the *Dichiaratione* to keep them separate for the purpose of his argument; this is clearer in the original Italian than in the translation in Strunk, *Source Readings in Music History,* 405–12.

## SOME ISSUES AND ARGUMENTS

If the agenda of the *Dichiaratione* was at least partly dictated by the *discorso*, one can go some way towards reconstructing Braccino's text. To judge by Giulio Cesare Monteverdi's responses, Braccino must have dissected Claudio Monteverdi's statement almost word-by-word, quibbling at his terminology, casting doubt on the composer's excuses for not having responded to Artusi,[21] and submitting the title of the proposed treatise, *Seconda pratica, overo Perfettione della moderna musica*, to a detailed critique. Braccino also seems to have drawn on Artusi's treatises of 1600 and 1603, reviving criticisms of Monteverdi's part-writing and dissonance treatment in "Cruda Amarilli, che col nome ancora" (now a topical example given its position at the head of the Fifth Book) as well as of his modal irregularities (witness the defense in the *Dichiaratione* of "O Mirtillo, Mirtillo anima mia," the second madrigal in the book). Similarly, Giulio Cesare Monteverdi occasionally resorts to points made in his brother's favor in Artusi's texts; for example, his claims that the modern style is effective in arousing the emotions and that it is widely adopted in the musical world echo L'Ottuso. But in general, the *Dichiaratione* tends to distance itself from the two defenses already offered for Monteverdi, by Luca in 1600 and L'Ottuso in 1603.

One can see why. That Monteverdi's dissonances are explicable in terms of contemporary improvisation and ornamentation practices, that they are fleeting enough not to offend the ear, that such dissonances are somehow metaphorical substitutes for consonances, that these pieces have to be judged as performed by good singers and not from score, were all arguments roundly (and rightly, given his frame of reference) dismissed by Artusi.[22] L'Ottuso was perhaps on a stronger tack in advocating novelty in music. Not that novelty *per se* was necessarily a good thing; Artusi dismissed that, too. But it pleased the senses by creating new ways of arousing new emotions—Luzzaschi had endorsed the point for both text and music in the dedication of his *Sesto*

---

[21]Braccino again noted Monteverdi's reluctance to respond to Artusi's letters written "piene d'amoreuolezza e ciuiltà" in the *Discorso secondo musicale* (1608) 6: "non ha mai (se bene più volte inuitato, e spronato) risposto cosa alcuna, ma sempre scusandosi e fuggendo, essendosi accorto del suo errore se ne stà così alla muta. . . ."

[22]These various defenses of Monteverdi are discussed in Palisca, "The Artusi-Monteverdi Controversy." Needless to say, Artusi neglected to point out that in Part III of Zarlino's *Istitutioni harmoniche* (Venice, 1558), the author had also argued that some dissonances could pass almost unnoticed by the ear. See the quotation in *ibid.*, 147.

*libro de' madrigali a cinque voci* of 1596[23]—and invention was to be more esteemed than the imitation of past models in advancing the art of music.[24] This final argument had some merit, not least because it could have been (but never was) supported by contemporary disputes in literary theory. Giulio Cesare Monteverdi, however, chose a safer course: first, he suggested that his brother did indeed adhere to models from both the near and the distant past; and second, he offered the possibility of a more rounded defense of the *seconda pratica*.

In his response to L'Ottuso's first letter, Artusi had requested a two-fold justification of the moderns by authority and (mathematical) demonstration. L'Ottuso generally fudged the question of demonstration (he had little choice), but he was not afraid to tackle Artusi on "authority": "scour the field of music yourself and you will find it to the full."[25] This may be obtuse: Artusi would doubtless have preferred the authority of approved theorists to that of composers. But the statement encourages all the participants in the controversy to scour the field for exemplars to support their various arguments, citing composers, and sometimes specific works, in their barrage of claims and counter-claims. The task was of course made all the easier by the evident impact of music printing on the transmission and dissemination of music in the period. Thus Giulio Cesare Monteverdi claims authority and precedent for his brother's apparent modal irregularities (citing mixed modes in plainchant and in works by Josquin Desprez, Alessandro Striggio, Cipriano de Rore and Adriano Willaert), for his modern style (the lists of *seconda pratica* composers), and for his new aesthetic (Plato).

---

[23]Printed in Ferrara by Vittorio Baldini; the dedication, written by Alessandro Guarini, is given in Anthony Newcomb, *The Madrigal at Ferrara, 1579–1597*, 2 vols. (Princeton: Princeton University Press, 1979) I: 118.

[24]L'Ottuso quoted in the *Seconda parte dell'Artusi* (1603) 19: "Et quanto à quello, che ella dice non esser ne Pittore, ò Scultore, ne Poeta, ouero Oratore, che non cerchi d'imitare gli Antichi, & massime gl'eccellenti. A questo io rispondo, che ue ne sono, & saranno sempre, quelli massime che stimano più la inue[n]tione, che la imitatione, nella qual parte, in questi suoi Madrigali esso Signor, &c. si ha fatta particolare professione, come che nella Musica questa sij di gran lunga più lodata di quella, oltra che in questa facoltà no[n] s'ha d'atte[n]dere alla imitatione de gl'Antichi, essendoui massime campo con la inuentione, & con questa noua modulatione d'auanzarli." By "antichi," L'Ottuso means "Iosquino, Clemens non Papa, Mouton, Crequilon, & altri di quella Classe..."(*ibid.*, 18).

[25]*Ibid.*, 17: "ma poiche ne addimanda autorità d'approuati autori, lei medesima scorri pel Campo della Musica, che ne lo ritrouerà pieno."

Naming composers of the *prima* and *seconda pratica* may have been prompted specifically by Braccino, who evidently dismissed Claudio Monteverdi's claim that there was indeed a practice distinct from that taught by Zarlino. The *seconda pratica* composers include two groups of powerful names nearly all active in publishing in the 1590s and/or early 1600s: first, Carlo Gesualdo, Emilio de' Cavalieri, Alfonso Fontanelli, the "Conte di Camerata,"[26] Giovanni del Turco, Tommaso Pecci "and other gentlemen of that heroic school"; and second, Marc'Antonio Ingegneri, Luca Marenzio, Giaches de Wert, Luzzasco Luzzaschi, Jacopo Peri, Giulio Caccini and other "loftier spirits." The two groups are introduced in different contexts. The first group includes dilettante composers of noble (or near-noble) standing; their evident aristocratic bearing may be more important than their music.[27] They have not deigned to write about music, only to compose, paying "no attention to nonsense and chimeras" such as criticisms from pettifogging theorists like Artusi. The second group is made up of professional musicians: composers who had a direct influence on Monteverdi (Ingegneri and Wert as teacher and colleague respectively); those whom he admired and arguably emulated (Marenzio and Luzzaschi);[28] and those who pioneered the "new music" in Florence (Peri and Caccini).

Combining these modern composers with those of the *prima pratica* (Ockeghem, Josquin Desprez, Pierre de la Rue, Jean Mouton, Crecquillon, Clemens non Papa, Nicolas Gombert, Adriano Willaert) produces a remarkable survey of music over the past century. It hints at the power of music printing to change the composer's perception of his

[26]The "Conte di Camerata" has commonly been identified as Giovanni de' Bardi, but Pietro Cerone, *El melopeo y maestro* (Naples: Giovanni Battista Gargano and Lucrezio Nucci, 1613) 150, notes "quan buenas son las obras musicales de d. Geronimo Branchiforte conde de Camerata. . ."; see Fabbri, *Monteverdi*, 369, note 75.

[27]But Wilfred Thomas Foxe, "Text Expression and Tonal Coherence in the Printed Madrigals of Tommaso Pecci (1576-1604): A Sienese Perspective on the Second Practice" (Ph.D. diss., University of Durham, 1991), places more emphasis on precise musical connections between Pecci and Monteverdi. I am grateful to Dr. Foxe for sharing his ideas with me.

[28]See Glenn E. Watkins and Thomasin La May, "*Imitatio* and *Emulatio*: Changing Concepts of Originality in the Madrigals of Gesualdo and Monteverdi in the 1590s," in *Claudio Monteverdi: Festschrift Reinhold Hammerstein zum 70. Geburtstag*, ed. Ludwig Finscher (Laaber: Laaber Verlag, 1986) 453–87; Tomlinson, *Monteverdi and the End of the Renaissance*, 33–72.

place in the musical world. Print gave the music of both past and present a permanence that encouraged the construction of historical processes within its development: composers were now better able to see their place within (and therefore, perhaps outside) one or more musical traditions. Here Giulio Cesare Monteverdi follows (but in much greater detail) the tendency in contemporary treatises to provide lists of composers grouped, say, as "antichi," "vecchi," and "moderni."[29] Thus he exploited the historical awareness of the age to persuade his readers that there was empirical evidence for style change in music. But Claudio Monteverdi seems to have sensed a more subtle lesson of history. According to his brother, he "honors, reveres and praises" both the *prima pratica* and the *seconda pratica*. Whether or not this was just an argument of convenience, the notion dawns that different groups of composers, regardless of their orientation, could and should now coexist in relative equanimity within a pluralist musical context.

The potential distinction of two musical practices, each equally justifiable on its own terms, was a cunning one that pulled the rug out from under the feet of Monteverdi's opponents. Artusi was not wrong to believe as he did—his mistake was simply to apply the standards of one practice to the music of another (*purpura iuxta purpuram diiudicanda*, as Giulio Cesare Monteverdi cited in a different context). The distinction was also a striking resolution of the dialectical confrontations that had dominated sixteenth-century theory. Yet Giulio Cesare's argument is not without its problems: historical awareness may provide a context for changes in musical style, but it does not necessarily sanction them. Plato was certainly a useful ally. So too was Cipriano de Rore, a distinguished (also dead) composer of unimpeachable reputation close

---

[29] A good example is provided by Lodovico Zacconi, *Prattica di musica* (Venice: Bartolomeo Carampello, 1596) fol. 7r: the "antichi" are "quei compositori che col mezzo delle figure Musicali composero tante cantilene, quante hoggi giorno si veggano ancor esser conseruate: i nomi de quali sono Iusquino, Gio. Mottone l'Ochghen, Brumello, Henrico Isaac, Lodouico Senfelio, & molti altri"; the "vecchi," "Adriano Vuilarth, Morales, Ciprian Rore, il Zerlino, il Palestina, & altri"; and the "moderni," those "che seranno le piu fresche, & le piu nuoue: delle quale gl'auttori sono ancora viui, ò se pur sono morti, sono mancati giouani, & inanzi l'età senile. . . ." A similar impetus is apparent in Seth Calvisius's "De origine et progressu musices" appended to his *Exercitationes musicae duae* (Leipzig: Apelij, 1600). The issue is discussed in Jessie Ann Owens, "Music Historiography and the Definition of 'Renaissance'," *MLA Notes* XLVII (1990) 305–30. I am indeed grateful to Professor Owens for so generously sharing her ideas on this and other matters with me.

enough to Willaert to be able to stand any comparison, and who, according to Vincenzo Galilei, was to be approved for composing not by rule but by judgment (*giuditio*).[30] However, authority (and, for that matter, taste) were fickle helpmates—as Braccino made clear in the *Discorso secondo musicale* (1608)—and there remained Artusi's request for an account of the modern style founded on "demostratione." If Monteverdi's claims for the "perfections of modern music" were not to ring hollow, he needed to produce a defense "to the satisfaction of reason" as well as "of sense."[31]

The partnership of *senso* and *ragione* in the formation of *giuditio* had been explored by Zarlino in the very last chapter of his *Istitutioni harmoniche* (1558). Artusi, too, was clear on the role of intellect (*intelletto*, of which *ragione* is a faculty) in musical judgment:

> after [the sense] has received [the sound], and has delighted in it, it presents it to the intellect, which then proceeds to consider what proportions those sounds, and those parts of that song, and those intervals, may contain among themselves, [and] the invention, the subject, the order, and the form given to that material, [and] whether the style is correct—[these are] all things which belong to the intellect to discern, understand, and judge; and this is that part which belongs to the intellect.[32]

As Artusi was happy to point out, Luca and L'Ottuso had each fallen into the trap of explaining the modern style by appealing to sense alone: although L'Ottuso had claimed that the new style operated "without

[30]Palisca, "The Artusi-Monteverdi Controversy," 156, note 82.

[31]See Monteverdi's 1605 letter in de' Paoli, *Claudio Monteverdi: lettere, dediche e prefazioni*, 392: "ma siano sicuri, che intorno alle consonanze, e dissonanze vi è anco un'altra consideratione differente dalla determinata, la qual con quietanza della ragione, e del senso diffende il moderno comporre. . . ."

[32]*L'Artusi, overo Delle imperfettioni della moderna musica* (1600) fol. 11r: "et dopò hauerlo riceuuto, e dilettatosi di lui, lo appresenta all'intelletto, che poi và considerando quali proportioni habbino fra di loro quei suoni, & quelle parti di quella Cantilena, e quelli interualli, l'inuentione, e'l soggietto, l'ordine, la forma data à quella materia; se il stile è purgato; cose tutte, che allo intelletto s'appartengono, il discernere, intenderle, & giudicarle; & questa è quella parte, che allo intelletto s'appartiene." For the general issues, see Michael Fend, "The Changing Function of *Senso* and *Ragione* in Italian Music Theory of the Late Sixteenth Century," in *The Second Sense: Studies in the History of Hearing and Musical Judgement*, eds. Charles Burnett, Michael Fend, and Penelope Gouk (London: Warburg Institute, forthcoming). I am grateful to Dr. Fend for allowing me to see his paper.

departing in any way from good reason," he never fully explained how the demands of reason would be met. Giulio Cesare Monteverdi promised to fill the gap. Not only was sense satisfied by the new style's ability to move the emotions, but also one could find rational foundations for the *seconda pratica* first in "the consonances and dissonances approved by mathematics," and second in the demands of *oratione*, "the chief mistress in the art of the perfection of *melodia*."[33] Such a reasoned account of the modern style could potentially produce a theoretical articulation of the *seconda pratica*—an *Istitutioni melodiche*—to match Zarlino's rationalization of the *prima pratica* in his *Istitutioni harmoniche*.

The mention of mathematics bows to the traditional domain of music theory. But it was dangerous—Artusi had demonstrated the mathematical irrationality of irregular intervals used in the modern style—and also potentially irrelevant: the limitations of rational proportions for music theory had already been exposed in contemporary debates on tuning and temperament. Certainly Giulio Cesare Monteverdi was on safer ground with Plato's (perhaps better, Ficino's) *melodia*, the trinity of *oratione, harmonia* and *rhythmus* which is used as a focus for the modern style in its search for emotional arousal. Of course, *melodia* simply provided an aesthetic framework for the *seconda pratica*; it did not offer a rational account of its licenses (nor, for that matter, did text-setting). But the concept was both strong and resonant enough to suggest a shift of the font of reason for musical composition away from the "nature" advocated by Zarlino and Artusi towards the aesthetic and affective demands of art.

Braccino was therefore forced to address the issue of *melodia* in his *Discorso secondo musicale* of 1608. As one might expect, he picks holes in Giulio Cesare Monteverdi's use of the term in an attempt to rescue Artusi's position. Even if Plato's ideas are relevant to modern music (and Braccino argues that they are not), advocating the primacy

[33]*Melodia* is of course to be understood in the sense of the total composition; see Palisca ("The Artusi-Monteverdi Controversy," 154–55), who also discusses Giulio Cesare Monteverdi's stretching of the terminology. The relevant passage is from Plato's *Republic*, 398c–d, as translated by Marsilio Ficino. The seeds for this defense may, ironically, have been sowed by Artusi himself: *melodia* is mentioned in the *Seconda parte dell'Artusi* (1603) 23, 31 (in the latter case, *harmonia* and rhythm are said to be "servants" of *oratione*). Zarlino's *Sopplimenti musicali* (1588) also merits examination in this light.

of *oratione* within *melodia* misses the point of its equal partnership with *harmonia* and rhythm. All three components have expressive powers, and all three must be perfect in the work of the perfect *melopeo*. Thus, however perfect Monteverdi's *oratione* may be, it remains irreparably disfigured by his "unnatural" harmony (hence Artusi's objections stand) and, it appears, by his imperfect control of rhythm (for this is the significance of Braccino's criticism of mensuration signs in the *Scherzi musicali*). Claudio Monteverdi, too, may have sensed the weakness of his brother's emphasis on *oratione*. His later plans for his treatise, now called *Melodia, overo Seconda pratica musicale*, divide the book into three parts devoted not just to *oratione*, but also to *harmonia* and rhythm.[34] Similarly, the *stile concitato* is one sign of the composer's later attempts to explore the expressive power of rhythm; and his Venetian works are rich in explorations of emotional arousal through a *harmonia* that may either reinforce or (and increasingly, in the case of aria) supersede the expressive function of *oratione* as it was understood in 1607.

### TOWARDS A POETICS OF MUSIC

Artusi was no ogre; nor was he the arch-pedant typecast by later generations. Certainly, he remained sensitive to the needs and aspirations of the modern musician, and although he was caustic when confronting the (often specious) arguments of Monteverdi's defenders, he retained a respect, even admiration, for the composer himself.[35] His sticking-point, however, was that it was impossible to give a rational explanation of modern musical practice within the parameters, however stretched, of a music theory true to nature, demonstrated by mathematics, and supported by the precepts of generations of distinguished theorists.

The evident failure of theory—turned *de facto* into a true epistemological crisis—was to be remedied by Monteverdi's long-promised account of the *seconda pratica*. This seems to have been intended as an

[34]Monteverdi outlines the organization of the treatise in his letter to Doni of 22 October 1633; see de' Paoli, *Claudio Monteverdi: lettere, dediche e prefazioni*, 319–24. According to his eulogist, Matteo Caberloti, he was working on the treatise until his death; see Fabbri, *Monteverdi*, 62.

[35]Braccino notes Artusi's view of Monteverdi in his *Discorso secondo musicale* (1608) 7: "egli loda l'opere sue, e 'l suo bello ingegno, in quella parte però che meritano esser lodate. . . ."

authoritative and comprehensive summary of the art and craft of modern musical expression (I use the term deliberately); the result would have been a fully fledged poetics of music. Vincenzo Galilei had already noted the issues that mattered:

> In the variety of books which are in print today written on the subject of the art of modern counterpoint which I have read diligently many times, I have never been able to know two very principal things. One of these pertains to the soul of the harmony, which is the conceit of the words; and the other pertains to the body, which is the diversity of successive sounds and voices by which the modulation proceeds. Regarding the soul, no one, as I have said, has yet, as far as I know, taught the way of accompanying the words, or rather the ideas behind them with the notes, in accordance with the end that one who is not a false musician should have before him.[36]

Monteverdi, too, felt that the stylistic and affective gains of modern music challenged theory to produce an explanation both of how texts should be expressed in music and (said his brother) of "the manner of employing the consonances and dissonances in actual composition." But he never finished his treatise.

The question of forging a poetics of music lies at the heart of the Artusi-Monteverdi controversy. In turn, the controversy has close conceptual (and terminological) parallels with contemporary debates in literary theory; the arguments over Guarini's *Il pastor fido* are an obvious example.[37] The claims of reason versus sense, tradition versus innovation, nature versus art, were all issues currently in hot debate. Even Artusi's expanded role of *intelletto* in musical judgment (quoted above) owes something to contemporary poetics. These debates in Italian academies and salons may have nudged the Artusi-Monteverdi controversy in new directions. Again, "print culture" may also have a bearing on the issue. Reification of the musical work on the printed

[36]*Discorso intorno all'uso delle dissonanze*, Florence, Biblioteca Nazionale Centrale, MS Anteriore Galileo, I, fol. 105v, translated in Palisca, "The Beginnings of Baroque Music," 364. See also *idem*, "The Artusi-Monteverdi Controversy," 156, note 84.

[37]See, for example, Tomlinson, *Monteverdi and the End of the Renaissance*, 17–21. As with Monteverdi's madrigals, *Il pastor fido* was subject to attack even while circulating in manuscript. L'Ottuso also cites the play (but in a different context) in the *Seconda parte dell'Artusi* (1603), 17.

page—and the broadening of the market for music through print—emphasized the need for a critical vocabulary through which to explain and evaluate the compositional process. Musical discussion was to be led out of the shadows of arcane mathematics and technical note-crunching into a world where professionals and intelligent amateurs could partake of critical discourse on musical composition and performance. Traditional theory was ill-designed to cater to such issues; indeed, its frames of reference, even its terminology, often relegated matters of function, style and aesthetic appreciation to the periphery of musical enquiry. But musical commentators now began to draw upon other traditions of critical and analytical thought.

It is precisely in the late-sixteenth century that style criticism starts to become an issue in contemporary prescriptive and descriptive writing on music.[38] So, too, does "analysis," a term seemingly first used in print in 1606 in a treatise by Joachim Burmeister with the significant title *Musica poetica* (Rostock: Stephan Myliander). As befits his training and career, Burmeister's models for the understanding and critical evaluation of musical works are drawn essentially from traditional grammar and rhetoric: thus in his analysis of Lassus's motet "In me transierunt," one strategy is to elucidate the composer's text-setting by way of musical techniques comparable with rhetorical figures.[39] Rhetoric provided a well-formed system of poetics, the authority and substance of which must surely have seemed seductive to a theorist contemplating the absence of a similarly authoritative and substantial poetics of music. The potential analogies between music and rhetoric, themselves sanctified by classical authority, were tempting indeed.

The Italian modernists never wholeheartedly adopted theories of musico-rhetorical figures, for reasons which merit exploration. Nevertheless they owe a debt to rhetoric and poetics not just in their oratorical ideals but also in their new emphases on genre, style, imitation, and

[38]See the discussion of Lodovico Zacconi in James Haar, "A Sixteenth-Century Attempt at Music Criticism," *Journal of the American Musicological Society* XXXVI (1983) 191–209. Also relevant in this context are *idem*, "Notes on the *Dialogo della musica* of Antonfrancesco Doni," *Music & Letters* XLVII (1966) 198–224; *idem*, "Cosimo Bartoli on Music," *Early Music History* VIII (1988) 37–79.

[39]See Claude V. Palisca, "*Ut oratoria musica*: The Rhetorical Basis of Musical Mannerism," in *The Meaning of Mannerism*, eds. Franklin W. Robinson and Stephen G. Nichols, Jr. (Hanover, NH: University Press of New England, 1972) 37–65.

purgation. An intriguing, if ill-formed, example is provided by Adriano
Banchieri's *Conclusioni nel suono dell'organo* of 1609. Here Banchieri
makes direct reference to the Artusi-Monteverdi controversy as it bore
on modern musical practice.[40] Theorists such as Zarlino and Artusi are
indeed worthy and deserve attention, but—here Banchieri follows Vincenzo Galilei—they have failed to show "how in practice to accom-
modate the words with imitated affections [*con imitati affetti*] in
whatsoever genre, whether Latin or vernacular." Their methods
produced pieces with "a most suave harmony of concent, but the said
harmony had no correspondence with the oration." Now most modern
musicians seek to compose in the manner of a "perfect orator," aiming
(following Cicero) to delight and move. Thus to "express" (*esprimere*)
a madrigal, motet, sonnet, or other kind of poetry, the musician must
"proceed imitating the affections with the harmony." Harmony must be
subject to the words, given that the words "express" the conceit (*il
concetto*) and must be clothed with "equivalent" (*equivalente*) harmony.
Music should "observe" the traditional rules in works without words
(toccatas, ricercares) and when the text does not require "unobservance" (*inosservanza*), but unobservance should be used to imitate the
word (*imitare la parola*), which is what "expresses the affections of the
most perfect orator." The discussion concludes in praise of Monteverdi—"for his most artful sentiments [*sentimenti*] in truth are worthy
of complete approval" by virtue of their being "industriously unfolded,
and imitated with equivalent harmony"—as well as of Gesualdo, Alfonso Fontanelli, Emilio de' Cavalieri, Benedetto Pallavicino, "and other

[40]"Parere delle mvsiche gia in vso à quelle, che modernamente vengono praticate,"
*Conclusioni nel suono dell'organo* (1609) 56–60. Some of this material was re-used in
Banchieri's *Cartella musicale nel canto figurato, fermo & contrapunto*, 3d ed. (Venice:
Giacomo Vincenti, 1614). He justifies (1609, 59) the composer who mixes modes and
uses irregular cadences: "non si deue però atribuirgli ch'egli dia vn colpo al cerchio, &
l'altro alla botte. . . ." According to Giulio Cesare Monteverdi in the *Dichiaratione* (de'
Paoli, *Claudio Monteverdi: lettere, dediche e prefazioni*, 403), Braccino said of such
solecisms: "è come sentire un pazzo ragionare il quale dia un colpo, come si dice, hor
sopra al cerchio e hor sopra la botte. . . ." Banchieri's two examples of modal irregularities for text-expressive ends are Tommaso Pecci's "O come sei gentile caro
augellino" (*Madrigali a cinque voci* [Venice: Angelo Gardano, 1602]) and Gabriele
Fattorini's "O quanto sei simile, ingrata rondinella" (*La Rondinella: secondo libro de
madrigali a cinque voci* [Venice: Ricciardo Amadino, 1604]).

modern and elevated spirits, whose worth is known today within honorable salons and heroic academies."[41]

Banchieri proposes a reconciliation between Artusi and Monteverdi, rescuing the Bolognese theorist from potential obsolescence by linking his position with incipient notions of genre-specific styles. Giulio Cesare Monteverdi had also hinted at the possibility in objecting that the rules of the *prima pratica* do not cater to all music because then "the harmony would be the same in all the types of songs" ("perchè l'armonia sarebbe sempre una in tutti li generi de cantilene"), while Claudio Monteverdi further explored theories of genre and style in the preface to his *Madrigali guerrieri, et amorosi... libro ottavo* (Venice: Alessandro Vincenti, 1638). Banchieri's solution (plus his notion of "observance" and "unobservance") becomes typical of Baroque theory and practice. However, more problematic, if no less typical, is the evident slippage in the terms adopted by Banchieri to explain how his musician-orator should approach a text. Does the composer imitate affections, sentiments, or words? Does music express texts, conceits or affections? What is imitation, what is expression, and how are they connected? What is the relationship between text, word, conceit, sentiment, and affection? And how should harmony (or even *harmonia*) be made "equivalent" to text?[42] Monteverdi's own "natural path to imitation" was a path through a terminological and philosophical minefield, as his later Venetian music was to prove.

---

[41]In the *Dichiaratione,* Giulio Cesare Monteverdi similarly used terms such as "questa Eroica scola" and "li spiriti più elevati" in connection with composers of the *seconda pratica*. It is not clear whether any reference is intended to the Florentine Accademia degli Elevati; see Edmond Strainchamps, "New Light on the Accademia degli Elevati of Florence," *The Musical Quarterly* LXII (1976) 507–35.

[42]L'Ottuso's claim (*Seconda parte dell'Artusi* [1603], 14) that the new style sought "to imitate thereby the nature of the verse, and justly represent the true sense of the poet" ("per imitare con essi la natura del verso, & giustamente rappresentare il senso uero del Poeta") was more concise, but no less problematic.

# VII

## 'SFOGAVA CON LE STELLE' RECONSIDERED:
## SOME THOUGHTS ON THE ANALYSIS
## OF MONTEVERDI'S MANTUAN MADRIGALS

Monteverdi's setting of (?) Ottavio Rinuccini's *Sfogava con le stelle* (in his Fourth Book of madrigals of 1603) has become something of a to-tem for the *seconda prattica* madrigal, both for its dissonance-treatment and given that it seems to offer a true composer's response to the Flor-entine 'new music'. In this latter context, Monteverdi's pioneering (but not unique) use of *falsobordone* in a secular setting has been construed as tending towards the declamatory flexibility of the new style while re-taining the possibility (amply realized by the composer) of using rich polyphony at particularly expressive moments within the text.[1]

More recently, Gary Tomlinson has focused on *Sfogava con le stelle* both for its apparent astrological implications and for its adherence to Renaissance articulations of resemblance in contrast to the newer no-tions of representation that seemingly underpin, say, the *Lamento della ninfa* in the *Madrigali guerrieri, et amorosi* of 1638.[2] Here, Foucault's ana-lysis of Renaissance and Baroque epistemes serves to explicate Tomlin-son's original sense of difference between Monteverdi's Mantuan and

---

[1] See, for example, the discussion in L. SCHRADE, *Monteverdi: Creator of Modern Music*, New York, Norton, 1950, pp. 190-193; and D. ARNOLD, *Monteverdi*, London, Dent, 1990³, p. 63.

[2] G. TOMLINSON, *Preliminary Thoughts on the Relations of Music and Magic in the Renais-sance*, in *In cantu et in sermone: for Nino Pirrotta on his 80th Birthday*, ed. by F. Della Seta and F. Piperno, Firenze, Olschki, 1989 ("Italian Medieval and Renaissance Studies", 2), pp. 121-139; ID., *Music in Renaissance Magic: Toward a Historiography of Others*, Chicago & Lon-don, Chicago University Press, 1993, pp. 229-246.

Venetian secular music explored in his earlier work on the composer.[3] However, it is possible to construe a slightly different relationship between *Sfogava con le stelle* and the *Lamento della ninfa*, focusing more on their similarities than on their differences.[4] And in general, it seems to me that we need to be very careful about our definitions of supposedly Renaissance and supposedly Baroque aesthetics and ideologies in this period, and that terms such as 'Baroque' (and associated concepts of Marinism, *concettismo*, *meraviglia* and the like) are due for reappraisal if we are effectively to confront what this period meant and means.

As for the structure of *Sfogava con le stelle*, both Tomlinson and Eric Chafe have made some attempt to get to grips with Monteverdi's harmonic and 'tonal' syntax, whether or not for rhetorical or text-expressive ends.[5] But both explicitly (if without explanation) reject the analytical strategies that perhaps best illuminate this syntax on both surface and deep-structural levels. For all the potential anachronisms of neo-Schenkerian and related reductive systems, they offer a powerful way of elucidating precisely what is not explained by Tomlinson, Chafe and their predecessors: the structural parameters within which (or against which) a given piece actually works.[6]

---

[3] As developed in particular in G. TOMLINSON, *Monteverdi and the End of the Renaissance*, Oxford, Clarendon Press, 1987. A number of other scholars have also started to exploit Foucault's ideas as useful tools to explicate Monteverdi; see J. KURTZMAN, *A Taxonomic and Affective Analysis of Monteverdi's 'Hor che'l ciel e la terra'*, «Music Analysis», XII, 1993, pp. 169-195; T. CARTER, *Resemblance and Representation: Towards a New Aesthetic in the Music of Monteverdi*, in «Con che Soavità»: *Studies in Italian Opera, Song, and Dance, 1580-1740*, ed. by I. Fenlon & T. Carter, Oxford, Clarendon Press, 1995, pp. 118-134.

[4] See T. CARTER, *'Possente spirto': On Taming the Power of Music*, «Early Music», XXI, 1993, pp. 517-523: here I explore the notion of triple-time aria assuming to some degree the expressive and formal functions of *seconda prattica* polyphony.

[5] TOMLINSON, *Monteverdi and the End of the Renaissance* cit., pp. 91-93; E. T. CHAFE, *Monteverdi's Tonal Language*, New York, Schirmer Books, 1992, pp. 82-86.

[6] Compare S. McCLARY, *The Transition from Modal to Tonal Organization in the Works of Monteverdi*, dissertation, Harvard University, 1976; F. SALZER, *Heinrich Schenker and Historical Research: Monteverdi's Madrigal 'Oimè, se tanto amate'*, in *Aspects of Schenkerian Theory*, ed. by D. Beach, New Haven & London, Yale University Press, 1983, pp. 135-152; G. CHEW, *The Perfections of Modern Music: Consecutive Fifths and Tonal Coherence in Monteverdi*, «Music Analysis», VIII, 1989, pp. 247-273; T. CARTER, *'An Air New and Grateful to the Ear': The Concept of 'Aria' in Late Renaissance and Early Baroque Italy*, «Music Analysis», XII, 1993, pp. 127-145; G. CHEW, *The Platonic Agenda of Monteverdi's 'Seconda pratica': A Case Study from the Eighth Book of Madrigals*, «Music Analysis», XII, 1993, pp. 147-168.

Also the subject of recent enquiry has been the social and func-
tional contexts of madrigals such as *Sfogava con le stelle* — although
we have still to identify the precise courtly, academic and other strains
invoked by their texts and music — and their place within the resonant
webs of reference and allusion that illuminate both the excitement and
the anxieties fostered by Renaissance notions of emulation, competition and homage:[7] for Monteverdi, we are just taking the first steps
into this rich vein of intertextuality. And the latest addition to the
melting-pot is the question of apparent representations of gender in
Monteverdi's music:[8] of course, *Sfogava con le stelle* is nothing if not
a gendered piece (although a key textual misreading has tended to obscure the point).

All in all, it seems that the time is ripe for a new attempt at reading
Monteverdi's totemic setting, one seeking to draw together some of
these various threads of recent Monteverdi studies and also to suggest
perhaps different directions as we move into a new musicological
age. My aim here is to open up a few lines of enquiry — I do not have
space to do more — both specific to this madrigal and broader in terms
of general cultural contexts. I also hope to suggest how we might gain a
multivalent view of the composer that, while conventionally fashion-
able in this post-modernist world, could also — dare I say it — get us
slightly closer to what Monteverdi somehow intended.

\* \* \*

Sfogava con le stelle
    un infermo d'Amore
    sotto notturno Cielo il suo dolore;
    e dicea fisso in loro:
5      O imagini belle

---

[7] To cite Howard Mayer Brown's well-known *Emulation, Competition, and Homage:
Imitation and Theories of Imitation in the Renaissance*, «Journal of the American Musicological
Society», XXXV, 1982, pp. 1-48. See also G. WATKINS & T. LA MAY, *«Imitatio» and «Emulatio»: Changing Concepts of Originality in the Madrigals of Gesualdo and Monteverdi in the
1590s*, in *Claudio Monteverdi: Festschrift Reinhold Hammerstein zum 70. Geburtstag*, hrsg.
von L. Finscher, Laaber, Laaber Verlag, 1986, pp. 453-487.

[8] See S. G. CUSICK, *Gendering Modern Music: Thoughts on the Monteverdi-Artusi Controversy*, «Journal of the American Musicological Society», XLVI, 1993, pp. 1-25.

> dell'idol mio, ch'adoro,
> sicome a me mostrate
> mentre così splendete
> la sua rara beltate
> 10     così mostraste a lei
> mentre cotanto ardete
> i vivi ardori miei.
> La fareste col vostro aureo sembiante
> pietosa sì, come me fate amante.[9]

[Under the stars in the night sky, a lovesick man proclaimed his grief. And he said, fixed on them: «O beautiful images of my idol whom I adore, just as you show to me – while you shinen her rare beauty, so show to her – while you burn – my ardent desires. With your golden semblance make her as pitying as you make me a lover.»]

Some nine settings of *Sfogava con le stelle* for a range of scorings survive in Italian music prints from 1602-1646. For Monteverdi, however, the most relevant were surely Salomone Rossi's five-voice setting in his *Secondo libro de madrigali a cinque voci* (Venezia, 1602) and Giulio Caccini's solo-song version in *Le nuove musiche* (Firenze, 1601 [= 1602]). Imogene Horsley has already discussed the possible connections between Monteverdi's and Caccini's settings, focusing on general similarities (and no less important, differences), on some seemingly direct quotations, and also on broader aesthetic issues: Caccini's famous condemnation of polyphony in the preface to *Le nuove musiche* finds a composerly riposte in Monteverdi's exaltation of five-voice textures in his own setting.[10] Among the direct 'quotations', Horsley explores how Monteverdi transforms a fairly innocuous passage in the Caccini

---

[9] The text here is drawn (with some editorial punctuation) from I-Fn, Palatino 251, p. 4. The poem also survives in *ivi*, Magliabechiano VII.907, f. 21r (line 9 = «la sua vera beltate»). While Palatino 251 is one of a nexus of Rinuccini manuscripts, it is not autograph, and indeed the attribution of this poem to Rinuccini is by no means secure. For Monteverdi's setting, see C. MONTEVERDI, *Madrigali a 5 voci: Libro quarto*, a cura di E. Ferrari Barassi, Cremona, Fondazione Claudio Monteverdi, 1974 ("Claudio Monteverdi: Opera omnia", 5), pp. 107-111.

[10] I. HORSLEY, *Monteverdi's Use of Borrowed Material in 'Sfogava con le stelle'*, «Music & Letters», LXIX, 1978, pp. 316-328. The Caccini is available in G. CACCINI, *Le nuove musiche (1602)*, ed. by H. Wiley Hitchcock, Madison, A-R Editions, 1970 ("Recent Researches in the Music of the Baroque Era", 9), pp. 88-91.

into one of the most trenchant – and well-known – dissonances in his piece, the famous C minor ninth chord towards the end of the second statement of «La fareste col vostr'aureo sembiante / pietosa sì» (Ex. 1a, b). She fails to note that the bass line of this celebrated passage seems taken from an earlier point in Caccini's song (Ex. 1c).[11] But this is grist to Horsley's mill: it is just one more example of how a great composer can make something significant, profound and intensely emotional out of mediocre ideas first presented in a rather muddled aesthetic and musical context.

Ex. 1a - Giulio Caccini, *Sfogava con le stelle* (*Le nuove musiche*, 1602), bars 33-41

The similarities revealed in Ex. 1 do seem to bolster Horsley's case for Monteverdi emulating Caccini (whose setting he knew either from first-hand experience or from the print). For that matter, there should be nothing surprising about the possibility of cross-references between solo songs and polyphonic madrigals: styles and genres which today we view as radically opposed were in fact both musically and conceptually much closer to each other in the early seventeenth century.[12] But Sa-

---

[11] Another interesting point of comparison is Caccini's rather vapid ornamental flourish on 'i vivi ar-*do*-ri miei', transformed into a structural melisma (if I may use the term) by Monteverdi and used on a more appropriate word ('i *vi*-vi ardori miei').

[12] As I have argued in *Giulio Caccini's 'Amarilli, mia bella': Some Questions (and a Few Answers)*, «Journal of the Royal Musical Association», CXIII, 1988, pp. 250-273; *Music in Late Renaissance & Early Baroque Italy*, London, Batsford, 1992, pp. 184-201.

Ex. 1b - Claudio Monteverdi, *Sfogava con le stelle* (*Il quarto libro de madrigali a cinque voci*, 1603), bars 47-54

Ex. 1c - Caccini, *Sfogava con le stelle*, bars 9-11

lomone Rossi's five-voice setting of 1602 seems to provide a much more obvious model for Monteverdi. Rossi himself seems to have acknowledged Caccini's song in his own setting: [13] there are significant motivic and structural parallels. The madrigal – certainly competent and at times inspired – is fairly typical of Rossi's style, focusing essentially on a homophonic presentation of the text, with some nice harmonic touches but little extended musical development and certainly few of the contrasts of style, texture and tonality that so distinguish Monteverdi's own reading. However, Rossi's setting of «La fareste col vostr'aureo sembiante / pietosa sì» provides a clearer precedent for Monteverdi's treatment of this text. As Ex. 2 reveals (compare Ex. 1b), his $a'$ suspended over a $B\flat$ – later transposed to a $d''$ suspended over an $e\flat$ – and its 'irregular' resolution (down a fifth) was reordered and reworked by Monteverdi (in the case of the $d''$, turning it into that famous ninth). Given that and the other clear relationships between Rossi's and Monteverdi's settings, there seems little doubt that Monteverdi set out to emulate his Mantuan colleague, and to confirm his technical and expressive credentials in the *seconda prattica* madrigal.

The question of the relationship between the Caccini, Rossi and Monteverdi is inevitably rendered problematic by as yet unresolved issues of dating. For example, we know that Monteverdi's Fourth Book contains material going back some six or seven years, if not further. The fact that Artusi did not cite *Sfogava con le stelle* in his criticisms of Monteverdi's irrational dissonance treatment in his *L'Artusi, ovvero Delle imperfettioni della moderna musica* (1600) [14] – that striking ninth, while properly prepared, is certainly open to objection on Artusi's terms – suggests that *Sfogava con le stelle* could (but it is a very

---

[13] Rossi's *Sfogava con le stelle* is in *Vocal Works by Salamon Rossi*, II, ed. by H. Avenary, Tel Aviv, Israeli Music Institute, 1989.

[14] Artusi did, of course, cite *Anima mia, perdona* from the Fourth Book (and *Cruda Amarilli, che col nome ancora, O Mirtillo, Mirtill'anima mia* and *Era l'anima mia* from the Fifth of 1605). For the controversy, see C. V. PALISCA, *The Artusi-Monteverdi Controversy*, in *The New Monteverdi Companion*, ed. by D. Arnold & N. Fortune, London, Faber, 1985, pp. 127-158; T. CARTER, *Artusi, Monteverdi, and the Poetics of Modern Music*, in *Musical Humanism and its Legacy: Essays in Honor of Claude V. Palisca*, ed. by N. K. Baker & B. Russano Hanning, Stuyvesant, NY, Pendragon Press, 1992 ("Festschrift Series", 11), pp. 171-194.

Ex. 2 - Salomone Rossi, *Sfogava con le stelle* (*Il secondo libro de madrigali a cinque voci*, 1602), bars 43-56

weak argument) be one of the later settings in the Fourth Book.[15] But we know that a good number of Caccini's songs had been circulating

[15] Tomlinson also reaches this conclusion on stylistic grounds, see *Monteverdi and the End of the Renaissance* cit., p. 110.

«tattered and torn» for some years before the publication of *Le nuove musiche*,[16] and Rossi's setting could well predate the publication of his own Second Book. At the very least, we have here an example of the networks of cross-reference and allusion typical of secular music in the late sixteenth century. And it is revealing to have so significant an example of Monteverdi looking both to his colleagues and to his competitors.

However, two differences between the Monteverdi and the Caccini and Rossi are worthy of immediate note. The first concerns the text. Line 11 of the poem as given above – «mentre cotanto ardete» (set by Caccini and Rossi) – is missing in the Monteverdi. Whether this is due to Monteverdi's own source for the poem or to a deliberate excision by the composer is, of course, as yet unknown, although the latter seems more likely given its presence in the Rossi. Such an excision doubtless plays into the hands of those critics who believe firmly in Monteverdi's sensitivity to poetry: the line is effectively redundant in terms of the meaning and is a clumsy, harsh echo of line 8 («mentre così splendete») – Monteverdi, ever sensitive to the sounds and senses of his poetry, makes a delicate editorial excision in the interest of euphony and compression.[17] Or, to play devil's advocate (and these things can always cut both ways), Monteverdi exhibits a cavalier approach to his poetry that betrays a none-too-literate mind sometimes insensitive to the demands of complex syntax and semantics.

The notion that Monteverdi is remarkably aware of the poetry he sets is, of course, a *sine qua non* of current appreciations of the composer, and one fostered by Monteverdi himself (or at least, his brother Giulio Cesare) in his account of the *seconda prattica*. We generally take

---

[16] As the singer claims in the preface to *Le nuove musiche*. However, Caccini did not include *Sfogava con le stelle* in his list of his earliest songs in the prefaces both to *L'Euridice composta in musica in stile rappresentativo*, Firenze, Giorgio Marescotti, 1600, and *Le nuove musiche*. On the possibility of Monteverdi being in Florence in October 1600 (for the wedding of Henri IV of France and Maria de' Medici), see CARTER, *Music in Late Renaissance & Early Baroque Italy* cit., p. 213. Certainly Monteverdi knew the opera performed then, Peri's *Euridice* (whether from having attended the event or from the print again remains unclear), as numerous passages in his *Orfeo* make clear.

[17] But if so – and if the poem *is* by Rinuccini (see note 9, above) – it conflicts somewhat with Monteverdi's fidelity to Rinuccini (and Rinuccini's own consummate craftsmanship) so lauded in G. TOMLINSON, *Madrigal, Monody, and Monteverdi's 'via naturale alla immitatione'*, «Journal of the American Musicological Society», XXXIV, 1981, pp. 60-108.

the Monteverdis at their word – and construct our images of the composer accordingly – without giving due weight to the complex ideological resonances that permeate the term and indeed the whole controversy with Artusi. Monteverdi had clear and precise reasons for latching on to his formula of the *oratione* as *padrona* of the *harmonia* – some, I suspect, not quite as noble as we tend to assume – and of course the question of whether and for how long Monteverdi actually adhered to his own creed (in whatever terms one chooses to define it) remains a matter for debate. But side-by-side with the image of Monteverdi, faithful servant of his poetry, is another common construct of the composer, as someone ferociously committed to his craft, sternly resisting modern trends for easy, instant gratification, and exploiting all the resources of his art in search of an intense – and intensely musical – expression. The question of how these two images of Monteverdi can co-exist – of how well he could serve both mistresses – has scarcely received an effective response in the literature and inevitably leads to unresolved tensions within it. Symptomatic is a kind of selective blindness to particular problems in Monteverdi's settings. For example, few have dared to expose Monteverdi's sometimes wayward treatment of his verse: missing out lines here, changing words and even *parole rime* there.[18] No less revealing is the frequent attempt

---

[18] An honourable exception is N. PIRROTTA, *Scelte poetiche di Monteverdi*, «Nuova Rivista Musicale Italiana», II, 1968, pp. 10-42, 226-254, translated as *Monteverdi's Poetic Choices* in ID., *Music and Culture in Italy from the Middle Ages to the Baroque: A Collection of Essays*, Cambridge, Mass., Harvard University Press, 1984, pp. 271-316. There are many examples: take the Guarini settings in Books III-V; the changes in *parole rime* in the *sestina Incenerite spoglie, avara tomba, Qui rise, o Tirsi, e qui ver me rivolse* (both in the Sixth Book, 1614) and *Zefiro torna, e di soavi accenti* (*recte: e di soavi odori*; in the 1632 *Scherzi musicali*); the famous «Notte» passage in the *Combattimento di Tancredi et Clorinda* (1624); and the *Lamento della ninfa* and the arrant nonsense of *Su, su, su pastorelli vezzosi* (both in the *Madrigali guerrieri, et amorosi*, 1638). One can, of course, find excuses for such lapses – for example, by blaming (now lost) textual sources or unsympathetic aesthetics – or even glorious justifications in terms of 'improving' the text. But clearing away the cobwebs of our own prejudices concerning Monteverdi has intriguing possibilities.

As a footnote to this footnote, one perhaps related aspect of *Sfogava con le stelle* caused some debate at the conference, namely the articulation of the last two lines: «La fareste col vostro aureo sembiante / pietosa sì come me fate amante». There is at least a potential ambiguity between «pietosa sì, come me fate amante» and «pietosa, sì come [i.e., *siccome*] me fate amante». The syntax would seem to favour the latter reading (and compare «sì come a me mostrate»), which was the preferred solution of a number

to turn the tensions between our conflicting images of Monteverdi into tensions played out in and through the music itself: this has the further advantage of absolving us of personal responsibility for our own critical dilemmas. The *locus classicus* is the opening of Monteverdi's *Sfogava con le stelle*: the introductory narration (lines 1-4) is set by three statements in *falsobordone* each leading to homophony (to large degree) – this choral 'recitative' (which will, of course, return later in the setting) is perhaps the most famous feature of the madrigal. However, at the moment of direct speech («O...»), the setting flowers into the most spectacular double counterpoint – and the texture expands to the highest and almost the lowest notes in the piece – as the intensity of the lover's invocation takes us beyond the realm of 'speech' into that of 'song' (Ex. 3). Thus do we reconcile our views of composer as poet and composer as musician (and thus do we argue that he is a musician when it really matters). Of course, in case we miss the words as a result, Monteverdi is careful to repeat them again. One also gets the feeling that he feels slightly guilty over his musical exuberance: the rest of the setting tends (rather self-consciously, in fact) to stay within respectable bounds of declamatory decorum (apart from some double statements of parallel text, worked carefully so that the meaning remains clear). However, this could equally well be due to the rather feeble ending of the poem (which even the excision of «mentre cotanto ardete» cannot rescue).

The second intriguing difference between Monteverdi and Caccini/Rossi is that of mode: given that one can reasonably expect emulatory settings to operate within the same or similar modal parameters as their model (if only for the sake of breaking the pattern so as to impress), Monteverdi's deviation here seems all the more striking. Indeed, his *Sfogava con le stelle* is somewhat unusual as regards its mode or tonal

---

of delegates, but Lorenzo Bianconi presented cogent syntactical and, still more important, metrical reasons for the former (the latter would create an illicit metrical accent on the fifth syllable of the line). Caccini and Rossi opt straightforwardly for «pietosa sì, come...», but Monteverdi's setting is a least slightly ambivalent (the first two statements of «pietosa» are minus the «sì»). I am indeed grateful to Francesca Chiarelli, a graduate student at Royal Holloway and Bedford New College, University of London, preparing a thesis on Monteverdi's text setting, for sharing her ideas on these and other matters with me.

Ex. 3 - Monteverdi, *Sfogava con le stelle*, bars 11-20

type.[19] The Caccini setting is straightforward, in the *chiavette* (G2, F3), one-flat, G-final tonal type that is a favourite in *Le nuove musiche* – what we would conventionally call a transposed Dorian mode. The Rossi, too, has a G final with a one-flat signature (this time in *chiavi naturali*: C1, C1, C3, C4, F4). Monteverdi uses Rossi's *chiavi naturali* – a point to which I shall return – and the one-flat signature, but his setting focuses

---

[19] For the terminology, see H. S. POWERS, *Tonal Types and Modal Categories in Renaissance Polyphony*, «Journal of the American Musicological Society», XXXIV, 1981, pp. 428-470.

instead on a D final: assuming a twelve-mode system for Monteverdi,[20] this is what would conventionally be called a transposed Aeolian mode. But the C1-♭-D tonal type is not common in Monteverdi's output (nor for that matter in that of his contemporaries). And despite the 'low' clefs, the *tessitura* (extending up to a *g″* in the *canto*) seems at least initially to belong more to a 'high'-clef piece.

For all its seeming Aeolian tendencies, in the context of the Fourth Book as a whole – and I shall attempt to show that this context is important for various reasons – *Sfogava con le stelle* separates untransposed Dorian (the exordium, *Ah dolente partita*, is a definable special case) from transposed Dorian pieces (C1-♮-d and C1-♭-g respectively). Logic would seem to suggest that *Sfogava con le stelle* is in some sense a representation of a Dorian mode: it is perhaps no coincidence (if in general, an inevitability) that the B flats dictated by the signature are initially introduced in *fa supra la* contexts that have obvious *ficta* overtones: the setting of «d'amore» in bar 4 – later to influence the treatment of «pietosa» – is a clear example (Ex. 4).[21] What might help clarify the potential confusion between Dorian and transposed Aeolian modes, or even the mode itself, are clear cadences on G or A. But curiously, and perhaps significantly, these cadences are conspicuously avoided by Monteverdi.[22] Certainly there are passages implying motion to G («sì come a me mostrate / mentre così splendete», but the missing third in the chord in bar 31 is significant) or 'phrygian' progressions to A («la sua rara beltate») – their close juxtaposition is significant – but they do not (at least until towards the end) involve *cadenze perfette* with suspensions.[23] Far more striking as alternative cadential and other sonorities are degrees VII and III (C and F): the first significant example is

[20] Few have broached the problem of mode for Monteverdi (Chafe's, *Monteverdi's Tonal Language* cit. – as its title reveals – is focussed somewhat differently). One important exception is POWERS, *Monteverdi's Model for a Multimodal Madrigal*, in *In cantu et in sermone* cit., pp. 185-219.

[21] CHAFE, *Monteverdi's Tonal Language* cit., pp. 82-85, argues that the flat signature/ system is important given that it permits the movement to even flatter domains (C minor) for the ending. There is surely some merit in his case, although it is weakened by a failure to explain the systemic and other exigencies that prompt movement through and between hexachords and systems in this music.

[22] It is perhaps significant that the other pieces before the Fourth Book in this (or a related) tonal type – for example, *Non si levava ancor l'alba novella* (Second Book, 1590) and «*Rimanti in pace*», *a la dolente e bella* (Third Book, 1592; compare also *La giovinetta pianta* here) – have a much clearer g/G focus.

[23] The cadence (with suspension) to A in bars 53-54 is 'fled' by the voice-leading; the one to G in bars 61-62 is 'fled' by an overlapping entry (in the tenor).

provided by the two statements of «O imagini belle» (cadence on C; new beginning on F). III is unexceptional by most standards; and VII may or may not be irregular depending on which theorist one chooses to read for analysing Monteverdi (the notion that Monteverdi is instead relying on psalm-tone cadential formulae – while attractive given the resonances of the *falsobordone* opening – is as yet unprovable). But whatever the case, the curious cadential articulations (or lack thereof) seem to enhance the modal inspecificity of the piece. Of course, the opening could not be clearer: a splendid unfolding (in the *canto*) of an octave descent from *d''* to *d'* divided at the fifth (*a'*) – this is surely an authentic rather than plagal mode, whatever that mode might be. What seems to cause the problems is the disruption – textual (and therefore – if I may be permitted the convention – musical) – of the lover's direct speech («O imagini belle»): this is where we seem to lose a sense of large-scale direction. The fact that the second statement of «O imagini belle» starts in F but moves resolutely back to D also seems symptomatic of a broader problem that has both structural and expressive implications.

Ex. 4 - Monteverdi, *Sfogava con le stelle*, bars 2-5, 45-47

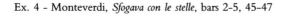

The modal inspecificity of *Sfogava con le stelle* may be related to the various modal inspecificities in the poem itself, which is not, it must be said, a masterpiece of design and expression. But Monteverdi's 'failure' to provide crystal-clear articulations of A and G has further ramifications. For one, it makes it rather difficult to produce a neat Schenkerian graph of this setting ($\hat{5}$ and $\hat{4}$ are never properly established, and a descent from $\hat{3}$ creates problems with the obligatory register), at least in terms of larger-scale middle- and background descents (even if individual sections are clearly structured). This may or may not be a cause for celebration depending on one's point of view on recent attempts to apply Schenkerian concepts and techniques to this repertory. But regardless of individual preferences – or prejudices –

the fact that Schenkerian methods 'work' straightforwardly for a good number of settings in the Fourth Book [24] but less so here suggests that there is indeed something different about *Sfogava con le stelle*, however we might choose to articulate that difference. The emphasis seems less on large-scale structural descents (for all their significance elsewhere in the book) than on contrasts of texture and tessitura, issues that have scarcely received their due in current analysis of this music. A clue seems offered by the wide ambitus of the piece as a whole (stretching a sixteenth from $F$ to $g''$). Monteverdi also appears to latch on to particular chords in particular spacings (Ex. 5): the striking 'D minor' of the opening, the 'D minor' triad in close spacing at «Sotto notturno ciel» (bar 6; echoed in bars 11 and 45) and the final chord (with a major third); the 'F major' triad at bar 21 (compare the same spacing in bars 36 – minus the tenor – and 55). He also seems to give these chords particular affective or narrative characterizations: note the association of the F sonority with the «imagini belle» (bar 21) which will show to the beloved the lover's ardour (bar 36) – when the lover refers to himself, D sonorities prevail – and which forms the final focus of the lover's plea («La fareste...»: three statements on D, G and F). All this may well suggest that texture and sonority could often be as important as cadences and descents for Monteverdi's structural articulations. Add to that the expansion of the texture at the first statement of «O imagini belle» and Monteverdi's choice of clefs perhaps becomes clearer. The *chiavi naturali* seem designed at least in part to avoid Monteverdi's remarkable and resonant sonorities being distorted by the downward transposition that could at least potentially be applied to pieces in *chiavette*.

The notion that *Sfogava con le stelle* focuses on Monteverdi's acute sense of texture, tessitura and sonority – for all the seeming limitations of the five-voice madrigal – opens up new areas in analysis that have broader ramifications for all his music. In part, this seems to result from the 'mixed' narrative mode of the piece, as the composer attempts to establish distinct tonal areas for the different 'functions' within the poem (for example, the shift from narration to 'direct' speech). But as in most of Monteverdi's madrigals, there remains the question of the speaking – and gendered – 'voice'. The 'mixed mode' madrigal (in the sense of al-

---

[24] I have proved the point, I hope (and with significant contemporary ramifications), in *'An Air New and Grateful to the Ear'* cit.

Ex. 5 - (a) Monteverdi, *Sfogava con le stelle*, bars 1, 6-7, 11, 45, 71;
        (b) bars 21, 36, 55

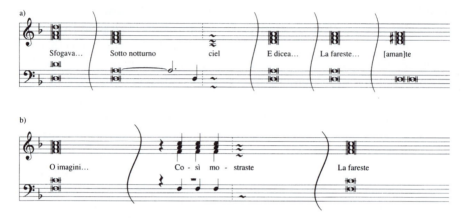

ternating narrative and 'direct speech') is of course standard within the repertory: witness the large number of pieces (particularly – and curiously enough – in Monteverdi) that comprise a narrative opening leading to a crucial «disse» («he [she] said») signalling a structural, conceptual and perceptual shift in the poem and therefore the music. In terms of the conventions of the genre, there is no difficulty in having five (four, three, two) voices 'speak' as or for one: it is this convention that permits – at least in theory – the easy transfer of the *Lamento d'Arianna* from one to five voices with little apparent conceptual dissonance. But how that speech is set apart from the non-speech portions of a given poem (by tonality, texture, pacing) remains a matter for individual exploration both within a composer's output and within a given work.

The 'speaker' in *Sfogava con le stelle* is «un'infermo d'amore» – one sick with love – to correct the famous misreading perpetuated by Malipiero («un'inferno d'amore», which is, incidentally, a more Marinist conceit). Like many misreadings, it is hard to not invest this one with significance, especially given its implications for the gender of the speaker in *Sfogava con le stelle*. For example, Suzanne Cusick's recent discussion of the gendering of Monteverdi's 'modern music' – via an analysis both of terms used in the Artusi-Monteverdi controversy and of two madrigals at its heart, *Cruda Amarilli, che col nome ancora* and *O Mirtillo, Mirtill'anima mia* – has focused on the problems posed by the perceived feminization of the *seconda prattica* style (which Artusi thus seeks to attack). «Further, with the domestic metaphor of *padrona-serva* as the best available defense for musical ingenuity, musical power needed constantly to be understood as a response to – and as controlled by – the composer's (masculine) intention. Thus, a man operating as a composer within this system of metaphors must make himself understood as manly and in control; a woman must be either masculinized or invisible, for her femaleness would break down the metaphor's only defense against the charge of womanish insubordination and irrationality in the modern musical style».[25] In our reconstructions of Monteverdi, we ourselves (for our own vested interests) take the game still further: «we position ourselves and music itself away from the submissive, feminized role that both Monteverdis believed it to play in the style then called modern. Instinctively, we seek to correct the Monteverdis' rhetorical lapse by ourselves re-gendering early modern music».[26] In the case of *Sfogava con le stelle*, however, the «re-gendering» of the piece is achieved not by some ideological manipulation on the part of modern criticism but by the simple correction of a mistake: it is clear that Monteverdi's setting was originally, and unambiguously, gendered.

The gender of the speaking voice in sixteenth-century madrigal texts – with the obvious exception of dialogues – often appears ambiguous (this is itself a result of a gendered language: «l'anima mia», say, can refer to either my female or my male lover), and often when a clear gender is implied (for example, by gendered pronouns) it is underplayed. Moreover, in his Mantuan madrigals Monteverdi is often reluctant (with only a few exceptions) to allocate gendered speech to appropriately gendered voices (soprano and alto for 'female' roles; tenor and bass for 'male' ones). This is what doubtless enhances – then as now – the universality of Monteverdi's musical and emotional world, a world that essentially hinges on the metaphorical nature of madrigalian discourse. This discourse focuses on modes of resemblance – of a particular relationship between art and life – that encourage 'literal' word-painting on the one hand, and on the other (not entirely paradoxically) permit a breaking of the canons of verisimilitude (five voices as one lover). However, new relationships between performers and listeners, the emphasis on solo song, new dramatic (indeed operatic) impulses in music over the 1600s,

---

[25] CUSICK, *Gendering Modern Music* cit., p. 24.
[26] *Ivi*, p. 25.

and a crucial shift from notions of resemblance to notions of representation (witness the *stile rappresentativo*), force distinct changes. Increasingly, madrigalian word-painting becomes a less prominent feature of a music which instead invokes affective codes whose significance is created more by convention (for example, the triple-time 'lament') than by any sense of literal mimesis. Similarly (and as a result), there is a tendency towards more structural, and structured, approaches to a given musical setting. But at the same time, canons of verisimilitude become increasingly enforced as regards the characterization of the speaking/singing voice (female as female, and male as male). This double sense of representation – invoking both a sense of distance through convention-generated affective codes and structural alienation, and one of closeness by the 'realism' of the representing voice – establishes the delicate ambiguities that thereafter play so powerfully through the Western art tradition.

But the period of change – precisely that of Monteverdi's own career – is one fraught with its own ambiguities, as new roles and role-models had to be found both for music and for those who brought it to life: Susan McClary has already made the point in connection with the gendering of music in *Orfeo*.[27] For example, the new canons of verisimilitude of the *stile rappresentativo* – and the questions of gender that emerge as a result – clearly created problems for the conventional five-voice madrigal with its no less conventional modes of metaphorical discourse. Not for nothing did the Florentine theorist, Giovan Battista Doni (followed by most modern critics), feel uncomfortable with the polyphonic version of the *Lamento d'Arianna* – for all that it fits squarely into the madrigalian tradition of (female) laments for five voices – in the light of the more properly representative (at least in one of my two senses of the term) solo-voice version.[28] And *Sfogava con le stelle* was very quickly depersonalized and de-gendered: the «inferno d'amore» (mis)reading first appears in the reprint of Monteverdi's Fourth Book issued by Ricciardo Amadino in 1611 and was fairly consistently adopted in reprints thereafter.[29]

---

[27] S. McClary, *Constructions of Gender in Monteverdi's Dramatic Music*, «Cambridge Opera Journal», I, 1989, pp. 203-223, also in Ead., *Feminine Endings: Music, Gender, and Sexuality*, Minnesota & London, University of Minnesota Press, 1991, pp. 35-52.

[28] For Doni's dismissive treatment of the polyphonic version of the *Lamento d'Arianna*, see P. Fabbri, *Monteverdi*, Torino, EDT, 1985, p. 193.

[29] For example, in the *cantus* and *bassus* of Amadino's 1615 reprint and in the reprints of 1615 (Antwerp, Pierre Phalèse), 1622 (Venezia, Bartolomeo Magni) and 1644 (Antwerp, Heirs of Pierre Phalèse); see the critical commentary on the poetic texts of the

One can get a further sense of the issues raised by new structural and expressive strategies – and Monteverdi's various attempts to manage them – in two settings in Monteverdi's *Concerto: settimo libro de madrigali* (1619) that both seem (deliberately?) to hark back to *Sfogava con le stelle*. The text of the duet (for two tenors) *Non vedrò mai le stelle* adopts a similar tactic, with an opening statement («Non vedrò mai le stelle / de' bei celesti giri...») leading to an invocation to the beloved's eyes («O luci belle / deh siate sì rubelle...»). The opening statement involves both voices moving in the contrapuntally enlivened homophony typical of Monteverdi's emerging duet style. The invocation, however, is set for solo voice: a harmonic disjunction (a major triad on E to one on C) emphasizes the modal shift (Ex. 6).

Ex. 6 - Monteverdi, *Non vedrò mai le stelle* (*Concerto: settimo libro de madrigali*, 1619), bars 20-29

The solo line is somewhat reminiscent of the soprano line at «O imagini belle» in *Sfogava con le stelle*, but for all its lyricism it lacks force when deprived of the rich double counterpoint: it is significant that Monteverdi soon shifts to the technique that in the new style arguably takes the expressive place of counterpoint, affective triple-time writing. Still more revealing is the four-voice setting

---

Fourth Book (by Gian Paolo Caprettini) in MONTEVERDI, *Madrigali a 5 voci: Libro quarto* cit., p. 62. Malipiero's perpetuation of this misreading presumably reflects his relying on one of these editions. However, it has certainly had a powerful influence on the literature: Wiley Hitchcock similarly 'misreads' (silently corrects?) the text in his edition of Caccini's *Sfogava con le stelle* in *Le nuove musiche*.

of Tasso's *Al lume delle stelle*, a poem that seems to have been a model for *Sfogava con le stelle*. Here contrapuntal writing is used for the opening narration as richly evocative scene-painting («Al lume delle stelle / Tirsi sott'un alloro / si dolea lagrimando»), but at the shift to 'direct speech' («O celesti facelle / di lei ch'amo e adoro») Monteverdi is again forced to make the point by writing for the tenor alone (if soon adding the bass) so as to represent the male 'speaker' (Tirsi) invoking the stars (Ex. 7). Again, a harmonic disjunction (a major triad on A to one on C) also marks the new section, which – as with *Non vedrò mai le stelle* – can no longer flow seamlessly from the preceding texture (compare Ex. 3). The composer's decision here – in the context of a four-voice setting – has further ramifications: Monteverdi needs to add two extra lines to Tasso's madrigal («Luci care e serene / sento gli affanni, ohimè, sento le pene») so as to give the soprano and alto their chance to shine before concluding the setting with all four voices.

Ex. 7 - Monteverdi, *Al lume delle stelle* (*Concerto: settimo libro de madrigali*, 1619), bars 27-38

The impact of the *stile rappresentativo* on contemporary secular genres relying on older modes of signification – and the fact that it created as many problems as it seemingly solved – clearly merits further exploration. But in the case of *Sfogava con le stelle*, the male lover's invocation to the stars, for all its musical power, seems singularly ineffectual. Even though his threefold plea («La fareste...») moves from the selfishly personal (the first 'D minor' statement) towards meeting the stars on what has been defined as their own tonal terms (the third 'F major' statement), it is a hollow gesture: the madrigal (both text and music) lapses into bathos, even banality, with the final D cadence. The attempted firmness of the ending (note the pedals) rings false, precisely because of the clear lack of structural direction to closure in the setting as a whole. It is hard to conceive the piece – and the (musical and emotional) issues it raises – actually ending here. But the next madrigal in the Fourth Book, *Volgea l'anima mia soavemente* (the text is by Guarini), is an entirely different case: it adopts a familiar tonal type (C1-♭-g) – the opening provides a 'tonic' for the D major triad at the end of *Sfogava con le stelle* – with clear structural descents and a well-formed progression to the final cadence. However, this madrigal also bears a number of similarities to *Sfogava con le stelle* in terms of texture, tessitura and motive. And as for the text, one cannot think of a better case of wish-fulfilment: in *Volgea l'anima mia soavemente*, the compliant – nay «pietosa» – beloved says precisely what the lover wishes her to say, and indeed wished for the stars to make her say. The effect in both expressive and structural terms is rendered all the more striking by the clear musical echoes of *Sfogava con le stelle*. One passage seems particularly significant (Ex. 8). The idea used in *Sfogava con le stelle* for the full statement of lines 4–5 («O imagini belle / dell'idol mio ch'adoro») is echoed in the second madrigal at «Mi rispos'ella in un sospir d'amore». In the former, a seemingly purposeful opening («O imagini belle», on F) dissolves as the lover hopelessly returns to the D (8?) of the opening (the 'hanging' $g''$ – so different from the $g''$ in 17–18 – is also significant). At «Mi rispos'ella», however, the harmonic direction is clear (a circle of fifths through D-g-(C)-F-B♭-E♭; omitting the C may be significant given its own resonances from *Sfogava con le stelle*), and the music moves strongly to a cadence on B♭ (thus 4̂–3̂). Even the key-word here, «amore», seems set more purposefully compared with the flaccid *la-fa-la* motion in *Sfogava con le stelle* (compare Ex. 4). It is but a small step to suggest that *Volgea l'anima mia soavemente* provides some kind of conceptual and musical resolution to *Sfogava con le stelle*, whose textual and mu-

Ex. 8 - (a) Monteverdi, *Sfogava con le stelle*, bars 21-25;
(b) Monteverdi, *Volgea l'anima mia soavemente* (*Il quarto libro de madrigali a cinque voci*, 1603), bars 69-73

a)

b)

sical meaning, in turn, is significantly enhanced by its place in the broader context of the book.

I am not the first to suggest that Monteverdi's madrigal books might be regarded as more than just a willy-nilly agglomeration of individual madrigals: indeed madrigals divided into two or more *parti* already provide one model, and the *Pastor fido* cycles in the Fifth Book have always been regarded as a special case. But few seem to have broached in any depth the various sequencing devices available to

168

Monteverdi and his editors and/or printers (cleffing, mode, scoring, textual association, emotional progression and doubtless more) that might help explain why – regardless of the (generally unknown) dates of composition of individual pieces – a given madrigal collection is ordered in a given way. This, in turn, invokes the broader narrative strategies embraced by the composer and required by the critic in giving an adequate account of this music. The stories told by Monteverdi, and thus to be re-told by modern scholars, are both rich and fertile: we have not yet reached their end.

# VIII

# Resemblance and Representation: Towards a New Aesthetic in the Music of Monteverdi

BY the mid-1620s, Claudio Monteverdi had been *maestro di cappella* of St Mark's, Venice, for over a decade. He was widely recognized as the leading composer in Italy, was head of a prestigious musical establishment, and was supported by gifted assistants who could carry the day-to-day burdens of administering, rehearsing, and directing music in the Basilica. As the composer entered middle age, his thoughts turned to more relaxing endeavours. There was still the unfinished business of the treatise he had (perhaps foolishly, he now felt) promised Artusi in his famous polemic with the Bolognese theorist in the early 1600s—we know that the treatise was still on his mind from two letters to Giovanni Battista Doni written in 1633–4[1]—but Artusi had died in the year Monteverdi moved to Venice (1613), and the composer claimed the satisfaction of seeing him reconciled with the modernist position.[2] For the moment, Monteverdi put all that aside in favour of a more

A first version of this essay was presented as a paper ('Monteverdi's *via naturale alla immitatione*: New Light on Opera and Song in Early Seventeenth-Century Italy') at the Conference on Seventeenth-Century Music, Washington University, St. Louis, Mo., in April 1993. It was then read by Susan McClary and Massimo Ossi. I am indeed grateful for their illuminating comments and criticisms which undoubtedly had their effect in various revisions, even if I have perhaps too stubbornly adhered to my original thesis.

---

[1] The letters to Doni of 22 Oct. 1633 and 2 Feb. 1634 are in *The Letters of Claudio Monteverdi*, trans. Denis Stevens (London and Boston: Faber & Faber, 1980), 406–16. According to the composer's eulogist, Matteo Caberloti, the composer was still working on the treatise at his death; see Paolo Fabbri, *Monteverdi* (Turin: EDT, 1985), 62.

[2] In his letter to Doni of 22 Oct. 1633; see *The Letters of Claudio Monteverdi*, trans. Stevens, 410: 'he calmed down in such a way that from thenceforward not only did he stop overruling me—turning his pen in my praise—but he began to like and admire me'. There may be a degree of wishful thinking here: we have no writings from Artusi directly praising the composer.

intriguing hobby, alchemy: five letters to the Mantuan court secretary Ercole Marigliani written between August 1625 and March 1626 (23 August and 19 September 1625, 15 and 24 February, and 28 March 1626)[3] suggest a lively exchange of ideas, materials, and equipment all the more surprising given that we have no other evidence of the composer being interested in much besides music.

This is not the place to discuss why Monteverdi should have gained so sudden an enthusiasm for his new hobby (nor, for that matter, where and how he learnt of it). But it is worth considering what benefits the composer might have drawn, however tangentially, from his pastime. For example, in the first of these five letters, Monteverdi discusses how to calcinate gold with lead (with a drawing of the necessary pot). Also:

> I must tell you how I shall be able to make mercury from unrefined matter which changes into clear water, and although it will be in water it will not however lose its identity as mercury, or its weight; because I have tested it by taking a drop, and have put it on a brass spoon and rubbed it, and it became all tinged with silver colour. From this purified water I shall hope to make something worthwhile, inasmuch as it is a powerful solvent of silver.[4]

The lesson is an interesting one. Something precious (*il mercurio*) can be made from something base (*del vulgo*), and it can look like something else (*acqua chiara*). Given its misleading appearance, some other test must be adopted for purposes of identification (*l'ho posta sopra un chuchiaro di ottone et fregatolo*). Nevertheless, Monteverdi's new cocktail has a powerful effect (*solve l'argento galiardamente*), suggesting that something useful might come of it.

Monteverdi's music is rich in examples of his making something precious from something base. But the question of appearances, however, is more intriguing. It was precisely in this decade that Monteverdi focused particular attention on the imitation of appearances in music, whether for serious (the *Combattimento di Tancredi et Clorinda* of 1624) or for comic (the unfinished *La finta pazza Licori* of 1627) effect. Such imitation, in turn, was predicated upon notions of (some might say, too literal) resemblance: witness the *concitato genere* or the dislocated succession of mimetic gestures that Monteverdi proposes to represent Licori's feigned madness.[5] Here a rather laboured concept

---

[3] Nos. 83, 84, 86, 87, and 89 in *The Letters of Claudio Monteverdi*, trans. Stevens.

[4] Ibid. 291. For the original, see *Claudio Monteverdi: Lettere, dediche e prefazioni*, ed. Domenico de' Paoli (Rome: De Santis, 1973), 222–4.

[5] It seems to me that there are distinct dangers in extrapolating from the well-known letters on the unfinished (uncomposed?) *La finta pazza Licori* (1627) evidence of a serious new aesthetic in Monteverdi's Venetian secular music, *pace* Gary Tomlinson, *Monteverdi and the End of the Renaissance* (Oxford: Clarendon Press, 1987), 204–5: it is, after all, a comedy. Moreover, all this needs grounding in 'mad scenes' on the contemporary stage (see below, ch. 8).

of verisimilitude—indeed, one easily open to ridicule—provided the touch-stone of what might be called a homologous approach to the *rappresentatione degli affetti* and consequently to emotional arousal: musical gestures should resemble as closely as possible the tenor of the words that they accompany, thereby facilitating and securing their action upon the senses. Of course, this was by no means a new idea—it provided the conceptual underpinning for much word-painting in, say, the Renaissance madrigal—and indeed it gives much of the music in which Monteverdi explores such an approach a some-what conservative air, for all its seeming adoption of modern elements. Not for nothing has this music received something of a bad press in the recent literature.

The importance of representation in early seventeenth-century musical endeavour goes without saying: witness the term *stile rappresentativo*, which could be, and was, applied widely to monody or to polyphony, and to music for the theatre, chamber, and church.[6] Exactly what is represented in the *stile rappresentativo* (the emotions, the text, the act of representation itself?) is open to debate. But one can usefully ask whether representation is best achieved by such resemblances or by some other means. Indeed, Monteverdi's little alchemical experiment suggests a different solution. His two substances (mercury and 'clear water') have no overt resemblance one to the other—their shared identity has to be discovered by experiment—and yet the visu-ally innocuous *acqua chiara* can have potent effects.

Today, the term *stile rappresentativo* is most often identified with the new music for the stage, which Giovanni Battista Doni called the 'stile detto recitativo'. He subdivided this style into three categories—'narrativo', 'recitativo' (or 'recitativo speciale'), and 'espressivo'. But for all his humanist enthusiasm for the recitative, Doni was somewhat less keen on its effects in the modern theatre, particularly the narrative style, which so often bored the listener due to its limited musical interest: at one point he suggested that such narrative recitative should be abandoned and replaced by speech de-livered over an instrumental accompaniment.[7] (Of course, Doni was by no means alone in objecting to 'the tedium of the recitative'.)[8] The expressive

---

[6] See my entry on 'Stile rappresentativo' in *The New Grove Dictionary of Opera*, ed. Stanley Sadie (London: Macmillan, 1992), iv. 543–4.

[7] For example, in Doni's *Discorso sesto sopra il recitare in scena*, published in his *Annotazioni sopra il Compendio de' generi e de' modi della musica* (Rome: Fei, 1640), transcribed in Claudio Gallico, 'Discorso di G. B. Doni sul recitare in scena', *Rivista italiana di musicologia*, 3 (1968), 286–302 at 295–6. Doni goes on to discuss the problem of mediating between speech and song.

[8] See Carolyn Gianturco, 'Nuove considerazioni su *il tedio del recitativo* delle prime opere romane', *Rivista italiana di musicologia*, 17 (1982), 212–39; Tim Carter, 'Non occorre nominare tanti musici: Private Patronage and Public Ceremony in Late Sixteenth-Century Florence', *I Tatti Studies: Essays in the Renaissance*, 4 (1991), 89–104.

style was somewhat more powerful—Doni cited Monteverdi's celebrated
*Lamento d'Arianna* in support (although much of its power, he said, was due
to the poet, Ottavio Rinuccini), not least for being 'more than the others
delightful, adorned and rich in varied intervals, which the stage requires both
to avoid tedium and engender greater delight in the listeners, and to be able
to express better all those diverse affects which underpin this type of poetry
and musical imitation'.[9] But Doni's preferences reveal a serious problem in
his conception (and in fact, most conceptions) of the ideal music for the
theatre. What happens when the need for delight and variety supersedes the
no less important need for verisimilitude on the dramatic stage?

Doni cites Plutarch in support of a style of theatre music that was 'variata
e artifiziosa', and in so doing he invokes a surprising model. He says that the
Florentine inventors of opera made a serious error in assuming

> that madrigalian music (which is today the most esteemed and artful) is worth
> little in producing those effects which one reads of ancient [music], and they
> persuaded themselves that this occurred because it was too *arioso* and scarcely
> similar to common speech, and not because of other, truer reasons, that is,
> because of the brevity of the verses, the frequent repetitions, and chiefly of
> the interweaving of so many airs together instead of forming one only, with
> the most beautiful flow of melody possible; and in having different words sung
> together, with great loss to the understanding, as well as the harm caused
> by the affected artifices of direct and retrograde fugues, and the excessive
> sprinkling of such lengthy and incessant passagework.[10]

---

[9] Doni, *Trattato della musica scenica* (1633–5), cited in Maurizio Padoan, 'Nature and
Artifice in G. B. Doni's Thought', *International Review of the Aesthetics and Sociology of Music*,
23 (1992), 5–26 at 17: 'più degli altri vago, e adorno, e ricco di variati intervalli, i quali
richiede la Scena sì per evitare il tedio, e recare maggior diletto agli uditori, come per poter
meglio esprimere tutti quei diversi affetti, che soggiaciono a questa sorte di Poesia, e Musicale
imitazione'. For Doni and Rinuccini, see Gary Tomlinson, 'Madrigal, Monody, and Monteverdi's "via naturale alla immitatione"', *Journal of the American Musicological Society*, 34 (1981),
60–108 at 86. Tomlinson is tempted 'to trust Doni's emphasis on Rinuccini's role in the
creation of *L'Arianna*' (ibid. 87), although it was doubtless coloured both by a dim view of
composers' intellectual abilities (even Monteverdi's; see Fabbri, *Monteverdi*, 292–3) and by a
degree of Florentine chauvinism.
[10] Doni, *Discorso sesto sopra il recitare in scena*, in Gallico, 'Discorso di G. B. Doni sul
recitare in scena', 294: 'che la musica Madrigalesca (ch'è oggi la più stimata e artifiziosa) poco
vale in produrre quegli effetti che dell'antica si leggono: onde si persuasero che ciò avvenisse
per essere troppo ariosa, e poco simile alla favella comune, e non da altre più vere ragioni:
cioè dalla brevità de' versi; da tante ripetizioni; e principalmente dall'intessere più arie insieme,
in vece di formarne una sola, con quel più bel procedere di melodia che si può; e nel far
cantare insieme parole diverse, con molta perdita dell'intelligenza; oltre il danno che recano
gl'affettati artifizii di fughe dritte e rovesce ecc., e i soverchi condimenti di passaggi tanto
lunghi e frequenti'.

But in fact

> experience shows us that to move the affects, this *arioso* music similar to madrigals (especially when it touches the notes of various modes) is much more effective than that simple and scarcely varied music which for the greater part is heard in the recitative. Whenceforth, just as I judge that the former should be perfected and applied to those parts of dramas that are appropriate, so do I believe that that other [style] which takes the place of real speech is to be spurned.[11]

Considering the arguments against the madrigal style that had formed so crucial a context for early opera and solo song in Florence, Doni's present argument marks a striking volte-face, however necessary it might have been in the changing musical climate of the 1620s and 1630s.

Doni's preference for a 'musica ariosa e simile a i Madrigali' did not necessarily extend to polyphonic madrigals—he made the usual criticism that counterpoint obscured the words—or to the *ariette* with which some composers were filling their stage music.[12] But he clearly wanted something more structured and more varied than the declamatory recitative that had played so great a part in early opera. So too, it seems, did a number of composers in the early seventeenth century. For example, Giulio Caccini and his successors had laid down important parameters for the solo song, consisting of declamatory solo madrigals on the one hand, and on the other, the 'canzonetta à uso di aria per poter usare in conserto di più strumenti di corde' (to use Caccini's own curious terminology for the strophic dance-songs that became characteristic of contemporary arias).[13] But these distinctions were being modified significantly by the second decade of the century. Indeed, Caccini's own stylistic boundaries were not always so clear-cut: his madrigals, while sometimes owing a debt to contemporary operatic recitative, often invoked more structured (and more melodic) *arioso* writing; and some of his arias could be only loosely strophic in any musical sense of the term, adopting a number of stylistic traits of the solo madrigal. By the late

---

[11] Ibid.: 'l'esperienza ci mostra che per muovere gl'affetti questa musica ariosa e simile a i Madrigali (massime quando tocca corde di varii Tuoni) è molto più efficace di quella semplice e poco variata, che per la maggior parte si sente nel Recitativo. Laonde, quanto più stimo che si debba perfezionare questa, e applicarla a quelle parti de Drammi, che ne sono capaci, altrettanto credo che sia da disprezzare quell'altra, che tiene il luogo del vero parlare.'

[12] Doni, for example, took significant exception to Cavalieri's *Rappresentatione di Anima, et di Corpo* (1600) because of its 'ariette con molti artifizi di ripetizioni, echi e simili, che non hanno che fare niente con la buona e vera musica teatrale' (*Trattato della musica scenica*, in Angelo Solerti, *Le origini del melodramma* (Turin: Bocca, 1903; repr. Hildesheim: Olms, 1969), 208).

[13] The description comes from the preface to Caccini's *Le nuove musiche* (Florence: I Marescotti, 1601 [= 1602]), sig. B1r.

1610s, however, the influence seems to have been moving the other way, as aria styles (for example, structured triple- or duple-time writing) started to have a significant influence on contemporary madrigals. Such stylistic cross-overs also become apparent in the increasing number of solo songs and duets—whether formal arias or formal madrigals (and there is an increasing lack of musical distinction between the two)—which involve shifts in style between declamatory writing and more focused passages in aria style. Nigel Fortune has already discussed one key example, Sigismondo d'India's 'Torna il sereno Zefiro' published in his *Le musiche . . . Libro quinto* (Venice: Alessandro Vincenti, 1623),[14] and I have pointed out some others (for example, by Jacopo Peri).[15] However, two specific duets by Monteverdi are particularly useful in the present context, another 'Zefiro' piece published by Monteverdi in the 1632 *Scherzi musicali* (Venice: Bartolomeo Magni), 'Zefiro torna, e di soavi accenti', and 'O sia tranquillo il mare, o pien d'orgoglio', published in his *Madrigali guerrieri, et amorosi . . . Libro ottavo* of 1638 (Venice: Alessandro Vincenti).

The well-known 'Zefiro torna, e di soavi accenti' sets a sonnet by Ottavio Rinuccini:

> Zefiro torna, e di soavi accenti
>    l'aer fa grato e 'l pié discioglie a l'onde,
>    e mormorando tra le verdi fronde,
>    fa danzar al bel suon su 'l prato i fiori.
> Inghirlandato il crin Fillide e Clori
>    note tempran d'amor care e gioconde;
>    e da monti e da valli ime e profonde
>    raddoppian l'armonia gli antri canori.
> Sorge più vaga in ciel l'aurora, e 'l sole
>    sparge piú luci d'or; piú puro argento
>    fregia di Teti il bel ceruleo manto.
> Sol io, per selve abbandonate e sole,
>    l'ardor di due begli occhi e 'l mio tormento,
>    come vuol mia ventura, hor piango hor canto.

(Zephyrus returns, and with sweet accents | makes the air pleasing and loosens his foot from the waves, | and murmuring among the green branches, | he makes dance to his sound the flowers in the meadows. || Phyllis and Chloris, garlands on their brow, | temper their sweet and joyous notes of love; | and from the mountains and the valleys low and deep | sonorous caverns echo

---

[14] In Nigel Fortune, 'Italian Secular Monody from 1600–1635: An Introductory Survey', *Musical Quarterly*, 39 (1953), 171–95.

[15] See Tim Carter, *Music in Late Renaissance and Early Baroque Italy* (London: Batsford, 1992), 250–1.

their harmony. || Dawn rises more lovely in the heavens, | and the sun spreads forth more rays of gold; | [while] purer silver adorns Thetis' fair cerulean mantle. || Only I, [wandering] through abandoned, lonely woods, | the brightness of two lovely eyes and my torment, | as my fortune wills it, now I weep, now I sing.)

Rinuccini's poem is a close imitation of Petrarch's sonnet 'Zefiro torna e 'l bel tempo rimena' (no. 310 in the *Canzoniere*)—set by Monteverdi in his Sixth Book of 1614—and there are also echoes of the nature imagery of Tasso (compare the *ottava rima* 'Vezzosi augelli infra le verdi fronde' from *Gerusalemme liberata*, XVI. 12, a popular text for sixteenth-century madrigalists); indeed, the resonances are clear enough to permit some syntactic obscurity in the present verse. The poem seems ready-made for musical setting, even if Monteverdi felt it necessary to clinch the point by changing the first *parola rima* (Rinuccini's first line is 'Zefiro torna, e di soavi odori', rhyming with 'fiori', 'Clori' and 'canori'). The composer's new 'accenti' prompts a setting for the most part over the syncopated *ciaccona* bass pattern in a jaunty triple time.[16] Nor does he lose any opportunity to 'paint' the specific images of the text—the 'sweet accents' 'murmuring' through the branches, the flowers made to 'dance' to the wind, the 'sweet and joyous notes' of the nymphs, and the (high) mountains, low valleys, and echoing caverns. But for the final tercet Monteverdi shifts to a dissonant madrigalian style, contrasting the joys of spring with the pains of the lover (Ex. 6.1): triple time returns only at the end as the poet counterpoints weeping and singing, the reference to 'canto' providing the final justification for the use of the two gestures that most obviously invoked 'song' in the early seventeenth century, triple-time writing and (in the final cadence) ornamental roulades. Thus Monteverdi's 'Zefiro torna' conventionally plays off aria styles (for the delights of spring) against 'recitative' (for the grieving lover). He also resorts to the literal mimetic gestures so redolent of sixteenth-century word-painting, and so criticized by some Monteverdi scholars in the composer's Venetian secular music. It is not entirely clear whether this is done seriously or in jest (the duet is, after all, one of a group of *scherzi musicali*, 'musical trifles'),[17] and whether we

[16] The technique is discussed in Massimo Ossi, '*L'armonia raddoppiata*: On Claudio Monteverdi's *Zefiro torna*, Heinrich Schütz's *Es steh Gott auf*, and Other Early Seventeenth-Century *Ciaccone*', *Studi musicali*, 17 (1988), 225–53.

[17] Massimo Ossi makes the point (private communication) that perhaps one should not be misled by the title (whose?) of the 1632 collection, *Scherzi musicali* (and the term 'scherzo' is notoriously difficult to translate), which is followed by an explicative subtitle, 'Cioè Arie, & Madrigali in stil recitativo, con una Ciaccona A 1. & 2. voci' ('that is, Arias, and Madrigals in recitative style, with a *Ciaccona*[,] for one and two voices'). Also, the last piece of the 1632 *Scherzi musicali*, 'Armato il cor d'adamantina fede', was later published in Monteverdi's *Madrigali guerrieri, et amorosi . . . Libro ottavo* (1638), and for that matter, both 'Zefiro torna, e di soavi

Ex. 6.1. Monteverdi, 'Zefiro torna, e di soavi accenti'

(. . . fair cerulean mantle. Only I, [wandering] through abandoned, lonely woods, the brightness . . .)

should be amused or moved (or both). But for all its modern medium (a duet), style (dancing triple time), and technique (the ground bass), this seems an essentially old-fashioned piece evoking, like Rinuccini's resonant sonnet, a past emotional world.

'O sia tranquillo il mare, o pien d'orgoglio' also plays off madrigalian 'recitative' against triple-time 'aria', but to very different effect. Again, the text is a sonnet (the poet is unknown):

> O sia tranquillo il mare, o pien d'orgoglio,
>   mai da quest'onde io non rivolgo il piede;
>   io qui t'aspetto, e qui de la tua fede,
>   tradito amante, mi lamento e doglio.
> Spesso salir su queste rupi io soglio
>   per veder se il tuo legno ancor se 'n riede.
>   Quivi m'assido e piango, onde mi crede
>   il mar un fonte, e 'l navigante un scoglio.
> E spesso ancor t'invio per messaggieri,
>   a ridir la mia pena e 'l mio tormento,
>   dell'aria vaga i zeffiri leggieri.

accenti' and 'Armato il cor d'adamantina fede' appeared in the posthumous *Madrigali e canzonette . . . Libro nono* (Venice: Alessandro Vincenti, 1651). But the same piece can, perhaps should, be 'read' differently in different contexts. It seems to me, too, that we have yet to reach an adequate sense of genres and their likely influence on critical interpretation for this period.

Ma tu non torni, o Filli, e 'l mio lamento
l'aura disperge; e tal mercè ne speri
chi fida a donna il cor e i prieghi al vento.

(Whether the sea is calm or haughty, | I never turn away from the waves;
| here I await you, and here I, | a betrayed lover, lament your ill faith. ||
Often I climb these cliffs | to see whether your ship returns. | Here I sit
and weep, so the sea believes me | a fountain, and the sailor a rock. || And
often I send you as messengers | to tell of my pain and torment | the light
breezes of the air. || But, o Phyllis, you do not return, and my lament | is
scattered by the air; such is the reward | of him who entrusts his heart to
women and his prayers to the wind.)

Here we have another representation of the pains of an abandoned lover,
but now things seem more serious: the piece is one of a set of *madrigali
amorosi*, not *scherzi musicali*. Moreover, the text lacks the binary oppositions
(for example, happy nature/sad lover) characteristic at various levels of
Rinuccini's pastoral verse. As a result, Monteverdi seeks a different motivation for the equivalent binary oppositions available to him in musical terms.
The first two-thirds of Monteverdi's setting is in a conventional madrigalian/
recitative style, but at line 12—'Ma tu non torni, o Filli'—the composer
devotes some fifty bars of expansive triple-time writing for the most part to
just half a line of verse (Ex. 6.2), returning to 'recitative' for the final ironic
epigram. In contrast to 'Zefiro torna, e di soavi accenti', the use here of
triple time—and the shift between 'recitative' and 'aria'—certainly does not
seem motivated by any desire for literal word-painting or pictorial madrigalism.
Moreover, it gives the text a musical weight seemingly disproportionate to
its role in the sonnet as a whole, a weight further emphasized by the function of this triple-time section in initiating the large-scale structural octave
descent of the piece. The long first section is an effective prolongation of
$d'$ ($\hat{8}$), the upper final of the modal octave reinforced by the main cadences
(and no less significantly, by the arrival of the two voices on a unison): this
explains its static feel. The triple-time section begins with a striking harmonic shift to F, then C, the C cadence providing support for $c'$ ($\hat{7}$) in the
voices (again emphasized by a unison) that is effectively prolonged for the
bulk of the section until the conclusion on a major triad on E, supporting
$b$ ($\hat{6}$). The remainder of the structural descent ($a$–$d$ = $\hat{5}$–$\hat{1}$) is passed over
quickly in the final lines, as the poet realizes the consequences of his
situation. I have argued elsewhere that this use of aria styles to provide a
rhetorical and emotional climax to a given setting marks a significant shift
in early seventeenth-century musical aesthetics, and obviously one with

Ex. 6.2. Monteverdi, 'O sia tranquillo il mare'

(. . . the light breezes of the air. But, o Phyllis, you do not return . . .)

significant resonances for the later Baroque period.[18] It also recovers the ground for music as music, rather than as some spurious form of speech. In this case, one interpretation of the result is that it transcends the text to produce a palpably real representation of grief.

Monteverdi well knew that dance-derived aria styles articulated the relationship between the triumvirate of *oratione*, *harmonia*, and rhythm that together made up *melodia* (the whole art of composition) in ways very different from the formula proclaimed as the credo of the *seconda prattica* in the 1600s (the oration as mistress, not servant, of the harmony). In a letter to Alessandro Striggio of 21 November 1615 Monteverdi discusses the recent commission

[18] Carter, *Music in Late Renaissance and Early Baroque Italy*, 253. Most recently, I have discussed the issues in '*Possente spirto*: On Taming the Power of Music', *Early Music*, 21 (1993), 517–23.

arrived from Mantua for a *ballo* in music. When Duke Vincenzo I Gonzaga used to commission such works in six, eight, or nine *mutanze*, Monteverdi says, he

> used to give me some account of the invention, and I used to try to fit to it both the harmony and the metres [*tempi*] that I knew to be most appropriate and similar.

The present commission, however, lacked any such detail, so the composer had come up with a *ballo* of six *mutanze* (a version of *Tirsi e Clori*, later published in the Seventh Book of madrigals of 1619). He also tells Striggio that:

> if His Most Serene Highness should want either a change of air in this [*ballo*], or additions to the enclosed [movements] of a slow and grave nature, or fuller and without fugues (His Most Serene Highness taking no notice of the present words which can easily be changed, though at least these words help by the nature of their metre and by imitating the melody [*canto*]), or if he should want everything altered I beg you to act on my behalf so that His Most Serene Highness might reword the commission . . .[19]

The notion that the present words 'can easily be changed'—although their metre is appropriate and they imitate the melody—is striking in the context of Monteverdi's earlier protestations over the *seconda prattica*. Of course, this is dance music—so the requirements are different—but Monteverdi's statement is easily applicable to many arias of the early (and for that matter, later) seventeenth century. The relative unimportance of the individual words of canzonetta texts and the dominance of metre and stereotyped subjects perhaps inspired a more compatible and less competitive relationship between poetry and music. The issues go beyond simple matters of genre to raise profound questions concerning the status of musical expression as the Baroque period came into its own.

In 'O sia tranquillo il mare', one textual (as opposed to affective) cue for the shift to triple time seems provided retrospectively in the poem by the reference to 'my lament' scattered by the air (and 'e 'l mio lamento' actually appears in the triple-time section).[20] But this is no tragic lament in the grand manner of the *Lamento d'Arianna* and its numerous imitations: even if the

[19] My translation differs slightly from the one in *The Letters of Claudio Monteverdi*, trans. Stevens, 107–8.

[20] I am grateful to Silke Leopold for suggesting (private discussion) that one common textual cue for triple time would seem to be notions of 'return' (as here: 'Ma tu non torni . . .'), and it is certainly true that 'tornare' and its derivatives can often be found in Monteverdi's and other's triple-time music, or is somehow present by implication (for example, in a nostalgic evocation of past pleasures). The whole issue seems to require fuller, and systematic, exploration.

apparent situations are similar—Ariadne, too, was left abandoned on a rocky beach—the laments of shepherds and their nymphs are cast in a more discrete vein. But they are no less impassioned, and the affective musical codes are equally clear. 'O sia tranquillo il mare' is one of the *canti amorosi* in Monteverdi's Eighth Book, and as in many of its counterparts, triple-time writing becomes one trait of the *molle* ('soft' or 'tender') *genere* that in the preface to the *Madrigali guerrieri, et amorosi* Monteverdi contrasts with the *temperato* and the *concitato*. The first madrigal in the Eighth Book further emphasizes the point: 'Altri canti d'Amor, tenero arciero', 'Let others sing of Love, the tender archer'. This begins in a sensuous triple time, and the descending tetrachord (*d'–c'–bb'–a*) implied in the bass through the opening turns into a true ground bass at the second line, 'i dolci vezzi, e sospirati baci' ('the sweet charms and sighed-for kisses'; Ex. 6.3)—here, it seems, less an 'emblem of lament' than of that which so often gives rise to lament.[21] As numerous passages in Monteverdi's late madrigals and operas make clear, the triple-time aria is the musical language of love.[22]

The processes whereby particular kinds of triple-time writing come to signify 'love' in early seventeenth-century secular music have yet to be traced, although the poet Gabriello Chiabrera had already made the connection between the pleasures or pains of love and the poetry most frequently associated with triple-time in the period, the canzonetta (often in metres other than the seven- or eleven-syllable *versi piani* of contemporary madrigals).[23] But whatever the case, the semiotic works in ways very different from the traditional associations of signifier and signified: having a lamenting lover sing in triple time is scarcely a plausible mimetic gesture, nor for that matter a particularly verisimilar one. In the Renaissance, the relationship between signifier and signified had been straightforwardly conceived in terms of the elaborate chains of resemblance dominating the Renaissance worldview. In a cosmos saturated by webs of analogy, the place of any element was fixed within a hierarchy from macrocosm to microcosm by virtue of its resemblance to elements both higher and lower on the scale. Identities were thus forged by similarities (whether revealed or hidden) that allowed the

---

[21] Compare Ellen Rosand, 'The Descending Tetrachord: An Emblem of Lament', *Musical Quarterly*, 55 (1979), 346–59.

[22] For example, see Tim Carter, '"In Love's harmonious consort"? Penelope and the Interpretation of *Il ritorno d'Ulisse in patria*', *Cambridge Opera Journal*, 5 (1993), 1–16.

[23] Gabriello Chiabrera's dialogue *Il Geri* of 1624–5 offers some useful suggestions; see most recently Robert R. Holzer, '"Sono d'altro garbo ... le canzonette che si cantano oggi": Pietro della Valle on Music and Modernity in the Seventeenth Century', *Studi musicali*, 21 (1992), 253–306. I have no doubt that the ideas presented in the present essay will eventually mesh with those suggested in Massimo Ossi, 'Claudio Monteverdi's *Ordine novo, bello et gustevole*: The Canzonetta as Dramatic Module and Formal Archetype', *Journal of the American Musicological Society*, 45 (1992), 261–304.

Ex. 6.3. Monteverdi, 'Altri canti d'Amor'

(. . . the tender archer, the sweet charms and sighed-for [kisses] . . .)

Renaissance to make sense of its world. Music reflected the harmony of the spheres; texts set to music were to be 'imitated' by musical homologues through word-painting; even the Florentine 'new music' sought validation on the grounds of resemblance (in this case, to oratorical speech), making it (in more than just the humanist sense) a profoundly 'Renaissance' genre.

The new modes of scientific endeavour and of philosophical thought in the seventeenth century encouraged an alternative construction of the relationship of signifier to signified as instead being one of difference, for all its possible grounding in similarity and identity: $x$ 'represents' $y$ but is (because it is?) different from $y$. The link was now forged less by resemblance—although that could still be an issue—than by conventions fostered by tradition or created by invention, establishing a code to be learned by and shared complicitly between producer and receiver. In contemporary terms, such notions of difference—and the emotional and other effects that such juxtapositions could produce—were intimately linked to the *concettismo* and *meraviglia* central to Marinist aesthetics. But they also had more far-reaching implications, for the increasingly autonomous sign also took on a life of its own, permitting an ever deeper exploration of its intrinsic nature and effects. As Foucault argues, the conceptual divorce of resemblance and representation was an intensely liberating experience: 'the sign . . . is charged no longer with the task of keeping the world close to itself and inherent in its own forms, but, on the contrary, with that of spreading it out, of juxtaposing it over an indefinitely open surface, and of taking up from that point the endless deployment of the substitutes in which we conceive of it'.[24] This, it seems to me, offers significant potential for viewing in a more positive light the aesthetic and other tendencies of the second, third, and fourth decades of the seventeenth century that have tended to receive so negative a press in recent years.[25]

The play of signs in Monteverdi's Venetian secular music—and for that matter, later music as well—can variously depend on both 'Renaissance' and 'Baroque' modes of signification. It should be clear from the above discussion that 'Zefiro torna, e di soavi accenti' seems to rely on the former, the composer perhaps being influenced by Rinuccini's echoes of older poets, not least Petrarch and Tasso. Of course, Tasso also inspired the development of the *stile concitato* in the *Combattimento di Tancredi et Clorinda* (based on an episode from *Gerusalemme liberata*). It is perhaps revealing that when

[24] Michel Foucault, *The Order of Things: An Archeology of the Human Sciences* (London: Tavistock Publications, 1970; repr. London: Routledge, 1989), 61. The original of this text, *Les Mots et les choses*, was published in 1966. I am not the first to use Foucault in this context: see, for example, Jeffrey Kurtzman, 'A Taxonomic and Affective Analysis of Monteverdi's "Hor che'l ciel e la terra"', *Music Analysis*, 12 (1993), 169–95; and note the comment on Tomlinson below, n. 28. I am indeed grateful to Professor Kurtzman for giving me a copy of his unpublished paper 'Monteverdi's Changing Aesthetics: A Semiotic Perspective' (presented at the Fifth Biennial Conference on Baroque Music, University of Durham, July 1992): we are moving on slightly different, if related, lines.

[25] For example, in Tomlinson's *Monteverdi and the End of the Renaissance*. I raised some of the issues in my review in *Early Music History*, 8 (1988), 245–60.

Monteverdi sought consciously to 'invent' a new *genere*—'In all the works of the former composers I have indeed found examples of the 'soft' [*molle*] and the 'moderate' [*temperato*], but never of the 'agitated' [*concitato*], a genus nevertheless described by Plato . . .'[26]—he adopted a conservative tack, using conventional mimetic gestures predicated upon their putative resemblance to the emotions being expressed (as Foucault says, 'keeping the world close to itself and inherent in its own forms'). The composer found it hard to play the intellectual, and the results ring false in an increasingly alien context (as many commentators on the *Combattimento* have claimed). But Monteverdi's musical instincts were much more assured. His exploration of the *molle genere* certainly seems to have been more intuitive, drawing on a wealth of experience (both from the work of 'former composers' and in his own output) in new conceptions and articulations of notions of representation, juxtaposing signs 'over an indefinitely open surface' with the possibility of an 'endless deployment' of new styles, sounds, and gestures.[27] Realizing such possibilities was, of course, the chief task of the years to come.

The fruits are apparent in 'O sia tranquillo il mare'. They are still more so in the most famous of the *canti amorosi* in Monteverdi's Eighth Book, the *Lamento della ninfa*.[28] Here a nymph laments her betrayal by her lover,

[26] From the preface to Monteverdi's *Madrigali guerrieri, et amorosi*, translated in Oliver Strunk, *Source Readings in Music History* (London: Faber, 1952), 413–15.

[27] Compare also Foucault, *The Order of Things*, 61–2: 'It had long been known—and well before Plato's *Cratylus*—that signs can be either given by nature or established by man. Nor was the sixteenth century ignorant of this fact, since it recognized human languages to be instituted signs. But the artificial signs owed their power only to their fidelity to natural signs. These latter, even at a remove, were the foundation of all others. From the seventeenth century, the values allotted to nature and convention in this field are inverted: if natural, a sign is no more than an element selected from the world of things and constituted as a sign by our knowledge. It is therefore strictly limited, rigid, inconvenient, and impossible for the mind to master. When, on the other hand, one establishes a conventional sign, it is always possible (and indeed necessary) to choose it in such a way that it will be simple, easy to remember, applicable to an indefinite number of elements, susceptible of subdivision within itself and of combination with other signs; the man-made sign is the sign at the peak of its activity. It is the man-made sign that draws the dividing-line between man and animal; that transforms imagination into voluntary memory, spontaneous attention into reflection, and instinct into rational knowledge.'

[28] See the discussion in Gary Tomlinson, *Music in Renaissance Magic: Toward a Historiography of Others* (Chicago and London: University of Chicago Press, 1993), 229–46, which I read after presenting my paper. Tomlinson's use of Foucault here is somewhat similar to mine— I am happy to acknowledge his precedence (along with Kurtzman's; see above, n. 24), and indeed his virtuosity—although we disagree on the extent to which Monteverdi 'lied— extravagantly, resonantly, and with rarely matched force—in the *Lament of the Nymph*' (ibid. 242). Tomlinson also praises 'Renaissance' notions of resemblance in Monteverdi's earlier madrigals (in particular, 'Sfogava con le stelle' from the Fourth Book of 1603) without acknowledging that (in my view) such notions underpin the mimetic gestures that he formerly criticized as anti-Renaissance in the Venetian music.

watched by three shepherds, who comment wryly on the situation. The opening narration exploits standard mimetic gestures (close imitation for the nymph trampling the flowers; a trenchant dissonance for her 'dolore'). But the nymph's complaint itself is set as the most sensuous triple-time aria over a descending tetrachord ground bass: here the focus is less on the words (which Monteverdi contorts freely) than on the raw power of the human voice, using melody, not the text, to achieve emotional representation and arousal. Again, one cannot imagine a greater contrast to that archetypal lament so lauded both by Monteverdi and in the literature, the *Lamento d'Arianna* of 1608. Yet both settings are avowedly in the *stile rappresentativo*, and both seek to represent the pains of love. In the *Lamento d'Arianna*, the success of the representation was to be judged by its adherence to Renaissance notions of verisimilitude, by its recognizable resemblance to heightened oratorical speech. However, the success and power of such new representations as the *Lamento della ninfa* must be judged not according to a Renaissance canon but instead by their immediate effect on the senses. Now the acid test is one of experiment and experience, whether rubbing 'clear water' on the back of a brass spoon or feeling ourselves moved to new heights by the power of a new kind of song.

The different world of the *Lamento della ninfa* may be conditioned not just by a new aesthetic but also by new constructions of gender.[29] The *molle genere* is itself explicitly gendered ('Io canto d'Amor'—'I sing of Love'—says the soprano in the counterpart to 'Altri canti d'amor, tenero arciero' in the *Madrigali guerrieri, et amorosi*, 'Altri canti di Marte e di sua schiera'); and there is some play to be made of the notion that 'old' modes of resemblance versus 'new' modes of representation can somehow carry 'masculine' and 'feminine' connotations. After all, the *Combattimento di Tancredi et Clorinda* is nothing if not a male show-piece, in several senses of the term; and the *Lamento della ninfa* offers a dramatic realization of different male (the shepherds) and female (the nymph) responses to emotional upheaval that in turn reifies the otherness of the lament, whether to signify madness (following Susan McClary) or (as I perhaps prefer) to emphasize the sense of distance newly required for true emotional expression. No less significant, however, is the question of genre: as with 'O sia tranquillo il mare' (and much of Monteverdi's other secular music) we are in the realms of the pastoral, where the problem of nature

---

[29] Compare, for example, the discussion of the *Lamento della ninfa* in Susan McClary, 'Excess and Frame: The Musical Representation of Madwomen', in ead., *Feminine Endings: Music, Gender, and Sexuality* (Minneapolis and Oxford: University of Minnesota Press, 1991), 80–111, although again I seem to be moving in a somewhat different direction. How my view meshes with Suzanne Cusick, 'Gendering Modern Music: Thoughts on the Monteverdi–Artusi Controversy', *Journal of the American Musicological Society*, 46 (1993), 1–25, is a matter for further study.

versus art comes to the fore. Pastoral conventionally extolled the virtues of nature, but any self-respecting pastoral poet knew full well that the artless 'nature' praised in verse conformed less to nature in 'real life' than to a nature modified and indeed improved by art: thus pastoral defined a space amenable to artistic experimentation of various kinds, and one of some significance for early Baroque endeavours in drama, poetry, and music. And Monteverdi must surely have realized that his 'via naturale alla immitatione' ('natural path to imitation')[30] was scarcely 'natural' in any realistic sense: his task, too, was to use art to improve upon nature. If that was not obvious enough in musical terms, it was clearly made apparent in alchemy, where art did indeed offer the possibility of creating things anew from the base substances of the real world.

Did Monteverdi learn some lessons from his little alchemical experiments? Perhaps we should not take them too seriously, for the composer ended his last letter on the subject (28 March 1626) on a whimsical note:

I am at present engaged in making a fire under a glass urinal with its cover on, to extract from it an I-don't-know-what and then make of it an I-don't-know-what so that (please God) I may then cheerfully explain this I-don't-know-what to my Lord Marigliani.[31]

One also wonders about the danger of taking Monteverdi's music a mite too seriously, ignoring the whimsy and fancy arguably at the heart of all musical entertainment in this (and perhaps any other) period. In other words, too intense a reading of, say, 'O sia tranquillo il mare' and the *Lamento della ninfa* might well be accused of gloriously missing the point: 'Ben, bene, tutto è zolfa, tutto è zolfa' ('Well, well, it's all sol-fa, it's all sol-fa'), Monteverdi would say benignly on looking over the feeble music of an aspiring pupil.[32] In the end, the composer left us in the dark, never completing the treatise to 'cheerfully explain this I-don't-know-what' that made his music work. But his delicate play of signs and his changing approaches to resemblance and representation were surely of profound significance for his time. They are also what challenge us most in his music today.

[30] The comment comes from Monteverdi's letter to Doni of 22 Oct. 1633; see *The Letters of Claudio Monteverdi*, trans. Stevens, 410; Tomlinson, 'Madrigal, Monody, and Monteverdi's "via naturale alla immitatione"'.
[31] My translation differs slightly from the one in *The Letters of Claudio Monteverdi*, trans. Stevens, 302–3.
[32] See the anecdote from Antimo Liberati, *Lettera scritta . . . in risposta ad una del sig. Ovidio Persapegi* (Rome: Mascardi, 1685), given in Fabbri, *Monteverdi*, 297.

# *Possente spirto*: on taming the power of music

1   Roelandt Savery (?1576–1639), *Orpheus* (1628) (London, National Gallery)

Monteverdi's great invocation to Charon and the powers of Hades in Act 3 of *Orfeo* (1607) has rung through the ages. Although he was not the first to pit himself against the challenge of representing Orphic song on the stage— Jacopo Peri had tried in his *Euridice* of 1600 (and for that matter, Angelo Poliziano in his *Orfeo* of over a century before)—he was the first to do so with such daring. 'Possente spirto e formidabil nume' certainly has its roots in earlier entertainment traditions, not least Peri's echo-song for another great musician of classical myth, Arion ('Dunque fra torbid'onde', in the fifth of the 1589 Florentine *intermedi*).[1] But Monteverdi's notation of the elaborate vocal embellishments (he provides a simpler version, too, but surely it was not meant to be sung) and of the equally virtuoso instrumental interjections and

ritornellos provides one of the most compelling visual and aural representations of the new-found power of music.

'Possente spirto' seems to have made an effect. For the second *intermedio* of Battista Guarini's *Idropica* staged in Mantua in June 1608 for the wedding of Prince Francesco Gonzaga (the patron of *Orfeo*) and Margherita of Savoy, Giovan Giacomo Gastoldi provided a piece in which 'Glaucus . . . sang in this manner, making his voice resound so that various instruments were heard in due order one after the other repeating his closing phrases as an instrumental echo from various parts [of the stage]'.[2] Monteverdi himself evoked the magical world of 'Possente spirto' in the large Magnificat of the 1610 'Vespers': the free exchange between 'secular' and 'sacred' repertories in this period merits continued discussion. And in a well known letter to Alessandro Striggio of 9 December 1616 the composer paired his 'giusta preghiera' for Orpheus with his no less renowned (and still more widely imitated) 'giusto lamento' for Ariadne (in the opera of 1608) as paragons of his ideal music for the theatre.[3]

But by the mid-1610s the musical world was fast changing. In vocal chamber music, the solo madrigal was declining alongside its polyphonic counterpart as monodists sought more structured musical styles to reclaim the ground for music as music rather than as some spurious form of speech. In keeping with contemporary trends in poetry, the seemingly 'lighter' styles of the canzonetta and aria were more amenable to contemporary tastes. Scholars have tended to be dismissive of early strophic arias, especially the triple-time dance songs that make up a large part of the repertory. But in his pioneering collection of solo songs, *Le nuove musiche* (1602), Giulio Caccini was anxious to give some status to what he called the 'canzonetta à uso di aria per poter usare in conserto di più strumenti di corde'[4]—his wording merits careful consideration. Monteverdi, too, attempted to dignify his own collection of, as it were, 'canzonettas in air style that can be used in concert with several stringed instruments', the *Scherzi musicali* 1607, not least by invoking the mystifying term 'canto alla francese', which, his brother said, had been newly introduced by him to Italy.[5]

Monteverdi well knew that aria styles articulated the relationship between the triumvirate of *oratione, harmonia* and rhythm that together made up *melodia* (the art of composition) in ways very different from the formula proclaimed as the credo of the *seconda prattica* in his polemic with the Bolognese theorist, Giovanni Maria Artusi, at the turn of the century (the oration as mistress, not servant, of the harmony).[6] In a letter to Alessandro Striggio of 21 November 1615, Monteverdi discusses the recent commission arrived from Mantua for a *ballo* in music. Given the lack of precise instructions, the composer had written a *ballo* with six *mutanze* (*Tirsi e Clori*, later published in the seventh book of madrigals of 1619). But

if His Most Serene Highness should want either a change of air in this [*ballo*], or additions to the enclosed [movements] of a slow and grave nature, or fuller and without fugues (His Most Serene Highness taking no notice of the present words which can easily be changed, though at least these words help by the nature of their metre and by imitating the melody [*canto*]), or if he should want everything altered I beg you to act on my

behalf so that His Most Serene Highness might re-word the commission . . .[7]

The notion that the present words 'can easily be changed'—although their metre is appropriate and they imitate the melody—is striking in the context of Monteverdi's earlier protestations over the *seconda prattica*. The relative unimportance of the individual words of the canzonetta and the dominance of metre and stereotyped subjects perhaps inspired a new relationship between poetry and music—a more compatible and less competitive relationship of profound significance for future developments. The issues go beyond simple matters of genre (although they are undoubtedly Monteverdi's chief concern in this letter) to raise profound questions concerning the status of musical expression as the Baroque period came into its own.

If Monteverdi eventually changed (or at least developed) his notion of the *seconda prattica*, it may or may not be necessary to invoke some new term to account for the aria-influenced styles of the 1620s and 30s: some have variously coined the term 'terza prattica'—whether felicitously or not is open to debate.[8] But whatever the case, clearly it is encumbent upon us to explore the implications of these styles as vehicles for a new conception of representing the emotions through music (which is perhaps how one can broadly interpret the term *stile rappresentativo* in all its resonances for the early Baroque period). The issues are particularly clear in those solo songs that seek to merge madrigal/recitative and aria styles in various ways. One such example, Sigismondo d'India's 'Torna il sereno Zefiro' published in his *Le musiche . . . libro quinto* (Venice, 1623) has already been discussed in the literature,[9] and other examples can easily be found. One, however, is particularly useful for my present argument.

In 1633 the obscure Italian composer Giovanni Battista Piazza published a curious setting of a corrupt version of Ottavio Rinuccini's canzonetta 'Non havea Febo ancora' (ex. 1) in his *Libro secondo: Canzonette a voce sola* (Venice: Bartholomeo Magni). Rinuccini's poem is a strophic canzonetta with ten stanzas: settings as a simple duple-time aria had been published by Antonio Brunelli (for solo voice) in 1614 and Johann Hieronymus Kapsberger (for two voices) in 1619.[10] Piazza, however, sets only the first strophe, altering the text accordingly. (In ex. 1 the Italian has been tacitly modernized.) The setting is in three sections. The scene is set in the style of a duple-time aria: 'Phoebus [= the sun] had not yet / brought light to the world, / when from her lodging / a young girl appeared.' There follows a brief passage in

Ex.1 Giovanni Battista Piazza, 'Non havea Febo ancora' (*Libro secondo: Canzonette a voce sola,* 1633)

'recitative': 'She said, grieving and sad—'. This leads to a concluding section in triple time: '"Wretched one, what shall I do? / I will not suffer such grief."' These last two lines correspond to (but are not the same as) the refrain in Rinuccini's original poem. The overall result is quite similar to (if much less effective than) d'India's 'Torna il sereno Zefiro'.

As with d'India's song, the use of a triple-time aria style at the end is somewhat problematic: the words are such that some kind of emotional recitative might plausibly be expected, at least according to the conventional canons of the 'new music'. Either the use of aria here is intended as somehow motivated by a lightweight view of the text (Rinuccini's poem is, of course, a canzonetta), or we have to come to terms with the notion that 'aria' has somehow taken over the expressive function of 'recitative' to mark an emotional climax, perhaps even of its having gained a new structural and affective eloquence in the context of an emerging Baroque (rather than dying Renaissance) aesthetic.[11]

Monteverdi's own response to changing tastes and styles needs further exploration: his seventh book of madrigals of 1619 (published with the significant title,

'Concerto') merits closer study than it has hitherto received in the literature (where comment has often been limited to the volume's role in Monteverdi's new formulation of the duet). As for 'Non havea Febo ancora', however, the composer produced a much more resonant—and more influential—setting of Rinuccini's complete poem in his eighth book of madrigals, the *Madrigali guerrieri, et amorosi* of 1638. Here the first two stanzas setting the scene are set as a trio for three shepherds, who remain 'on stage' (after all, the piece is said to be *rappresentativo*) to comment on the nymph's lament and to offer a peroration. The nymph's poignant lament (sung not 'al tempo della mano' as the opening, but 'al tempo dell'affetto'; not to the beat but to the time of the emotions) is in a rhapsodic triple time over a ground bass formed of a descending tetrachord, for the moment less an 'emblem of lament' (although that was to be one of its later significances) than one of what so often causes lament, love (ex.2).[12] Monteverdi uses the style to affirm his absolute control over the expression of the verse. He also thereby emphasizes the new power of aria as the chief force for representing powerful emotions in music.

Assuming that the *Lamento della ninfa* is in some way

Ex.2  Monteverdi, *Lamento della ninfa* (1638)

Ex.3  Monteverdi, 'Sfogava con le stelle' (1603)

a serious piece (the possibility of reading it in other ways must be left for another occasion), clearly it is very different from what has been claimed the archetype of the early Baroque 'serious' lament, the *Lamento d'Arianna*.[13] Perhaps that is because we are now in the world of the pastoral, and not of the tragedy (again, questions of genre merit further exploration). But one also wonders whether the manifest power of aria is a product of new approaches to aria texts by contemporary poets. Rinuccini's 'Non havea Febo ancora', ostensibly a fairly straightforward canzonetta, is one of several examples of a more expressive—some might say dramatic—approach to such strophic poetry.[14] Indeed, the poet displays more than an inch of Freudian slip in an earlier version of his last stanza of the poem, which in Monteverdi's setting begins 'Sì tra sdegnosi pianti / Spargea le voci al ciel' ('Thus amid scornful tears / she left forth her words to the sky'). The reading in one of the Rinuccini manuscripts (Florence, Biblioteca Nazionale, Fondo Palatino 250, f.147v) has 'Sì tra sdegnosi pianti / sfogava il suo dolor' ('Thus amid scornful tears / she poured forth her grief'),[15] and it seems that the echo of Rinuccini's own madrigal 'Sfogava con le stelle' was so obvious as to demand excision.

But just as Rinuccini assimilates his canzonetta to the serious madrigal, so does Monteverdi, whose well known setting of 'Sfogava con le stelle' appeared in his fourth book of madrigals of 1603. Here, the opening description—telling how a man 'sick with love poured forth his grief to the stars'—is set for the five voices in a recitational *falsobordone* style, breaking out into rich imitative polyphony at the speaker's exclamation 'O immagini belle / dell'idol mio ch'adoro' ('O beautiful images / of my idol whom I adore') (ex.3). So, too, in Monteverdi's 'Non havea Febo ancora' an opening narration for the three shepherds breaks out into triple-time aria for the nymph's invocation to 'Amor'. The expressive effect seems much the same, for all the differences in style and medium (and perhaps still more, gender).[16] There are some merits in the notion that Monteverdi attributes to the triple-time aria affective and structural attributes formerly allocated to imitative counterpoint in the transformation of the *seconda prattica* ideals that accompanied his relentless search for 'the natural path to imitation', a path that took him away from the pseudo-natural speech of the *Lamento d'Arianna* to a much more profound sense of how emotions could and should be 'naturally' imitated in and through the raw power of the voice.

By the 1630s Monteverdi's notion of how best to invoke a 'powerful spirit' through music had changed remarkably. But as many have noted, his acutely musical perception of his texts—for all the differences in style between his early and late works—remained constant, informed by an extraordinary understanding of emotional arousal through music. Whether we view Monteverdi as the last great composer of the Renaissance or the first great composer of the Baroque (or both), we must bow to his unique ability to move us even today. That is what is surely best celebrated on this the 350th anniversary of his death.

*Tim Carter is Reader in Music at Royal Holloway and Bedford New College, University of London. He has published widely on music in the late Renaissance and early Baroque periods and is currently preparing a book on solo song in Italy, 1580-1630.*

[1] *Musique des intermèdes de 'La pellegrina': les fêtes de Florence, 1589*, ed. D. P. Walker (Paris, 1963, R/1986), pp.98-106.

[2] From Federico Follino's *Compendio delle sontuose feste fatte l'anno MDCVIII nella città di Mantova, per le reali nozze del serenissimo prencipe d. Francesco Gonzaga con la serenissima infante Margherita di Savoia* (Mantua, 1608), in A. Solerti, *Gli albori del melodramma* (Milan, 1904-5; R/Hildesheim, 1969), iii, p.219.

[3] *The letters of Claudio Monteverdi*, trans. D. Stevens (London, 1980), pp.115-18, discussing plans to set to music Scipione Agnelli's *Le nozze di Tetide*: '*Arianna* led me to a just lament, and *Orfeo* to a righteous prayer, but this fable leads me I don't know to what end.'

[4] The description comes from the preface to Caccini's *Le nuove musiche* (Florence: I Marescotti, 1601 [=1602]), f.Br.

[5] For the *Scherzi musicali* and the 'canto alla francese', see most recently M. Ossi, 'Claudio Monteverdi's *ordine novo, bello et gustevole*: the canzonetta as dramatic module and formal archetype', *Journal of the American Musicological Society*, xlv (1992), pp.261-304.

[6] For the Artusi–Monteverdi controversy, see C. V. Palisca, 'The Artusi–Monteverdi controversy', *The new Monteverdi companion*, ed. D. Arnold and N. Fortune (London, 1985), pp.127-58; and T. Carter, 'Artusi, Monteverdi, and the poetics of modern music', *Musical humanism and its legacy: essays in honor of Claude V. Palisca*, ed. N. K. Baker and B. R. Hanning (Stuyvesant, NY, 1992), pp.171-94.

[7] My translation differs slightly from the one in *The letters of Claudio Monteverdi*, trans. Stevens, pp.107-8.

[8] The notion of a 'terza prattica' has been alive in the world of Monteverdi scholarship for a few years now: Ellen Rosand reminds me that Gary Tomlinson deserves the credit. I explored a few of the issues in my *Music in late Renaissance and early Baroque Italy* (London, 1992), pp.250-53: some seem to like the idea (e.g. Michael Talbot in his review of my book in *Early music*, xx (1993), pp.111-12), but Jeffrey Kurtzman has voiced reasonable objections (*Music and letters*, lxiii (1992), pp.438-40).

[9] In N. Fortune, 'Italian secular monody from 1600-1635: an introductory survey', *Musical quarterly*, xxxix (1953), pp.171-95.

[10] For the Brunelli, see P. Aldrich, *The rhythm of seventeenth-century Italian monody* (New York, 1966), p.166; for the Kapsberger, see J. Whenham, *Duet and dialogue in the age of Monteverdi* (Ann Arbor, MI, 1982), ii, pp.332-3. There is another (anonymous) solo-voice setting in manuscript in Florence, Biblioteca Nazionale Centrale, Banco Rari 236 (*olim* Magliabechiano XIX.114). To the best of my knowledge, the Piazza setting has not hitherto appeared in print, but note the dis-

IX

cussion in Ossi, 'Claudio Monteverdi's *ordine novo, bello et gustevole'*, pp.291-301.

[11]"I shall explore this issue further, with specific reference to the duet 'O sia tranquillo il mare, o pien d'orgoglio' in Monteverdi's *Madrigali guerrieri, et amorosi* (1638), in my contribution to *'Recitar cantando': essays on seventeenth-century Italian opera and song*, ed. I. Fenlon and T. Carter (Oxford University Press, forthcoming).

[12]Compare E. Rosand, 'The descending tetrachord: an emblem of lament', *Musical quarterly*, lv (1979), pp.346-59. For another use of the descending tetrachord ground bass, see the first section of 'Altri canti d'Amor, tenero arciero' at the beginning of the *Madrigali guerrieri, et amorosi* (1638): its significance ('love' rather than 'lament'?) merits closer examination. On the triple-time aria as the 'language of love', see my '"In Love's harmonious consort"? Penelope and the interpretation of *Il ritorno d'Ulisse in patria'*, *Cambridge opera journal*, v (1993), pp.1-16.

[13]See the discussion in G. Tomlinson, 'Madrigal, monody, and Mon-teverdi's "via naturale alla immitatione"', *Journal of the American Musicological Society*, xxxiv (1981), pp.60-108.

[14]Gabriello Chiabrera's dialogue *Il Geri* of 1624-5 offers some useful suggestions: see most recently R. R. Holzer, '"Sono d'altro garbo . . . le canzonette che si cantano oggi": Pietro della Valle on music and modernity in the seventeenth century', *Studi musicali*, xxi (1992), pp.253-306.

[15]The reading is also found in the settings by Brunelli and Kaps-berger, see Ossi, 'Claudio Monteverdi's *ordine novo, bello et gustevole'*, p.292.

[16]It will be clear that I disagree somewhat with Gary Tomlinson's reading of 'Sfogava con le stelle' and the *Lamento della ninfa* as two set-tings contrasted by different notions of resemblance and represen-tation (in his *Music in Renaissance magic: toward a historiography of others* (Chicago, 1993), pp.229-46), although, as I shall discuss else-where, the ideas of Michel Foucault adopted by Tomlinson do indeed have considerable potential for our understanding of this period.

# X

# Intriguing Laments: Sigismondo d'India, Claudio Monteverdi, and Dido *alla parmigiana* (1628)

IN 1627–28, CLAUDIO MONTEVERDI set to one side his duties as *maestro di cappella* of St. Mark's, Venice, to write music for the festivities in Parma celebrating the wedding of Duke Odoardo Farnese and Margherita de' Medici of Florence.[1] He faced stiff competition for the commission, not least from the distinguished madrigalist and monodist Sigismondo d'India, and Monteverdi's recruitment was in part the result of an intrigue that extended even to the performers enlisted for the festivities, especially the Florentine soprano Settimia Caccini and her husband, Alessandro Ghivizzani. Moreover, this intrigue brought specific musical works into play in ways that suggest the rich debate, then as now, over stylistic and aesthetic issues in a complex period of change and experiment. The documentary, textual, and musical sources are somewhat fragmentary. Nevertheless, they permit a fuller exploration of the background to the 1628 festivities in

Early versions of this paper were presented at the Sixth Biennial Conference on Baroque Music, University of Edinburgh, 7–10 July 1994, and at the Sixtieth Annual Meeting of the American Musicological Society, Minneapolis, October 1994. I am truly grateful to Dinko Fabris for reintroducing me to all this material, and for his help with sources and matters of interpretation. I have also benefited from the close reading and careful comments of Annegret Fauser, Kelley Harness, Wendy Heller, John Walter Hill, Anne MacNeil, and Margaret Murata.
    [1] For the 1628 festivities, see Paolo Minucci del Rosso, "Le nozze di Margherita de' Medici con Odoardo Farnese Duca di Parma e Piacenza," *La rassegna nazionale* 21 (1885): 551–71; 22 (1885): 550–70; and 23 (1885): 19–45; Irving Lavin, "Lettres de Parme (1618, 1627–28) et débuts du théâtre baroque," in *Le Lieu théâtral à la Renaissance*, ed. Jean Jacquot (Paris: Centre National de la Recherche Scientifique, 1964), 105–58; Stuart Reiner, "Preparations in Parma—1618, 1627–28," *The Music Review* 25 (1964): 273–301; Alois M. Nagler, *Theatre Festivals of the Medici, 1539–1637* (New Haven and London: Yale University Press, 1964; reprint, New York: Da Capo Press, 1976), 139–61; Paolo Fabbri, *Monteverdi* (Turin: EDT, 1985), 268–79 (idem, *Monteverdi*, trans. Tim Carter [Cambridge: Cambridge University Press, 1994], 206–19); Irène Mamczarz, *Le Théâtre farnèse de Parme et le drame musical italien (1618–1732): Étude d'un lieu théâtral, des représentations, des formes; drame pastoral, intermèdes, opéra-tournoi, drame musical* (Florence: Olschki, 1988).

Parma than has been achieved to date, and also pose intriguing questions about changing notions of musical structure and expression as the Baroque period came into its own.

The Medici-Farnese wedding of 1628 was no diplomatic triumph.[2] As early as 1615, Ranuccio Farnese, then duke of Parma, approached Grand Duke Cosimo II de' Medici concerning an alliance between his son Odoardo, born in 1612, and one of the grand duke's daughters. The bride was to have been Cosimo's eldest daughter, Maria Cristina, but she was a hunchback, and in the early 1620s she entered a convent. Next in line were Margherita, also born in 1612, and Anna. The Farnese claimed Margherita, although Archduchess Maria Magdalena (wife of Cosimo II and regent with Grand Duchess Christine after the grand duke's death) hoped to wed her to Prince Władisław of Poland. The Farnese refused Anna and negotiated an agreement over Margherita, but then in 1627 Gaston, duke of Orléans and son of Maria de' Medici (the dowager queen of France), made an offer for her hand. Odoardo, now duke of Parma, was again offered the unfortunate Anna, and the Farnese again refused. In the end, the question of the young duke's marriage—both he and his bride were but sixteen years old in 1628—provoked a power struggle between pro-Medici and pro-Farnese cardinals at the papal court, and between the Farnese and the French queen. And having bested the Medici in the political arena, the Farnese seem to have set out to do the same in that of theatrical entertainments.

The marriage ceremony took place in Florence on 11 October 1628, and it was followed by the usual festivities: balls, banquets, a tournament, and an opera, *La Flora*, to a libretto by Andrea Salvadori and with music by Marco da Gagliano and Jacopo Peri. The Medici's evident lack of enthusiasm for their latest political union may explain why these celebrations were on a less extravagant scale than the most spectacular of Florentine wedding entertainments, for the marriages of Grand Duke Ferdinando de' Medici and Christine of Lorraine in 1589, of Maria de' Medici and Henri IV of France in 1600, and of Cosimo de' Medici and Archduchess Maria Magdalena of Austria in 1608. The Farnese, in contrast, staged a lavish series of spectacles in Parma. When Margherita arrived there on 6 December she received a triumphal entry and witnessed a rich program of entertainments,

---

[2] The following details of the marriage negotiations are drawn from Tim Carter, "Jacopo Peri (1561–1633): His Life and Works," 2 vols. (Ph.D. diss., University of Birmingham, 1980; reprint, New York and London: Garland, 1989), 1:96–97, with further information provided by Kelley Harness.

X

34

including a performance of Tasso's *Aminta* with grand *intermedi* and an elaborate tournament, *Mercurio e Marte*.

The impresario for the Parma festivities was Marquis Enzo Bentivoglio, a prominent Ferrarese patron well known for his involvement in court and civic spectacles. During the summer of 1627, word seems to have spread that he was seeking one or more composers to provide the music for the forthcoming entertainments. One composer who saw himself a prime candidate was Sigismondo d'India. D'India had been dismissed in 1623 from his position as *maestro di musica da camera* to Carlo Emmanuele I, duke of Savoy, because of malicious gossip from courtiers, he claimed. He now pursued a somewhat roving career, associating himself both with the Este dukes of Modena (from October 1623 to April 1624, and from early 1626 until his death) and with Cardinal Maurizio of Savoy, then living in Rome, for whom he wrote his now lost sacred opera *Sant' Eustachio* (1625). On 26 August 1627, d'India, in Modena, sent a fairly unspecific letter to Bentivoglio, perhaps in response to a query from the marquis, signaling his readiness for some kind of musical employment:[3] he notes that he has always professed to be Bentivoglio's "most devoted servant" and is free to leave Modena once he has presented to the duke "a work of which I believe I shall be disencumbered within eight or ten days."[4] He concludes: "It remains only that you put me to use, anywhere at all that you may think good, as I am eager for your commands."

Bentivoglio must have replied almost immediately, prompting d'India to send a much more detailed letter one week later on 2 September wherein he proclaims his preeminence in writing music for the stage. This letter has already been reproduced in part by Stuart Reiner, but the important ramifications of the whole have not yet been explored fully.[5] D'India does not make anything of his former attachments to the Farnese: his first book of solo songs (1609) had

---

[3] The letter survives in Ferrara, Archivio di Stato, Archivio Bentivoglio (henceforth *AB*) 208, fol. 379r, translated in Reiner, "Preparations in Parma," 286; the original (not given by Reiner) will be included in Dinko Fabris's forthcoming edition of correspondence in the Bentivoglio archive.

[4] D'India writes "un'opera," which was most likely a collection of printed music, now lost (see below, n. 16).

[5] Stuart Reiner, " 'Vi sono molt'altre mezz'arie . . . ,' " in *Studies in Music History: Essays for Oliver Strunk*, ed. Harold Powers (Princeton: Princeton University Press, 1968), 248, 256. Dinko Fabris drew this letter once more to my attention and gave me a copy; it, too, will be included in his forthcoming edition of correspondence in the Bentivoglio archive.

been dedicated to Duke Ranuccio Farnese,[6] and we have evidence of the composer being in the duchy of Parma and Piacenza in 1609 (writing sacred music) and in 1610 (providing music for festivities).[7] But d'India's renewed emphasis on his earlier connections with Enzo Bentivoglio suggests that he was looking toward the forthcoming wedding entertainments.

## My Most Illustrious Lord Most Respected[8]

I received Your Most Illustrious Lordship's letter and give you infinite thanks for the memory you hold of me, stating always that I am one of

[6] Sigismondo d'India, *Musiche . . . da cantar solo* (Milan: Heirs of Simon Tini and Filippo Lomazzo, 1609).

[7] D'India's presence in Piacenza in August 1609 is revealed in a letter of 24 August 1609 from Ludovico Caracci in Piacenza to Gioseffo Guidetti in Bologna (given in *Gli scritti dei Caracci: Ludovico, Annibale, Agostino, Antonio, Giovanni Antonio*, ed. Giovanna Perini [Bologna: Nuova Alfa Editoriale, 1990], 118): "Il Signor Sismondo d'India appunto quella matina che ebbe sue letere si trovasimo insieme tutte due a una tavola de la Signora Barbara Baratiera dove lui si tratiene continuamente, e vi era uno pavese che canta uno soprano che si chiama il Pigamondo, il primo soprano d'Italia, così dice il Signor Gismondo, mandato a piliare da questa Serenissima per fare cantare quatro messe votive le più eccelentemente cantate che si possa in queste bande. Il Signor Gismondo le à composte co' li moteti fra megio, dicano cosa rara" ("On that very morning when I received your letter, Signor Sigismondo d'India and I found ourselves together at table at Signora Barbara Baratiera's, where he entertains himself continually, and there was one from Pavia who sings soprano who is called Il Pigamondo, the first soprano of Italy—so Signor Sigismondo says—who was sent for from the Serenissima [Venice] so as to have sung four votive Masses sung as most excellently as one can in these parts. Signor Sigismondo has composed them with the motets in the middle, which they say are rare"). I am grateful to Dinko Fabris for this reference. For other connections with Parma during this period, see John J. Joyce, *The Monodies of Sigismondo d'India* (Ann Arbor: UMI Research Press, 1981), 5.

[8] *AB* 209, fols. 39r–40r (all abbreviations and contractions have been "silently" expanded, "v"/"u" and "i"/"j" standardized, and upper case applied where appropriate): "Illustrissimo Signor mio Colendissimo // Ho ricevuta la lettera di Vostra Signoria Illustrissima e le rendo infinite gratie della memoria che tiene da me professando sempre esserli de suoi servitori vecchi havendo fortuna sino da miei primi anni di doverla servire per la Bonarella che si dovea rappresentare a Ferrara quando ella mi trattene per simil effetto in quella città. Ora mando a Vostra Signoria Illustrissima questa mia opera messa pur ora al luce quivi vedra a l'ultimo il lamento di Armida composto da me in due ore a Tivoli avanti al Signor Cardinale da questo potra comprendere la mia maniera d'uscir in scena la quale lei trovera ch'e è sola potendo sentir cantare detto lamento da la Settimia la qual liele scritto a mano quando io passai per Fiorenza, desidererai poter volare ove lei fosse perche ella sentisse la forza di tal maniera e stile et son sicuro non lo sentira da nessun altro [fol. 39v] anzi s'ella si trattenesse a Ferrara alcuni giorni vorrei venire a spasso sin la accio si degnasse dar orechio a quanto le scrivo ne piu ne manco. Io ho tempo di star a spasso per tutto il mese d'ottobre e piu ancora, e s'assicuri che de la maniera l'e piu di quello io le so dire poiche in Roma il principe Aldobrandino mi diede l'opera del' Adone a me benche si trovo poi ch'io ero amalato e non lo potei servire fui pero sforzato di rifare

your old servants since I had the fortune in my early years to be required to serve you for *La Bonarella* which was to be performed in Ferrara when you kept me for such matters in that city. Now I send to Your Most Illustrious Lordship this my work now published, where you will see at the end the *Lamento d'Armida* composed by me in two hours at Tivoli before the Lord Cardinal [Maurizio of Savoy?]. From this you will be able to understand my manner of broaching the stage, which you will discover is unique by being able to hear the said lament sung by Settimia [Caccini] for whom I wrote it out by hand when I passed through Florence. I would like to fly to where you are so that you might hear the force of this manner and style, and I am sure that you will hear it from no other. Indeed, if you were to stay in Ferrara for a few days I would like to come there for a vacation so that you might deign to listen to what I am writing to you, no more no less. I have time to take a vacation for the whole month of October and indeed longer, and be assured that concerning this manner there is more that I can tell you, for in Rome Prince Aldobrandino gave me the work *Adone*, although it then turned out that I got sick and could not be of service. Then I was forced to rewrite the part for Lorenzino [Sances], who brought it to me when I was overwhelmed by fever in bed, and it was done in a morning.[9] You will be able to inform yourself of all this from Rome. Furthermore, you know very well that he who composed *Adone* has not written any other work than this one, [and] think how it could have succeeded being entirely full of canzonettas since there was no recitative style—indeed very far from it—and you know that in such works it is necessary that one should be born to it.

It would please me, Most Illustrious Lordship, if you would listen to the *Lamento di Didone* [sung] by Signora Settimia in Florence, for from this you will see whether I tell lies or the truth, and [if you] would seek information from the Lord Duke of Fano and others to see from this lament whether my style is thus, even though I well know that you know me. I am forced only by affection for my service to tell you this, begging you to make me worthy of your commands, which I esteem more than those of any other patron which I have in this world. And I pay Your

---

tutta la parte di Lorenzino il quale me la porto ch'io hero assediato de la febre in letto dove ando fatta in dimatina. Di questo ella se ne potra informare da Roma che sopra il tutto oltra ch'ella sa molto bene che chi compose l'Adone non ha fatto altra opera sol che quella [fol. 40r] pensi come potea riuscirne essendo tutta piene di canzonette non vi essendo proposito di stile recitativo anzi lontanissimo sapendo lei che bisogna in simil opre esserli nato dentro. / Mi facci gratia di sentir Vostra Signoria Illustrissima da la Signora Settimia in Fiorenza il lamento de Didone che da quello comprendera s'io le dico buggie o verita e ne domandi informatione dal Signor Duca di Fiano e d'altri che vedra da tal lamento se'l mio stile e tale se ben so ch'ella mi conosce, son solo sforzato da affetto della servitu mia a dirli questo suplicandola mi faccia degno de suoi comandi, i quali stimo piu che di nessun altro padrone ch'io vi habia, in questo mondo et a Vostra Signoria faccio riverenza di Modena li di 2 di settembre di Vostra Signoria Illustrissima // obligatissimo servitore // Sigismondo d'India."

[9] Reiner (" 'Vi sono molt'altre mezz'arie . . . ,' " 248) reads "doue ando tutta in limatura" ("there, it got polished up completely").

Lordship reverence, from Modena the 2d of September. Your Most
Illustrious Lordship's

most obliged servant
Sigismondo d'India

Several important points emerge, not least d'India's hitherto unknown
involvement in some way in an earlier theatrical entertainment for
Bentivoglio, here called "la Bonarella." This seems to have been a
pastoral entertainment with *intermedi* planned for performance in
Ferrara in Carnival 1611/12,[10] shortly after d'India's appointment to
Turin in April 1611. And Stuart Reiner has already explored d'India's
assertions that he originally received the commission for the opera
"l'Adone"—Domenico Mazzocchi's *La catena d'Adone*, first performed
in the Palazzo Conti, Rome, on 12 February 1626—and that despite
being ill and therefore having turned down the offer, he managed to
rewrite some of the music on command while in his sickbed.[11] But all
this forms part of a larger claim on d'India's part, that he was well
qualified to write music for the stage under pressure of time, at a high
musical standard, and to the satisfaction of virtuoso singers.

D'India's overt dismissal of Mazzocchi may well reflect the fact
that Mazzocchi himself is thought to have entered the competition for
the commission for the Parma music: the print of *La catena d'Adone*
(Venice: Alessandro Vincenti, 1626) had already been dedicated to the
young Duke Odoardo Farnese on 24 October. But the grounds for

---

[10] See the *Manuscrito osia Cronaca di Claudio Rondoni* in Ferrara, Biblioteca
Comunale, MS Cl.A.250 (a copy made in 1783 of a seventeenth-century original),
fols. 282v–283r, concerning entertainments (including a tournament) planned for a
visit of the duke of Mantua: "li Accademici procurorono di dar l'ultima mano al
Teatro per rapresentare la Bonarella Egloga pastorale abelita d'intramezzi, et diversità
di Machine, che in diverse ocasioni fingevano varietà de Paesi, et diversità di Stati"
("the academicians sought to complete the theater so as to stage *La Bonarella*, a
pastoral eclogue ornamented by *intermedi* and a diversity of machines which at
different moments displayed a variety of countries and a diversity of states"). I am
grateful to Dinko Fabris for this reference. The entertainments were curtailed by the
untimely death of Duke Vincenzo Gonzaga. John Walter Hill discusses them in his
forthcoming *Roman Monody, Cantata, and Opera from the Circles around Cardinal
Montalto* (Oxford: Clarendon Press) and suggests that "la Bonarella" is a pastoral by
Alessandro Guarini. A possible connection with Guidobaldo Bonarelli's *Filli di Sciro*,
first performed in Ferrara in 1607 and repeated there quite regularly, remains unclear.

[11] The composer notes "un poco d'indispositione qual credo al tutto per questa
settimana mi terra un poco impedito" in a letter to the duke of Modena from Rome,
3 February 1626, given in Federico Mompellio, *Sigismondo d'India: Musicista palermi-
tano* (Milan: Ricordi, 1956), 78. Reiner (" 'Vi sono molt'altre mezz'arie . . . ,'" 250–54)
goes so far as to claim that the published score of *La catena d'Adone* (Venice:
Alessandro Vincenti, 1626) reflects the work as heard at the first performance and
therefore includes unacknowledged recitative music by d'India.

d'India's disapproval of Mazzocchi are intriguing: Mazzocchi lacked operatic experience apart from *La catena d'Adone*, and that work gives scant indication of any true theatrical ability owing to the predominance therein of "canzonette." D'India's criticism presumably refers to the arias and so-called *mezz'arie* that Mazzocchi himself considered essential to breaking "the tedium of the recitative" ("rompono il tedio del recitativo").[12] D'India, on the other hand, seems to have felt that the stylistic and affective heart of music for the theater—and the true mark of the theatrical composer—lay precisely within the *stile recitativo*.

Mazzocchi's concern over the "tedium of the recitative" fits squarely within the context of the problematic reception of the *stile recitativo* in early seventeenth-century Italy. The Florentine "new music" and early operatic recitative by composers such as Giulio Caccini, Jacopo Peri, and Claudio Monteverdi prided itself on, and achieved its power by, the verisimilar representation of heightened speech: singer-actors literally "spoke in song." But audiences were quick to complain about tedious recitatives being too much "like the chanting of the Passion,"[13] and by the 1620s duple- and triple-time aria styles had become, in operas and songbooks, an increasingly significant force for emotional arousal through music, using the seductive power of song, not speech, to make their effect.[14] The new-found popularity of the aria and related styles is striking in an age that prized some notion of verisimilitude—lamenting lovers rarely sing in triple time—on the stage and in the chamber. It also requires much closer study.

In the light of such changing musical fashions, d'India's objection to Mazzocchi's "canzonettas" may well reflect an old-fashioned, perhaps courtly, view of contemporary opera and related genres. But it also formed part of a broader strategy to establish his credentials in

[12] Discussed in Reiner, " 'Vi sono molt'altre mezz'arie . . . ,' " passim; and Carolyn Gianturco, "Nuove considerazioni su *il tedio del recitativo* delle prime opere romane," *Rivista italiana di musicologia* 17 (1982): 212–39.

[13] This was a contemporary comment on early Florentine recitative as heard in Jacopo Peri's *Euridice* and Giulio Caccini's *Il rapimento di Cefalo*, both performed at the wedding festivities for Henri IV of France and Maria de' Medici in Florence in 1600; see Claude V. Palisca, "Musical Asides in the Diplomatic Correspondence of Emilio de' Cavalieri," *The Musical Quarterly* 49 (1963): 351. Another noted that "il modo di cantarla venne facilmente a noia"; see Tim Carter, "*Non occorre nominare tanti musici*: Private Patronage and Public Ceremony in Late Sixteenth-Century Florence," *I Tatti Studies: Essays in the Renaissance* 4 (1991): 102 n. 32.

[14] See my " 'In Love's harmonious consort'? Penelope and the Interpretation of *Il ritorno d'Ulisse in patria*," *Cambridge Opera Journal* 5 (1993): 1–16.

writing music for the stage. To that end, he cites two specific works that seem to have been sent to Bentivoglio, a recent *Lamento d'Armida* and a *Lamento di Didone*, and suggests that the affective power of these works can be projected only by a virtuoso singer, specifically the Florentine Settimia Caccini. Here he seeks the double advantage of associating himself with Florence, widely acknowledged as the birth-place of the *stile recitativo*, and with the designated "star" singer of the 1628 festivities, the younger daughter of the virtuoso tenor Giulio Caccini.[15]

D'India's *Lamento d'Armida* is now lost, along with, I suggest, the publication that originally contained it, possibly a sixth book of *Musiche*.[16] But his *Lamento di Didone* had already been published, together with other laments for Jason and Olimpia, in his *Le musiche ... libro quinto* of 1623.[17] The *Lamento di Didone*, setting the com-poser's own text in free-rhyming seven- and eleven-syllable *versi sciolti*, provides in effect a reworking of the rhetorical, topological, and

---

[15] For Settimia Caccini, see Warren Kirkendale, *The Court Musicians in Florence during the Principate of the Medici, with a Reconstruction of the Artistic Establishment*, Historiae Musicae Cultores Biblioteca 61 (Florence: Olschki, 1993), 337–46. She married the Lucchese musician Alessandro Ghivizzani (ibid., 333–37) shortly before they entered the Medici payroll on 3 November 1609. Enzo Bentivoglio had been involved in attempts to engineer a marriage between Settimia and Girolamo Frescobaldi in early 1609; see Anthony Newcomb, "Girolamo Frescobaldi, 1608–15," *Annales musicologiques* 7 (1976): 111–58. She found employment in Mantua in 1613–19 and hoped to sing the title role in Monteverdi's *Andromeda* in 1620; see Kirkendale, *Court Musicians in Florence*, 341–43.

[16] Reiner (" 'Vi sono molt'altre mezz'arie ... ,'" 256–58) associates the lost *Lamento d'Armida* with what appears to be a strophic aria or part thereof copied in d'India's hand at the end of the copy of his *Liber primus motectorum quatuor vocibus* (Venice: Alessandro Vincenti, 1627), formerly owned by the Bentivoglio family and now in Bologna, Civico Museo Bibliografico Musicale (shelf-mark AA122). Of course, this is strong evidence of a connection between d'India and Bentivoglio, but this aria seems unlikely to be associated with any *Lamento d'Armida*. First, "questa mia opera messa pur ora al luce" containing "a l'ultimo" the *Lamento d'Armida* described in d'India's letter to Bentivoglio of 2 September 1627 is probably the work to be presented to the duke of Modena, "of which I believe I shall be disencumbered within eight or ten days," noted in his letter of 26 August: the *Liber primus motectorum quatuor vocibus* was dedicated to Cardinal Federico Borromeo, archbishop of Milan, on 8 April 1627. Second, the text of the aria, "Son tanti e lo sapete," is a conventional complaint from a lover denied a kiss; this scarcely seems right for Armida.

[17] Sigismondo d'India, *Le musiche ... da cantarsi nel chitarrone, clavicembalo, arpa doppia, & altri stromenti da corpo ... libro quinto* (Venice: Alessandro Vincenti, 1623). The *Lamento di Didone* is edited in Sigismondo d'India, *Le musiche a una e due voci: Libri I, II, III, IV e V*, 2 vols., ed. John J. Joyce, Musiche Rinascimentali Siciliane 9 (Florence: Olschki, 1989), 2:295–304. D'India's laments are discussed in Mompellio, *Sigismondo d'India*, 54; Nigel Fortune, "Sigismondo d'India: An Introduction to His Life and Works," *Proceedings of the Royal Musical Association* 81 (1954–55): 41–44; and Joyce, *The Monodies of Sigismondo d'India*, 43–47.

musical tropes that characterized the most famous lament of the early seventeenth century, Monteverdi's *Lamento d'Arianna*, from his opera *Arianna* of 1608 (to a libretto by Ottavio Rinuccini) and published as a chamber monody in the same year as d'India's *Le musiche . . . libro quinto*. Contemporary evidence of the dissemination and popularity of the *Lamento d'Arianna* reveals how easily d'India could have come to know the piece, while the concurrent dates of publication of d'India's and Monteverdi's laments by the Venetian presses of Alessandro Vincenti and Bartolomeo Magni, respectively, suggest the rivalry between music printers that may also have influenced earlier "competitions" involving Monteverdi and his contemporaries.[18] The close relationship between the *Lamento di Didone* and the *Lamento d'Arianna* extends to both text and music. In his poetry, d'India exploits much of the imagery, turns of phrase, and rhetorical repetition so characteristic of Rinuccini's virtuosic verse. And the music follows Monteverdi in terms of declamatory pacing, angular melodic lines, sequential repetitions, and *concitato* semiquavers; indeed, at times d'India verges on direct quotation (Ex. 1).

D'India clearly prized the *Lamento di Didone* as a paragon of his recitative style for the theater. But his emulation of Monteverdi went a stage further. Monteverdi reworked his operatic *Lamento d'Arianna* as a five-voice madrigal cycle included in his Sixth Book of madrigals of 1614. Thus it is one of a surprising number of pieces from the period that survive in several formats, including versions both for solo voice and for, say, five-part ensemble, giving the lie to the clear-cut stylistic and affective distinctions between "new" styles of solo song for voice and continuo and "old"-style polyphony often, if erroneously, maintained in historical studies of this period.[19] D'India's *Lamento di Didone* underwent a similar process. An undated but clearly early

[18] See my "Artusi, Monteverdi, and the Poetics of Modern Music," in *Musical Humanism and Its Legacy: Essays in Honor of Claude V. Palisca*, ed. Nancy Kovaleff Baker and Barbara Russano Hanning (Stuyvesant, N.Y.: Pendragon Press, 1992), 171–94. Another *Lamento d'Arianna* (this time to a text by Marino) was also published by Bartolomeo Magni in 1623, in Pellegrino Possenti's *Canora sampogna*; while Francesco Costa's setting of Rinuccini's text appeared in his *Pianto d'Arianna: Madrigali e scherzi . . . a voce sola* (Venice: Alessandro Vincenti, 1626). On these and other chamber laments, see the discussion in William V. Porter, "*Lamenti recitativi da camera*," in "*Con che soavità*": *Studies in Italian Opera, Song, and Dance, 1580–1740*, ed. Iain Fenlon and Tim Carter (Oxford: Clarendon Press, 1995), 73–110.

[19] Examples of multiple versions of works in different formats are given in my "Giulio Caccini's *Amarilli, mia bella*: Some Questions (and a Few Answers)," *Journal of the Royal Musical Association* 113 (1988): 250–73. I have also explored some of the broader issues in my *Music in Late Renaissance and Early Baroque Italy* (London: Batsford; Portland, Oreg.: Amadeus Press, 1992), 184–201.

X

Example 1

(a) Monteverdi, *Lamento d'Arianna*

(b) D'India, *Lamento di Didone*

seventeenth-century partbook in the Biblioteca Estense in Modena (F1530) contains the alto parts of five settings published in d'India's Eighth Book of five-voice madrigals (1624)[20]—"Godea del sol i rai," "Pallidetto mio sole," "Lidia, ti lasso, ahi lasso," and two of the five *partes* of "Se tu, Silvio crudel, mi saettasti"—plus an alto part setting the text of the first section of the monodic *Lamento di Didone*.[21]

D'India had dedicated his Eighth Book to the Infante Isabella, princess of Modena, seeking to cement his new links with the Este family. In the dedication, he notes the presence in Modena of "a musical *concerto* formed by a gathering . . . of the best singers that Europe can hear today" ("un musico concerto, formato da una adunanza (dirò forse) de' megliori cantanti, ch'hoggi ascoltar possa l'Europa"). To judge by the rich vocal *passaggi* throughout the Eighth Book, the Modenese singers were indeed virtuosos, and d'India provides them with continuo madrigals in the style established by the last six pieces of Monteverdi's Fifth Book of 1605, which permitted the exploitation of various textures—solos, duets, trios, and so forth—as well as the full ensemble. D'India's Eighth Book opens with "Se tu, Silvio crudel, mi saettasti," Dorinda's well-known appeal to Silvio from Guarini's *Il pastor fido* (act 4, sc. 9), which Monteverdi also set (from "Ecco, Silvio, colei che in odio hai tanto") in his Fifth Book. After fifteen measures for solo soprano and continuo, d'India writes largely for the full ensemble even though only one character is still "speaking," with brief duets and trios for rhetorical emphasis or wordplay. The texture is largely homophonic, indeed often four-squarely so (Ex. 2),[22] although d'India sometimes moves to more expansive counterpoint, both to highlight expressive points in the text and to provide appropriate concluding gestures, as at the end of "Ma se con la pietà non è in te spenta."

[20] Sigismondo d'India, *L'ottavo libro de madrigali a cinque voci* (Rome: Giovanni Battista Robletti, 1624).

[21] The manuscript is cited in Fortune, "Sigismondo d'India," 42, and in Sigismondo d'India, *Ottavo libro dei madrigali a cinque voci — 1624*, ed. Glenn Watkins, Musiche Rinascimentali Siciliane 10 (Florence: Olschki, 1980), xxix. There are some significant variants not noted by Watkins: "Ma se con la pietà non è in te spenta," m. 42, alto, last note, c♯'; "Godea del sol i rai," m. 8, alto, third note, c♯'; m. 46, alto, first note, e'; "Pallidetto mio sole," mm. 51–52, alto is an octave higher; m. 69, alto, third note, a'. There are also differences in terms of rhythmic placement, and some evidence of recomposition (for example, in "Godea del sol i rai" the manuscript contains two additional passages: five measures between mm. 64–65 and two measures between mm. 107–8).

[22] Example 2 follows the edition of the madrigal in d'India, *Ottavo libro dei madrigali a cinque voci*, ed. Watkins, 2–5, mm. 29–35.

Example 2

D'India, "Se tu, Silvio crudel, mi saettasti"

These observations provide a useful basis for the conflation of the monodic *Lamento di Didone* and the alto part in F1530 presented in Appendix A, below. The alto part fits well enough with the solo song to suggest that it originally formed part of what I assume was a five-voice version of the lament in the manner of Monteverdi's polyphonic *Lamento d'Arianna*. For the first seventeen lines of the text (mm. 1–36), the vocal and bass lines of the monody combine easily with the alto part; a fuller reconstruction would require only the minor rhythmic changes and adjustments to the bass that one would expect in moving from a solo song to a polyphonic madrigal or vice versa. The setting appears to have been even more homophonic than "Se tu, Silvio crudel, mi saettasti": only for the final two lines ("Ahi, ch'a le mie querele e gravi pene / rispondon per pietà l'aure e l'arene") does d'India seem to have moved to expansive counterpoint for an expressive conclusion. This conclusion appears to have been modally closed with a final cadence on A (the "key" of the opening), whereas the equivalent cadence in the monodic *Lamento di Didone*, on E, is modally open, implying some manner of continuation.

We cannot be sure which version of the *Lamento di Didone* came first. If the apparently strict homophony in the first half of the five-voice setting suggests an arrangement of the solo song, some of the evident harmonic discrepancies between the two versions shift the argument in favor of the solo song itself being some kind of reworking. For example, in measure 14 of the alto part, the final two quarter notes, d'–a, imply an attempt to avoid consecutive octaves against a bass consisting of whole note d (figured 9–8) to whole note e: the more exotic shift from a "major" triad on d to one on B is easier to handle in a monodic texture. Similarly, the repeated a''s in the alto in measures 17–19 seem odd in the context of a harmonic progression created by the soprano and continuo lines that is perfectly manageable within a five- (four-, three-) part texture; this suggests that the monodic version reflects a later revision.

The possibility that d'India composed first the polyphonic version of the *Lamento di Didone* casts a somewhat different light on his claims for the theatrical perfection of his recitative lament. Ultimately, however, the question of chronology seems less important in the context of the evident proximity of solo song and polyphonic madrigal in the early seventeenth century: composers could draw upon either genre/style and were often equally effective and affective in both. D'India's own career as a composer well illustrates the point: he published polyphonic madrigals and solo songs more or less in tandem throughout his life, and they interact in intriguing ways. Of course, one can discuss whether the solo song is any more or less dramatic or "representative," to use a contemporary term, than the five-voice madrigal.[23] But the two versions of the *Lamento di Didone*, plus d'India's own comments in his letter to Enzo Bentivoglio of 2 September 1627, suggest that d'India's true theatrical style was threatened less by stylistic or generic cross-dressing between monody and madrigal than by external contamination from the canzonettas which d'India criticized in Mazzocchi's *La catena d'Adone* and which were gaining such prominence both in songbooks and on the stage at the time.

[23] I discuss the question of "representation" in *"Possente spirto:* On Taming the Power of Music," *Early Music* 21 (1993): 517–23; "Resemblance and Representation: Towards a New Aesthetic in the Music of Monteverdi," in *"Con che soavità,"* ed. Fenlon and Carter, 118–34; and " 'Sfogava con le stelle' Reconsidered: Some Thoughts on the Analysis of Monteverdi's Madrigals," in *Claudio Monteverdi: Convegno di studi,* ed. Claudio Gallico (Florence: Olschki, forthcoming).

D'India himself had a significant part to play in the changing status of the canzonetta-aria, as his celebrated "Torna il sereno Zefiro" reveals.[24] And he could write seductive triple- or duple-time melodies with the best of his contemporaries. But he also retained a clear sense of propriety, considering such trifles appropriate only in their proper place. The *Lamento d'Apollo* in his *Le musiche . . . libro quarto* (1621)[25] offers a revealing comparison. Even when his own poetic muse (and doubtless Apollo's mythical associations) led d'India to shift into strophic structures within a conventional lament, he resisted any drastic musical implications. Apollo twice has two-stanza groupings of four *endecasillabi*, and each time, the second stanza is printed just as text underneath the music of the first. And this music remains in a conventional declamatory style, distinguished from the rest of the recitative only by its rather foursquare structure, somewhat in the manner of the earlier improvisatory formulas then formalized in operatic prologues. Farther than this he would not go: just as he decried the modern tendency toward facile melody at the expense of serious counterpoint in the preface to his *Liber primus motectorum quatuor vocibus* (1627), so, surely, would he have resented the degradation of laments of noble characters by the current vogue for aria and related styles.

This vogue may account in part for d'India's eventual failure to secure the commission for the 1628 festivities, notwithstanding his claims for the superiority of his music, and indeed of the recitative style in general. His submission to Enzo Bentivoglio of two laments for Armida and Dido seems more than coincidence. First, Monteverdi, too, had recently been working on a *Lamento d'Armida*.[26] And second,

[24] The significance of "Torna il sereno Zefiro" and its mixture of "recitative" and "aria" styles is discussed in Nigel Fortune, "Italian Secular Monody from 1600 to 1635: An Introductory Survey," *The Musical Quarterly* 39 (1953): 191. The song appears in d'India's *Le musiche . . . libro quinto* (1623), i.e., the same volume as contains his *Lamento di Didone*.

[25] Sigismondo d'India, *Le musiche . . . a una et due voci . . . libro quarto* (Venice: Alessandro Vincenti, 1621).

[26] Monteverdi's now lost *Lamento d'Armida*—setting Tasso's *Gerusalemme liberata*, XVI.40 ff.—is first mentioned in his letter to Alessandro Striggio of 1 May 1627; see *The Letters of Claudio Monteverdi*, trans. Denis Stevens, 2d ed. (Oxford: Clarendon Press, 1994), 315. The piece is also mentioned in letters of 25 September, 2 October, and 18 December 1627, and 4 February 1628 (ibid., 374, 378, 387, 395). Monteverdi's letter of 18 September 1627 refers to his not having "completely finished *Aminta*" (ibid., 369), which Stevens takes to refer to the 1628 Parma music, although Fabbri (*Monteverdi*, 266; *Monteverdi*, trans. Carter, 204) believes this to be a mistake for *Armida*. Striggio seems to have been intending to use the work for performance in Mantua; Monteverdi's letter of 4 February 1628 also associates it with his Venetian

a lamenting Dido, with Settimia Caccini singing the role, did indeed appear in Parma in 1628, in the second of the *intermedi* accompanying Tasso's *Aminta*. Whether or not Bentivoglio had already released details of the subject matter of some or all of the proposed *intermedi*, the musical grapevine in the mid 1620s appears to have been remarkably efficient.[27] Whatever the case, d'India seemed to feel that the setting of a lament was significant proof of a composer's ability to write music for the stage. As we shall see, however, developments in Parma in 1627–28 suggest that the conventional approach to laments by way of *versi sciolti* set in recitative no longer sufficed to secure the prize.

In any event, d'India's carefully constructed letter of 2 September proved redundant: on 4 September Enzo Bentivoglio told Dowager

---

patron Girolamo Mocenigo, who provided the venue for the premiere of Monteverdi's more famous adaptation from Tasso, the *Combattimento di Tancredi et Clorinda* of 1624.

Here and below, references to Monteverdi's letters are for convenience made in the first instance to Stevens's translation (the second edition introduces important revisions to the first [1980], which is now superseded). I have also used these translations where possible, with minor changes in styling, there being scant reason to introduce new readings into the literature save where there are errors to be corrected. In the latter case, I cite Claudio Monteverdi, *Lettere*, ed. Éva Lax, Studi e Testi per la Storia della Musica 10 (Florence: Olschki, 1994); Lax's new edition is much to be preferred over Claudio Monteverdi, *Lettere, dediche e prefazioni: Edizione critica con note*, ed. Domenico de' Paoli (Rome: Edizioni de Santis, 1973).

[27] A number of the stage effects of the 1628 *intermedi* and tournament drew on entertainments planned for the original opening of the Teatro Farnese in 1618 (see Reiner, "Preparations in Parma")—including in the second *intermedio* the appearance of the dragon and the descent of Iris—but Dido and Aeneas were not part of the subject matter. Nevertheless, work on the 1628 Dido *intermedio* seems to have begun early on in the proceedings. In his letter to Enzo Bentivoglio of 18 September 1627, Monteverdi claimed that he was hoping to send "the intermezzo of *Dido* in its entirety" on the forthcoming Saturday (*The Letters of Claudio Monteverdi*, 372), although on 30 October he admitted that it was still not finished (ibid., 380). Meanwhile, on 24 October 1627 the stage designer Francesco Guitti reported to Bentivoglio on the near completion of the Carthage set (Mamczarz, *Le Théâtre farnese de Parme*, 125).

Guitti had the texts of at least three of the *intermedi* on 7 September 1627: see his letter to Enzo Bentivoglio given in Lavin, "Lettres de Parme," 120–22. Revisions occurred as work continued on the entertainments, however: for example, on 1 October 1627 Goretti sent Monteverdi a new set of texts for the *intermedi*—see his letter to Bentivoglio given in Mamczarz, *Le Théâtre farnese de Parme*, 460–61—and words were still being added on 21 October 1628 (Goretti to Bentivoglio in ibid., 475). Similarly, the ending of the third *intermedio* was likely altered at some stage: in his letter to Bentivoglio of 10 September 1627 (*The Letters of Claudio Monteverdi*, 358), Monteverdi refers to Diana falling in love with Endymion, but in the final text she snubs her "pastore," who is no longer Endymion: Margherita de' Medici's beauty has rendered Cupid's weapons impotent.

Duchess Margherita of Parma (the widow of Duke Ranuccio Farnese) of his pleasure at the fact that the choice had been made in favor of Monteverdi, "as much for the man's rare quality as also for being able to get down to work."[28] We do not know who made this choice, and on whose recommendation. But whatever its artistic or other grounds, d'India also fell victim to a good deal of backstage maneuvering for the commission. According to Monteverdi, "about six or seven applied for the appointment,"[29] who seem to have included, besides d'India and Mazzocchi, Antonio Goretti, Alessandro Ghivizzani (Settimia Caccini's husband), and possibly Giovan Battista Crivelli.[30] Word of d'India's presence on a shortlist for the commission had already spread before his own first letter to Bentivoglio of 26 August. On 13 August 1627, Goretti wrote to Bentivoglio with his own rather acerbic view of d'India's suitability: "he is capable—nor can anything be said to the contrary; but it is also true, however, that he has in his head certain ideas of wishing to be considered the foremost man in the world, and that no one but he knows anything; and whoever wishes to be his friend, and deal with him, has to puff him up with this wind." Goretti also claimed that d'India was always reluctant to heed "the necessity of putting the pieces into practice and having them sung with the appropriate harmonies and accompaniments—for here is the whole point with regard to making the work turn out well." One should not forget, he said, the lessons of Turin, where "the poor virtuosos had to go crazy."[31]

Despite Goretti's personal interest in the proceedings, his comments may well contain more than a grain of truth given the self-important tone of d'India's letter of 2 September. And musicians at the Farnese court shared this negative view. On 28 August 1627, Alessandro Ghivizzani wrote to Dowager Duchess Margherita stating that he was as good a musician as d'India, and that if the latter wrote the music for Parma, his wife Settimia Caccini was not prepared to

---

[28] See Umberto Benassi, "I natali e l'educazione del duca Odoardo Farnese," *Archivio storico per le provincie parmensi pubblicato dalla R. Deputazione di Storia Patria,* n.s. 9 (1909): 213; see also *The Letters of Claudio Monteverdi,* 361. Bentivoglio repeated the point in his letter to the duchess of 6 September.

[29] In his letter to Alessandro Striggio of 10 September 1627 (*The Letters of Claudio Monteverdi,* 362).

[30] Crivelli dedicated his *Primo libro delli madrigali concertati a due, tre, & quattro voci* (Venice: Alessandro Vincenti, 1626) to Duke Odoardo Farnese on 30 March 1626; see Reiner, "Preparations in Parma," 286.

[31] *AB* 208, fols. 241r–242r, translated in Reiner, "Preparations in Parma," 286–87. The original will be included in Dinko Fabris's forthcoming edition of correspondence in the Bentivoglio archive.

renounce the right to sing only her husband's music; but "if a Monteverdi—to whom all must yield—were to compose the music, Settimia will sing most willingly, and I, if required, would serve him as copyist."[32] Ghivizzani wrote to Monteverdi (so the composer reported) in even stronger terms: "If anybody—other than you yourself—has a right to look after that music, I should do so more than anyone else, because I am not inferior . . . in any aspect of the art."[33]

Monteverdi entered the lists in early to mid August 1627 in response to a specific invitation from Bentivoglio, or so he claimed, perhaps disingenuously, to Alessandro Striggio. His apparent eagerness to work for the Farnese does not entirely square with his normal reluctance to fulfill commissions for the Mantuan court: the conventional view has Monteverdi much happier working in a republic such as Venice than for a duke, given his unhappy experiences during the later years of his service to the Gonzagas. But in fact Monteverdi was surprisingly anxious to retain connections with, or even return to, courtly music making: he pursued the possibility of employment with Prince Władisław (later, King Władisław Sigismund IV) of Poland, and he later became associated with the Habsburg court in Vienna, in part by way of Mantuan connections. For all Monteverdi's complaints about his earlier treatment in Mantua, the court continued to hold its attractions for the composer.

As for the 1628 commission, Monteverdi managed to give an impression of rising above the bickering among the Parma musicians, doubtless because his appointment had already been decided by the time of his first surviving letter (which was his second, at least) to Enzo Bentivoglio. On 10 September 1627, the composer acknowledged the receipt from Bentivoglio the day before of both the text of one of the *intermedi* (the third) and a partial copy of a letter from Dowager Duchess Margherita of Parma confirming the commission.[34] But the smooth formality of Monteverdi's letter to Bentivoglio could well mask his relief at having achieved a delicate diplomatic and tactical

---

[32] Benassi, "I natali e l'educazione," 212–13: "quando componesse la musicha un Monteverde, al quale ognun deve cedere, la Settimia volentierissimo canterà, et io, bisognando, lo servirò da copista." Benassi is reporting and quoting from a letter in the "Carteggio farnesiano generale"; I have not been able to trace this letter. The musician who eventually took on the job of Monteverdi's copyist was Antonio Goretti, whose connection with the composer went back some thirty years (the performances of Monteverdi's madrigals in Ferrara which led to the Artusi-Monteverdi controversy took place in Goretti's house).

[33] Given in Monteverdi's letter to Ercole Marigliani of 10 September 1627; see *The Letters of Claudio Monteverdi*, 367.

[34] *The Letters of Claudio Monteverdi*, 358–59.

victory; as always with Monteverdi, one needs to read carefully between his lines. And while it is hard to gauge the extent of his direct involvement in any competition, this was clearly a sensitive matter from several points of view. For example, again on 10 September Monteverdi wrote to his old friend Alessandro Striggio in Mantua in response, it seems, to a slightly querulous request for information (given the composer's unimpressive track record in writing music for recent Mantuan court entertainments, Striggio may well have felt disgruntled at news of the Parma commission). In this letter, Monteverdi emphasizes that he enjoys a special relationship with Bentivoglio (for which scant evidence survives before 1627), who had written "as long as a month ago" about the commission; that he is to write music for *intermedi* and not an opera (perhaps a potential sore point in the context of Monteverdi's earlier collaborations with Striggio); that the task should not take up too much time (a vain hope, in the event); and that the appointment does him great honor. He also appears to tell a fib: assuming that the *intermedio* text just sent by Bentivoglio was the first he received, he could scarcely "have already half finished" setting verses which had reached him the day before, even if, as he said, "they are almost all soliloquies."[35]

On that busy day in September, Monteverdi wrote a third letter, this time to Ercole Marigliani (Marliani), a Mantuan count with whom he had collaborated on *Andromeda* (1620). This letter gives stronger hints of Monteverdi's involvement in some element of intrigue.[36] Clearly the composer had sought to enlist in his cause Alessandro Ghivizzani, the Florentine-trained musician now working in Parma who had collaborated with Monteverdi and others in writing the music for the *sacra rappresentazione La Maddalena* (Mantua, 1617). Ghivizzani certainly wrote at least twice to Monteverdi in Venice, as Monteverdi reported to Marigliani on 10 September. According to Monteverdi, Ghivizzani's latest letter "speaks of little else but his certainty about the shortness of time for what those Most Serene Princes intend to do, and as yet nothing in the way of poetry or any kind of beginning is to be seen." Also, "Once again he kindly assures me that he will not allow his wife to obey anyone else but myself in singing," which is probably closer to the truth than Ghivizzani's claim

[35] Ibid., 361–64. This is Monteverdi's first mention of the 1628 commission to Mantua, although some hint of a "busy state of affairs" can be found in his letter to Striggio of 17 August 1627 (ibid., 351).

[36] Ibid., 366–67. This has been a problematic letter in the literature, and one plagued by misreadings corrected only in Monteverdi, *Lettere*, ed. Lax, 175–76 (followed by Stevens in the second edition of his translation of the letters).

to Dowager Duchess Margherita of Parma on 28 August that Settimia Caccini was able to choose whose music she sang.[37] And Ghivizzani's dispute with d'India seems to have escalated, "since he [Ghivizzani] could not suffer the friend he loves to be hurt by anyone, either rightly or wrongly."[38]

Monteverdi himself probably knew d'India in person, since d'India had visited Venice in 1621, as well as through his music, although we cannot tell whether or how that acquaintance—and the knowledge that d'India had been involved in the competition for the Parma commission—influenced his own work for the 1628 festivities.[39] This work is well documented in his own letters, and in those from Antonio Goretti, who was appointed his assistant. We also have other contemporary accounts and Marcello Buttigli's official description of the festivities,[40] though the latter makes scant reference to music. Monteverdi composed the prologue *Teti e Flora* (text by Claudio Achillini) and five *intermedi* (by Ascanio Pio di Savoia, Enzo Bentivoglio's son-in-law) for Tasso's *Aminta*, performed on 13 December 1628 in a

[37] The issue is none too surprising given the condition of women performers in early seventeenth-century Italy and their subservience to their husbands, fathers, or guardians. It may also have a bearing on the often problematic attributions of musical works associated with husband-wife pairs in this period, such as Vittoria and Antonio Archilei, Ippolita Recupito and Cesare Marotta, and indeed Settimia Caccini and Alessandro Ghivizzani. For Vittoria Archilei, see the conflicting attribution of the opening song of the first of the 1589 Florentine *intermedi*, "Dalle più alte sfere," to Emilio de' Cavalieri (in the 1589 *descrizione* of the festivities by Bastiano de' Rossi) and to Antonio Archilei (in the 1591 print of the music); see *Les Fêtes du mariage de Ferdinand de Médicis et de Christine de Lorraine, Florence 1589*, vol. 1, *Musique des intermèdes de "La pellegrina,"* ed. D. P. Walker (Paris: Centre National de la Recherche Scientifique, 1963; reprint, 1986), xxxvii–xxxviii. Songs by Settimia Caccini and Alessandro Ghivizzani are variously attributed one to the other, and to other musicians, in the paired manuscripts Bologna, Civico Museo Bibliografico Musicale, Q49, and Prague, Národní Muzeum, Hudebni Oddělení, Lobkowitz MS II.La.2. Husbands may well haved claimed authorship of music sung or even written by their wives.

[38] It is not clear whether Ghivizzani has responded to another letter from d'India pursuing his claim for the 1628 music, and one maligning Monteverdi directly, or whether Ghivizzani has seen a version of d'India's letter to Bentivoglio of 2 September, and thus that the maligned "friend" is Domenico Mazzocchi.

[39] The purpose of D'India's 1621 visit was to receive a knighthood from the doge; see Roark Miller, "New Information on the Chronology of Venetian Monody: The 'Raccolte' of Remigio Romano," *Music and Letters* 77 (1996): 30 n. 27. Miller notes in addition that the texts of d'India's laments for Apollo and Orpheus (in his *Le musiche . . . libro quarto*, 1623) were also published in Remigio Romano's *Nuova raccolta di bellissime canzonette* (Venice: Salvadori, 1623).

[40] Marcello Buttigli, *Descrizione dell'apparato fatto per honorare la prima e solenne entrata in Parma della serenissima principessa Margherita di Toscana, duchessa di Parma, Piacenza* (Parma: Seth Viotto, 1629).

X

temporary theater erected in the courtyard of S. Pietro Martire in the confines of the ducal palace. He also provided music for the tournament *Mercurio e Marte* (again, by Achillini) marking the long-delayed opening of the Teatro Farnese on the twenty-first. The performance of a play with *intermedi* is symptomatic of the continuing favor found in the North Italian courts by ostensibly old-fashioned theatrical genres even after the invention of opera:[41] it is revealing that on 4 September 1627, Enzo Bentivoglio told Dowager Duchess Margherita of Parma that "as regards staging a *commedia di buffoni* or an *opera recitata*, either one or the other will do well, but there is no doubt that a tragicomedy will have more of the aristocratic."[42] But the Farnese may also have sought to make a broader competitive point, given the special place reserved for *intermedi* within Florentine traditions of courtly entertainment.

The subjects of the *intermedi* were Ruggiero and Bradamante, Dido and Aeneas, Diana victorious over Venus and Cupid, Jason and the Argonauts, and the appearance of the four continents and the gods (prefacing a brief tournament itself heralding *Mercurio e Marte*). This combination of themes typically exploited mythology, classical sources (Virgil), and Renaissance epic (Ariosto and Tasso) to generate the range of princely encomiums, spectacular settings (landscape, sea scene, inferno, the heavens), and stage machines conventional of the genre. Although the music for the *intermedi* is lost, the surviving texts offer at least a possibility of assessing how Monteverdi might have approached his task.[43]

[41] See my comments in "The North Italian Courts," in *Man and Music: The Early Baroque Era; From the Late Sixteenth Century to the 1660s*, ed. Curtis Price (London: Macmillan, 1993), 23–48.

[42] "E l'uno e l'altro starà bene circa il far comedia di bufoni o opera recitata. Non è però dubio che avrà più del nobile una tragicomedia" (Benassi, "I natali e l'educazione," 213 n. 4). What to stage with the *intermedi* was still undecided on 1 October 1627. Reiner ("Preparations in Parma," 288 n. 73) cites Bentivoglio's letter in translation (giving its location as Parma, Archivio di Stato, Carteggio farnesiano inedito, busta 372) and takes "comedia di bufoni" as an "improvised" *commedia dell'arte* production, and "opera recitata" as a more formal play (hence, the "tragicomedia" eventually chosen). But *Aminta* was performed, in effect, by "buffoni"—just as the play was premiered in 1573 by the Gelosi company—and by "opera recitata" Bentivoglio could have meant to include a work "recited" in music, that is, an opera as we would understand the term. I would not press the point, however.

[43] The texts are edited in Angelo Solerti, *Musica, ballo e drammatica alla corte medicea dal 1600 al 1637: Notizie tratte da un diario con appendice di testi inediti e rari* (Florence: Bemporad, 1905; reprint, New York: Broude Brothers, 1968), 429–79. Solerti also includes the texts of the prologue, *Teti e Flora*, and of the tournament.

The text of the second *intermedio* merits closer study in this light, not least because of the apparent, if partial, precedent of d'India's sample lament. The story comes from Virgil, with accretions drawing upon Ariosto and Tasso. The scene represents Carthage in the process of construction, with the sea in the distance. Aeneas enters with Achates; (l. 16) Mercury descends to urge Aeneas to fulfill his destiny in Italy, Aeneas wishes to take farewell of Dido, and Mercury tells Achates to lead the fleet offshore to await Aeneas's arrival; (l. 81) Ascanius looks forward to triumphs in Italy; (l. 127) Fame descends with two trumpets in hand and accuses Aeneas of treachery; (l. 151) Dido argues with Aeneas; (l. 212) Juno expresses her sympathy for Dido; (l. 238) Dido enters with Aeneas's sword in hand and accuses her lover, who makes his escape flying overhead on a dragon; (l. 294) Dido curses Aeneas, laments her fate, and resolves to die; and (ll. 362–74) Iris descends on a cloud to pronounce the moral of the tale:

> Messaggera non men l'alma Giunone,
> o bellissime Dame, a voi m'invia,
> e vuol che specchio all'alme vostre sia
> il caso della misera Didone.

(Kind Juno as a messenger, no less, / O most beautiful ladies, sends me to you, / and wishes that an example to your souls should be / the fate of the wretched Dido.)

This conclusion is conventional enough both within the *intermedio* tradition and in terms of contemporary perceptions of Dido. Similarly, the accretions to Virgil sit squarely within this theatrical context, and served to display the scenic possibilities of the temporary theater constructed in Parma in 1628 for the performance of *Aminta* and its *intermedi:* witness the descent not just of Mercury, following the *Aeneid,* but also of Fame, Juno, and Iris. Aeneas's escape by dragon is part of the same trend, but it evokes other resonances as well: Mercury arranges the dragon's appearance "dal mauritano Atlante" (l. 73), a reference to the African necromancer in Ariosto's *Orlando furioso* who also appears in the first of the 1628 *intermedi*. Other comments by Mercury further associate "effeminato Enea" (l. 16), as he was commonly viewed in the sixteenth century, with those famous Renaissance heroes seduced from the path of duty by women-magicians, Ariosto's Ruggiero and Tasso's Rinaldo. Dido, on the other hand, is explicitly equated with Rinaldo's captress, the pagan Armida. When Dido curses Aeneas, she does so with a series of strophic texts, in the

second of which the first line of each strophe begins "Vattene pur . . ."
(". . . fellone," ". . . o crudo," etc.). The poet seals the reference to
Armida's "Vattene pur, crudel, con quella pace" (*Gerusalemme liberata*,
XVI.59) with a direct quotation from Armida's invective, "tanto
t'agitarò quanto t'amai," which recurs as a refrain.[44] The association
of Dido with Armida reminds us of d'India's two laments submitted to
Bentivoglio on 2 September 1627. It also turns Virgil's heroine into a
type much closer to one late Renaissance notion of the feminine: the
lamenting, perhaps mad, woman betrayed and abandoned by her
lover.[45]

Monteverdi himself remarked on the "molte e variate orazioni" in
the Parma *intermedi*,[46] and in the second *intermedio* this variety
extends even to the verse structure in several striking and apparently
unconventional ways. In particular, the free-rhymed seven- and
eleven-syllable *versi sciolti* typical of stage recitative (and of d'India's
text for his *Lamento di Didone*) are interspersed with regular strophic
units, often with refrains. The pattern is established by Ascanius, who
has a three-stanza canzonetta (for want of a better term)—"Ecco pur
giunto il giorno" (ll. 89–124)—mixing *settenari* and *quinari* with a final

---

[44] The quotation is extended in the second strophe: "nova furia co' serpi, ove sarai,
/ tanto t'agitarò quanto t'amai" (ll. 304–5; compare Tasso's "Nova furia, co' serpi e
con la face / tanto t'agiterò quanto t'amai" in *Gerusalemme liberata*, XVI.59).
Monteverdi had already set Tasso's text in his *Terzo libro de madrigali a cinque voci*
(Venice: Ricciardo Amadino, 1592). As for the Tasso quotation(s) in Dido's speech,
there are strong links with a set of *intermedi* by Battista Guarini reworking Tasso's
Armida story, which Guarini provided for Enzo Bentivoglio(!) in 1612. These
*intermedi* were staged, with alterations, in Ferrara in early 1614 and 1616. John Walter
Hill (*Roman Monody, Cantata, and Opera*) gives useful extracts from Antonio Ongaro,
*L'Alceo, favola pescatoria . . . con gl'intramezzi del Sig. Cavalier Batista Guarini* (Ferrara,
1613/14). In Guarini's third *intermedio*, Armida says to Rinaldo, "Ove ne vai crudele?"
(Dido says the same in l. 151 of the second of the Parma *intermedi*); then "Vattene pur
crudele. / Ch'avrai me tosto a tergo / nuova furia; va pur, ch'ovunque andrai / tanto
t'agiterò quanto t'amai" (compare Dido's ll. 298–99, 302, 304–5 in Appendix B,
below). It seems clear that Ascanio Pio di Savoia had sight of some version of
Guarini's *intermedi*.

[45] I am grateful to Wendy Heller for our discussion on this and other issues; see
also her "Chastity, Heroism, and Allure: Women in the Opera of Seventeenth-
Century Venice" (Ph.D. diss., Brandeis University, 1995).

[46] In his letter to Enzo Bentivoglio of 25 September 1627 (Monteverdi, *Lettere*, ed.
Lax, 180–81): "chè non sarà così facil cosa (secondo me) il concertar le molte e variate
orazioni che veggo in tali bellissimi intermedi." Stevens (*The Letters of Claudio
Monteverdi*, 376–77) translates this as "many and varied soliloquies," but when the
composer (in his letter to Alessandro Striggio of 10 September 1627) referred to the
ease with which he would set the *intermedi* "because they are almost all soliloquies"
(*The Letters of Claudio Monteverdi*, 362) he used the Italian "soliloqui" (Monteverdi,
*Lettere*, ed. Lax, 106). In this context, "orazioni" may simply mean "speeches,"
although there is another possible reading, to be discussed below.

*endecasillabo* refrain ("Ceda amor ad onor, diletto a gloria"). Fame's speech (ll. 127–44) consists of three stanzas of *endecasillabi* and *settenari*, and Juno's (ll. 212–27) of four stanzas of *endecasillabi*, each ending with a *quinario*. Contemporary librettists often gave gods and allegorical figures such repetitive poetic structures, to be set to music as strophic variations or arias, and Ascanius's song can be excused as the outpourings of youth (compare Telemachus at the opening of act 2 of Monteverdi's *Il ritorno d'Ulisse in patria*). And one might well justify the two *ottava rima* stanzas for Dido (ll. 185–200) as appropriate for so seemingly noble, indeed "epic," a character, especially given the broader echoes of Tasso;[47] here, though, and toward the end of the *intermedio* as we shall see, the metrical structure also seems designed to give force to her accusations and threats.

But the second half of the *intermedio* is more surprising. Here Dido berates Aeneas, laments her fate, and leaves the stage to die (the text is given in Appendix B, below). Dido enters in high dudgeon at the news that Aeneas has left Carthage. As Aeneas flies overhead on the dragon, he proclaims his escape, introducing a two-line refrain ("Ferma, ferma la mano; / cangia, cangia consiglio"; "Stay, stay thy hand; change, change your counsel") in the context of *versi sciolti*. Dido picks up on the refrain ("Ferma tu pure, o mio Signore, il volo"; "Stay thou, my lord, thy flight") in the first line of a strophic text in four stanzas with the refrain "O core del mio cor, riedi, deh riedi" ("O heart of my heart, return, ah return"), separated by freer speeches for Aeneas, as she pleads with her beloved. Though moved to pity, he pursues his flight, at which point Dido embarks on a second strophic text, "Vattene pur, fellone" ("Go then, villain") with the refrain "tanto t'agitarò quanto t'amai" ("I will harass thee as much as I loved thee," the quotation from *Gerusalemme liberata*, XVI.59). Then, as she shifts to referring to Aeneas in the third person, she begins a third sequence at "Ma l'empio se n'è gito" ("But the wicked one has gone"), the opening of which suggests some kind of strophic organization with the refrain "Che più tardo a morire?" ("Why do I delay my death any longer?"), although it gradually dissolves into looser structures. To be

---

[47] "Non ti generò Anchise, e non sei nato / da l'amoroso sen di Citerea; / un uomo così perfido e spietato / esser parto non può di quella Dea. / Te l'Arimaspe o 'l Caucaso gelato / produsser forsi, o mostruoso Enea; / ma te ne pentirai: sdegno e furore / scaccin dal petto mio l'infame amore. // Che vad'io più dissimulando invano / e perchè getto le querele e i pianti? / Col destino si scusa, empio ed infame [*sic*], / e del suo fallo accusa i regni santi: / ah, non fia ver che 'l menzogner Troiano / d'aver calcato l'onor mio si vanti; / armi e foco prendete, o gente fida, / s'arda ogni nave, ogni Troian s'uccida."

sure, refrains were by no means unusual in laments—Andrea Salvadori's *Didone abbandonata* included in the first volume of his *Poesie* (Rome, 1668) has two[48]—and Dido's speeches shift conventionally enough from accusation through curses and remorse to resignation. But in terms of structure, at least, her verse clearly does not conform to standard poetic treatments of the abandoned woman. This is no *Lamento d'Arianna*, nor is it, for that matter, a *Lamento di Didone* as d'India construed it.

The topos of the lamenting abandoned woman, and its expression in *versi sciolti* set in recitative, remained prevalent within theatrical and nontheatrical (if there is a difference) monodic repertories at least until the 1630s. Thus serious questions are raised by deviations from that norm, such as the range of poetic structures invoked in this second *intermedio*. The curious nature of Dido's laments may come down to questions of genre and of practical exigency. Perhaps one should not expect *intermedi* to conform to conventional canons of operatic expression in the period, despite d'India's apparent assumption to the contrary in his letter of 2 September 1627. *Intermedi* generally relied on a free succession of vocal and instrumental items focusing more on visual and aural effect, as in the well-known case of the 1589 Florentine *intermedi*. Also, despite the comments in d'India's letter, Settimia Caccini was judged weak at putting across the words in her singing,[49] and hence the *stile recitativo* would not display her talents in

---

[48] "Torna, torna crudele" and "Mori, misera, mori" in the context of free-rhyming *endecasillabi* and *settenari*: the lament is included in the section headed "Recitativi." I am grateful to Kelley Harness for pointing out this text to me, and also for her ideas on the 1628 Dido text that have influenced my discussion below. I have not been able to consult the *Lamento di Didone per musica*, "Quando miro l'innamorata Dido," given as a text in Rome, Biblioteca Nazionale, MS 43, fols. 11r–12v.

[49] Antonio Goretti later wrote to Enzo Bentivoglio from Parma on 28 October 1627 (*AB* 210, fols. 382r–383r, given in Fabbri, *Monteverdi*, 270; idem, *Monteverdi*, trans. Carter, 209): "We have looked over the musicians who are to come, and as regards women there is none other than Signora Settimia, who, to tell Your Most Illustrious Lordship the truth, I doubt will do as well as one thinks, and Signor Claudio thinks the same. For the rest, these singers are a pretentious bunch, to the extent that we are amazed." Goretti also complained about Settimia Caccini to Bentivoglio on 2 November 1627—"she is unlikely to have the success one believes, since she does not let the words be understood well as we have heard" ("non debba fare quella riuscita che si crede, non lasciando bene intendere le parole come l'abbiamo sentita")—and discussed plans to bring in Settimia's elder sister, Francesca Caccini (recently remarried and living in Lucca), although the two are "mortal enemies" ("nemiche mortali"); see the letter transcribed in Mamczarz, *Le Théâtre farnese de Parme*, 463–64. Both Monteverdi and Goretti continued to grumble about the singers.

the best light. This may have prompted the poet and composer to seek more strongly articulated forms of dramatic and musical expression.

The issue, however, may also extend to matters of characterization. D'India presents Dido as the conventional abandoned lover, noble enough in thought and deed, whereas the 1628 Dido is construed more complexly. Iris's final warning to the ladies of the audience that the "fate of the wretched Dido" should be "an example to your souls" is perhaps best read as an exhortation against excessive, immodest passion: Dido is "killed by love and madness" ("dall'amore e dal furore uccisa"). Even in Virgil—if not always Virgil as we choose to read him today—Dido was a problematic character, at once the noble queen and the seductive siren, and in this second *intermedio* Dido swings rather wildly between pleas and curses, and self-control and despair. The structural shifts of her verse reflect such emotional instability. It may be going too far to argue that the different poetic registers also seek to destabilize, if not undermine, a character of dubious morals too much swayed by love. But there are three issues that may give further clues for the use of strophic texts in Dido's laments. First, such texts and their related musical styles were often associated with seduction. Second, given Dido's reputed engagement in witchcraft, this would have all the hallmarks of an incantation scene were it not for the lack of, in a later period, signifying *versi sdruccioli*. Third, notions of madness are invoked if not in Dido's rhetoric at least in Iris's moral and in Dido's final stage direction as she leaves "furiosa" to commit suicide by Aeneas's sword.

Armida, too, went mad after Rinaldo's desertion. And in the contemporary theater, the singing of strophic canzonettas had long assumed the signifying function of madness. For example, in the 1589 *commedia dell'arte* performance of *La pazzia d'Isabella*, a prototype of dramatic mad-scenes, Isabella Andreini "as a madwoman went running through the city, stopping now one person and now another, and speaking now in Spanish, now in Greek, now in Italian and many other languages, but all without reason, and among other things she began to speak French and to sing certain canzonettas in the French style."[50] Monteverdi, too, had recently considered the representation

---

[50] Giuseppe Pavoni, *Diario . . . delle feste nelle solennissime nozze delli serenissimi sposi il sig. duca Ferdinando Medici e la sig. donna Christina di Lorena* (Bologna: Rossi, 1589), 29–30, cited in Paolo Fabbri, "On the Origins of an Operatic Topos: The Mad-Scene," in *"Con che soavità,"* ed. Fenlon and Carter, 157–95: "come pazza se n'andava scorrendo per la cittade, fermando or questo ed ora quello, e parlando ora in spagnuolo, ora in greco, ora in italiano, e molti altri linguaggi, ma tutti fuori di proposito, e tra le altre cose si mise a parlar francese et a cantar certe canzonette pure

of madness in the theater while working on *La finta pazza Licori* for Mantua in May–September 1627. In his letter to Striggio of 22 May 1627 confirming the decision to set Giulio Strozzi's libretto, he said that he would encourage the poet, "as is my habit," to enrich his text with "varied, novel, and diverse scenes" and "other novelties" so that "each time [Licori] comes on stage she can always produce new moods and fresh changes of music [*novi gusti e nove differenze di armonie*], as indeed of gestures."[51] Representing madness required a loosening of the conventional constraints upon genres and styles appropriate for representing particular types of characters. This not only served the cause of verisimilitude, but also provided a convenient justification for musical variety.

We do not know whether Monteverdi also exploited his "habit" of telling poets what to do in the case of Ascanio Pio di Savoia's texts for the 1628 *intermedi*. But whatever the case, Monteverdi's comment on the "molte e variate orazioni" in these texts now takes on a somewhat richer hue, especially if one chooses to read *orazione* in the broader sense of rhetorical delivery.[52] This poses the obvious burning question: how did these varied "orazioni" (whether "speeches" or "modes of delivery") fare in their musical setting? In their extensive correspondence on the 1628 festivities, neither Monteverdi nor Goretti makes much mention of the second *intermedio*. For all its apparent novelty, it seems to have been one of the more straightforward elements of an otherwise problematic entertainment.[53] Thus we can only speculate about the kinds of music Monteverdi wrote for his lamenting Dido, and about the extent to which they provided "novi

---

alla francese" (p. 164). See also Anne E. MacNeil, "Music and the Life and Work of Isabella Andreini: Humanistic Attitudes toward Music, Poetry, and Theater in the Late Sixteenth and Early Seventeenth Centuries" (Ph.D. diss., University of Chicago, 1994). Fabbri, "On the Origins of an Operatic Topos," charts the whole range of signifiers of madness in seventeenth-century opera: unusual musical behavior figures prominently. As for "canzonette pure alla francese," and as Anne MacNeil notes, this has obvious resonances for the debate over Monteverdi's ever problematic *canto alla francese*.

[51] *The Letters of Claudio Monteverdi*, 322–23. On *La finta pazza Licori*, see also Gary Tomlinson, "Twice Bitten, Thrice Shy: Monteverdi's 'finta' *Finta pazza*," this JOURNAL 36 (1983): 303–11.

[52] This, I think, is how the term should be read in the famous defense of the *seconda prattica*, with "orazione" (delivery, not just "words") deemed mistress, not servant, of the "armonia"; see, most recently, Suzanne Cusick, "Gendering Modern Music: Thoughts on the Monteverdi-Artusi Controversy," this JOURNAL 46 (1993): 1–25.

[53] The only matter for discussion was its eventual position within the set of *intermedi*; see the letter from Ascanio Pio di Savoia to Enzo Bentivoglio, Ferrara, 8 February 1628, given in Lavin, "Lettres de Parme," 145–46.

gusti e nove differenze di armonie" on the model of *La finta pazza Licori*. The use of strophic texts with refrains—in technical terms, arias—implies that the poetry requires a musical style in some way more structured than the norm in the *stile recitativo*. But we cannot know whether Monteverdi obtained such structure within the context of a more exalted style of recitative (whether or not with strophic variation) or by invoking duple- or triple-time aria styles, or both. Even in the most straightforward circumstances, predicting the musical outcome of setting a given text in the early seventeenth century is a perilous task, and Monteverdi's later Venetian madrigals and operas suggest that he, much more than many of his contemporaries, freely manipulated or ignored the structural implications of his verse in the pursuit of dramatic or affective expression, whether treating "aria" verse as recitative or, perhaps more commonly, vice versa. Given the ever-problematic mismatches between verse and music in Monteverdi's secular and theatrical music, a topic yet to be explored by those of us too willingly seduced by contemporary claims for the *seconda prattica*, one can do little but establish a range of options available to the composer.

Such options were perhaps most straightforward in the first and last of Dido's four text-complexes in this concluding section of the *intermedio*, respectively "Come, com'è fuggito" ("What, what, has he fled"; l. 228) and "Ma l'empio se n'è gito" (l. 318). "Come, com'è fuggito" suggests some kind of declamatory recitative, as does "Ma l'empio se n'è gito," with its loose refrain, *versi sciolti*, and careful rhetorical construction as Dido addresses the sword ("Tu ferro amato tanto / . . . / Tu mi traffigi il core /. . . / tu mi cura la piaga / . . . / tu questo seno impiaga / . . .") and then her hand ("E tu, per darmi aita / . . . / tu ch'il pegno di fede / . . . / lacera, o destra, tu l'indegno imago / . . . / tu chiudi questi lumi / . . ."). One can also well imagine the refrain in this last section ("Che più tardo a morire?") being set off by lyrical arioso. But more complex issues are raised by Dido's two strophic texts: "Ferma tu pure, o mio Signore, il volo" (from l. 248; separated by Aeneas's "recitatives") and "Vattene pur, fellone" (l. 294). The former a seductive plea and the latter an incantatory curse, they both lack the rhetorical strategies associated with recitative, and, of course, their poetic structures have other musical implications.

Nothing in Monteverdi's surviving output from this period bears comparison. But in fact, such strophic texts in *settenari* or *endecasillabi* with or without refrains figure commonly enough in the songbooks of the 1620s by composers close to Monteverdi in Venice. For example, they take up over two-thirds of the Third Book of cantatas and arias

(1626) by Alessandro Grandi, Monteverdi's deputy at St. Mark's.[54]
This emphasis on strophic texts suggests a new seriousness of purpose
and design for a poetic vein associated in the first two decades of the
century with amorous trifles (and with other line-lengths such as
*ottonari* or *quinari*).[55] The music, too, becomes more subtly cast than
in earlier examples of strophic canzonettas in the monody repertory.
Grandi's strategies for dealing with such texts involve setting them
entirely in declamatory "recitative," or entirely in some kind of "aria"
style, whether in triple time or, less often, in duple time over, say, a
walking bass. Another of Monteverdi's colleagues at St. Mark's, the
singer Giovanni Pietro Berti, apparently preferred to mix "recitative"
and "aria" styles. The first stanza of "Da grave incendio oppresso"—a
text elsewhere labeled a "Canzonetta Pietosa"—in his Second Book of
cantatas and arias (1627) provides a good example:[56]

> Da grave incendio oppresso
>   chiamo soccorso e la pietate invoco,
>   e in suon funesto e spesso
>   grida il cor palpitando al foco al foco;
>   e ben ch'arda mia vita
>   in vivo ardor nessun però m'aita.
>   Soccoretemi voi con largo humore
>   dunque occhi miei, che lo dimanda il core.

---

[54] Grandi's *Cantade et arie a voce sola . . . libro terzo* (Venice: Alessandro Vincenti,
1626) is included in facsimile in vol. 6 of *Italian Secular Song, 1606–1636*, ed. Gary
Tomlinson (New York and London: Garland, 1986), which also contains a number of
other Venetian songbooks with useful examples.

[55] See the discussion in Robert R. Holzer, "Music and Poetry in Seventeenth-
Century Rome: Settings of the Canzonetta and Cantata Texts of Francesco Balducci,
Domenico Benigni, Francesco Melosio, and Antonio Abati" (Ph.D. diss., University
of Pennsylvania, 1990), esp. 52–60; idem, " 'Sono d'altro garbo . . . le canzonette che
si cantano oggi': Pietro della Valle on Music and Modernity in the Seventeenth
Century," *Studi musicali* 21 (1992): 253–306. For later laments in strophic verse or
verse with elements derived from the canzonetta, see Holzer's discussion of Domenico Benigni's "Mortalmente ferito" (set by Mario Savioni) and "Lasciatemi qui
solo" (set by Luigi Rossi and Orazio Tarditi), in "Music and Poetry in Seventeenth-
Century Rome," 307–21.

[56] The song is in Berti's *Cantade et arie . . . libro secondo* (Venice: Alessandro
Vincenti, 1627). There are four stanzas, the last of which has new music. This song
was discussed in Fortune, "Italian Secular Monody from 1600 to 1635," 191–92; and
in a paper by Roark Miller, "Between Imitation and Plagiarism: Modes of Borrowing
in the Solo Canzonetta," presented at the Sixth Biennial Conference on Baroque
Music, University of Edinburgh, 7–10 July 1994. Berti's song is in fact earlier than,
and the model for, the setting included by Pellegrino Possenti—a fervent admirer of
Monteverdi—in his *Accenti pietosi d'Armillo, canzonette & arie* (Venice: Bartolomeo
Magni, 1625), from where the label comes.

Example 3

Giovanni Pietro Berti, "Da grave incendio oppresso"

(Burdened by harsh burning / I call for help and invoke pity, / and in sad sound and often, / my heart in palpitation cries "Fire, fire!" / And although my life burns / in lively flames, yet no one helps me. / Assist me with welling tears / then, my eyes, for the heart demands it.)

Here Berti sets the first six lines in "recitative," shifting to an extended lyrical triple-time passage for the refrain, "Soccoretemi voi . . ." (Ex. 3). The tantalizing suggestion that Monteverdi similarly made at least some reference to structured triple- or duple-time "aria" styles in his settings of Dido's two strophic texts would certainly be consistent with his remarks on Licori, with the notion that he was somehow responding to a challenge from d'India, and also with apparent trends both in Venetian secular music and in his own later works as aria and the musical styles associated with it increasingly gained aesthetic credibility as a significant means of emotional arousal.[57] If so, and even if Monteverdi's Dido concluded with impassioned recitative, d'India presumably would have objected, just as he did to the "canzonette" in Mazzocchi's *La catena d'Adone*. But d'India's conception of the *stile recitativo* as the most effective musical vehicle for representing the suffering and pleas of his abandoned Dido missed the point as a relic of a courtly art now superseded by newer musical and expressive demands.

Perhaps it would be unwise to polarize the issues too strongly. Even the most literal interpretation of the text structures of this *intermedio* does not support any clear-cut affective distinction between "recitative" and "aria," nor should it, for this period. At most the text seems distinctly casual in its exploration of different, at times inconsistent, ways of expressing the emotions of an abandoned woman. And as I have already suggested, d'India's failure to gain the 1628 commission probably owed as much to practical concerns as to any putative stylistic conservatism on his part. The Florentine courtier Luigi Inghirami sent four letters to Archduchess Maria Magdalena in Florence describing the festivities in Parma.[58] According to him, the wedding guests had an unhappy time, not least because of the December snow, fog, rain, and freezing temperatures. In the courtyard theater with its thin canvas roof, few paid serious attention to *Aminta*; indeed, the royal party left to take refreshment during the third act. The play was too well known and thus regarded as an unwise choice, and the actors found it hard to project their speeches above the coughing and sneezing in the audience, and the sound of feet stamping to keep warm. But in the case of the *intermedi*, Inghirami roundly praised both the stage machines (the descent of Fame's chariot in the second *intermedio* receives a special mention) and the music, "the spirit and soul of everything" ("lo spirito e l'animo di tutto"). He was no less enthusiastic about the prologue *Teti e Flora*, performed "with rare music and exquisite voices, this being the work of Monteverdi, today the best musician of Italy" ("con musiche rare e voci squisite, essendo

[57] See my "*Possente spirto*." It is also tempting to suggest that the *Lamento della ninfa* ("Non havea Febo ancora") in Monteverdi's *Madrigali guerrieri, et amorosi* of 1638 is the next link in the chain. This text (in *settenari piani* and *tronchi*, with a partial refrain in *ottonari tronchi*) is by Rinuccini, who died in 1621, and it had already been set as a canzonetta by Antonio Brunelli (in 1614, for solo voice and continuo) and Girolamo Kapsperger (in 1619, for two voices and continuo). See also Massimo Ossi, "Claudio Monteverdi's *Ordine novo, bello et gustevole*: The Canzonetta as Dramatic Module and Formal Archetype," this JOURNAL 45 (1992): 261–304.

[58] These letters are transcribed in Minucci del Rosso, "Le nozze di Margherita de' Medici con Odoardo Farnese Duca di Parma e Piacenza."

composizione di Monteverdi, oggi il migliore musico d'Italia"). Securing the "best musician of Italy" surely mattered most to Enzo
Bentivoglio during those hectic negotiations in August–September
1627. But he thereby gave Monteverdi a unique opportunity to return
to the stage, and to explore issues that would surely come to fruition
in his theatrical endeavors in Venice in years to come.

X

## Appendix A

### Sigismondo d'India, *Lamento di Didone*

The vocal line and basso continuo are taken from d'India's *Le musiche . . . da cantarsi nel chitarrone, clavicembalo, arpa doppia, & altri stromenti da corpo . . . libro quinto* (Venice: Alessandro Vincenti, 1623), 4–5; the alto part from Modena, Biblioteca Estense, F1530, fol. 6r–6v.

X

fug - gi    Che ti    fe - ci    cor    mi - o         Per - che ne - gar-mi oi -

fug - gi    che ti    fe - ci    cor    mi - o         per - che ne - gar-mi ohi -

me l'ul - ti-mo à Di - o              Non m'o - di    tù    mio so - le

me l'ul - ti-mo à Di - o              non m'o - di    tu    mio so - le

Deh    por - tas - se-ro i ven - ti    Co - me por - tan le    ve - le i miei

dhe    por - tas - se-ro i ven -

Sop. (1623)

la - men - ti          Ahi    ch'a le mie que - re - le e gra - vi

B.c. (1623)

11    #    11                            #              11

pe - ne    Ri - spon-don per pie - tà    l'au - re e l'a - re - ne

#        7        6        11        #

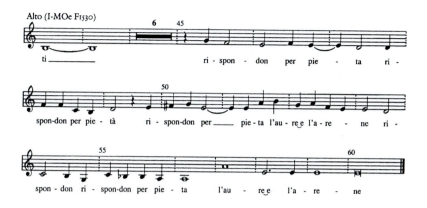

Alto (I-MOe F1530)

ti ___ ri - spon - don per pie - ta ri - spon-don per pie - tà ri - spon-don per___ pie - ta l'au - re e l'a - re - ne ri - spon - don ri - spon-don per pie - ta l'au - re e l'a - re - ne

## APPENDIX B
### Dido Berates Aeneas

The following text is the second half (from the departure of Juno) of the second of the *1628 intermedi* by Ascanio Pio di Savoia. It is taken, with some minor amendments, from the edition in Angelo Solerti, *Musica, ballo e drammatica alla corte medicea dal 1600 al 1637: Notizie tratte da un diario con appendice di testi inediti e rari* (Florence: Bemporad, 1905; reprint, New York: Broude Brothers, 1968), 445–49. Refrains are highlighted in bold type.

> *Esce di nuovo Didone dalla porta di Cartagine infuriata, con la spada di Enea in mano.*

Didone

> Come, com'è fuggito
> fuor delle mura della mia Cartago,
> quello stregon, quel mago?           230
> Dove, dove s'asconde?
> Non è chi me l'insegni,
> ch'io l'uccida e lo sbrani,
> e getti i membri indegni
> per degno pasto ai cani?             235

> *Intanto passa Enea per l'alto de l'aria sopra un gran drago, e verso Didone parla.*

Enea

> Tu mi ricerchi in vano
> ch'io son fuor di periglio;
> innalza il ciglio
> e mira, alta Reina,
> che mal s'oppugna ciò che 'l ciel destina!    240
> **Ferma, ferma la mano;**
> **cangia, cangia consiglio;**
> conosci che già mai non manca 'l cielo
> a chi 'l serve con puro e santo zelo:
> scaccia 'l furor insano,              245
> **ferma, ferma la mano,**
> **cangia, cangia consiglio.**

*Did.*                Ferma tu pure, o mio Signore, il volo;
                    cangia pur tu pensiero,
                    e 'l gravissimo duolo                       250
                    mi diverrà leggiero.
                    Deh ritorna, o pietoso cavaliero,
                    e farò quanto chiedi.
                    **O core del mio cor, riedi, deh riedi.**

*En.*                Deh, come volentieri io tornerei         255
                    se non me l'impedisse il re de' Dei.
*Did.*                Deh, non fidar te stesso ad un dragone,
                    che gli uomini divora,
                    più tosto che a Didone
                    che te qual nume adora.                   260
                    All'amor nostro, alla mia vita ancora
                    pochi giorni concedi.
                    **O core del mio cor, riedi, deh riedi.**

*En.*                Se non m'intenerisce il suo cordoglio
                    se non mi muove il mar di quel tormento,   265
                    se non mi crolla de' sospiri il vento,
                    certo ch'io sono in aria alzato scoglio.
*Did.*                Tu, che pretendi posseder il nome
                    glorioso di pio,
                    deh come poi, deh come                 270
                    voler il martir mio?
                    E come dare a me la morte, s'io
                    a te la vita diedi?
                    **O core del mio cor, riedi, deh riedi.**

*En.*                Come potrò lasciarti                275
                    in preda a sì gran pianto, o mio bel volto?
                    E come abbandonarti,
                    o sol de gli occhi miei fra nubi involto?
*Did.*                Non andar d'un dragon reggendo 'l freno
                    per l'aria peregrino,                  280
                    ma torna del mio seno
                    ad esser cittadino.
                    Fra i rischi a che cercar regno Latino
                    se l'African possiedi?
                    **O core del mio cor, riedi, deh riedi.**   285

*En.*                Ahi qual battaglia fan dentro 'l mio core,
                    coi divini precetti,
                    la pietade e l'amore.
                    Ma cedan pur al ciel terreni affetti;
                    empio sono a me stesso, empio a colei,   290
                    ch'amo più del cor mio,
                    per non esser già mai empio co' dei.
                    Ahi con quanta ragion son detto pio!

                  *Ciò detto Enea se ne va.*

*Did.*                Vattene pur, fellone,
                    da l'uno a l'altro polo,              295
                    che seguiratti a volo
                    la tradita Didone.
                    Vanne veloce pur, ch'ovunque andrai
                    **tanto t'agitarò quanto t'amai.**
                  Vattene pure, o crudo,               300
                    fuggi pur questo albergo,
                    ch'avrai me tosto a tergo
                    spirto di corpo ignudo;

nova furia co' serpi, ove sarai,
**tanto t'agitarò quanto t'amai.**                    305
Vattene pur, ingrato,
perfido mancatore,
nulla di cui peggiore
ha la terra creato;
vanne, che senza perdonarti mai,                    310
**tanto t'agitarò quanto t'amai.**
Vanne pur, disleale,
nel Cielo e ne l'Inferno,
ch'io ti sarò in eterno
indivisibil male;                                    315
vanne, che l'ombra mia, tosto il vedrai,
**tanto t'agitarà, quant'io t'amai.**
Ma l'empio se n'è gito,
e i duri miei tormenti
non ha voluto udire;                                 320
ahi ch'i pianti e i lamenti,
se ne portano i venti.
**Che più tardo a morire?**
Non han de l'infedele,
più crudo e più fellone                              325
del suo stesso dragone,
potuto l'amarissime querele
fermare almen la furia del partire:
**che più tardo a morire?**
Tu ferro amato tanto,                                330
e caro agli occhi miei,
mentre piacque alli dei
omai fa' che succeda il sangue al pianto.
Tu mi traffigi il core,
e col dolor mortale                                  335
da' fine al mio dolore:
tu mi cura la piaga
de l'amorosa strale;
tu questo seno impiaga,
e levane l'asprissimo martire.                       340
**Che più tardo a morire?**
E tu, per darmi aita,
mano, divieni ardita,
tu ch'il pegno di fede
già desti all'infedele,                              345
spingi il ferro pietoso, e non crudele,
ch'a fin funesto il traditor mi diede:
e col tormi di vita,
abbrevia il mio lunghissimo languire.
**Che più tardo a morire?**                          350
Nel magnanimo core
della Reina della gran Cartago
lacera, o destra, tu l'indegno imago
che del vile Troian v'impresse Amore;
tu chiudi questi lumi,                               355
già divenuti fiumi;
omai, con profondissima ferita,
medica il cor che langue;
omai lava col sangue
la macchia ch'io mi fei col mio fallire.             360
A morire, a morire.

*E ciò detto, risoluta di morire, se ne entra furiosa nella città.*

*Vedesi Iride, messaggia di Giunone, accompagnata da
bellissima nube, in cui scorgesi formato l'arco celeste.*

Iride          Nunzia son io della pietosa Dea,
    del gran Tonante in un moglie e sorella,
    e mandami a ciò 'l crin dorato svella
    a la tradita dal fugace Enea.                              365
Anzi tempo ella muora, e non dal Fato
    ma da l'amore e dal furore uccisa;
    onde pur troppo penarebbe Elisa,
    se non le fosse il fatal crin levato.
Messaggera non men l'alma Giunone,                                          370
    o bellissime Dame, a voi m'invia,
    e vuol che specchio all'alme vostre sia
    il caso della misera Didone.

# 'In Love's harmonious consort'?
# Penelope and the interpretation of
# *Il ritorno d'Ulisse in patria*

Recent Monteverdi scholarship has set great store by the composer's last work for the new 'public' opera houses of Venice, *L'incoronazione di Poppea* (1643).[1] The problematic status of the sources for *Poppea* – at least some of its music is not by Monteverdi – and a rather prurient fascination with its supposed amoral excess have provided ample scope for scholars to play their textual and critical games, often with impressive results.[2] But this has deflected attention from Monteverdi's first Venetian opera, *Il ritorno d'Ulisse in patria* (1640), written to a libretto by Giacomo Badoaro. Once a cause of some debate – Wolfgang Osthoff carried the torch in the 1950s[3] – *Il ritorno d'Ulisse* is now seen as a much less complicated work. We have only one manuscript of the score – *A-Wn* MS 18763 – the uncertain provenance of which has caused scant musicological anxiety; nor have the surviving copies of the libretto, with their divergent readings, excited much recent comment

---

[1] A first version of this paper was presented at the 27th Annual Conference ('Music and Eroticism') of the Royal Musical Association, Oxford, 27–9 March 1992; it also develops ideas presented rather primitively in my 'Monteverdi Returns to his Homeland', in Nicholas John, ed., *The Operas of Monteverdi*, English National Opera Guides, 45 (London, 1992), 71–81. I am grateful to Susan McClary, Ellen Rosand and Frederick W. Sternfeld for reading various drafts: their perceptive comments helped me realise still more the significance of the problems raised (if not always solved) here. I also owe an obvious debt to Gary Tomlinson, *Monteverdi and the End of the Renaissance* (Oxford, 1987); Susan McClary, 'Constructions of Gender in Monteverdi's Dramatic Music', this journal, 1 (1989), 203–23; Ellen Rosand, 'Iro and the Interpretation of *Il ritorno d'Ulisse in patria*', *Journal of Musicology*, 7 (1989), 141–64; *idem.*, *Opera in Seventeenth-Century Venice: The Creation of a Genre* (Berkeley, Los Angeles and London, 1991); and Iain Fenlon and Peter Miller, *The Song of the Soul: Understanding 'Poppea'*, Royal Musical Association Monographs, 5 (London, 1992). *Il ritorno d'Ulisse in patria* is in *Claudio Monteverdi: Tutte le opere*, ed. Gian Francesco Malipiero, 17 vols., 2nd edn (Vienna, 1954–68), vol. 12, from which the present music examples are drawn (with minor amendments). Quotations from the libretto are taken (with some editorial punctuation) from *The Operas of Monteverdi*, 87–128; translations are my own.
[2] The most recent, and best, example is Alan Curtis, '*La Poppea Impasticciata*, or Who Wrote the Music to *L'incoronazione* (1643)?', *Journal of the American Musicological Society*, 42 (1989), 23–54.
[3] Wolfgang Osthoff, 'Zu den Quellen von Monteverdis "Ritorno di Ulisse in patria"', *Studien zur Musikwissenschaft*, 23 (1956), 67–78; 'Zur Bologneser Aufführung von Monteverdis "Ritorno di Ulisse" im Jahre 1640', *Österreichische Akademie der Wissenschaften: Anzeiger der phil.-hist. Klasse*, 95 (1958), 155–60; *Das dramatische Spätwerk Claudio Monteverdis* (Tutzing, 1960).

from scholars.[4] Thus the text is seemingly secure. Moreover, the supposed 'moral' of *Il ritorno d'Ulisse* – 'the rewards of patience, the power of love over time and fortune'[5] — seems unproblematic, nay predictable, perhaps tedious. Even Ellen Rosand's noble attempt to inject a fly in the ointment by focusing on the seemingly minor character of Iro, the social parasite, has scarcely troubled complacent critical comment on an essentially straightforward opera with an essentially straightforward message.

Whether the 'power of love' is precisely the 'message' of *Il ritorno d'Ulisse* is open to question, as we shall see. But the work merits close study if only for the fact that it is Monteverdi's first surviving attempt to consolidate in the field of opera some three decades of drastic style-change in music. When he wrote his first operas, *Orfeo* (1607) and *Arianna* (1608), the problem, so to speak, was to legitimise the recitative – a style taking 'an intermediate course, lying between the slow and suspended movements of song and the swift and rapid movements of speech' developed by Jacopo Peri and his Florentine colleagues[6] – as a plausible and verisimilar representation of human speech. However, by the 1630s, whether through serious academic debate or simply (and more likely) by default, that battle was more or less won. The issue now brought to the fore, in contemporary madrigal books as much as on the operatic stage, was the status of song (aria) rather than sung speech (recitative) as a verisimilar mode of representation for characters in highly emotional states. *Orfeo* and (presumably) *Arianna* certainly contained formal arias – strophic settings of canzonetta-like texts, generally in a well-articulated triple or duple time. But as a matter of principle, these songs were placed in contexts where singing rather than speaking could plausibly be expected of operatic characters. However, the current trend – settings in Monteverdi's Seventh (1619) and Eighth (1638) Books of madrigals make the point – was to exploit the formal and formalist possibilities of aria and related styles in a less 'natural' (whatever that means) context in order to articulate an emotional crux and in turn to provide the musical focus of a given setting. Some might doubt the possibility of serious emotional statement within ostensibly light-hearted

---

[4] With the honourable exception of Rosand, 'Iro' (see n. 1). Of the nine extant manuscript librettos, Rosand allocates some priority on chronological grounds to the one in *I-Vmc* MS Cicogna 564 (hereafter *L*); see pp. 142n3, 148n18 (and I am grateful to Professor Rosand for providing me with a copy). As will become clear, the format of *L* – a first layer presenting the text, with a second layer of additions/corrections following the score – reveals intriguing divergences between the text here and that set by Monteverdi. However, attempts to play on their significance must be tempered by an acknowledgement that the lack of a thorough codicological study of the sources for *Il ritorno d'Ulisse* renders suspect any evidence drawn from them. For the most part, I shall not build such evidence into the core of my argument, suggestive though it may be about individual points therein.

[5] To quote Rosand, 'Iro' (see n. 1), 142.

[6] Peri discusses his formulation of the recitative in the preface to *Le musiche sopra L'Euridice* (Florence, 1600[ = 1601]), translated in Oliver Strunk, *Source Readings in Music History: From Classical Antiquity to the Romantic Era* (London, 1952), 373–6. Nino Pirrotta, *Music and Theatre from Poliziano to Monteverdi* (Cambridge, 1982), 237–80 ('Early Opera and Aria'), remains a crucial introduction to the problems raised here.

forms such as the canzonetta and its derivatives.[7] But for better or for worse, it was precisely the notion of some serious statement that lay at the heart of modern musical endeavour, with composers now reclaiming the ground for music as music, rather than as some spurious form of speech.

The anonymous Florentine author of *Il corago*, a treatise on opera of the early 1630s, was clear on the kinds of subjects best suited to the genre:

To begin with characters or interlocutors that musical setting seems to suit best, for secular plots the ancient deities such as Apollo, Thetis, Neptune and other respected gods seem very appropriate, as do demigods and ancient heroes, among whom one might especially list rivers and lakes, and especially those most famous among the Muses, such as Peneus, the Tiber, and the Trasimenus, and above all those personages whom we consider to have been perfect musicians, such as Orpheus, Amphion and the like. The reason for all this is that since each listener knows all too well that at least in the more familiar parts of the earth ordinary men do not speak in music, but plainly, speaking in music is more consonant with one's conception of superhuman characters than with the notion and experience one has of ordinary men; because, given that musical discourse is more elevated, more authoritative, sweeter, and more noble than ordinary speech, one attributes it to characters who, through a certain innate feeling, have more of a sublime or divine quality.

He also noted the fundamental problems created as opera left behind its origins within classical myth and the pastoral Age of Gold:

If we take as characters people close to our times, and of manners more obviously similar to ours, all too clearly this manner of sung speech soon presents itself to us as improbable and not lifelike [*inverisimile*].[8]

For Orpheus, music is a natural part of daily existence; whether it is so for Penelope and Ulysses, or indeed Nero and Poppaea, is another matter. Of course, opera could never be verisimilar in this sense, as contemporaries admitted in terms ranging from despair to complacency. Moreover, one early argument indirectly sanctioning the lack of verisimilitude in opera – that the genre was a revival of classical practice – was no longer appropriate for the anti-Humanist climate of the 1630s and 1640s. Contemporaries needed somehow to privilege the voice and singing as a 'natural'

---

[7] See, for example, Tomlinson, *Monteverdi* (n. 1), 231. This book is a powerful climax to a host of wide-ranging arguments first exposed in his 'Ancora su Ottavio Rinuccini', *Journal of the American Musicological Society*, 26 (1973), 240–62; 'Madrigal, Monody, and Monteverdi's "via naturale alla immitatione"', *Journal of the American Musicological Society*, 34 (1981), 60–108; 'Music and the Claims of Text: Monteverdi, Rinuccini, and Marino', *Critical Inquiry*, 7 (1982), 565–89. I made my broad views known – perhaps intemperately – in my review in *Early Music History*, 8 (1988), 245–60. I shall be making the changing status of aria-styles in the secular vocal music of Monteverdi and his contemporaries the subject of a forthcoming study.

[8] Anon., *Il corago o vero alcune osservazioni per metter bene in scena le composizioni drammatiche* [MS in *I-MOe* γ.F.6.11], ed. Paolo Fabbri and Angelo Pompilio (Florence, 1983), 63; this is among the passages given in Rosand, *Opera in Seventeenth-Century Venice* (see n. 1), 428 (for the first extract, I have used the translation on p. 39).

# XI

4

response to highly emotional situations,[9] one offering insights into human behaviour that were inherently more penetrating, and more trustworthy, than those gained by other modes of sensory perception. The latter argument was played out, with some degree of self interest, within the Accademia degli Incogniti, whose members acted as patrons, librettists and ideologues for much early Venetian opera.[10]

But the fact that song, rather than sung speech, still posed profound problems is clear from the attempts of contemporary librettists and composers to locate arias according to at least vestigial canons of verisimilitude.[11] Realistic songs in a 'natural' setting (that is, in which a character could plausibly sing rather than speak) posed few problems: as we have seen, they were sanctioned in the first operas in Florence and Mantua. Song was also appropriate for certain kinds of characters: gods and allegorical figures (song signifies superhuman powers), inhabitants of a pastoral world (song is the natural language of shepherds and shepherdesses in the Age of Gold) and characters of 'low', often comic, status (drawing in part on the conventions for song within the *commedia dell'arte*). And song had its place in situations where 'reality' itself was suspended, for example, in magic or sleep scenes. The more opportunities there were for such songs within a libretto, the better: this is one explanation for the formulaic character of much Venetian opera in this period.

In *Il ritorno d'Ulisse*, Badoaro and Monteverdi follow these patterns within the constraints of their plot: there are few realistic songs, which poses some logistic problems, but gods, shepherds (Eumete), nurses (Ericlea) and other comic characters (Iro) sing in structured triple and duple time to obvious effect. However, given the taste for aria in contemporary Venetian opera, both librettist and composer also had to justify song (rather than sung speech) for characters lying outside the range of those for whom aria was a more or less automatic right. The situation is straightforward enough for the two courtly lovers, Melanto and Eurimaco, whose flirtatious behaviour conventionally justifies song (compare Valletto and

[9]  This was Giovanni Battista Doni's tack in the *Trattato della musica scenica* (1633–5) in his *De' trattati di musica ... tomo secondo*, ed. Anton Francesco Gori (Florence, 1763); see the comments in Rosand, *Opera in Seventeenth-Century Venice* (n. 1), 246n2.

[10] See Fenlon and Miller, *The Song of the Soul* (n. 1), 32–44, although some may feel the point not entirely proven there. In general, the arguments presented by members of the Incogniti are slippery, not least because of their penchant for intellectual role- (and game-) playing that makes nothing quite what it seems. The situation is not helped by the tendency of some scholars to rely on texts and translations of doubtful status and accuracy; a study of the academy and its contribution to Venetian ideas and cultural endeavour remains to be written.

   *Il ritorno d'Ulisse*, however, is placed clearly in the context of the Incogniti in Badoaro's dedication to Monteverdi in *L*, which makes prominent mention of Pietro Loredano and Gasparo Malipiero. Federico Malipiero also refers to the opera in his *La peripezia d'Ulisse overo la casta Penelope* (Venice, 1640); this Malipiero later produced a translation of the *Iliad*, *L'Iliada d'Omero trapportata dalla Greca nella Toscana lingua* (Venice, 1642), dedicated to the leader of the Incogniti, Giovanni Francesco Loredano, and promised one of the *Odyssey*, which seems never to have appeared.

[11] This paragraph owes a great deal to Rosand, *Opera in Seventeenth-Century Venice* (see n. 1), 245–80. Most recently, see her 'Operatic Ambiguities and the Power of Music', this journal, 4 (1992), 75–80, which frames the issues in the context of a debate to which my study may well offer a further contribution.

Damigella in *L'incoronazione di Poppea*), and even for the three royal suitors (Pisandro, Antinoo and Anfinomo), whose triple- and duple-time antics are no less demeaning than their scurrilous behaviour at Penelope's court. But the issue is more difficult in the case of those 'noble' characters – Telemaco, Ulisse and Penelope – whose status is potentially threatened rather than enhanced by so problematic a musical mode of dramatic discourse.

That decisions about when and where to use aria-styles were the concern of the librettist, not just of the composer, is clear from any analysis of the interaction of poetic and musical structures in contemporary opera. The first librettist, Ottavio Rinuccini, had established paradigms for recitative and aria (or ensemble, chorus, etc.) verse that were to last through the nineteenth century and beyond: recitative verse is in free-rhyming seven- and eleven-syllable *versi piani* (with the accent on the penultimate syllable), whereas more regular patterns in terms both of rhyme-scheme and of line-length become characteristic of aria texts. The latter may invoke strophic structures, although this is by no means essential, and may also adopt other line-lengths (say, of five, six, eight or ten syllables) and/or other verse types (*versi tronchi* and *versi sdruccioli*, with the accent on the final and antepenultimate syllable respectively).

As a result, within any seventeenth-century (or for that matter, later) libretto, changes of line-length, metre and rhyme offer clear instructions which the composer may follow or ignore, the latter of course being the more interesting possibility.[12] The opening scene of Act II of *Il ritorno d'Ulisse* provides a straightforward example. Here Telemaco is brought to Ithaca by Minerva and is greeted by the shepherd Eumete and the disguised Ulisse. The text is given below, with indications of rhyme and metre, and of the musical style chosen for each section (a straight line indicates an aria-style in duple time; a wavy line an aria-style in triple time; and a dotted line, recitative):

TELEMACO:
Lieto cammino,　　　　　　　　　　　　　A5
dolce viaggio,　　　　　　　　　　　　　　B5
passa il carro divino　　　　　　　　　　　A7
come che fosse un raggio.　　　　　　　　　B7

MINERVA/TELEMACO:
5　Gli dei possenti　　　　　　　　　　　C5
navigan l'aure,　　　　　　　　　　　　　D5
solcano i venti.　　　　　　　　　　　　　C5

MINERVA:
Eccoti giunto alle paterne ville,　　　　　　E11
Telemaco prudente.　　　　　　　　　　　F7

[12] As we shall see, Tomlinson's claim that 'Monteverdi rarely evaded the formalism of Badoaro's and Busenello's texts' (*Monteverdi* [see n. 1], 231) does not ring quite true. Similarly, as the present argument implies, I am not convinced that for *Il ritorno d'Ulisse* and *L'incoronazione di Poppea* 'the rhetoric of Petrarchism ... remains their expressive essence' (232).

6

| | | |
|---|---|---|
| 10 | Non ti scordar gia mai de' miei consigli, | G11 |
| | che se dal buon sentier travia la mente | F11 |
| | incontrerai perigli. | G7 |
| | | |
| | TELEMACO: | |
| | Periglio invan mi guida, | H7 |
| | se tua bontà m'affida. | H7 |
| | | |
| | EUMETE: | |
| 15 | Oh gran figlio d'Ulisse, | I7 |
| | è pur ver che tu torni | J7 |
| | a serenar della tua madre i giorni, | J11 |
| | e pur sei giunto al fine | K7 |
| | di tua casa cadente | L7 |
| 20 | a riparar l'altissime ruine? | K11 |
| | Fugga, fugga il cordoglio e cessi il pianto; | M11 |
| | facciam, o pelegrino, | N7 |
| | all'allegrezze nostre honor col canto. | M11 |
| | | |
| | EUMETE/ULISSE: | |
| | Verdi spiagge, al lieto giorno | O8 |
| 25 | rabellite herbette e fiori, | P8 |
| | scherzin l'aure con gli amori, | P8 |
| | ride il ciel al bel ritorno. | O8 |
| | | |
| | TELEMACO: | |
| | Vostri cortesi auspici a me son grati. | Q11 |
| | Manchevole piacer però m'alletta, | R11 |
| | ch'esser calma non puote alma ch'aspetta. | R11 |

[TELEMACO: Happy journey, sweet voyage, the divine chariot passes as if it were a ray of light. MINERVA/TELEMACO: The powerful gods navigate the breezes and plough the winds. MINERVA: Now you have reached your father's domains, wise Telemachus. Never forget my counsels, for if your mind strays from the right path, you will meet with dangers. TELEMACO: Danger leads me in vain if your grace is entrusted to me. EUMETE: O great son of Ulysses, is it indeed true that you return to brighten your mother's days, and have you come to repair the most noble ruins of your fallen house? Let grief flee, flee, and weeping cease. O wanderer, let us honour our joy with song. EUMETE/ULISSE: Green shores, to the happy day set forth grasses and flowers again, let the breezes play with the cupids, let the sky smile on the fair homecoming. TELE-MACO: Your kind auspices are welcome to me. However, an incomplete pleasure charms me, for a soul that is waiting cannot be tranquil.]

Telemaco's quatrain of five- then seven-syllable lines (verses 1–4) praising his 'happy journey' is followed by a tercet of five-syllable lines (5–7) for him and

Minerva invoking the power of the gods, and then a group of seven- and eleven-syllable lines (8–14) as Minerva tells Telemaco that he is in his homeland. The loose rhymed seven- and eleven-syllable lines continue as Eumete greets Telemaco (15–23); then the text shifts to rhymed eight-syllable lines (24–7) when Eumete and Ulisse urge the return of spring as happiness comes to Ithaca. Finally, Telemaco acknowledges their welcome (28–30) in eleven-syllable lines (with a final rhyming couplet). These changes in metre and rhyme reflect the dramatic function of the various sections of the text: the free-rhymed seven- and eleven-syllable lines (6–23, 28–30) represent action-dialogue, with one character speaking to another, while the sections in other line-lengths and more regular patterns involve more passive statement or commentary.

No less straightforward, with one notable exception, is the correlation between these verse structures and Monteverdi's music. Telemaco's first quatrain becomes a duple-time aria extended, by repetition of the first two lines at the end, into a rounded ABA form. The duet for Minerva and Telemaco (5–7) adopts a suave triple time, a style also used in the duet for Eumete and Ulisse (24–7). But when the text first shifts to dialogue in seven- and eleven-syllable lines at verse 8, as Minerva tells Telemaco that she has brought him to his father's domains, the music changes to free recitative.

The exception to this scheme is Eumete's speech greeting Telemaco as the 'great son of Ulysses' in verses 15–23. The structure of the text, and its status as speech directed to another character, prompts recitative: only the last line, 'honour our joy with song', with its reference to 'canto', suggests literal imitation in song; Monteverdi acts accordingly, preceding it with one line of 'recitative' to make the point. But the decision to begin Eumete's speech as a triple-time aria overrides the text. It is certainly an appropriate gesture – Eumete's joy at seeing Telemaco bursts the bounds of controlled speech – but the effect is produced solely by Monteverdi. Not for the first time, and most certainly not for the last, a composer exerts his right to prevail over his librettist in producing drama through music. Yet Monteverdi thereby causes himself problems, for in constructing an aria from verse that the librettist has devised for recitative (with long lines and a lack of patterning), he has to mangle the text: 'Oh gran figlio, gran figlio d'Ulisse, oh, oh, oh, oh gran figlio d'Ulisse … e pur sei giunto, sei giunto al fine, al fine …'. We can see why Badoaro claimed, 'I no longer know how to recognize this work as mine'.[13]

The opening of Act II is reasonably typical of Monteverdi's approach: he is happy to respond to (indeed, sometimes to create) textual cues for passages in aria-style; and he is willing to set recitative verse as aria should the need arise. Moreover, the sequence of arias and duets here is also used for conventional ends. It is (deliberately?) reminiscent of the beginning of Act II of *Orfeo* and serves a similar function, preparing a *coup de théâtre* as Ulisse disappears into the earth and re-emerges in his own form (compare the much more effective arrival of

---

[13]  In his dedication (to Monteverdi) in *L*, given in Rosand, *Opera in Seventeenth-Century Venice* (see n. 1), 408–9 (my translation).

the Messenger to tell of Euridice's death in *Orfeo*). The musical styles are entirely appropriate for Minerva and Eumete, goddess and shepherd respectively, but less so for Telemaco and Ulisse. However, the conceptual dissonance is not great. One can plausibly sing while flying through the air in a divine chariot. And Ulisse is in disguise – indeed, the fact that he 'sings' rather than 'speaks' enhances the disguise:[14] significantly, when he resumes his true form, he reverts to his 'normal' musical language (compare his following duet with Telemaco). Most important, the opening of Act II is a moment of celebration, and celebration is always a matter for song, not speech.

These issues become particularly important, and gain still more dramatic point, in the handling of Penelope. As yet she has nothing to celebrate: indeed, her refusal (inability?) to sing rather than speak is one of the most striking features of *Il ritorno d'Ulisse*, exposing the dramatic and aesthetic dilemmas that lie at the very heart of the opera. We first see her right at the opening of Act I, establishing her considerable presence with a recitative lament that, as many commentators have noted, vies with Monteverdi's celebrated 'Lamento d'Arianna' in expressive power and dramatic effect. Penelope's long speech picks up themes from Monteverdi's prologue.[15] There Humana Fragilità (Human Frailty) lamented the onslaughts of Tempo (Time), Fortuna (Fortune) and Amore (Love), none of whom offers pity or escape. As Penelope makes clear, Time and Fortune have also been against her as she has long awaited Ulisse's return. In this overwhelming context of recitative, Penelope's one brief shift to an aria-style at 'Torna il tranquillo al mare' (Calm returns to the sea) seems no more than a nostalgic hankering for the joys of the past, when she did indeed know how to sing.[16] But she can sing no more.

Penelope has been able to resist Time and Fortune. However, Love – 'blind archer, winged, naked: no defence or shield can withstand my arrow', he says in the prologue[17] – poses a different threat, one that will besiege her throughout the opera. Love's blandishments are clear in the very next scene (I.2), where Melanto and Eurimaco introduce the third of Human Frailty's oppressors, significantly in a mellifluous triple time, its first extended appearance in the opera proper. In the prologue, Fortune, Love and (in the final trio) Time had each appropriated

---

[14]  See Rosand, *Opera in Seventeenth-Century Venice*, 120–1. It is significant that Ulisse's first extended aria, 'O fortunato Ulisse', occurs after he has assumed the disguise of an old man at Minerva's prompting (I.9), for all this aria's basis in a refrain established earlier in Act I scene 8.

[15]  The prologue in *L* is different, involving a debate between Fato (Fate), Fortezza (Bravery) and Prudenza (Prudence) emphasising the power of Fate over the dealings of mankind. It is not known when, why and by whom this prologue was removed – it gives a different slant to the story of the opera proper. However, secular 'fate' was a tricky concept to get past the church censors in Venice (and indeed anywhere else in Counter-Reformation Italy). See, for example, the dedication of Federico Malipiero's *L'Iliada d'Omero trapportata dalla Greca nella Toscana lingua* (1642), where Malipiero adds the standard caveat that words such as Fate and Destiny have been changed for being contrary to the Catholic faith.

[16]  The score emphasises the point still more: 'Torna il tranquillo al mare' comes much earlier in the longer version of this scene in *L*.

[17]  'Cieco saettator, alato, ignudo, / contro il mio stral non val difesa o scudo.'

triple-time aria-styles; but in the opera itself it is clear that this is the musical language of Love. Apparent changes to the libretto make the point stronger still. 'Ama dunque, che d'Amore / dolce amica è la beltà' (Love, then, for beauty is a sweet friend of Love) sings Melanto (twice) in a seductive triple time in C major (I.10);[18] 'Ama dunque, sì, sì / dunque riama un dì' (Love then, yes, yes / then love again one day) sing Pisandro, Antinoo and Anfinomo (three times), again in triple time in C major (II.5).[19] Not for nothing do the suitors proclaim in Act II scene 8 that 'Amor è un'armonia / sono canti i sospiri' (Love is a harmony, the sighs are songs), singing in solemn three-part harmony (starting in C major).[20] Their view echoes arguments held by members of the Accademia degli Incogniti over whether weeping or singing is more likely to produce affection. As the leader of the Incogniti, Giovanni Francesco Loredano, concluded:

If Love is the child of delight and Song is nothing but sweetness and joy, who does not see that from it must come Love. If Love is a little spirit, and if indeed it resembles what produced it, one can never judge it born of weeping but rather from the spirits which emerge with Song. ... Who does not know that Love can indeed be born of Music, but never of tears.[21]

For Penelope, however, 'canti' (songs) all too easily become 'incanti' (enchantments) – Eurimaco makes the pun in Act I scene 2 – and thence 'bugie' (lies).[22] Victorious over Time and Fortune, she cannot afford defeat at the hands of Love. So, too, must she not give way to aria: just as Penelope encloses herself within her palace and within her chastity, she is no less enclosed in the joyless world of recitative. 'Non dee di nuovo amar / chi misera penò; / torna stolta a penar / chi prima errò' (She who has suffered should not love again; only a fool comes back to suffer after a first mistake), she says to Melanto (I.10), in a bare recitative to a text that in most circumstances Monteverdi would have been happy to style

---

[18]  For the second appearance of Melanto's 'refrain', *L* provides a second stanza, 'Fuggi pur d[e]l tempo i danni / tosto vien nemica età' (Yet flee the losses of time, the enemy age comes soon). This may also relate to the expunging of references to Penelope's beauty, see p. 11–12.

[19]  The second statement is omitted in *L*.

[20]  Or in Anne Ridler's memorable translation for the English National Opera, 'In Love's harmonious consort, sweetest singing is deep sighing'. In *L*, the suitors' speech begins 'Sono canti i sospiri', with 'Amor è un'armonia' a later insertion, which is, of course, all grist to my mill.

[21]  Fenlon and Miller, *The Song of the Soul* (see n. 1), 39 (my translation). For this debate – which took place within the Accademia degli Unisoni – see also Ellen Rosand, 'Barbara Strozzi, *virtuosissima cantatrice*: The Composer's Voice', *Journal of the American Musicological Society*, 31 (1978), 241–81. *Pace* Fenlon and Miller, the argument in favour of tears was presented not by Giovanni Francesco Loredano but rather by Matteo Dandolo. And compare the dedication to Barbara Strozzi's *Diporti di Euterpe overo cantate & ariette a voce sola* (Venice, 1659), in Rosand, 'Barbara Strozzi', 280n118: 'Queste harmoniche note ... son lingue dell'Anima, ed istromenti del Core' (These harmonic notes ... are tongues of the Soul, and instruments of the Heart).

[22]  Compare Penelope's brief shift to triple time at 'questo di tua bugia' in Act III scene 10. Other brief triple-time passages for Penelope occur only in Act I scene 10, conventionally enough at 'cangia il piacer in duolo' (*changes* pleasure into grief); Act II scene 12, 'Concedasi al mendico la prova' (Grant the beggar the test); and Act III scene 5, for 'gioco' (plaything).

as an aria, a homely moral in *versi tronchi*. His reluctance to have Penelope sing in structured triple and duple time – all the more striking given his commitment to aria at the beginning of Act II – is clearer still in Act II scene 5. Here Penelope's response to the suitors' 'Ama dunque, sì, sì' is a foot-stamping refrain, 'Non voglio amar, no, no' (I will not love, no, no), which denies its status as aria even as it runs its petulant triple-time course (See Ex. 1a). By the third statement (see Ex. 1b), Penelope seeks comfort in her familiar recitative, again despite Badoaro's *versi tronchi* later in the passage. This is scarcely Love's triumph.

Penelope's recitative is surely the 'normal' language for so serious a character; indeed, many will claim it the most ennobling aspect of her music. However,

Ex. 1 *Il ritorno d'Ulisse in patria*, II.5.

if one can be forgiven the conceit, Melanto, Ericlea and the suitors – perhaps even that large part of early seventeenth-century operatic audiences always bored by the *stile recitativo*[23] – would surely see her commitment to recitative as a gesture no less arid than her refusal to acknowledge the 'obvious' solution to her problems: she is alone and so must love and sing anew. Her commitment to Ulisse is depicted as a hardness of heart that contravenes even the laws of nature.[24] The result can only be an 'unnatural' sexual frustration. Penelope reacts bitterly to Telemaco's description of the charms of Helen of Troy (II.11). And her test for the suitors (made from her lips, not her heart, she says) to fire Ulisse's bow, although presumably prompted by Minerva, is a splendid Freudian slip. But Penelope's situation gets worse still. Trapped by the conflicting demands of heart and mind, and by the pressures of peers and circumstance, she eventually succumbs to emotional paralysis, unable to react even to the death of the suitors (III.3): 'Dell'occhio la pietate / si risente all'eccesso, / ma concitar il core / a sdegno et a dolore / non m'è concesso' (My eyes feel pity to the extreme, but to arouse my heart to scorn or grief is not permitted me). Even the evidence of Ulisse's return offered by her servant Eumete and her son Telemaco cannot arouse her from a catatonic state of disbelief. Still more notable is Ulisse's failure to convince her that he is indeed her husband: 'incantator o mago' (enchanter or wizard), she calls him in Act III scene 10, perhaps a fitting response to his earlier penchant for aria. Eumete, she says (III.4), is 'stolto e cieco' (foolish and blind), accusing him of the failings she has previously attributed to Love: but in fact she herself is now made to seem foolishly blind to the truth.

Penelope's increasing passivity begins early in the opera: not for nothing is her first scene (I.1) her longest. In part, one suspects, this is because of the fear that she herself – and her womanhood – could threaten the potency of the messages she is meant to convey.[25] In the libretto, her opening lament is longer still –

[23]  See the comments in Carolyn Gianturco, 'Nuove considerazioni su *il tedio del recitativo* delle prime opere romane', *Rivista italiana di musicologia*, 17 (1982), 212–39; Tim Carter, '*Non occorre nominare tanti musici*: Private Patronage and Public Ceremony in Late Sixteenth-Century Florence', *I Tatti Studies: Essays in the Renaissance*, 4 (1991), 89–104.

[24]  Compare Melanto on Penelope in Act I scene 2: 'ritoccherò quel core / ch'indiamante l'honore' (I will revive that heart which honour has made [as hard] as diamonds). Similarly, in Act II scene 4, Melanto says that Penelope has a 'cor di sasso' (heart of stone). The question of nature and the natural becomes most prominent in Act II scene 4, where the suitors invoke horticultural images to represent love – the vine (Pisandro), the cedar (Anfinomo) and ivy (Antinoo). In *L*, Penelope responds: 'L'edra, il cedro, e la vite / altre leggi non han, che di natura; / ogni suo pregio oscura / bella donna e regina, / s'à natura s'inchina' (The ivy, the cedar and the vine have no laws other than nature's; [but] a beautiful woman and a queen blots out all her worth if she inclines to nature). She is deprived of this defence in the score.

[25]  Compare Eurimaco's 'E pur udii sovente / la poetica schiera / cantar donna volubile e leggiera' (And yet I have often heard the poets' band call woman loquacious and flighty) in Act II scene 4. The Incogniti could argue in much the same way. One wonders whether the doubts sown in Ariosto's *Orlando furioso* (XXXV.27) were not also a factor. In a curious passage, St John the Evangelist invokes the power of poets who, given the right patronage, will readily spread lies. See Ludovico Ariosto, *Orlando furioso*, trans. Barbara Reynolds (Harmondsworth, 1975), 342: 'Homer makes Agamemnon win the war; / The Trojans cowardly and weak he shows. / Although the suitors so persistent are, / Penelope is faithful to her spouse. / But if for truth you are particular, / Like this, quite in reverse, the story goes: / The Greeks defeated, Troy victorious, / And chaste Penelope notorious.'

seeming like so much whingeing – and one of its themes, that her beauty is fast fading (and therefore that she fears her ability to arouse desire in Ulisse), is entirely missing from the score. Similarly, subsequent (often extended) references to Penelope's physical beauty, and hence her sexuality, are systematically expunged from the text set by Monteverdi. Such a strategy had its advantages: the Incogniti were clear that beauty could all too easily be an instrument of deceit (Loredano quoted Tasso: 'Beauty is an infamous monster, an unworldly monster, heaven's scourge with which to beat the world').[26] It also defused the potentially damaging comparison with those beautiful women who 'ungratefully' deny love so condemned in Monteverdi's *Ballo delle ingrate*, recently published in his Eighth Book of madrigals, the *Madrigali guerrieri, et amorosi* of 1638. But all this makes the resolution of the opera, which requires the re-awakening of Penelope as a sentient woman, much more problematic. Indeed, Penelope's need to recover herself becomes specifically a matter of reviving her sexuality: only thoughts of Ulisse naked (so Ericlea sees him in the bath) and of her marriage bed, the site of sexual pleasure for all its virginal quilt, show her some way out of the psychological crisis into which she has been manipulated (or has manipulated herself).

It is curious, if typical, that Penelope's fate is ignored by all the characters in *Il ritorno d'Ulisse*. That Melanto, Eurimaco and the suitors treat her as a mere commodity subject to their whims comes as no surprise.[27] But the gods, who have the power to resolve the plot, say absolutely nothing about her: when Juno intercedes with Jove (compare Proserpina and Pluto in *Orfeo*), then Jove with Neptune, the arguments are made entirely on Ulisse's part. Even Eumete and Telemaco explode in frustration (III.9): Penelope is 'Troppo incredula, / troppo ostinata' (Too incredulous, too stubborn) – remarks worthy of a Melanto. But Penelope does have one champion: Monteverdi. Even if the changes to the libretto in the prologue and the opera proper were not his, the composer clearly became fascinated with Penelope. The suitors' deaths offer no lesson to the audience and thus appear gratuitous; at least, there was indeed a lesson to be learnt – that all human sins receive divine punishment – but the scene expounding it (III.2) was cut from the score for being 'too melancholic' (a nice Incognito gesture?).[28] The other candidate for presenting a message, Iro, remains – for all Rosand's perceptive analysis – a 'parte ridicola'.[29] Monteverdi's attention, and ours, is focused on Penelope.

[26] Fenlon and Miller, *The Song of the Soul* (see n. 1), 35n14.

[27] The suitors' final strategy to win Penelope is to woo (buy?) her with gold: 'Amor è un'armonia, / sono canti i sospiri, / ma non si canta ben se l'or non suona; / non ama chi non dona' (Love is a harmony, the sighs are songs, but one does not sing well if gold does not ring forth; he who does not give does not love). This echoes another Incognito debate, 'Perche si paghino le Donne de' congressi amorosi' (Why Women are Paid for Amorous Congresses), in Giovanni Francesco Loredano, *Bizzarrie academiche* (Bologna, 1676), part II, 49–55, esp. 52 (my translation): 'A woman does not love without self-interest. She does not give herself as booty to one who does not give. Therefore the purchase of feminine hearts is gained by the profusion of gold.'

[28] The text of the omitted scene is given and discussed in Rosand, 'Iro' (see n. 1), 160–2.

[29] So he is called in the rubric to Act III scene 1. For Rosand's view, see 'Iro' (n. 1), and *idem.*, 'Operatic Madness: A Challenge to Convention', in *Music and Text: Critical Inquiries*, ed. Steven Paul Scher (Cambridge, 1992), 241–87.

Confused as she is (or as she is forced to be), she sees her acknowledgement of Ulisse as a choice between Love and Honour.[30] Penelope picks Love, prompting a drastic reversal in her role. Having spent the whole opera resisting, so to speak, the blandishments of the triple-time aria, in the final scene she gives herself to them body and soul. Badoaro provides a straightforward recitative in eleven- and seven-syllable *versi piani*: 'Hor sì ti riconosco, hor sì ti credo / antico possessore / del combattuto core' (Now I recognise you, now I believe you, former possessor of my besieged heart). But Monteverdi sets this in an excited triple-time aria style with hints of the *stile concitato* (see Ex. 2). Penelope returns to musical recitative

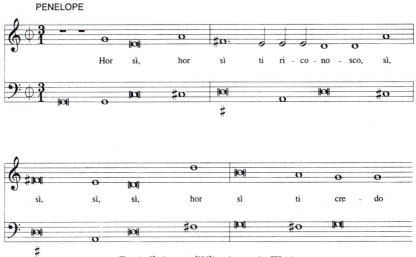

Ex. 2 *Il ritorno d'Ulisse in patria*, III.10.

only to confirm her decision: 'Honestà, mi perdoni: / dono tutto ad Amor le sue ragioni' (Honesty, forgive me: I give all the arguments to Love). Ulisse senses the change and meets her on this new ground, urging Penelope in a seductive triple time, again to 'recitative' verse: 'Sciogli la lingua, sciogli / per allegrezza i nodi. / Un sospir, un ohimé la voce snodi' (Untie your tongue, untie for joy the knot. Let your voice loose forth a sigh, an alas). Penelope knows full well that 'sighs are songs' (she heard the suitors?), and she lets forth the most stunning aria in the opera, 'Illustratevi o cieli' (Shine bright, o heavens), once more in C major (see Ex. 3). And significantly, the instruments – rarely heard in the opera – join the voice in celebratory refrains. Penelope's song is an ecstatic moment of emotional release as she once more learns to sing the language of love.

Whether Penelope's climactic adoption of aria marks triumph or capitulation

---

[30] Act III scene 10: 'Creder ciò ch'è desio m'insegna [*L* has the more plausible 'm'invita'] Amore; / serbar costante il sen comanda honore' (Love invites me to believe what is [my] desire, but honour commands my breast to stay constant).

Ex. 3 *Il ritorno d'Ulisse in patria*, III.10.

– the character forcibly subjugated by the pressures of the genre and its (male) protagonists – remains a matter for debate. But for Monteverdi, her song itself was enough to ensure the happy ending and the final love duet of the opera.[31] Yet although Penelope sees her choice as being for Love rather than Honour, it is surely Honour that wins the day: for Love to claim victory in *Il ritorno d'Ulisse*, Penelope should have submitted to Melanto's exhortations on the one hand, and to the suitors on the other. Instead, the 'message' of the opera – if message we need – is that Human Frailty, so belaboured in the prologue and through Penelope in the opera, has one invincible weapon against Time, Fortune *and* Love – Constancy. Such constancy, placed within a Neostoic framework, was also to be an issue in Monteverdi's last opera, *L'incoronazione di Poppea*. But given the havoc that Amore wreaks in the decadent world of the late Roman Empire, *Poppea* might indeed be subtitled 'Love's Revenge'. Certainly, Nerone and Poppea need no lessons in the musical language of love; they know it right from the start. Where that leads them is, of course, a different matter.

In 1651, Francesco Sbarra happily admitted in the preface to his *Alessandro vincitor di se stesso*:

I know that the *ariette* sung by Alexander and Aristotle will be judged as contrary to the decorum of such great personages; but I also know that musical recitation is improper altogether, since it does not imitate natural discourse and removes the soul from dramatic compositions, which should be nothing but imitations of human actions, and yet this defect is not only tolerated by the current century but received with applause. This kind of poetry today has no purpose other than to give delight; thus we should adjust to the practice of the times.[32]

But in 1640 the new Venetian opera was still in its early development. And Monteverdi always had an acute sensitivity to his characters and to the musical and dramatic issues they raised. Thus it is not surprising that *Il ritorno d'Ulisse* should have problematised the status of aria within operatic endeavour. Many contemporaries felt, along with Penelope (III.9), that 'Le favole fan riso e non dan vita' (Tales cause laughter and do not offer life); operas are *favole per musica*. For Monteverdi, however, opera was indeed some kind of representation of life in its truest form. He shows us how individuals can – must – sing rather than speak, exploiting the perennial problem of opera to make precise points both about his characters and about sung drama as a whole. Badoaro caught something of this in his dedication of the libretto when he claimed that Monteverdi had made known to

---

[31] *L* follows the love duet with a short speech for Ulisse – he will go to Minerva's altar – a brief duet for Ulisse and Penelope urging the bystanders to sing of the renewed marriage of their king and queen, and a final chorus of Ithacans saying that the wise and brave man armed with virtue can indeed conquer fortune and fate. This invokes the original prologue: it also, of course, shifts the focus back to Ulisse.

[32] Translated in Rosand, *Opera in Seventeenth-Century Venice* (see n. 1), 45. For the original see p. 421, and note also a further passage here: 'If the recitative style were not mingled with such *scherzi*, it would give more annoyance than pleasure' (my translation).

the world 'the true spirit of theatrical music [which is] not well understood by modern compositions' ('il vero spirito della Musica teatrale non bene intesa da moderni compositioni'). The result had profound implications not just for his time, but also for the whole of operatic history.

# Re-Reading *Poppea*: Some Thoughts on Music and Meaning in Monteverdi's Last Opera

THERE is a convenient fiction maintained by all but the most fervent postmodernist concerning the interpretation of opera: that the music somehow reveals how a particular drama should be played out on the stage. Whether a reading (or a production) is supposedly authentic, traditional or modernist in intent and delivery, support is invoked for it within the musical score by assuming a clarity in the semiotic play of signifier and signified that in turn validates our various responses to opera as drama. We know an aria signifying 'love', 'triumph', 'rage' or 'lament' when we hear one, and we respond accordingly, indeed conventionally to the extent that we often focus less on what is being sung about than on how it is being sung. And whether or not one agrees with Joseph Kerman's battle-cry 'In opera, the dramatist is the composer',[1] the notion of the composer as musician–orator, persuading and moving at will, is a powerful one, reinforcing deep-seated beliefs concerning the transcendental truths about the human condition conveyed by the canon of operatic masterpieces. It is also a trope adopted early in the history of opera. When the unknown librettist of Claudio Monteverdi's *Le nozze d'Enea in Lavinia* (1641; now lost) praised its composer for

> adapting in such a way the musical notes to the words and to the passions that he who sings must laugh, weep, grow angry and grow pitying, and do all the rest that they command, with the listener no less led to the same impulse in the variety and force of the same perturbations[2]

---

This article starts from two important readings of Monteverdi's last opera: Ellen Rosand, 'Seneca and the Interpretation of *L'incoronazione di Poppea*', *Journal of the American Musicological Society*, 38 (1985), 34–71; and Iain Fenlon and Peter Miller, *'The Song of the Soul': Understanding 'Poppea'*, Royal Musical Association Monographs, 5 (London, 1992). It also seeks to develop my ideas on changing functions of 'aria' in the early seventeenth century most recently expressed in my ' "In Love's harmonious consort"?: Penelope and the Interpretation of *Il ritorno d'Ulisse in patria*', *Cambridge Opera Journal*, 5 (1993), 1–16, and 'Resemblance and Representation: Towards a New Aesthetic in the Music of Monteverdi', *'Con che soavità': Essays in Italian Baroque Opera, Song, and Dance, 1580–1740*, ed. Iain Fenlon and Tim Carter (Oxford, 1995), 118–34. The music examples are drawn from the sources listed in their captions, with some minor editing and emendation: original note-values have been given where possible. All translations are my own. I am indeed grateful to Lorenzo Bianconi, Annegret Fauser, Iain Fenlon, Wendy Heller, Robert Holzer, Susan McClary and Anne MacNeil for their comments on earlier drafts of this essay. I must also thank Clifford Bartlett and Paolo Fabbri for providing copies of original source material.

[1] *Opera as Drama* (New York, 1956; rev. edn, Berkeley and Los Angeles, 1988; repr. London, 1989), 91.

[2] *Argomento et scenario delle Nozze d'Enea in Lavinia, tragedia di lieto fine da rappresentarsi in musica*, trans. in *Composing Opera: From 'Dafne' to 'Ulisse errante'*, ed. Tim Carter and Zygmunt Szweykowski, Practica musica, 2 (Cracow, 1994), 147–79 (p. 177).

he was not only invoking a topos drawn from classical antiquity; he was also affirming an aesthetic stance that retains its fascination even today.

Of course, the understanding of any musical semiotic is largely acquired rather than innate, and it is necessarily conditioned by an awareness of historically contingent processes of signification: few can still sustain a faith in the transcendent power of specific musical gestures to convey specific musical or extra-musical meanings. The judging of individual musical acts against the background of the stylistic, generic or other norms of a particular period is now widely viewed as a precondition for some kind of contextual reading of a given work, validating – even authenticating – our interpretation(s) within their proper frame. That an understanding of such stylistic and generic norms can substantially affect and inflect our reading of familiar operas is clear from recent work on gestural signification in Mozart by scholars such as Wye Jamison Allanbrook.[3] Presumably the task of reading operas less firmly in the canon would benefit still more from similar historically sensitive treatment.

Early seventeeth-century opera, however, poses particular problems. On the one hand, the extent to which the aesthetic, structural and practical paradigms of opera were established at the outset of its long history is striking: the prefaces, librettos and scores of operas by Jacopo Peri, Giulio Caccini and Claudio Monteverdi establish basic premises and musical outcomes that hold true for much opera of subsequent periods, for all its changes of style.[4] Characters sing out their lives, loves and sorrows in musical speech (recitative) or song (aria) in ways that make these early works recognizable as operas in more recent senses of the term. On the other hand, these works emerged during a period of questioning and exploration where the aesthetic ground was shifting significantly in the move from 'Renaissance' to 'Baroque' modes of technique and expression, producing a striking lack of fixity in styles, structures and meanings. Monteverdi is particularly problematic in this light depending on whether one views him as a late Renaissance, Mannerist or proto-Baroque composer. Musical codes became obscure as old signifier–signified relationships were dismantled and reconfigured in the forging of a new musical language the essence of which lay not so much in new compositional techniques as in new ways of generating and conveying musical and emotional meaning. For example, although the Florentine 'invention' of musical recitative for solo voice and basso continuo responded to a Humanist need to privilege the oratorical act of musical 'speech' over the musical act of 'song', yet 'song' quickly, perhaps inevitably, began to reclaim its ground from 'speech', shifting the operatic balance of expressive power from recitative to aria in various intriguing ways through the first half of the seventeenth century. For all the difficulties of verisimilitude that ensued, the singing, rather than musically 'speaking',

---

[3] See, for example, Wye J. Allanbrook, *Rhythmic Gesture in Mozart: 'Le nozze di Figaro' and 'Don Giovanni'* (Chicago and London, 1983), and compare (for instrumental music) V. Kofi Agawu, *Playing with Signs: A Semiotic Interpretation of Classic Music* (Princeton, 1991).

[4] I have explored the issues in my chapter on seventeenth-century opera in *The Oxford Illustrated History of Opera*, ed. Roger Parker (Oxford and New York, 1994), 1–46.

voice came to dominate the genre in ways that brought increasing pleasure to the ear, if not to those ascetic theorists for whom opera was to be made of sterner stuff.

Pleasure was a byword for opera as it emerged in the 'public' opera houses of Venice from 1637 onwards, where commercial success was largely dependent on audience appeal. Therefore it is not surprising that song occupied the high ground, sometimes for sound dramatic reasons and at others for a sheer delight in vocality. Boundaries between recitative and aria became blurred, as did the musical handling of the conventional poetic distinctions between texts for these various musical styles: on the one hand, free-rhyming seven- and eleven-syllable *versi sciolti* for recitative, and, on the other, more regular metrical and rhyming structures, usually in strophic forms, for aria. In Monteverdi's two surviving Venetian operas, *Il ritorno d'Ulisse in patria* (1640) and *L'incoronazione di Poppea* (1642-3), the composer may adhere to and reflect the poetic distinctions of his librettos (by Giacomo Badoaro and Gian Francesco Busenello respectively), but equally he can ignore or manipulate them at will. In the latter case, the choice (more often) of aria over recitative can sometimes be read, if one so chooses, as made for dramatic or emotional effect, but it can also appear a matter of whim, if not whimsy. The result is a flexible shifting of recitative and aria styles, plus various points in between, where recitative can last only a short while before flowering into aria (and vice versa). This permeability of the recitative–aria divide (or perhaps better, the complex continuum from 'pure' recitative to 'pure' aria) permits a wide range of functions for a wide range of triple- and duple-time aria styles: word-painting, rhetorical emphasis, affective expansion, lyrical expression.[5] The result is to produce a work that is, in effect, a mosaic of speech- and song-like fragments. Whether this mosaic can or should cohere into a single musical or dramatic whole is a matter for debate.[6]

A shift from recitative to aria, whether or not prompted by metrical or semantic cues in the libretto, can easily be understood when applied specifically to affective situations (e.g. celebration), to character-types (e.g. pastoral, comic, mythical), or in diegetic contexts (e.g. lullabies, incantations). However, significant interpretative difficulties are raised when other characters in other situations adopt aria as a common form of utterance. There is some point to be made from Penelope's succumbing to aria at the end of *Il ritorno d'Ulisse in patria* as she is reunited with her long-lost husband; and Nerone and Poppea's frequent recourse to sensual triple times in *L'incoronazione di Poppea* serves to emphasize their

---

[5] See Ellen Rosand, 'Monteverdi's Mimetic Art: *L'incoronazione di Poppea*', *Cambridge Opera Journal*, 1 (1989), 113–37; *eadem*, 'Operatic Ambiguities and the Power of Music', *Cambridge Opera Journal*, 4 (1992), 75–80.

[6] I use the word 'mosaic' deliberately given its rich echoes of a statement by Simone Luzzatto in his *Discorso circa il stato de gl'Hebrei* (Venice, 1638) which Fenlon and Miller take as a motto for '*The Song of the Soul*' (see pp. viii, 18): 'The internal image of our soul is like a mosaic, which seems to be a single shape, and on closer inspection shows itself to be made up of various fragments of small stones both cheap and precious, joined and assembled. Even more so is our soul made up of various differing and conflicting pieces, any one of which can appear distinctly at various times. Consequently, describing the nature and condition of a single man is very arduous and difficult; and it is more difficult still to aim to explain a man's actions in terms of a single norm or principle.' Luzzatto's reasoning provides several lessons for the Monteverdi critic.

176

yielding of body and soul to Love, the protagonist of the prologue and, arguably, of the whole opera. But here other 'noble' characters – Ottone, Drusilla, Seneca (Ottavia is a case apart)[7] – also sing their songs with seeming abandon. The hardened seventeenth-century theorist would doubtless have viewed such emphasis on song as confirming the effeminate degeneracy rendering impotent so noble an art-form.[8] Modern commentators appear to have a more difficult time of it.

Ever since its revival early this century, critics have found L'incoronazione di Poppea fraught with dramatic and musical problems. The fact that it was to be Monteverdi's last opera, composed at the grand old age of 75, has inevitably encouraged a search for grand statements and valedictory messages. But there are notable difficulties with the sources and the attribution of the music: certainly, not all the music in the two surviving manuscripts of the opera is by Monteverdi,[9] and these manuscripts contain revisions and additions that take the text well beyond the original version staged at the Teatro SS Giovanni e Paolo in the 1642-3 season, less than a year before Monteverdi's death.[10] Moreover, the questionable decorum of the plot – glorifying the illicit passion of Emperor Nero and his mistress Poppaea – is unsettling, with apparent evil triumphing over apparent good in a reversal of the moral principles which conventionally underpin our readings of operatic masterpieces. The resulting discomfort has led to a remarkable amount of special pleading, and rather as with another morally 'problematic' opera, Mozart's Così fan tutte, critics seem prepared to blame almost anything or anyone other than the composer. The librettist Gian Francesco Busenello is decried as a cynic and a libertine; so, too, is the academy whose dealings provide an important context for Venetian opera in this period, the Accademia degli Incogniti. Excuses are found in the new social, political and economic circumstances for the production of opera in the 'public' (if it was) opera house rather than the court theatre: the bourgeois audience generally (if wrongly) assumed to have dictated the content of Venetian operas can conveniently be blamed for questionable ethical standards or even moral disinterest.[11]

---

[7] The best treatment of Ottavia, and in a critical and methodological context to which I owe a debt, is in Wendy Beth Heller, 'Chastity, Heroism, and Allure: Women in Opera of Seventeenth-Century Venice' (Ph.D. dissertation, Brandeis University, 1995), 225–85.

[8] On the pleasures and perils of song as viewed by contemporary theorists, see Ellen Rosand, Opera in Seventeenth-Century Venice: The Creation of a Genre (Berkeley, Los Angeles and Oxford, 1991), 40–5.

[9] Venice, Biblioteca Nazionale Marciana, MS It. IV.439 (9963); Naples, Biblioteca del Conservatorio S. Pietro a Majella, MS Rari 6.4.1.

[10] The most recent discussion of the sources is Alan Curtis, 'La Poppea impasticciata, or Who Wrote the Music to L'incoronazione (1643)?', Journal of the American Musicological Society, 42 (1989), 23–54. However, reference must still be made to Wolfgang Osthoff, 'Die venezianische und neapolitanische Fassung von Monteverdis "Incoronazione di Poppea"', Acta musicologica, 26 (1954), 88–113; idem, 'Neue Beobachtungen zu Quellen und Geschichte von Monteverdis "Incoronazione di Poppea"', Die Musikforschung, 11 (1958), 129–38; and Alessandra Chiarelli, 'L'incoronazione di Poppea o Il Nerone: Problemi di filologia testuale', Rivista italiana di musicologia, 9 (1974), 117–51. Paolo Fabbri, 'New Sources for "Poppea"', Music and Letters, 74 (1993), 16–23, reports the discovery of a new libretto and provides a useful, concise overview of the sources.

[11] Contrast these conventional arguments with the remarks on the not-so-public nature of 'public' opera in Venice in Lorenzo Bianconi and Thomas Walker, 'Production, Consumption and Political Function of Seventeenth-Century Opera', Early Music History, 4 (1984), 209–96. Similarly, notions of a bourgeoisie (and therefore of a bourgeois morality) are highly contentious for this period.

Some condemn the empty Marinist aesthetic of a dying cultural age as a frivolous Baroque overtook a noble Renaissance.[12] And there is one final, if somewhat desperate, strategy: although the opera ends with the coronation of Poppaea, we know from our history books that she will soon meet a violent death at Nero's hand, and that her cuckolded husband Otho will gain (if briefly) the imperial throne.[13] Thus honour is satisfied and moral equilibrium restored. But on the whole it might have been easier for our music history if Monteverdi's last opera had been the more straightforward *Il ritorno d'Ulisse in patria,* where the messages appear clear and the musical outcomes unequivocal.

The search for stable meanings and clear binary oppositions implicit in much opera criticism forces a rationalization of *Poppea*'s apparent subversion of ethical and generic norms. Thus an opera as immoral as *Poppea* can still be construed as containing a 'moral', be it the superiority of modern republican Venice over ancient imperial Rome (and, by implication, its modern equivalents), to follow Ellen Rosand, or, according to Iain Fenlon and Peter Miller, the virtues of *constantia* in a fickle world over which contemporary Venetian Tacitists and Neostoics were struggling to gain conceptual control. Rosand's notion of *Poppea* (and much other Venetian opera) as anti-Roman propaganda squares with the well-known hostility between Venice and Rome dating from before the Interdict of 1606. But there was a further potential target: the modern successors to the Roman Emperors, the Habsburgs. In a period when it was treasonable to advocate in Venice the cause of empire, as Monteverdi discovered to his discomfort,[14] any representation thereof on the operatic stage would probably have been viewed in a negative light. Not for nothing does *Poppea* play itself off against a knowledge of the historical Nero, Poppaea, Seneca, Octavia and Otho – even though Busenello had distanced himself from history in his synopsis of *Poppea,* and

---

[12] The most powerful articulation of Monteverdi in broader cultural contexts is Gary Tomlinson's *Monteverdi and the End of the Renaissance* (Oxford, 1987). I have engaged with Tomlinson's tendency towards a rather old-fashioned *Geistesgeschichte* in my review in *Early Music History,* 8 (1988), 245–60. His reading (and at times dismissal) of Monteverdi's Venetian music in the context of Marinism is both powerful and problematic: it is one reason why several recent Monteverdi scholars, myself included, have tried to explore this repertory in new, more sympathetic ways. Some of the fruits of this reassessment will also be apparent in Massimo Ossi's *Divining the Oracle: Aspects of Monteverdi's 'Seconda prattica'* (Chicago and London, forthcoming).

[13] Fenlon and Miller are only the latest to argue that by the end of the opera 'there could hardly have been any doubt in the mind of any contemporary Venetian, familiar with subsequent events and in particular with Poppea's death at Nero's hand three years after their marriage, of the illusory character of this seeming Triumph of Love' (*'The Song of the Soul',* 92). Compare also *ibid.,* 74: 'ultimately, as any seventeenth-century audience would have known, Ottone was to get his revenge by ascending the Imperial throne after the reigns of Nero and Galba'. For Poppaea's murder see Tacitus' *Annals,* XVI, 6; and for Nero's own sorry death and Otho's eventual assumption of the throne, see Suetonius, *Lives of the Caesars,* VI, VIII. Similarly, another classical source to which Busenello refers, the tragedy *Octavia* then attributed to Seneca, would have informed audiences of the troubles lying ahead for Poppaea: the Roman people rise up against her in favour of Octavia, dashing to the ground statues of Nero's new bride. Ellen Rosand notes both general and specific connections between the pseudo-Senecan *Octavia* – the first extant *fabula praetexta* or historical play – and *Poppea* in 'Seneca and the Interpretation of *L'incoronazione di Poppea',* 42–5; see also Heller, 'Chastity, Heroism, and Allure', 243–7.

[14] Monteverdi was denounced anonymously (at an unknown date, but after 1623) for expressing pro-Habsburg/Spanish sentiments in public; see Jonathan Glixon, 'Was Monteverdi a Traitor?', *Music and Letters,* 72 (1991), 404–6.

therefore from the notion that this is in any real sense a 'historical' opera[15] – and the two soldiers' reference (in Act 1, scene ii) to Armenia in rebellion and Pannonia up in arms had clear contemporary resonance in the context of the Thirty Years War. Fenlon and Miller's reading, however, raises greater difficulties. Like their predecessors, they acknowledge a crucial problem with any attempt to find a moral in *Poppea*: the fact that the one character seemingly able to convey such a moral with *gravitas* and probity, the aged philosopher Seneca, dies about half-way through the work, in Act 2, scene iii. Although Seneca's death is thus the centre-piece of the opera (rather like Orfeo's 'Possente spirto e formidabil nume' in *Orfeo*), it imposes something of a structural and dramatic vacuum (again, as in *Orfeo*) on its remainder. Fenlon and Miller's consequent strategy of transferring the virtues of Senecan *constantia* to the character of Drusilla meets at least one need – she is alive, if in exile, at the end of the opera – and it seems confirmed by Nerone, who (in Act 3, scene iv) applauds her 'costanza' as an example of and to her sex. However, their touching faith in Drusilla (and, curiously, in an epithet delivered by a moral degenerate) does not quite square with a rather self-interested character who is complicit in the attempted murder of Poppea and who lies to proclaim her innocence (Act 3, scene iii: 'Innocente son io, / Io sa la mia coscienza e lo sa dio'; 'I am innocent: my conscience knows it, and God knows it'). Drusilla does not entirely rescue the opera for the moral cause, for all her new-found place in Busenello's and Monteverdi's worlds.

So we are left with Seneca. Not only is his early death an inconvenience; he, too, is open to the taint of degeneracy. As both Rosand and Fenlon and Miller have variously and ably revealed, there were two sides to Seneca as he was perceived in early seventeenth-century Venice (and earlier): the wise, noble philosopher willing to die happily for his beliefs versus the wastrel and lush cynically exploiting his position at Nero's court for fame and fortune.[16] This reflects broader ambivalences in contemporary Venetian political and historical writings concerning the life and principles of the philosopher. Busenello knew his Seneca well, making direct or indirect reference to a number of his texts in the libretto,[17] and he would have been aware of current arguments on the merits and demerits both of Seneca as an individual and of the Neostoic ideals traced

---

[15] See the preface to the 1656 edition of the libretto, *L'incoronatione di Poppea di Gio: Francesco Busenello: Opera musicale rappresentata nel Teatro Grimano l'anno 1642* (Venice, 1656): 'Nerone innamorato di Poppea, ch'era moglie di Ottone, lo mandò sotto pretesto d'ambascaria in Lusitania per godersi la cara diletta, così rappresenta Cornelio Tacito. Ma qui si rappresenta il fatto diverso . . .' ('Nero, in love with Poppaea, who was Otho's wife, sent him as a pretext on an embassy to Lusitania so as to enjoy his chosen beloved – this according to Cornelius Tacitus. But here the action is represented differently . . .'). This is the libretto commonly described as having been printed in Busenello's 'collected works' (*Delle hore ociose*), but the copy in the British Library, London, is a separate fascicle. The text was undoubtedly revised for this 'literary' publication, but in some areas it may be closer to the original text than scholars have assumed.

[16] The latter view derives from Dio Cassius; see Fenlon and Miller, 'The Song of the Soul', 7–8. In the prologue to *Poppea*, Fortuna accuses Virtù of selling privileges and titles for personal gain, which may be an indirect reference to Seneca.

[17] See the excellent discussion in Robert R. Holzer, review of Fenlon and Miller, 'The Song of the Soul', *Cambridge Opera Journal*, 5 (1993), 79–92.

back through his teaching. Such ideals focused on the related notions of dispassion towards pain (*apatheia*), a withdrawal from public life in favour of the *vita contemplativa*, and an emphasis on the virtue of *constantia* in the face of mutable fortune. They may have matched the tenor of the period – Venice kept its distance from the horrors of the Thirty Years War – but the Republic's tendency towards passivity (and its presumed bedfellow, hypocrisy) had already been cause for complaint in the 1610s by the popular Venetian propagandist Paolo Sarpi, who instead argued passionately for the virtues of the active life and of political engagement.[18] Both Seneca and Senecan ideals also prompted significant criticism from more recent Venetians. The issue was in part played out in the Accademia degli Incogniti. The academy's leader, Giovanni Francesco Loredano, included among the monologues by various historical figures in his *Scherzi geniali* (1632) one entitled 'Seneca prudente', a sympathetic elaboration of Seneca's retirement speech in Tacitus' *Annals* (XIV, 53–4) defending himself against the accusations of his jealous rivals.[19] Loredano's colleague Federico Malipiero took the negative view of Seneca as an opportunist, cheat, pimp and hypocrite.[20] These two sides to Seneca are certainly present in the libretto of *Poppea* and perhaps even in its music. His preparations for death at the opening of Act 2 would appear to present him in a favourable light. But in Act 1, scene ii the two soldiers call the 'pedant' Seneca 'quel reo cortigiano / che fonda il suo guadagno / sul tradire il compagno' ('that guilty courtier who founds his gain on betraying his friend'); in Act 1, scene vi Valletto unleashes a plethora of insults against 'il filosofo astuto, il gabba Giove' ('the sly philosopher, the fake Jove'); while in Act 1, scene x Nerone calls him a 'decrepito pazzo' ('decrepit madman') fit only for 'concetti' and 'sofismi'. Even the noble (at least for the moment) Ottavia remains unmoved by Seneca's counsel, deploring (again, in Act 1, scene vi) his 'vanità speciose' and 'studiati artifici'. If Seneca's later actions in the opera are indeed to be admired, it demands some readjustment of our perceptions of the character presented thus far.

[18] See William J. Bouwsma, *Venice and the Defense of Republican Liberty: Renaissance Values in the Age of the Counter-Reformation* (Berkeley and Los Angeles, 1968), 527–8.
[19] Loredano's *Scherzi geniali* (Venice, 1632) contains 'Agrippina calunniata' (scherzo 2; pp. 21–38), 'Poppea supplichevole' (scherzo 9; pp. 145–64) and 'Seneca prudente' (scherzo 11; pp. 181–96). The last two are briefly discussed in Fenlon and Miller, 'The Song of the Soul', 46–8. 'Poppea supplichevole', a devious if passionate farrago of lies (against Octavia) and sexual promises, seems prompted in part by events in the pseudo-Seneca *Octavia*. In 'Seneca prudente', Seneca repeatedly invokes Fortune, Virtue and Moral Philosophy. Only Fortune and Virtue can withstand the attack of Envy, and all three can be protected only by Seneca's withdrawal from Nero's court and renouncing his riches: 'Lo dico per facilitare con l'esperienza l'asprezza de' miei precetti, e per autenticare col'essempio i tratti della mia penna. Lo dico anco per sottrarmi una volta di tanto peso, e vivere à me stesso in riposo sotto l'ombra della virtù' (p. 191: 'I say it to enact with experience the harshness of my precepts, and to authenticate by example the writings of my pen. I say it also to free myself for once of so great a weight, and to live by myself in calm under the shadow of virtue'). Compare *L'incoronazione di Poppea*, Act 2, scene i: 'Or confermo i miei scritti, / autentico i miei studi' ('Now I confirm my writings, I authenticate my studies'; see Example 2 below). Most would have spotted the irony of Loredano having Seneca claim ('Seneca prudente', 193) that he is eternally grateful to Nero, and whoever wishes to erase that memory will have to kill him.
[20] Malipiero's *L'imperatrice ambiziosa* (Venice, 1642) is discussed in Rosand, 'Seneca and the Interpretation of *L'incoronazione di Poppea*', 47–52.

Seneca is in effect extraneous to the story of Nero and Poppaea as told by Tacitus and other Roman historians:[21] the real-life Seneca died in AD 65, after the events recounted in the opera and for other reasons, his supposed involvement in the plot against Nero headed by Gaius Calpurnius Piso. Seneca's nephew and co-conspirator, the poet Lucan, who also took his own life at the same time, also appears in *Poppea* (as Lucano) and, ironically, in a drunken celebration of Seneca's death with Nerone (Act 2, scene v). Lucano's presence certainly offers a clue to any reading of the opera (or at least, of Busenello's libretto).[22] According to Suetonius' *Life of Lucan*, the poet was one of the emperor's *cohors amicorum*, and his epic poem *Pharsalia* (or *De bello civili*) – on the battle of Pharsalus waged between Julius Caesar and Pompey in 48 BC – begins with a lavish encomium (I, 33–66) in praise of the emperor. In the course of writing the *Pharsalia*, however, Lucan became alienated from Nero's court (Tacitus speaks of Lucan's violent hatred in *Annals*, XV, 49), and his poem turned into a diatribe against Caesar and in favour of the Republic. Accordingly, in the Renaissance (when Lucan was widely read) the fawning eulogy of Nero was generally construed as a masterpiece of irony.[23] It was also taken as one model for a rhetorical genre that gained some currency during the sixteenth and seventeenth centuries, the so-called paradoxical encomium, an exercise in praising that which cannot be praised.

Erasmus's *Moriae encomion* (*Praise of Folly*, 1509) is one in a long line of paradoxical encomia covering a number of standard topics, one of which is the praise of Nero (others include madness and the French pox).[24] The *Neronis encomium* of Girolamo Cardano (1501–76) is one example;[25] another is Henri de Boulay's *Il Nerone difeso di Luciano*, published in 1627 by the Venetian printer Evangelista Deuchino as the

---

[21] As Wendy Heller pointed out, responding to an earlier version of this essay presented as a paper at the Fifth Annual Meeting of the Society for Seventeenth-Century Music, Florida State University, Tallahassee (USA), 10–13 April 1997. I have drawn significant benefit from her response; her forthcoming 'Tacito incognito: Opera as History in *L'incoronazione di Poppea*' also promises an important new political–historical reading of the opera.

[22] The point is noted, but not developed, in Holzer's review of Fenlon and Miller, 'The Song of the Soul', 80, and will be taken further by Heller in her forthcoming study (see n. 21 above). Busenello may well have been influenced by Lucan's *Pharsalia*, particularly in its treatment of history in an epic mode and in its downplaying the role of the gods therein. Lucano appears alone in the 1643 scenario; in the 1656 libretto he is joined by Petronio and Tigellino (P. Turpilianus Petronius and C. Ofonius Tigellinus, two of Nero's intimates in Tacitus' *Annals*).

[23] John Dilwyn Knox, 'The Concepts of Rhetorical and Socratic Ironia in the Renaissance (Latin and Italian Sources)' (Ph.D. dissertation, University of London, 1984), 111–14, to which the following discussion of paradoxical encomia is indebted. See also Henry Knight Miller, 'The Paradoxical Encomium, with Special Reference to its Vogue in England, 1600–1800', *Modern Philology*, 53 (1956), 145–78; Rosalie L. Colie, *Paradoxia epidemica: The Renaissance Tradition of Paradox* (London, 1966).

[24] Compare George Chapman, *A Iustification of a Strange Action of Nero; in burying with a solemne funerall, one of the cast hayres of his mistresse Poppaea. Also a iust reproofe of a Romane smell-feast, being* [a translation of] *the fifth Satyre of Iuvenall* (London, 1629); and S. S., *Paradoxes, or Encomiums in the praise of: Being Lowsey; Treachery; Nothing; Beggery; the French Pox; Blindnesse; the Emperor Nero; Madnesse* (London, 1653). The latter condemns (p. 21) 'that very *Seneca* who wrot[e] so much in the praise of *temperance*, and *fortitude*, yet lived like an absolute epicure, and dyed like an effeminate coward'. In the preface, the author claims that 'I have attempted by a kind of novel Alchemy to turn Tin to Silver, and Copper into Gold'; of these paradoxes 'there hath none more intricate, been discussed, and canvased, among the Stoicks in *Zenos Porch*, [and] if thy sense besot not thy understanding, I do not doubt a welcome'.

[25] There are several editions of *Hieronymi Cardani Neronis encomium* including one published in Amsterdam in 1640 and the one in Cardano's *Opera omnia*, 10 vols. (Lyons, 1663), i, 179–220.

third of *Tre discorsi del Signor Henrico De Bullay, gentil'huomo francese*.[26] Henri de Boulay was a Frenchman who had established his home in Venice seeking, it seems, to earn his living as a tutor to young members of the nobility. His fanciful dialogue is set in the Underworld, with Nero summoned before the judge Minos for his crimes and specifically for the murder of his mother, Agrippina. In Greek myth, Minos heads the three judges of the Underworld (the others are his brothers Rhadamanthys and Aeacus) who decide the fate of newly dead souls: there are three outcomes, consignment to the Asphodel Meadows for those neither virtuous nor evil, punishment in Tartarus, and admission to Elysium. Minos normally tries the most difficult cases, into which category Nero clearly falls.

In response to Minos' questioning, Nero asks for Seneca to be called as a witness, at which point the emperor presents an extraordinary defence of his life hinging on three arguments: first, his immoral excesses can be blamed on his family, his poor upbringing and destiny, all of which he could not avoid and which therefore absolve him from personal blame; second, his actions were justifiable by reason of state[27] and indeed were approved by the Roman senate; and third, his erstwhile tutor Seneca (also responsible for his poor upbringing) both encouraged and was complicit in his crimes and benefited materially from them. Nero also draws to Minos' attention his own good points – including his artistic talents – and his achievements for the glory of Rome and the Empire, whether military or architectural. But it is the attack on Seneca that provides the focus of De Boulay's text, which goes further than most in accusing the philosopher not just of luxury and wantonness – Seneca gained 'da 7. in 8. millioni d'Oro' from Nero and owned villas and gardens that exceeded the emperor's own[28] – but also of sexual excess (with Agrippina, among many others) and of murder for political gain. Nero turns Seneca's learning against him – he is 'attracted only to vain, pedantic studies which serve to amuse children'[29] – and claims that the philosopher was feeble even in death, persuading his wife Paulina to commit suicide with him for fear of dying alone (Nero takes credit for saving her life). All in all, Nero argues, if Seneca had been of a different cast, things might not have turned out as they did. On the other hand,

---

[26] The collection is dedicated (12 April 1627) by Deuchino to the young Todaro Minio, who has already published anonymously with the printer. The two other discourses are *Dell'historia scritta, e non scritta* and *Della vanità dell'astrologia giudiciaria*; *Il Nerone difeso di Luciano* takes up pages 126–61. According to the dedication (p. 4), these are among several discourses 'già fatti per sua [De Boulay's] memoria, ed esercitio' and presented to 'un religioso Claustrale'; further translations from French into Italian are promised depending on the success of the present volume.

[27] Incidentally, this was a criticism often made of the Venetians; see Bouwsma, *Venice and the Defense of Republican Liberty*, 503.

[28] *Tre discorsi del Signor Henrico De Bullay*, 144. Compare Loredano's 'Seneca prudente' in *Scherzi geniali*, 187: 'Quai pensieri devono formare i Romani, i miei medesimi amici sovra l'immensità di tante mie ricchezze? Mi veggono adornare superbi giardini, trattenermi in così magnifiche Ville, havere possessioni così grandi, raccorre entrate così abbondanti. Non hò dubbio, che l'invidia gli haverà co' suoi fiati infetti. E quei medesimi, che vengono alle mie case, per servirmi di corteggio, fanno voti per la mia caduta.' Similarly (*ibid.*, 191), Seneca admits to having 'sette millioni, e cinquecento mille ducati di facoltà'.

[29] *Tre discorsi del Signor Henrico De Bullay*, 143: 'avezzo alli soli studij vani, e pedanteschi, che servono a dar trattenimento a' fanciulli'.

182

De Boulay's Seneca makes only two points in his own favour, doubtless heeding the real-life Seneca's advice (in *De constantia*) that the wise man should remain indifferent to insult: his fortune was received unasked from Nero, and he had saved Otho from death. But Minos is unimpressed. Having started with the assumption that Seneca was a man of 'tante virtù', the judge is moved by Nero's argument, praising his rhetorical power, and is suspicious of the philosopher's reticence. The dialogue ends with Minos adjourning the case to give Seneca time to prepare his defence; he also promises to summon Agrippina as a further witness.

Of course, none of this is to be taken seriously. If that were not clear from the text – which is surprisingly persuasive – and its offence against common sense, it is so from De Boulay's title, *Il Nerone difeso di Luciano*. However one reads the ambiguous wording – Nero 'defended by Lucian' or 'Nero defended', by Lucian – the author plays with the notion that his dialogue is in the manner of the Greek author, if not a translation of him. It is not the latter (the dialogue bears no relation to the pseudo-Lucianic *Nero*), as any literate reader would have known, but the merest mention of Lucian is sufficient to anchor both the genre and the mode of the piece.[30] De Boulay's text is written in the manner of Lucian's *Dialogues of the Dead*, a number of which focus on similar Underworld scenarios (although having Minos as the judge comes from Lucian's *Menippus*),[31] and like much of Lucian it is intended to be read satirically. For the Renaissance, Lucian, Juvenal and others established a sophist–satirical mode that gained some popularity in Italian and north-European political and moral tracts, especially when the tenor was anti-intellectual, anti-monarchical and/or anti-clerical. Lucian himself wrote vehemently against the Stoics; and Socrates, Seneca's great predecessor in noble suicide (the two were often conjoined), receives harsh treatment in *Dialogues of the Dead*, IV (which may have influenced De Boulay's criticisms of Seneca). Lucian also advocated 'the way ordinary men live' (*Menippus*, IV) in the face of the vanity of human endeavour and the mutability of fortune. His cynicism, plus the strong whiff of anti-establishment subversion (his writings were on the *Index librorum prohibitorum*), must have struck a chord in Venice, and especially within the Accademia degli Incogniti.[32]

Lucian certainly makes his presence felt in the librettos of Monteverdi's late operas: his *The Parasite* has direct bearing on the treatment of the character Iro in *Il ritorno d'Ulisse in patria*, and the dispute between Fortuna, Virtù and Amor in the prologue to *L'incoronazione di Poppea* is a Lucianic topos.[33] It is no doubt useful to politicize in the manner of Rosand these and other allusions as indicative of Venetian republican sentiment (or at least, one strain thereof) and of the political and social theories

[30] Christopher Robinson, *Lucian and his Influence in Europe* (London, 1979) remains the standard text on Lucian and his reception through to the eighteenth century.
[31] But see also Virgil, *Aeneid*, VI, 432.
[32] See Rosand, 'Seneca and the Interpretation of *L'incoronazione di Poppea*', 37: 'Most members of the [Incogniti] could boast at least one book on the *Index librorum prohibitorum*.'
[33] Compare the Lucianic play of Fortune versus Virtue in Leon Battista Alberti's *Virtus dea* (one of his *Intercoenales*) discussed in Robinson, *Lucian and his Influence in Europe*, 86.

underpinning it. However, paradoxical encomia and other satirical genres cut both ways – they may have moral or political points to make, but they also exhibit a pleasure in rhetorical play for its own sake: Erasmus's *Moriae encomion* was avowedly written to pass the time on a long journey and merely to entertain the author's old friend Thomas More (punned in the title). And there is some merit in dissecting *Poppea* with just such a double-edged blade, whether as a paradoxical encomium of Nero and Poppaea or, more intriguingly, as one of the Love (false and politically dangerous) that the Incogniti were to denounce in a different context as 'a plague and a defect, not an affect, of the heart'[34] and which appears so prominently in the prologue and throughout the opera. Thus Amor's victory over Virtù in this prologue, and for which the opera is proclaimed an exemplar, may be read paradoxically. Indeed, one might also go further to see *Il ritorno d'Ulisse in patria* and *L'incoronazione di Poppea* as counterpointing each other in terms of presenting different faces of love, whether 'true' (constant Penelope) or 'false' (debauched Poppaea) in the manner of a textual and musical debate much in the vein of innumerable debates within the Accademia degli Incogniti, an exercise *in utramque partem disputare* that was a basic feature of rhetorical training and of academic discussion. Whether such debates were to be taken seriously is an entirely different matter.

For De Boulay and his contemporary Venetians, the jury was clearly out on Seneca. And the jury remains out on the musical Seneca in Monteverdi's *L'incoronazione di Poppea*. The problems are caused precisely by the ambivalences of his music in its frequent shifts from recitative through arioso to aria that veer uncomfortably between seriousness and pompous vacuity. The latter is certainly close to the surface in his dialogue with Ottavia and Valletto in Act 1, scene vi, where the empress's claims for Seneca's 'specious vanities' and 'studied artifices' are matched in his music by a bombast that wilfully misaccentuates the text.[35] All his precepts are mere 'canzoni', says Valletto in one of those typical self-referential moments in opera emphasized in Monteverdi's setting by a prominent signifier of 'song' in his own musical semiotic, a passage in triple time over a repeating *ciaccona* ground bass (Example 1).[36] And in

[34] In the preface to *Novelle amorose de' Signori Academici Incogniti publicate da Francesco Carmeni, segretario dell'Academia* (Venice, 1641), f. [A4]': 'è una pesta, & un difetto, non un'affetto del cuore'. For other Incogniti statements on Love, see Fenlon and Miller, 'The Song of the Soul', 35.

[35] Rosand ('Seneca and the Interpretation of *L'incoronazione di Poppea*', 44) notes of this scene that 'Seneca's attempts to preach stoicism to Ottavia are singularly lacking in compassion; they are ineffective, even repressive', although this is in the section of her article dealing with the libretto; perhaps significantly, she does not consider this scene in her discussion of Monteverdi's score (but see below, note 43), for all that it surely sits uncomfortably with her view of the 'moral integrity' of Seneca's music (*ibid.*, 55). Act 1, scene vi is also handled somewhat ambivalently by Fenlon and Miller ('The Song of the Soul', 63–7), who associate Seneca's madrigalesque word-painting (for example, a 'long, virtuosic melisma on the word "bellezza" '; *ibid.*, 64) with notions of irony (whether on Seneca's or on Monteverdi's part remains unclear). Heller ('Chastity, Heroism, and Allure', 272–3) is less equivocal – Monteverdi's 'representation of the philosopher's advice to Ottavia seems pregnant with satire' – which seems entirely justified given the deliberate oddities in Seneca's music (for example, and as Heller notes, Fenlon and Miller's 'long, virtuosic melisma' is not on 'bellezza' at all, but on the immediately preceding definite article, '*la* bellezza').

[36] There may be a further resonance here: Seneca was Spanish, as was the *ciaccona* in origin. As a potentially 'low'-class genre, the *ciaccona* is also, of course, appropriate for Valletto.

Example 1. Monteverdi, *L'incoronazione di Poppea*, Act 1, scene vi, Venice MS (compare Claudio Monteverdi, *L'incoronazione di Poppea*, ed. Alan Curtis, London, 1989. 65–6): Valletto.

(These mere inventions of his brain he sells as mysteries, and they are songs. Madama...)

general Seneca does indeed seem rather too willing to move into lyrical triple time – to sing his songs – at every opportunity, whether for word-painting or to emphasize the sententious maxims piously littering his speeches. When Monteverdi gives him a gloriously extended passage in triple time on the blessings of death ('L'uscir di vita è una beata sorte' Act 2, scene i), we are left wondering whether this is an emotional out-pouring, a rhetorical emphasis or just yet another of Valletto's 'canzoni' (see Example 2).

Susan McClary has no doubt whatsoever. For her, Monteverdi's Seneca, like Ottone and Nerone, is 'depicted as profoundly passive and impotent': 'Seneca habitually reverts to silly madrigalisms, which destroy the rhetorical effect of most of his statements'.[37] Accordingly, the music of

---

[37] Susan McClary, 'Constructions of Gender in Monteverdi's Dramatic Music', *Feminine Endings: Music, Gender, and Sexuality* (Minnesota and London, 1991), 35–52 (p. 49). This important article first appeared in *Cambridge Opera Journal*, 1 (1989), 203–23.

Example 2. *L'incoronazione di Poppea*, Act 2, scene i, Venice MS (compare *L'incoronazione di Poppea*, ed. Curtis, 112–13): Seneca.

(Now I confirm my writings, I authenticate my studies. The leaving of life is a blessed fate...)

*Poppea* causes 'crucial assumptions concerning the potency of patriarchy, male domination and masculine sexuality' to evaporate, and it liberates the female voice in 'an anomalous moment in culture when power relationships associated with gender and rhetoric were oddly reconfigured'.[38] Ellen Rosand, however, takes a different tack. Her crucial interpretation of *L'incoronazione di Poppea* focuses precisely on the character of Seneca so as to draw out the moral of an immoral opera and to rescue Monteverdi from the censure of those critics troubled by the difficulties of its plot. She acknowledges that at least some members of the Accademia degli Incogniti, and by extension Busenello, adopted the cynical view of Seneca as, at best, a figure of fun and, at worst, a hypocrite: in effect, Valletto is one authentic voice of the Incogniti. However, Rosand then argues that Monteverdi's music places Seneca in a light very different from that cast by the libretto ('In opera, the dramatist is the composer'!): the essential truths revealed by Seneca's songs give the character a depth, honesty and integrity that make him the true hero of the piece, steadfast and wise in a world of otherwise relentless degeneracy. Her reading of Seneca's 'L'uscir di vita è una beata sorte' is very different from McClary's dismissive treatment of Seneca's 'silly madrigalisms': Monteverdi 'shifts into triple meter and a beautifully arched stepwise melodic line of successively smaller curves descends to

---

[38] *Ibid.*, 49, 51.

XII

a cadence, sealing [Seneca's] happy acceptance of his fate and emphasizing his union with the gods'.[39]

Rosand's faith in Monteverdi's music seems to chime with one strand of Incogniti thinking. As Fenlon and Miller have noted, the members of the Accademia degli Incogniti tussled with the relationship between appearances and reality (a key feature, we learn, of their Tacitist stance). Physical beauty can be recognized by proportion, body and voice, and these appearances of beauty reflect the internal beauty of the soul. However, appearances can be deceiving, and, in the analytical process required to distinguish truth from falsehood, one must weigh the evidence of the eyes against that of the ears; in cases of doubt, the sound of the voice, rather than beauty of appearance, reveals the truth of the soul.[40] Fenlon and Miller never quite come to terms with a major problem of their 'reliance upon the musicality of the human voice to ascertain the true disposition of the soul':[41] (false) love deceives. Nor does their subsequent account quite reconcile faith in music with the fact, palpable in the opera (indeed, one cause for its frequent critique), that the devil has all the best tunes. But Fenlon and Miller's conclusion accords well with common aesthetic prejudices concerning the nature of opera: 'Only the voice can cut through the realm of appearances. In its beautiful harmonies we hear a song of the soul, a song that cannot mislead.'[42] Music is taken as being pre-eminently trustworthy in its sounds and meanings.

For Rosand, the issue comes to a head at the opening of Act 2, where Seneca is visited by Mercury announcing his imminent demise, and by Liberto as Nerone's emissary bearing the death-sentence, leading to the affecting scene between Seneca and his 'famigliari' (traditionally interpreted as his friends and/or students) as the philosopher takes leave of his companions: they try to dissuade him from the task by extolling the pleasures of life on earth, and he gently orders them to prepare the bath in which he will open his veins and die. In Rosand's view (at least, as expressed in 1985),[43] Monteverdi clearly empathizes with Seneca, and thus we are moved to feel for rather than against him, his fate going to the core of our emotional being. Certainly this is the response of the Famigliari, whose poignant plea to Seneca that he should not die ('Non morir, Seneca, nò'; see Example 3) is given powerful force through

[39] 'Seneca and the Interpretation of *L'incoronazione di Poppea*', 66.
[40] Fenlon and Miller discuss the ideas of Giovanni Battista Doglioni and Giovanni Francesco Loredano in *'The Song of the Soul'*, 35–40.
[41] *Ibid.*, 38.
[42] *Ibid.*, 40.
[43] It would be unreasonable to assume that Rosand's views have remained fixed, for all their subsequent influence on reading *Poppea*. Her 1985 article is a revision of papers presented in 1981 and 1982; it was also written in response to the Jean-Pierre Ponnelle/Nikolaus Harnoncourt *Poppea* (Zurich, 1975), where Seneca was patently mishandled, which may explain Rosand's special pleading for the character (curiously, the 1984 revival of the Peter Hall/Raymond Leppard *Poppea* at Glyndebourne – for all its controversial approach to the sources – came much closer to Rosand's proposed reading). Rosand's 'Monteverdi's Mimetic Art' (published in 1989 but originally written in 1983) suggests a slight but perhaps significant shift. Although Rosand does not deal primarily with Seneca in this article, there is one telling remark (p. 122): in his encounter with Mercurio in Act 2, scene i, 'music sustains Seneca's moral conviction here, just as earlier [in Act 1, scene vi, with Ottavia] it had helped to undermine it' (compare note 35 above).

Example 3. *L'incoronazione di Poppea*, Act 2, scene iii, Venice MS (compare *L'incoronazione di Poppea*, ed. Curtis, 122–3): Famigliari.

XII

Rosand's rhetoric: 'The effect of this chromatic passage is remarkable. In texture, melody, and harmony it is unique in the opera, emphasizing the followers' pain above their hedonistic denial of philosophical principle.'[44]

One cannot gainsay so moving a response to the Famigliari's music – with which many will feel in sympathy – but it is harder to demonstrate that it is historically appropriate or even authentic. Yet the question of authentication is pertinent if only because it exposes the difficulties of generating a context-sensitive reading of *Poppea*. Thus it is worth examining this scene (Act 2, scene iii) in some detail:[45]

| | |
|---|---|
| *Seneca* | Amici, è giunta l'ora<br>di praticare in fatti<br>quella virtù che tanto celebrai.<br>Breve angoscia è la morte,<br>un sospir peregrino esce dal core,<br>ov'è stato molt'anni,<br>quasi in ospizio, come forestiero,<br>e sen vola all'Olimpo,<br>della felicità soggiorno vero. |
| *Famigliari* | Non morir, Seneca, nò. |
| *Uno* | Questa vita è dolce troppo,<br>questo ciel troppo sereno,<br>ogni amaro, ogni veleno<br>finalmente è lieve intoppo. |
| *Fam.* | Io per me morir non vuò.<br>Non morir, Seneca, nò. |
| *Uno* | Se mi corco al sonno lieve<br>mi risveglia in sul mattino,<br>ma un avel di marmo fino<br>mai non dà quel che riceve. |
| *Fam.* | Io per me morir non vuò.<br>Non morir, Seneca, nò. |
| *Sen.* | Supprimete i singulti,<br>rimandate quei pianti |

[44] 'Seneca and the Interpretation of *L'incoronazione di Poppea*', 69. Rosand continues: 'Monteverdi's vivid setting of Seneca's final words, projecting his impending death as he depicts the life flowing from his open veins, is one more instance of the composer's empathy with the heroic aspect of the act.' True, Rosand has earlier (p. 46) raised doubts about this scene: 'When, in Act II, scene 3, Seneca announces his decision to his followers, we may be moved, but they are not. Their brief plea for him to reconsider gives way to complete dissociation from the act. They would not do the same. Life is too sweet. There is nothing worth dying for . . .'. But again (compare note 35 above) this comes in her discussion of the libretto: the music is kept apart. As for 'Non morir, Seneca, nò', Fenlon and Miller follow Rosand closely here, as elsewhere: 'This remarkable passage begins with rising chromatic lines in all voices to the words "Non morir, Seneca", the music gradually growing in intensity through the cumulative effect of pungent suspensions . . .' ('The Song of the Soul', 79). Wolfgang Osthoff (*Das dramatische Spätwerk Claudio Monteverdis*, Tutzing, 1960, 98) takes a more detached view; he also notes the connection with 'Non partir, ritrosetta' on which I elaborate below.

[45] I give the text as it was printed in the 1656 libretto, which for various reasons seems close enough to what Monteverdi had before him when he put pen to music paper.

dai canali degl'occhi
alle fonti dell'anime, ò miei cari.
Vada quell'acqua homai
à lavarvi dai cori
dell'inconstanza vil le macchie indegne.
Altr'essequie ricerca
che un gemito dolente
Seneca moriente.
Itene tutti a prepararmi il bagno
che se la vita corre
come il rivo fluente,
in un tepido rivo
questo sangue innocente io vò che vada
a imporporarmi del morir la strada.

(*Seneca*: Friends, the hour has come / to practise in deed / that virtue which I so much celebrated. / Death is brief anguish, / a wandering sigh leaves the heart, / where it had stayed for many years / like a guest, as a stranger, / and flies towards Olympus, / the true resting-place of happiness. // *Famigliari*: Do not die, Seneca, no. // *One*: This life is too sweet, / this sky too serene, / all bitterness and poison / finally is a light burden. // *Fam.*: For myself, I would not die. / Do not die, Seneca, no. // *One*: If I lie down to feathery sleep / I wake up in the morning, / but a tomb of fine marble / never yields up what it receives. // *Fam.*: For myself, I would not die. / Do not die, Seneca, no. // *Sen.*: Suppress your sobs, / send back your tears / from the channels of the eyes / to the wellspring of your soul, o my dear ones. / Let that water now go / to wash out of your hearts / the unworthy stains of vile inconstancy. / Other obsequies are demanded / than a grieving groan / by Seneca's dying. / Go, all of you, to prepare the bath for me, / for if life runs by / like the flowing river, / in a warm river / I wish this innocent blood to run / so as to empurple for me the path to death.)

The structure of the scene presented here is straightforward. Nine lines of *versi sciolti* for Seneca – the verse cues recitative – are followed by a single *verso tronco*, 'Non morir, Seneca, nò', for the Famigliari and then two six-line stanzas for one of their number (incorporating a two-line refrain by all: 'Io per me morir non vuò. / Non morir, Seneca, nò') in eight-syllable lines: the shift of metre and the strophic structure cue aria. The scene then concludes with 16 lines of *versi sciolti* – back to recitative – for Seneca, only six of which (from 'Itene tutti a prepararmi il bagno') are set in the Venice manuscript of the opera (all are set in the Naples manuscript). There are grounds for considering that the short version of Seneca's final speech in the Venice manuscript reflects a later cut; that is, the Naples manuscript appears to preserve the 'original' in some (even if revised) form. Or, to put the point another way, the longer version of the text seems better to reflect what Busenello originally wrote, whether or not it was reworked for publication in the 1656 libretto.[46]

---

[46] In the case of the two manuscripts of the music for *Poppea*, the assumption has tended to be that the Naples manuscript presents a revised version (associated with a performance in Naples in 1651?). Thus Curtis suggests of nearly all the Naples 'additions' (given in an appendix to his 1989 edition) that they were the result of 'afterthoughts' and, it is implied, by

Monteverdi's setting of this text – and for all the problems of the sources for *Poppea* it is evident that this scene was indeed by him, with or without subsequent revision – follows reasonably closely the musical implications of Busenello's verse. True, Seneca begins in triple time rather than recitative (another of his 'canzoni'?),[47] but Busenello's 'aria' for one of the Famigliari (Monteverdi sets it as a trio) is duly marked out by strophic setting with the two strophes preceded, separated and followed by an instrumental ritornello (only the bass line survives), and then there is a final recitative for Seneca. The 'aria' (trio) at 'Questa vita è dolce troppo' even adopts the standard hemiola patterns associated with eight-syllable lines from the late sixteenth century onwards. The one significant variant between the libretto (as printed in 1656, admittedly, but arguably close to the original) and the score – the handling of the first *verso tronco* for the Famigliari, 'Non morir, Seneca, nò' – may be a result of later revision. In the score Busenello's anticipation of the impending refrain is expanded by setting 'Non morir, Seneca, nò. / Io per me morir non vò [*sic*]' (the two lines are reversed in the refrain). Incorporating both lines of the refrain before the fact, and reversing their order, makes dramatic sense (the Famigliari ask Seneca not to die, then 'Io per me morir non vò' provides the justification for the song apostrophizing the sweetness of life).[48] This, together with the omission of the refrain from

---

composers other than Monteverdi. But the stemma of the sources for *Poppea* is extremely complex, and although apparently later sources (including, of course, the Venice manuscript, which also dates from the 1650s) may well contain later music, the proportion of revisions to additions remains unclear. For example, the Udine libretto discovered by Paolo Fabbri (Udine, Biblioteca Comunale, Fondo Joppi 496; see 'New Sources for "Poppea" ') seems to derive from a now-lost score closer to the version used at the première than the surviving Venice and Naples manuscripts, and yet it includes a number of the Naples 'additions' (but not the longer version of Seneca's final speech).

The present case is an instructive example. The long version of Seneca's speech (and its opening 'Supprimete i singulti') seems closer to Busenello's main source for Seneca's death scene, Tacitus' *Annals* (XV, 60–4; compare also Lipsius' *Life of Seneca* discussed in note 62 below). There is also fairly strong musical evidence to suggest that Seneca's final speech did not originally start at 'Itene tutti a prepararmi il bagno'. The immediately preceding ritornello cadences on D minor (with or without a *tierce de picardie*; I use the language of major–minor tonality for convenience), and 'Itene tutti' begins on a chord of G major (Monteverdi, *L'incoronazione di Poppea*, ed. Curtis, 129), whereas the setting of the beginning of Seneca's final speech in the Naples manuscript, at 'Supprimete i singulti' (*ibid.*, 273), starts on a chord of D minor, the 'key of the ritornello and also of Seneca's final cadence. There is a clear tendency in *Poppea* as it survives for ritornellos to maintain tonal continuity with preceding and succeeding recitatives/arias, failing strong dramatic reasons to the contrary (e.g. the introduction of a new character) or obvious difficulties in the sources (e.g. the problem of Ottone's ritornellos in Act 1, scene i). And in general, Seneca's music is often in D minor (or else some kind of C): witness Act 1, scenes vii–viii and Act 2, scene i, and indeed the beginning of the present Act 2, scene iii. Having Seneca begin with 'Itene tutti a prepararmi il bagno' (on G) creates a tonal disjunction, whereas the D minor of 'Supprimete i singulti' does not.

[47] Fenlon and Miller speak of 'a steady, lilting, evenly phrased *arioso*' (*'The Song of the Soul'*, 78): evidently, in their eyes, this opening is to be taken seriously.

[48] This may not have been done by Monteverdi, at least in his original version. The Udine libretto (Fondo Joppi 496) does not give the first appearance of 'Io per me morir non vò' (it has only 'Non morir, Seneca, nò', just as the 1656 libretto) and yet this libretto derives (according to Fabbri) from an early score, a suggestion reinforced by its allocation of different lines of the Famigliari's quatrains to 'Vno', 'Altro' and 'Terzo', i.e. in a trio format. (But the Udine libretto also corresponds to the 1656 libretto in having the refrain 'Io per me morir non vò, / Non morir, Seneca, nò' at the end of each of the Famigliari's quatrains.) Again, musical evidence may be helpful, for all its obvious dangers. 'Non morir, Seneca, nò' cadences on D minor

the first stanza for the Famigliari, produces a symmetrical structure start-ing and ending with what seems to be the main point of the Famigliari's contribution, the poignant 'Non morir, Seneca, nò' singled out by Rosand (and now, it seems, by Monteverdi and/or his revisers) as the key element of the scene.

The question, then, is the emotional veracity of 'Non morir, Seneca, nò', and whether (to return to Fenlon and Miller) 'In its beautiful har-monies we hear a song of the soul, a song that cannot mislead'. If this is a serious moment seeking to move, then it sits rather uncomfortably with the subsequent disclaimer, 'Io per me morir non vò', and with the bouncing hemiola rhythms of the two strophes of 'Questa vita è dolce troppo' (not to mention its dance-like ritornello). Nevertheless the prima-facie arguments seem to come down in Rosand's favour. The chromaticism that permeates 'Non morir, Seneca, nò' is traditionally associated with serious expressive intent, and the tetrachordal structure hints at what Rosand has called in a different context 'an emblem of lament'.[49] Nor can one deny the rhetorical power of this passage as the carefully con-structed contrapuntal patterning produces a stretto effect rising to a climax on the upper *bb'* falling dejectedly to the cadence on D. On the face of it, the Famigliari appear moved by Seneca's impending death: their plea seems genuine. But how can we be sure?

This goes to the heart of the problems of early opera, and, given the systemic confusions inherent within a semiotic (both text- and music-based) now in a state of flux, one is tempted, perhaps naively, to answer by recourse to extrinsic evidence. There is a range of material upon which one might draw to determine how Seneca and his Famigliari might have been, or might have been intended to be, read in 1643, including the contemporary political and other writings referred to above (although Rosand in effect excludes them from her account of Monteverdi's own contribution to *Poppea*), the generic parameters of the opera, accounts of 'readers' of the time, and the resonant networks of reference and allu-sion invoked and evoked in the score. All these may help define a field of possible meanings for Monteverdi's music.

*Poppea* does not fall conveniently into one or other of the generic categories – tragedy, comedy, tragicomedy, pastoral – that would set con-ventional limits on its interpretation, and as an 'opera regia' (something

---

(there may or may not be a *tierce de picardie*), and 'Io per me morir non vò' moves from D minor to a final cadence on A minor, followed by the ritornello in D minor (which, following the argument in note 46 above, would follow on better from a D cadence). 'Io per me morir non vò' sits better in the tonal context of the end of the 'aria': 'mai non dà quel che riceve' cadences on D minor, 'Io per me morir non vò' begins in D minor and ends in A minor, and 'Non morir, Seneca, nò' starts on A as V of D minor and cadences on D minor followed by the ritornello in D minor: in other words, the final sequence where 'Non morir, Seneca, nò' leads directly to the ritornello (cadence on D minor; start in D minor) may have been intended for its first appearance. The Naples manuscript takes the worst of both worlds: after 'mai non dà quel che riceve' it has 'Io per me morir non vò' followed by 'Non morir, Seneca, nò' (thus as the Venice manuscript) then followed by 'Io per me morir non vò' and the ritornello.

[49] Ellen Rosand, 'The Descending Tetrachord: An Emblem of Lament', *The Musical Quarterly*, 55 (1979), 346–59. Rosand is, of course, primarily discussing descending, not ascending, tetrachords, and in fact the inversion of the figure in 'Non morir, Seneca, nò' may add further to its ironic/parodic overtones discussed below.

XII

192

of a default term deriving from *commedia dell'arte* scenarios involving royal or noble characters but which cannot be called tragedies)[50] it lacks the theoretical underpinning provided by classical and Renaissance poetics. Therefore appropriate audience responses are not generically determined. But we do have evidence of how the Seneca seen in *Poppea* was construed by at least one 'reader', the unknown author (Busenello?) of the scenario printed for the première in the 1642-3 season (*Scenario dell'opera reggia intitolata La coronatione di Poppea*, Venice, 1643). This scenario was presumably sold to the public as preparation for, or a souvenir of, the performance, and it presents a brief but surprisingly accurate synopsis of the plot as we know it from the various surviving librettos and the two musical manuscripts of *Poppea*: almost certainly it was written with a libretto in hand. Like any synopsis, it also suggests possible interpretations, and the accounts of the scenes involving Seneca are particularly revealing.[51] For example, in Act 1, scene vi:

> Seneca consola Ottavia ad esser constante. Valletto paggio d'Ottavia per trattenimento dell'imperatrice burla Seneca al quale Ottavia si raccomanda, e va a porger preghiere al tempio.

> (Seneca encourages Octavia to be constant. Valletto, Octavia's page, for the empress's entertainment makes fun of Seneca, to whom Octavia commends herself; she then leaves to offer prayers at the temple.)

And in Act 1, scene viii:

> Pallade in aria predice la morte a Seneca, promettendoli che se doverà certo morire glielo farà di novo intender per bocca di Mercurio, e ciò per esser come uomo virtuoso suo caro e diletto; venendo ringraziata sommamente da Seneca.

> (Pallas Athene in the air foretells death to Seneca, promising him that if he is certain to die she will let him know again through the mouth of Mercury, and this because he, a man of virtue, is her loved one and delight; whereupon she is thanked greatly by Seneca.)

In both these cases, the author of the synopsis introduces a gloss that finds no direct (or even indirect) basis in the text of the equivalent scene in the opera: Valletto mocks Seneca 'for the empress's entertainment'; and as for Pallas Athene's intervention on Seneca's behalf, 'this [is] because he, a man of virtue, is her loved one and delight'.[52] Similarly, the

[50] *Poppea* is called an 'opera reggia' in the title of the 1643 scenario: other sources (see Chiarelli, '*L'incoronazione di Poppea o Il Nerone*') adopt generically neutral labels such as *opera musicale*, *dram(m)a* or *dram(m)a musicale*: the 'trag[edia]' in the libretto in Florence, Biblioteca Nazionale Centrale, Magl. VII.66 (*ibid.*, 119) appears to be an eighteenth-century addition. Compare *L'Alvida, opera regia* (giornata 43) and *La fortuna di Foresta prencipessa di Moscou, opera regia* (giornata 50) in Flaminio Scala's collection of scenarios, *Il teatro delle favole rappresentative* (Venice, 1611), mentioned in Louise George Clubb, *Italian Drama in Shakespeare's Time* (New Haven and London, 1989), 255. See also Nino Pirrotta, '*Commedia dell'arte* and Opera', *Music and Culture in Italy from the Middle Ages to the Baroque: A Collection of Essays* (Cambridge, MA, 1984), 343–60 (see p. 355); Rosand, *Opera in Seventeenth-Century Venice*, 34–65 (ch. 2: 'The Question of Genre').
[51] The text of the 1643 scenario forms the basis of the rubrics which Alan Curtis places at the head of each scene (where possible) in his 1989 edition of *Poppea*. The texts below follow Curtis, although I have modified his translations.
[52] Compare Mercurio's reference to Seneca as 'vero amico del cielo' at the very beginning of his speech in Act 2, scene i. Mercury's arrival has been announced by Pallade in Act 1, scene viii (see the relevant section of the scenario given above): productions that omit the role (and many do) miss an important point.

scenario for Act 2, scene ii calls Seneca 'costante' as he prepares for death, invoking the concept of *constantia* that for Fenlon and Miller provides the key to reading the character. Thus there emerges a clear tendency in the scenario to play up the nobility and dignity of Seneca's actions – or at least, not to make explicit the Incogniti's alternative view of him – and to moderate thereby the sometimes harsh treatment of Seneca in the libretto. Valletto's scorn of the pedant–philosopher is given new, almost honourable reason (Valletto teases Seneca to distract Ottavia).[53] And Seneca is explicitly made a man of virtue in the eyes of Pallas Athene. Of course, the reasons for these two glosses remain unclear – perhaps they present an acceptable public face masking the private scepticisms of the Incogniti – as does their relation to any reading of the character apparent in the music. Nevertheless, the glosses and general tenor of the synopsis as regards Seneca do not militate against Rosand's interpretation of Monteverdi's (as distinct from the libretto's) treatment of the character: rather, they work in favour of it.

However, the music is much more ambivalent, even at the simplest level of voice-type and scoring. Seneca's deep and wide-ranging bass, unique in the opera, would seem to confer a philosophical *gravitas* on the character, and even perhaps a god-like status.[54] But one should be wary of applying later eighteenth- and nineteenth-century characterizations of specific voice-types to early seventeenth-century opera, and even in later operas not all basses are wise old men. Although Monteverdi often scored the roles of mythical gods for bass voice – Caronte and Plutone in *Orfeo*, Plutone in the *Ballo delle ingrate*, Nettuno in *Il ritorno d'Ulisse in patria* – this was not always for serious effect. The rough humour traditionally associated with Caronte in performances of *Orfeo* (accentuated by Monteverdi's specification of a regal in the accompaniment) may or may not be warranted by the text. But Plutone in the *Ballo delle ingrate* (as we have it in the Vienna version published in the *Madrigali guerrieri, et amorosi* of 1638) is clearly a whimsical figure, at least in some performances, whose interventions prompt wry amusement. Reading Seneca in the light of Plutone (their music is at times very similar) prompts a degree of scepticism as regards his *gravitas* and decorum.[55]

---

[53] Although this may not have been enough: in the Venice manuscript the bulk of Valletto's comments against Seneca are struck through, implying a cut in performance.

[54] Rosand, 'Seneca and the Interpretation of *L'incoronazione di Poppea*', 55: 'Even Monteverdi's casting of Seneca as a bass contributes to his characterization, exploiting, as it does, a rather natural if not yet conventional association between vocal range and age, in this case the low voice with authority.' The distinguishing of Seneca is clearer still if one accepts that Mercurio, originally a *bassetto*, was transposed 'alla quinta alta', as it is marked in the Venice manuscript.

[55] Rosand would presumably disagree, given that (*ibid.*) his 'music is unlike that of any of Monteverdi's other basses. It uses a range that extends both lower and higher than usual, from low *E* to high *d'*, and exploits both extremes. It is more independently melodic, more affective and expressive, and more responsive to text, eschewing excessive doubling of the basso continuo and the cadential movement in large intervals that characterize most previous operatic music for bass.' Compare also Nino Pirrotta, 'Falsirena and the Earliest *Cavatina*', *Music and Culture*, 335–42, discussing the music of Arsete, scored for bass, in Domenico Mazzocchi's *La catena d'Adone* (Rome, 1626), the 'role of the philosophic sage' which offers a direct model for Seneca: Arsete's 'singing reflects the noble, concerned, and yet disinterested ponderings of a man whose age and wisdom have placed him beyond the reach of the passions, even though he has not lost the ability to be saddened by the folly of others' (*ibid.*, 337).

Nor does another of Monteverdi's bass roles, the fatuous Antinoö in *Il ritorno d'Ulisse in patria*, help Seneca's cause. But the writing for Antinoö and his fellow suitors (the Proci), Pisandro and Anfinomo, does bear directly on the Famigliari. The scoring for the three suitors besieging Penelope is precisely the same as that for the Famigliari: alto (C3), tenor (C4) and bass (F4). And their music merits comparison. For example, the suitors' trio in Act 2, scene v of *Il ritorno d'Ulisse in patria* ('Ama dunque, sì, sì', as the suitors urge Penelope to love; see Example 4) is closely related in gesture and structure to 'Non morir, Seneca, nò'; the latter is a chromatic counterfeit of the former. The chromaticism of 'Non morir, Seneca, nò', and of course the sentiment, may be sufficient to distinguish the earnest pleas of the Famigliari from the uncouth promptings of the Proci; but the Famigliari need to overcome a less than illustrious precedent if we are to take them seriously.

Furthermore, the three-male-voice scoring had an iconic significance for Venetians that without a doubt has a bearing on its interpretation at least in the case of the Proci: the *giustiniana*, a 'popular' genre one topos of which is three ludicrous old men singing of their supposed sexual exploits, was a favourite in the sixteenth century, and similar pieces kept their place in *commedia dell'arte* and carnival entertainments (which operas, of course, were).[56] Monteverdi certainly alluded to the genre – and invoked its interpretative resonances – in the male-voice trios (AAB, ATB and TTB) in his Seventh (1619) and particularly Eighth Book (1638) of madrigals: for the Seventh, the ribald setting for two tenors and bass of Marino's 'Eccomi pronta ai baci' (a poem written, significantly, in the female voice) is a splendid example,[57] and in the Eighth, the trio of shepherds (TTB) in the *Lamento della ninfa* prompts interesting reading in this light.[58] But another of the 'madrigal amorosi' in the Eighth Book, 'Non partir, ritrosetta' (for AAB, although the range suggests ATB), is of more direct musical relevance. The text is a straightforward (anonymous) canzonetta:

[56] The connection was suggested by Denis Arnold in his article 'Giustiniana', *The New Grove Dictionary of Music and Musicians* (London, 1980), vii, 418. See also Ellen Rosand, '*Il ritorno d'Ulisse in patria* and the Power of "Music" ', *Cambridge Opera Journal*, 7 (1995), 179–84 (see p. 181). Also typical of the *giustiniana* is the presence of comical stammers: these are not so apparent in the music for the Proci, but, and curiously enough for my developing argument, the repeated 'nò' in the Famigliari's 'Io per me morir non vò' – emphasized to excess in the Venice manuscript (Curtis for the most part follows the underlay in the Naples manuscript here) – comes close to stammering.

[57] See Massimo Ossi, ' "Excuse me but your teeth are in my neck": Of (Love) Bites, Jokes, and Gender in Claudio Monteverdi's "Eccomi pronta ai baci" ', paper presented at (among others) the Seventh Biennial Conference on Baroque Music, University of Birmingham (UK), 4–7 July 1996.

[58] The *Lamento della ninfa*, 'Non havea Febo ancora', published in Monteverdi's *Madrigali guerrieri, et amorosi . . . libro ottavo* (Venice, 1638) is in many ways a test case; see my '*Possente spirto*: On Taming the Power of Music', *Early Music*, 21 (1993), 517–23. Its text (a canzonetta by Ottavio Rinuccini) does not conform to standard lament types, and its music, in a sensuous triple time over a descending tetrachord ground bass, differs strikingly from, say, the *Lamento d'Arianna* (and, for that matter, the recitative laments for Penelope in *Il ritorno d'Ulisse in patria* or Ottavia in *L'incoronazione di Poppea*). The three shepherds who introduce and conclude the nymph's lament, and interject therein, also threaten a possible spanner in the works (see Susan McClary, 'Excess and Frame: The Musical Representation of Madwomen', *Feminine Endings*, 80–111). However, the tendency has been to treat the *Lamento della ninfa* as a somehow serious piece; indeed, there is a considerable vested interest on the part of Monteverdi scholars in viewing it as such. See, for example, the important discussion in Lorenzo Bianconi, *Music in the Seventeenth Century* (Cambridge, 1987), 204–19.

XII

Example 4. Monteverdi, *Il ritorno d'Ulisse in patria*, Act 2, scene v, after Claudio Monteverdi, *Tutte le opere*, ed. Gian Francesco Malipiero (2nd edn, Vienna, 1954–68), xii, 107: Proci.

(Love then, yes, yes; so love again one day.)

Non partir, ritrosetta,
troppo lieve e incostante,
senti me non fuggir, aspetta, aspetta,
odi il pregar del tuo fedel amante.
Tu non senti i lamenti,
ah tu fuggi, io rimango,
ah tu ridi e io piango.

L'alma vola disciolta,
teco parte il mio core,
ᶜᵒrma il piè, non fuggir, ascolta, ascolta,
torna a gioir almen d'un che si more.
Tu non miri i martiri,
tu non odi, ah, io ti chiamo,
tu mi sprezzi, ah, io ti bramo.

Tu crudel più mi offendi
quanto più sei fugace,
già dal sen l'alma fugge, attendi, attendi,
se il mio languir a te cotanto piace.
Tu non ri[e]di, non ri[e]di,
tu mi sprezzi, ah, io t'adoro,
tu mi lasci, ah, e io moro.

(Do not leave, bashful one,/too flighty and inconstant,/listen to me, do not flee, wait, wait,/hear the prayer of your faithful lover./You do not hear my laments,/ah you flee and I remain,/ah you laugh and I weep.//My soul flies unleashed,/my heart leaves with you,/stay your foot, do not flee, listen, listen,/ return to give joy at least to one who dies. / You do not see my suffering, / you do not listen, ah, I call you,/you scorn me, ah, I long for you.//You, cruel one, offend me/the more you are fleeing,/already from my breast my soul flees, wait, wait,/if my languishing so much pleases you./You do not return, you do not return, / you scorn me, ah, I adore you, / you leave me, ah, and I die.)

Monteverdi's setting is strophic and in a typical triple time, with three shifts to duple time for drawn-out cadences (to be played for laughs?). The obvious point of contact with the Famigliari comes at 'Tu non senti i lamenti' (juxtaposed with 'ah tu fuggi') with music more or less the same as 'Non morir, Seneca, nò', an imitative point passing through the three voices rising chromatically through the tetrachord (see Example 5; compare Example 3 above). When revising this passage for the Famigliari, Monteverdi rearranged the voice-leading (in part because of the different tonal context) and added another imitative entry in stretto (he has space to do so, having removed the 'ah tu fuggi' counterpoint); he also produced a more structured climax and fall to the cadence. But there is no doubting the direct relationship between the two passages.

It comes as a shock to find the Famigliari's supposedly painful, intense plea directly linked to a light love-song that, if 'Eccomi pronta ai baci' is anything to go by, was intended for humorous effect. The textual prompt for the chromatic passage in 'Non partir, ritrosetta', unheeded 'lamenti', may offer a clue for the apparent association (the Famigliari's

XII

Example 5. Monteverdi, 'Non partir, ritrosetta', *Madrigali guerrieri, et amorosi . . . libro ottavo* (1638), after Monteverdi, *Tutte le opere*, ed. Malipiero, viii, 305–9.

'Non morir, Seneca, nò' is a lament at least in embryo, and it will be unheeded by its recipient); the whole canzonetta's repeated references to the soul fleeing the lover's breast (just as Seneca's soul will fly to Olympus) provides another possible connection. But for all the relations between the texts, the clear disjunction between their contexts is worrying. Perhaps performance style (tempo, expression, gesture) could be enough to distance the two pieces.[59] And one should doubtless beware the too easy assumption of gestural–affective equivalence in different stylistic, generic and textural environments (Rosand's 'emblem of lament' is a case in point: in the 1630s and 40s it does not always appear in lamenting contexts). But at the very least, there now is the possibility of playing 'Non morir, Seneca, nò' not so seriously. This, in turn, works against Rosand's reading of the scene and therefore, perhaps, of Monteverdi's Seneca as a whole: the composer may be no less detached from, or even cynical about, the character than some of his colleagues in the Accademia degli Incogniti.

Fenlon and Miller could have made capital from the connection between 'Non morir, Seneca, nò' and 'Non partir, ritrosetta': for them, one point of this scene is the contrast between Seneca's constancy and the rejection of such constancy by the Famigliari[60] – how better to invoke the Famigliari's position than by direct reference to a canzonetta itself focusing on the inconstancy of a fickle woman? Gary Tomlinson, too, would doubtless add this connection to his armoury of critical barbs against Monteverdi's Venetian music, where he notes the ever-diminishing potency of Humanist musical discourse and the ascendancy of a Marinist-derived musical *concettismo*. Whatever the case, one has to admit that a less painful reading of 'Non morir, Seneca, nò' sits more easily in the context of the scene as a whole. For all the chromatic astringency of 'Non morir, Seneca, nò', the following 'Io per me morir non vò' is oddly bland – and the extravagant repetitions of 'nò' are cumbersome – while the subsequent 'aria' (trio), 'Questa vita è dolce troppo', with its ritornello (see Example 6) creates an awkward juxtaposition that is at best difficult to handle in performance.

Here Monteverdi invokes another intertextual resonance, not to a canzonetta published a few years earlier but instead right back to his first opera, *Orfeo*, premièred in Mantua in 1607. The melodic, harmonic and rhythmic similarities between 'Questa vita è dolce troppo' and Orfeo's 'Vi ricorda, o boschi ombrosi' (in Act 2 of *Orfeo*; see Example 7) –

---

[59] The relevant passage in 'Non partir, ritrosetta' is notated in triple-minim (C3), whereas its equivalent in 'Non morir, Seneca, nò' is in triple-semibreve (3/1), to use Curtis's terminology for identifying different layers of triple-time writing in the surviving sources for *Poppea* (although the present example should urge a degree of caution in Curtis's positing of a chronological order between the two versions of triple-time notation, with triple-semibreve being more old-fashioned). On the face of it, triple-semibreve would seem to suggest a slower pace, but the relationship between various triple-time notations and either tempo or proportion (i.e. the relation with contiguous duple-time music) is highly problematic: compare, for example, the *furor* that has greeted the suggestions in Roger Bowers, 'Some Reflection on Notation and Proportion in Monteverdi's Vespers of 1610', *Music and Letters*, 73 (1992), 347–98.

[60] Fenlon and Miller note the sharp pointing-up in this scene of 'The contrast between the heroic possessor of *constantia* and the undisciplined, wavering masses of humanity' ('The Song of the Soul', 78).

Example 6. *L'incoronazione di Poppea*, Act 2, scene iii, Venice MS (compare *L'incoronazione di Poppea*, ed. Curtis, 123–6): Famigliari. The ritornello has blank upper staves (G2, G2, C1 clefs).

Example 7. Monteverdi, *Orfeo*, Act 2, after Monteverdi, *Tutte le opere*, ed. Malipiero, xi, 48–9 (but with original note-values): Orfeo.

(Do you recall, o shady woods, my [long, harsh torments]…?)

including their (danced?) ritornellos – seem due to more than just the metrical similarities of their texts (four-line stanzas in *ottonari* rhyming ABBA). Orfeo's song to the woods plays his former suffering as he wooed Euridice against his happiness at impending marriage: he 'blesses' his torment because it makes his joy so much the sweeter ('dopo il duol vi è più contento, / dopo il mal vi è più felice'; 'after grief there is more contentment; after pain there is more happiness'). The Famigliari's song also picks up on the theme of suffering ('ogni amar, ogni veleno / finalmente è lieve intoppo') if for a different end: it is still better to be alive than dead. As in the case of the possible textual connections between 'Non partir, ritrosetta' and 'Non morir, Seneca, nò' (lament, departure or inconstancy), the relationship between 'Questa vita è dolce troppo' and 'Vi ricorda, o boschi ombrosi' (suffering compared with pleasure) may be prompted simply by a textual association perceived on the micro- rather than the macro-level. In both cases, the further generic associa- tions ('Non partir, ritrosetta' as a canzonetta; *Orfeo* as a court opera) may also be relevant. But if they are, it is hard to know whether the courtly resonances of 'Questa vita è dolce troppo' ennoble the sentiments or satirize them.

All these issues render still more problematic a scene already difficult to play convincingly on the stage: it appears to have been cut in at least one performance of the time.[61] And it is no wonder that the Venice manuscript does not contain Seneca's subsequent reference to the Famigliari's 'singulti' and 'pianti': their 'sobs' and 'tears' now seem too ambivalent for his comment to carry any conviction.[62] Instead, Seneca has just six more lines (the last six of his speech as given above from the 1656 libretto) to take his leave. He is mentioned again only twice in the opera as first Nerone and then Poppea start a scene with 'Hor che Seneca è morto' (Act 2, scenes v, x), his demise providing proof of the emperor's degeneracy and Poppea's power more than any moral exemplar. The speed of his dispatch – and its ultimate irrelevance for the plot – are made still clearer by the immediately following scene in both scores, where Valletto and Damigella enjoy a flirtatious romp concluding (in the Venice manuscript) in a love duet vying with those of Nerone and Poppea in erotic intensity.

Seneca is silenced both in and by death: he ignores the injunctions of his Famigliari and is not given a formal lament of his own. Even if such a lament would have been dramatically inappropriate (perhaps even improper, given the status of laments as essentially feminine discourse),[63] one feels a certain lack of musical and dramatic weight to his final act. Such a lack may also have been noted at the time. It is significant that the 1656 libretto – whether before or after the musical fact remains unclear – does indeed give Seneca one more chance to speak in a scene directly after Act 2, scene iii with Virtue and a Chorus of Virtues.[64] Virtù had of course appeared in the prologue (with Fortuna and Amor) and Seneca, at least in his noble guise, is her protagonist in the

---

[61] It is omitted from the libretto usually associated with a performance in Naples in mid-century, *Il Nerone overo L'incoronatione di Poppea* (Naples, 1651). Rosand ('Seneca and the Interpretation of *L'incoronazione di Poppea*', 45) explains this as a response to the demands of Catholic censors, whose power was much more effective outside Venice than within.

[62] Seneca's injunction to the Famigliari draws directly upon Lipsius' *Life of Seneca*; see Fenlon and Miller, 'The Song of the Soul', 29. Fenlon and Miller (*ibid.*, 79) note the reference to 'dell'inconstanza vil le macchie indegne' in the omitted portion of Seneca's speech but present that speech in a curiously garbled version.

[63] My argument here and below owes an obvious debt to Heller, 'Chastity, Heroism, and Allure'.

[64] The scene for 'La Virtù con un Choro di Virtù, Seneca' is given in the 1656 libretto (from which the text below is taken) and also in three of the manuscript librettos ('La Virtù in machina . . .'): Rovigo, Biblioteca dell'Accademia dei Concordi, Silvestriana 239; Warsaw, Biblioteka Narodowa, BOZ 1043; and Venice, Museo Civico Correr, Cicogna 585. It is not present in the Udine libretto (Fondo Joppi 496), and the 1643 scenario makes no reference to this scene; it surely did not appear in the first performance. However, it may not just be a 'literary' addition for the 1656 libretto: although Chiarelli places the Rovigo and Venice librettos (she did not know of the Warsaw one) in the same stemma as the 1656 libretto, neither derives directly from the print, and indeed they may contain readings anterior to it (see '*L'incoronazione di Poppea o Il Nerone*', 128–33); Fabbri draws the same conclusion concerning the Warsaw libretto ('New Sources for "Poppea" ', 16–18).

Curiously, *Il ritorno d'Ulisse in patria* also contains a 'missing' scene set in the afterlife following a significant death, Act 3, scene ii for Mercury and the shades of the suitors (in a 'desert',, during which Hell opens) following immediately upon the 'suicide' of Iro; see Rosand, 'Iro and the Interpretation of *Il ritorno d'Ulisse in patria*', *Journal of Musicology*, 7 (1989), 141–64 (pp. 160–2). This scene was omitted from the score (we do not know whether it was ever set to music) 'per esser maninconica'.

XII

202

opera.[65] Now Busenello has them appear together, allowing Seneca to turn death into glory, and Virtù a (silent) opportunity to enjoy her one triumph in the opera:

| *Ch[oro]*. | Lieto e ridente<br>al fin t'affretta,<br>che il Ciel t'aspetta. |
| *Sen[eca]*. | Breve coltello,<br>ferro minuto<br>sarà la chiave<br>che m'aprirà<br>le vene in terra<br>e in ciel le porte dell'eternità. |
| *Ch.* | Lieto e ridente &c. |
| *Sen.* | À Dio grandezze,<br>pompe di vetro,<br>glorie di polve,<br>larve d'error,<br>che in un momento<br>affascinate, assassinate il cor. |
| *Ch.* | Lieto e ridente &c. |
| *Sen.* | Già, già dispiego il volo<br>da questa mia decrepità mortale,<br>e verso il choro vostro<br>adorate virtudi inalzo l'ale. |

(*Chorus*: Happy and smiling / hasten to your end, / for heaven awaits you. // *Seneca*: A short cut of the knife, / a tiny blade, / will be the key / which will open for me / my veins on earth / and in heaven the gates of eternity. // *Ch.*: Happy and smiling etc. // *Sen.*: Farewell grandeurs, / splendours of glass [i.e. fake jewellery], / glories of dust, / phantoms of error, / which in one moment / both fascinate and assassinate the heart. // *Ch.*: Happy and smiling etc. // *Sen.*: Now, now, I take flight / from this my mortal decrepitude, / and towards your chorus, / adored virtues, I spread my wing.)

This scene may or may not have been intended for the theatre, but its absence in any of the musical sources for *Poppea* is scarcely surprising: it is religiously suspect, the jogging *quinari* are unamenable to music, and one wonders how such a curiously banal apotheosis would have been staged. However, this apotheosis also runs counter to the apparent programme of the opera as defined in the prologue: for all the association of Seneca and Virtù, it is clear from the outset that *L'incoronazione di Poppea* is to be about the triumph of Love, the one allegorical figure from the

---

[65] Fenlon and Miller ('*The Song of the Soul*', 76) note the further connection between Seneca's notion (Act 2, scene iii) of the virtuous soul which 'se ne vola all'Olimpo' and Virtù's (in the prologue) 'Io son la tramontana / che sola insegno agl'intelletti umani / l'arte del navigar verso l'Olimpo'.

prologue to appear (twice) in the opera proper and who is repeatedly invoked by Poppea both in her texts and in her sensuous music. That song was the natural language of Love – 'a child of harmony'[66] – had been made clear in *Il ritorno d'Ulisse in patria*, and for Nino Pirrotta it is the sensuous excess of love in *Poppea* that explains (but cannot quite justify) its hedonistic music.[67] Even Seneca's death becomes dominated (or contaminated) by the music of love-songs, as the references to 'Non partir, ritrosetta' and 'Vi ricorda, o boschi ombrosi' now reveal. Perhaps there was little choice but to truncate his death scene and its aftermath: given the dangers of song as a signifier of feminine or feminized excess, the only way to retain a masculine *gravitas* and nobility for Seneca was through silence. A delicious paradox emerges: if one wishes to pursue Rosand's (and Fenlon and Miller's) 'serious' reading of Seneca, one might better do so less through his presence in Monteverdi's score than through his absence. His early death not only precipitates the moral collapse of Nerone and Poppea's world; it also permits that world to be represented in a music no longer burdened with a vestigial need for moral rectitude. In this sense, Busenello's premature removal of Seneca from the reckoning may have made Monteverdi's task much easier.

This is perhaps the best strategy for rescuing any 'serious' reading of Monteverdi's Seneca; it also obviates the need for any other character (e.g. Drusilla) to take his place. However, there remains the question of how to read the music for Seneca and those associated with him prior to his death. For Robert Holzer, the apparent critique of Seneca contained in the libretto of *L'incoronazione di Poppea* (at least in the voices of the two soldiers and Valletto) are tempered by 'a Tacitean emplotment that relegates such critique to inferior characters'.[68] But, so it now appears, the ostensible musical support for Seneca is similarly tempered by a stylistic and generic emplotment alluding to 'inferior' love-songs. Commentators may be forced to refer to events outside the opera (Poppaea's death by Nero's hand; Otho's assumption of the imperial

---

[66] Giovanni Francesco Loredano, *Bizzarie academiche* (Bologna, 1676), 217–18: 'Amore è figliuolo dell'harmonia, e però quegli amanti, che vorrebono farlo nascere nelle loro amate hò ben io veduti cantare, ma non versar lagrime, indegne dell'huomo, e che sarebbero atte a produrre il riso in vece d'Amore' ('Love is child of harmony, and therefore I have seen those lovers who wish to give rise to it in their beloveds sing, but not release tears, which are unworthy of man and which would be more apt to produce laughter instead of Love'). This is from the celebrated 'Contesa del canto e delle lagrime' discussed in Ellen Rosand, 'Barbara Strozzi, *Virtuosissima cantatrice*: The Composer's Voice', *Journal of the American Musicological Society*, 31 (1978), 241–81 (pp. 278–80); Fenlon and Miller, *The Song of the Soul*, 38–40. Compare Fenlon and Miller, *The Song of the Soul*, 39: 'Amore potrà ben nascere dalla Musica.'

[67] Nino Pirrotta, 'Monteverdi and the Problems of Opera', *Music and Culture*, 235–53 (pp. 251–3). As an aside, it is curious that Busenello and Monteverdi did not take advantage of Nero's musical prowess to justify the use of music on the stage. Compare Giulio Cesare Corradi's *Il Nerone, drama per musica* (Venice, 1679), set to music by Carlo Pallavicino for the Teatro S. Giovanni Grisostomo, where Nero both sings and acts as part of his attempted seduction of Gilde, wife of Tiridate, proclaimed king of Armenia. The plot here is interesting. There is a dispute between Nero and Seneca (Act 1, scene ii) rather close to *Poppea* (Act 1, scene ix), but Seneca stays on Nero's side in the Pisonian conspiracy, and at the end of the opera he receives Nero's vow to reform his wicked ways ('De l'opre tue fedeli / Seneca in guiderdone / giura, e promette Augusto / d'esser sul Tebro un Regnator più giusto').

[68] Review of Fenlon and Miller, *The Song of the Soul*, 86.

throne) in order to support and clarify their 'moral' readings of occur-rences within it, but adopting a similar strategy for the music scarcely supports and clarifies the notion of it strengthening any such moral or other outcome. The weakened integrity of the frame places the onus of reading the musical Seneca on that character's music, rather than on what surrounds it, and yet Seneca's music can itself be read in contradictory ways (as Rosand's and McClary's conflicting interpretations reveal): when all is said and done, his 'canzoni' remain just that, songs.

It will now be clear that the notion of a musically serious Seneca steer-ing *Poppea* straight on a moral course – a notion central to Rosand's and still more to Fenlon and Miller's readings of the opera – is problematic. The dramatic and musical ambiguities of the character might be amenable to clarification in and through performance – 'Non morir, Seneca, nò' can be played seriously if one chooses – or they might be left uninter-preted, the opera maintaining an ironic, carnivalesque detachment from its Grand Guignol world much in the manner of the paradoxical encomia and related satirical genres that formed one strand of early-modern literary traditions.[69] But in the end, this music is not amenable (why should it be?) to the strongly interpreted readings that post-Enlightenment critics, producers and performers seek to place on it according to their various ideological and other agenda: every argument has its counter. Moreover, the close reading of works and their contexts practised in this essay may refine the limits of interpretation, but it cannot fix those limits with any precision. Such ambivalence – perhaps polyvalence – may be a counsel of (postmodernist) despair; it may be an authentic response to the practicalities of the mid-seventeenth-century Italian opera house, where focused articulations of characters and actions surely did not come high on any list of priorities; or it may be seen as exuberantly liberating for future readings of this rich, magnificent work. It also suggests a pleasure in rhetorical play that may, in the end, prove to be the valedic-tory message of Monteverdi's last opera.

---

[69] Compare Edward B. Savage, 'Love and Infamy: The Paradox of Monteverdi's *L'incorona-zione di Poppea*', *Comparative Drama*, 4 (1970), 197–207. Savage invokes dramatic irony in Montever-di's music in terms typical of literary criticism; it is also typical that musicologists have tended not to follow his perceptive lead. I read too late a pre-publication copy of Robert C. Ketterer, ' "Militat omnis amans": Ovidian Elegy in *L'incoronazione di Poppea*', forthcoming in *The Interna-tional Journal of the Classical Tradition*, 4 (1997). Ketterer's placing of the opera in the context of carnivalesque subversion meshes nicely with my remarks.

# INDEX